T0355081

The AI Military Race

The AI Military Race

*Common Good Governance in the Age of
Artificial Intelligence*

Denise Garcia

OXFORD
UNIVERSITY PRESS

Great Clarendon Street, Oxford, OX2 6DP,
United Kingdom

Oxford University Press is a department of the University of Oxford.
It furthers the University's objective of excellence in research, scholarship,
and education by publishing worldwide. Oxford is a registered trade mark of
Oxford University Press in the UK and in certain other countries

Published in the United States of America by Oxford University Press
198 Madison Avenue, New York, NY 10016, United States of America

British Library Cataloguing in Publication Data

Data available

Library of Congress Control Number: 2023937959

ISBN 9780192864604

DOI: 10.1093/oso/9780192864604.001.0001

Printed and bound by
CPI Group (UK) Ltd, Croydon, CR0 4YY

I dedicate this book to José Garcia Gasques e Sonja Enie Garcia, meus pais amados.

Foreword

By her Honorable Beatrice Fihn, former Director of the International Campaign to Abolish Nuclear Weapons, Nobel Peace Prize Laureate 2017

Military developments in artificial intelligence (AI) demand our attention, urgently. Autonomous Weapon Systems (AWS) will drastically change how our world operates, and it's imperative that what we're trying to undo at the International Campaign to Abolish Nuclear Weapons (ICAN)—decades of indoctrination that said that a particular type of weaponry, in our case nuclear weapons, was special, magical, stability-creating, powerful—is not repeated here. Not only do AWS heighten existing risks of nuclear weapons, in both predicted and unpredicted ways, but emerging autonomous technologies have the potential for unprecedented unintended consequences that we have no capacity to understand. If we're going to automate military systems, and, further, if we're going to automate responses to adverse military action, including with nuclear weapon systems, we very well could start a nuclear war.

As we learned with the 2017 Treaty to Prohibit Nuclear Weapons, it gets a whole lot harder to deal with something once it's been developed. Thus, it is extremely urgent that we deal with military AI systems and autonomous weapons alike now, in a preventive state, rather than wait for countries to develop them. The Campaign to Stop Killer Robots, of which my organization is member, calls upon all states to commit to an immediate moratorium on autonomous weapon systems so that this regulatory framework can be created. As more and more states realize the full extent of harm that autonomous weapons present, and as the space for freely developing them decreases, we can and will slowly chip away at the legitimacy of these weapons. That begins with this book.

At ICAN, we've built a campaign around the humanitarian consequences of nuclear weapons, and in this book Denise Garcia builds her own campaign around the consequences of the militarization and weaponization of AI and also the unrestrained use of autonomous weapons. This book explores the complexities of the humanitarian processes and high-level diplomacy surrounding these pressing matters around the world. There is no doubt that this book's proposal for inclusive and humane ways to forge cooperation between states will be the impetus for an age of common good governance, in all areas of international cooperation, starting with AI. Human control over the use of violent force is essential for ensuring the protection of civilians, and we must do everything in our power to ensure it remains the centerpiece of weapons development around the world to ensure humanity's security, as Garcia proposes.

Acknowledgments

This book was the result of a long, exciting, and exploratory journey. I met wondrous people. I visited many of the key diplomatic capitals where multilateral diplomacy in the matters studied here happens: Geneva, New York, Berlin, Brussels, Brasilia, and Oslo. Meeting caring and generous people nurtured and inspired me along the way. Francesca and Stefania Batault were staunch and faithful supporters; without them, this journey would have been impossible because their trust carried me all the way. My thanks to Beatriz Garcia and Isabela Abdala for all the inspiration they bring to both my academic and my personal life. Thanks also to my husband, Jeremy V. Lapon, for the pragmatism he instills and for his constant love and faith, along with my fantastic American family.

For more than a year, I counted on the extraordinary research assistance of Emerson Johnston, who patiently kept me on track even as she was progressing on her own arduous journey. It was an inspiration to work with you, Emerson. Several brilliant students have assisted me as research assistants throughout the years; it was a treat to work with Kelsey Taeckens, Jillian Jacobson, Joshua Burns, and Shane Gravel.

Many thanks to Edwin Hees, a talented and patient editor extraordinaire. Sebastian Chávez Da Silva, the guardian of the text, assisted me in finalizing everything with a detailed and vigilant eye. I would not have been able to do without his pragmatic engineering mindset to the project.

Alumni and PhD students are a constant enrichment to my life and they keep me up to date with the world: Ximena Tovar, Rebecca Leeper (for helping me to learn AI), Elina Mariutsa (for friendship and guidance in Geneva), and, for their love and unwavering support, Justin Haner, Valeria P. Hernandez, Maria Virginia Olano Velasquez, Klara Đurkin, Matthew Kokkinos, Will McDermott, Maisam Alahmed, Kenneth Iannuzzi, Bailey Rose Marcus, Adam Dolce, Carlos Arriaga Serrano, Paula Soumaya Domit (so many thoughtful revisions), Drew Baldwin, Daniela Lacal Rodriguez, Nikolas Beimler, Margarida Soares Rodrigues, and Sara Morrell.

Heather Roff, Peter Asaro, and Rebecca Leeper: again, I thank you for countless conversations. Robert Mason: my gratitude for sharing your engineering expertise and for furthering my knowledge of AI.

Thanks to Michael Biontino, Jody Williams, and Steve Goose for the initial motivation, and, later, for the conversations with Eugenio V. Garcia, Guilherme Patriota, Flávio Soares Damico, Ousman Noor, Augusto López-Claros, and Deeph Chana.

I was fortunate to be part of the International Panel for the Regulation of Autonomous Weapons from 2017 to 2022: the essential years of writing the manuscript. The conversations I had with the wonderful members of the group and our guests during our many visits to Berlin, Geneva, and Brussels were invaluable.

I am grateful, with all my heart, for the hospitality, generosity, and eternal friendship of Frank Sauer, Peter Asaro, Marcel Dickow, AJung Moon, Anja Dahlmann, Vadim Kozyulin, Heigo Sato, Thompson Chengeta, Erin Hahn, Ian MacLeod, Binxin Zhang, and Elisabeth Hoffberger-Pippan. Frank and Peter, so many thanks for the revisions at different points, and for the light and clarity you bring.

For every project I write, fortitude comes from Robert I. Rotberg. This project is in memory of the beloved Christof Heyns, who showed the way to all us first; and of the professor who inspired me to study international law: the late honorable International Court of Justice judge, Antônio Augusto Cançado Trindade, my professor at the University of Brasília.

I thank Toby Walsh, Kerstin Vignard, and Stuart Russell for all they have done to make things clear for everyone discussing autonomous weapons and the militarization of AI. More recently, as a member of the Institute of Electrical and Electronics Engineers Global Initiative on Ethics of Autonomous and Intelligent Systems, and the IEEE-SA Research Group on Issues of Autonomy and AI for Defense Systems, I was fortunate to meet and work with Ariel Conn.

At Northeastern University, I am very fortunate to have wondrous friends: Thomas Vicino, Amilcar Barreto, Berna Turam, Luis Dau, Rick Davis, Mai'a K. Davis Cross, Joseph Aoun, Taskin Padir, Julie Boudoukara, Costas Panagopoulos, Janet Louise-Joseph, Uta Poiger, and Roxanne Palmatier. Northeastern is my academic home, and I am thankful to be a part of such an encouraging and supportive place. Beyond Northeastern, my long-standing partnership with Professor Monica Herz is always a part of it all.

At the United Nations Library in Geneva, nothing would be possible without Adriano Gonçalves and Cristina Giordano. Pedro da Silva's hospitality is, every time, irreplaceable. In Geneva, so much is about the excitement of meeting the people who are making a difference in the world: Beatrice Fihn, Stefano Toscano, Pascal Rapillard, Kerry Brinkert, María Merchán Rocamora, Peter Kolarov, John Borrie, and Carolyne-Mélanie Régimbal.

In 2017, I was a research fellow at the place where many of the ideas of *common good governance*, and *humanity's security*, were born: the Norwegian Nobel Institute, Oslo. Ingvild Bode and Rebecca Crootof for all the inspiration they provide. Rebecca Crootof for all the inspiration she provides. I am grateful for the opportunity to present my initial book project at Yale Law School in March 2019 and for the engagement with the Information Society Project Fellows; and to visit Bode's Autonorms project in Denmark in 2022. Finally, via my participation at We Robot 2019 (Miami Law School) and at the 2022 International Conference on Robotics and Automation (ICRA), I had the privilege of meeting and presenting with Lisa Miracchi Titus and Daniel E. Koditschek, and of working again with Michael C. Horowitz. At the International Committee for Robot Arms Control, thanks to Noel Sharkey for leading all of us from the beginning, along with Peter Asaro and Frank Sauer, always. Finally, I would like to thank my editor at Oxford University Press, Dominic Byatt, for believing in this project right from the beginning, and for supporting me with fortitude and thoughtfulness; the conversations at the International Studies Association were a must. To the production team at Oxford: much gratitude to Karen Bunn and Raja Dharmaraj.

Contents

List of figures

List of tables

Introduction
Artificial intelligence to benefit humanity

The world is at a critical juncture. Ill-considered conceptions of national security have led to imprudent wars, millions of lives lost, and trillions of dollars wasted without making anyone more secure. Now, the world is at an extreme point of insecurity. The very same permanent members of the United Nations Security Council, charged with saving future generations from the scourge of war, flagrantly violate international law and threaten to undermine nearly a century of progress toward peace. Great power competition is a folly that must end, as it diverts critical resources away from truly important global issues. Its worst possible outcomes range from nuclear war to dystopian autonomous weapons and surveillance systems in the hands of despots. It is not possible to achieve genuine security on a unilateral basis in the world today. *Common good governance* toward *humanity's security* is the way forward.

We must face the interconnected catastrophic global risks—from climate change to pandemics to nuclear weapons and militarized artificial intelligence (AI)—with governance toward the global common good. The proliferation of military AI is making the world less safe. The unrelenting pursuit of more militarization does not protect; it imperils future generations. It happened with nuclear weapons proliferation and it is happening with AI-enabled weapons as well. Our efforts must rise in ambition to meet the scale of our problems. They must include structural reforms to our aging global political infrastructure, beginning with comprehensive United Nations reform. This book urges a return to constructive international cooperation so that we may all enjoy global public goods and build humanity's security together on a planetary scale.

The book's significance

Autonomous weapons threaten to become the third revolution in warfare. Once developed, they will permit armed conflict to be fought at a scale greater than ever, and at timescales faster than humans can comprehend. These can be weapons of terror, weapons that despots and terrorists use against innocent populations, and weapons hacked to behave in undesirable ways. We do not have long to act. Once this Pandora's box is opened, it will be hard to close.[1]

The AI Military Race. Denise Garcia, Oxford University Press. © Denise Garcia (2023).
DOI: 10.1093/oso/9780192864604.003.0001

The epigraph to this introduction comes from a letter published in 2017 by a group of concerned people convened by the Future of Life Institute, and signed by more than 250 companies, including Google Deepmind and Tesla, and more than 30,000 technology professionals and researchers, alerting the world to the perils of weaponizing AI and committing not to participate in or support the development of autonomous weapons. Autonomy refers to a machine's ability to carry out a function or a mission on its own.[2]

This missive was preceded by a historic letter, published in July 2015, in which the unique problems arising from autonomous systems were powerfully highlighted by the world's foremost scientists in the field of AI. They warned that an AI militarization race would be detrimental to humanity, but also reminded us that AI has great potential to benefit humanity in many ways. They go on to state:

> Just as most chemists and biologists have no interest in building chemical or biological weapons, most AI researchers have no interest in building AI weapons—and do not want others to tarnish their field by doing so, potentially creating a major public backlash against AI that curtails its future societal benefits. Indeed, chemists and biologists have broadly supported international agreements that have successfully prohibited chemical and biological weapons, just as most physicists supported the treaties banning space-based nuclear weapons and blinding laser weapons.[3]

In this book, intended for readers with an interest in rapid technological developments that have an impact on war and peace, I delve into the complexities involved in setting global governing rules on the deployment of autonomous weapons, restraining the weaponization of AI, and exploring the intricacies of regulating the militarization of AI, inspired by a goal to improve the common good of humanity. This book is not about a dystopian future wherein machines will kill humans autonomously, either embodied as robots or operating in cyberspace. It makes the point that this "future" is already here; it is impacting on our lives right now in the way that nations continue to divert funds to create technologically ever more advanced ways to kill and impose control, rather than tackling other pressing concerns of global cooperation of a nonmilitary nature, such as confronting the climate crisis or preventing the next pandemic.[4] With this in mind, I investigate ways to establish a peaceful future global order characterized by a concern for the common good, where future generations will have a chance to live in a nonviolent world and without the constant fear of an impending state of war. The only way to attain this goal is to look at the concept of national security in an updated way that matches the challenges humanity faces. Inward looking, solely military-focused ways to conceive security will do more harm than good. The means to attain global cooperation shall also be updated and I offer possible avenues here.

> Our challenge is to maximize the benefits of the technological revolution while mitigating and preventing the dangers. The impacts of new technologies on warfare are a direct threat to our common responsibility to guarantee peace and security.[5]

For all the reasons mentioned above in Guterres' quote, I introduce three novel humanistic conceptions: *common good governance, transnational networked cooperation*, and *humanity's security*. By exploring all the entities and actors involved, I investigate the threats to peace in the shifting world order by exploring existing initiatives to set global norms and principles, by a broad set of entities—not only states—with a focus on the most daunting aspect of the rise of AI, which is its militarization. To this extent, I depict the already occurring utilization of autonomous systems for military applications, and contend that the integration of AI in weapon systems is perhaps the most far-reaching development in the history of conflict since the advent of nuclear weapons, as it is likely that this will entirely remove the actions performed by autonomous weapons from any human purview and authority.[6]

Many autonomous systems are already being deployed, gradually incorporating AI, designed to search, track, and target to kill under the control of algorithms and not human beings. Systems with various levels of autonomy are already in operation. However, thus far they are mostly deployed via preprogrammed and stationary platforms to perform reiterated actions—for instance, the American Phalanx defense system, used to protect vessels at sea.[7] The same is true for the Israeli Iron Dome, which can defend an area against incoming missiles by deciding on the target from a library of preprogrammed algorithms. The new wave of weapon systems is prominently represented by the Israeli Harpy, which operates with full autonomy and is a loitering defensive weapon system. This sensor signature-detecting weapon system can remain operationally active in the air for hours, continuously seeking the enemy's radar signal.[8] When it detects a signal, the Harpy can destroy it autonomously without human input, at the moment of action. If the final attack takes place in a heavily populated area, surrounded by civilians or near a school or hospital, it is unlikely that the Harpy would make the necessary distinctions, as required by international humanitarian law. Other countries, such as China, Germany, Russia, the United Kingdom, and the United States, have started to acquire or already possess similar systems.

The AI scientists who contributed to the 2015 letter made this urgent call to action:

> AI technology has reached a point where the deployment of such systems is feasible within years, not decades, and the stakes are high...If any major military power pushes ahead with AI weapon development, a global arms race is virtually inevitable, and the endpoint of this technological trajectory is obvious: autonomous weapons will become the Kalashnikovs of tomorrow. Unlike nuclear weapons, they require no costly or hard-to-obtain raw materials, so they will become ubiquitous and cheap for all significant military powers to mass-produce. It will only be a matter of time until they appear on the black market and in the hands of terrorists, dictators wishing to better control their populace, warlords wishing to perpetrate ethnic cleansing, etc.[9]

These scientists urged policymakers and others to recognize that the key question for humanity is whether to continue a global military AI race, or to act preventively and show restraint. If humanity fails to respond appropriately, the scientists warn that militarized AI will be used in assassinations, to destabilize nations, and to eliminate particular ethnic groups or political dissidents. This race to use AI to harm will not serve humanity well. In the 2015 letter, the signatories indicate that "there are many ways in which AI can make battlefields safer for humans, especially civilians, without creating new tools for killing people." Over the last two decades, the dominant trend has been to use robotic and increasingly autonomous systems in aerial, land, and maritime operations. Such systems have been weaponized in certain instances, such as with unmanned aerial vehicles, known as drones. In many instances, drones have been deployed to save lives, distribute vaccines, and predict the weather. However, the proliferation of drone weaponization has occurred rapidly and has been widespread. This general trend will be a permanent feature in the future, and it does not look as if these technologies will be applied to save lives.

My broader argument is that the militarization of AI, especially in the absence of any oversight rules and globally agreed forms of governance, is a developing phenomenon that will impact appreciably on international relations in three ways. First, the militarization of AI will mean higher risks for global stability. The still unpredictable behavior of machine-learning AI systems when algorithms control weapon engagements means that they may respond too quickly for humans to intervene in case of faulty behavior.[10] A consequence of this may be that the ability to maintain global peace and security is severely compromised. What is at stake is the potential loss of human control to machines that will kill autonomously in response to an algorithm, with no humans involved. Consequently, the threshold for initiating war and conflict may be lowered. The use of autonomy and AI computation techniques in weapon systems is not the problem per se. Instead, what is uncertain and raises several questions is the inadequacy of the human element in overseeing each of the operational stages of weapon systems deployment.[11] Increased autonomy in weapon systems means that human decisions are made only in the early stages of the mission. There may be a disconnection from what occurs at the end, which may contravene not only commonly agreed rules of international law, but also the principles of ethics and morality.[12] Human control means that systems should operate within proper time limits and geographical constraints that can be deemed acceptable even while performing functions without direct human intervention.[13] Throughout this book I highlight the need for, and the presence of, human control over the weapon's operation in a context-dependent and differentiated manner, to ensure that the use of autonomous functions remains sound, protective of human dignity, and future-proof.[14] It is likely that exerting human control over AI-enabled systems will be highly complex, or not feasible at all.[15]

Second, an ongoing military race is already underway, with appreciable sums of money allotted to research on and development of AI systems by the major militarized powers. The United States is seeking to spend $1.8 billion dollars on the development of AI in defense in 2024.[16] Intensifying rivalries among states is again becoming a reality—especially in the search for supremacy in AI—and this signals an impending transformation of the global order.[17] By surveying the shifting global order, one notes a few characteristics that may impact on the current discussion: the rise of China; superpower rivalry to attain preeminence in AI knowledge; a tendency by the United States to disregard the rules-based order and an accompanying disdain for global cooperation; fragmentation of power; the fourth industrial revolution, wherein the digital economy and connections prevails; and a public health pandemic that, compounded by the climate crisis, is eroding economic and social stability. In this new environment, the advanced technological powers have engaged in fierce competition for supremacy. In the contest to gain a strategic edge in this new rivalry, the development of AI takes center stage.

This situation points to a lacuna in the current geopolitical landscape—namely, the lack of norms. Hence, the need to build international norms and global public goods on the basis of the principles of *common good governance* forms the framework that must incorporate the ideas of other groups beyond states, such as scientists and civil society. Global public goods benefit everyone's well-being, promote prosperity, increase international security, and can only be attained by global cooperation.[18] These ideas privilege the well-being of humanity and not of any state in particular. A characteristic of the shifting world order is a decline in the levels of peace. According to the Global Peace Index, the levels of world peace have fallen by 2.5% worldwide since 2008.[19] The Index—the only one to measure levels of peace—adopts 23 indicators, including military expenditure, and applies them in 163 countries. The decline in peace comes with a record increase in global military spending amounting to $1.9 trillion dollars in 2019, which rose to close to $2 trillion in 2020 during the pandemic, and exceeded $2 trillion for the first time in 2022 (reaching $2.1 trillion).[20] Global military spending on AI is expected to reach about $11.6 billion dollars by 2025.[21] A global public good attained by *common good governance* would be a rise in the levels of peacefulness, building a global governance framework for AI, or reaching climate stability at less than 1.5 °C; countries have to build these together.

Third, I contend that the weaponization of AI will disrupt the existing architecture of peace and security; compounding this dilemma is uncertainty as to whether existing international law will suffice to preserve the peace. The accelerated pace of AI technological advancements may be perilous for the future of peaceful relations. The overall architecture of peace is based upon the regulation of the use of force and the accompanying norms associated with the peaceful settlement of disputes (through negotiation, mediation, conciliation, arbitration, and adjudication).[22] This architecture is supported by dense networks of global norms that constrain states' behavior with mechanisms for ensuring transparency, confidence-building, and checks on what is permissible in war and during hostilities. This understanding aligns with a recent adjustment in the normative foundations of the international legal order from being purely state-centric to being aligned with human security interests.[23] In this human-centric international legal order, more voices are included in making new global norms, not only states. My *common good governance* views align with such a shift.

I provide an account of how the global order is transforming, with a growing number of voices insisting on privileging human security, but at the same time there is rivalry amongst the major military powers. I propose that AI should be concomitantly harnessed for humanity's common good. The ominous march toward algorithmic killing—autonomous weapons and the ongoing militarization of AI— further risks the precarious shifting order. Several countries are developing AI for military applications, with the United States, the United Kingdom, Russia, China, India, Israel, South Korea, and some countries within the European Union leading the charge. Such applications include intelligence collection and analysis, logistics, information-gathering, command and control, and various semi-autonomous and autonomous vehicles.[24] My concern is that the increased speed at which this is occurring increases the risk of global instability. The possibility of manipulation and hacking by a multitude of ill-intentioned people would be considerable. The increasing tempo of operations could become so rapid that humans would no longer be able to exercise proper oversight. Escalations and unintended wars would prevail.[25]

I view the creation of a global framework on military AI as an indispensable global public good to maintain world peace. To chart possible avenues toward the creation of common good governance to govern the military use of AI, I address both current and future problems and challenges at the intersection of renewed great power rivalry and loss of human dignity. At present, this includes the intensified use of autonomy in weapons and the trend toward incorporating AI computational techniques such as machine learning into parts or functions of weapon systems, along with developing new ones—in other words, the weaponization of increasingly autonomous technologies, including autonomy that is incorporated into weapon systems. Furthermore, I also warn of the problems that can arise in the near and the long-term future: AI systems will be programmed to kill people and change the course of operations as they proceed without any human involvement and oversight. War would lose its last modicum of humanity. Machines would decide the fate of combatants and civilians alike. The future we want to ensure is one wherein humanity can hold firmly onto its moral and legal obligations to present and future generations by creating *common good governance* for these emerging technologies.

Common good governance arises from the combined efforts of multiple governments and other entities' endeavoring to create global public goods to ensure the mutual benefit and common good of all peoples. Examples would be a global framework on AI, combating the climate crisis, preventing the next pandemic, and eliminating nuclear weapons, leading to the better living conditions that those commitments would create for the whole of humanity, including for future generations. As a result, *common good governance* would arise from the collective attempts to create processes of global cooperation involving a multitude of actors (states and civil society alike), mainly within the frameworks sustained by the different transnational networks that form anew or within existing international and regional organizations. Their iterated practices promote cooperation. *Common good governance* is operationalized when different networks combat a mutual challenge cooperatively and create new global public goods.[26]

One prominent area where AI is being used for the common good is in scaling up the application of AI for climate action. The estimation is that greenhouse gas emissions will be cut by almost 16% through AI-enabled projects over the next five years.

The use of AI-enabled climate action projects is also expected to improve power generation for electricity and industrial efficiency, and to reduce waste.[27] Another prominent area where AI could be used exclusively for the common good of humanity is in achieving the United Nations Sustainable Development Goals (Chapter 3).[28] To help attain these goals, the more AI is integrated into cities' electrical grids, countries' financial systems, autonomous cars, and healthcare provision, the more it becomes essential that AI algorithms are robust and beneficial, especially in areas where their misuse "could have catastrophic effects, such as with autonomous weapons."[29]

Most of the energy in AI innovation in the United States and Europe is generated within academic institutions, as well as prominently within the private sector, large and small companies, and innovators. Names that come to mind immediately are Apple, Google, Facebook, and Microsoft. As Maaike Verbruggen says, "autonomy is mostly a software endeavor," and it is not a given that innovations made in the civilian sector will be transferred to the defense sector. The former is more agile, with larger network collaborations and open-source technologies.[30] Batteries, sensors, and other components have become abundant and accessible, but these and other systems must be robust and safe when they are applied to the military sphere, especially when issues of life and death are on the line. It is not clear that safety concerns are at the forefront. It seems that there are already premature applications, and that the military AI race is leading to hastiness where judicious and meticulous actions should be applied instead.[31] Compounding the concern expressed here is the fact that dual-use technologies always proliferate faster.[32] Take drones, for example, and bear in mind that there is still a human being in remote control in their deployment: The United States started using drones in Iraq in 2003, and their use grew more widespread even in countries that the United States is not at war with, such as Pakistan, Yemen, and Somalia. Now almost 100 countries use drones, and nearly 20 of these have armed them. If this development is a yardstick of what will occur in times to come, the world is facing a precarious future where countries will arm themselves with autonomous weapons (with no human in control) and will more easily initiate war, lowering the acceptable threshold for making the initiation of war permissible under established international law.[33]

In sum, the story I tell is an account of how a few technologically powerful countries are seeking to weaponize AI. Just as troubling, they may want to employ AI in military situations that are not clearly defined as wars under international law, with a concomitant deterioration of human security worldwide. With no global framework to regulate the military use of AI, the world is heading for perilous uncharted waters. The power and ingenuity of humanity must prevail to create a better world for future generations by containing the capacity for autonomous killing, which is a mounting affront to human dignity. Fundamentally, the purpose of my research is to address the foundations for the means—technological, legal, and moral—to constrain the surge of the capacity for autonomous killing, enhanced by militarizing AI. I intend to sound the alarm about how this process foreshadows an uncertain future that may be unstable and destabilizing for future work on peace, development, and prosperity.

Civil and military AI

The AI-enabled technologies that are useful to and that may appeal to human beings now—such as speech and object recognition (smartphone voice assistants), favorite pattern selection (Netflix movie choices), navigation (GPS), and autonomous vehicles, amongst others—are all already also being used to identify targets and attack them on the battlefield. Such uses are often already occurring without human control or supervision. Since 2014, I have met several of the scientists involved in the creation of the movement responsible for the scientists' letters mentioned earlier, including Max Tegmark (MIT), Toby Walsh (University of New South Wales), and Stuart Russell, professor of Computer Science and founder of the Center for Human Compatible Artificial Intelligence at the University of California, Berkeley, and author of the most influential AI manual, adopted worldwide. Russell cautions against the perils of weaponizing AI, a technology that could and should be used solely for the common good.[34] Russell, Walsh, and I have participated in several meetings at the United Nations and have given our testimonies to the member states. They and others represent a convincing mosaic of change makers who are reshaping the global debate about what is morally and ethically acceptable. This work has started to influence the creation of a different and more beneficial future for humanity. My concept of *common good governance* aligns with this more humane orientation to forge global public goods.

AI is already being used for military purposes, primarily to assist physical military hardware with specific functions and tasks such as flight, surveillance, and navigation. Autonomous systems are increasingly being deployed to kill in war, as well as in extra-legal (or extrajudicial) conflicts—with countries not at war—in law enforcement situations (police operations) and cyberspace. Cyberattacks do not necessarily kill individuals directly, but instead can cause great harm by dismantling or disabling infrastructure (electricity grids, hospitals, power sources) or damaging it; furthermore, autonomous systems can be hacked, such as the Solar Winds cyberattack on the Pentagon, the State Department, and others.[35] Stuart Russell warns that autonomous weapons will greatly reduce human security at all levels: personal, local, national, and international.[36]

To create *common good governance* frameworks, it is essential to make a distinction between the global attempts at creating governance mechanisms within the civilian realm and the uses of AI in the military realm.[37] I focus on the latter but will discuss aspects and major initiatives relevant to the former throughout the book. It is essential to note that states are much more willing to create principled AI and ethical principles on the civilian realm of AI, but are less inclined to specify the contours of governance mechanisms in the military realm. This reluctance is an aspect of the ongoing race in AI militarization that is leading to states being rather secretive about their aims and ultimate objectives—even the United States, which generally tends to be more transparent. For instance, the Global Partnership on AI—initiated by France and Canada, and involving the European Union and the United States—is a welcome multistakeholder initiative, based upon shared values and human rights, but it does not address the military aspects of the use of AI. This reaffirms the point that there is a rich landscape of global *transnational networked cooperation* in the realm of civilian AI applications, but highlights the dearth of similar global initiatives in the military domain. The exception is the first summit of military AI held February 15–16, 2023, organized by the Netherlands and the Republic of Korea, that called for the responsible use of AI in the military.[38] The new concept of "responsible AI" remains an empty shell, but reinforces the need for action in networked cooperation including multiple actors, as I contend here.[39]

This book is the first to attempt to address the formation of what I call *transnational networked cooperation* in the military AI domain, where there is little explicit motivation from the major technological powers to cooperate. Since 2014, the major powers have relegated part of the discussion to the United Nations in Geneva, within a negotiating forum called the Convention on Certain Conventional Weapons (CCW), where the use of autonomous weapons started to be discussed and then evolved to become more formal deliberations within the CCW Group of Governmental Experts (GGE), also at the United Nations in Geneva, on emerging technologies in the area of lethal autonomous weapon systems. But the pace has been glacial in this negotiating forum, where everything moves by consensus and where the wider discussion on the broader aspects of the militarization of AI has been avoided by the major powers by attempting to focus solely on autonomous weapons. When I started observing these critical deliberations back in 2014, there was a fairly open window of opportunity as there were only prototypes of autonomous weapon systems at the time, and the utilization of AI in these systems was not yet widespread. This window has now virtually closed. Therefore, it is has become even more urgent to discuss the way forward in a collective way. Autonomous systems, and increasingly AI-assisted systems, are progressively being deployed ubiquitously—for example, algorithms for facial and voice recognition are now prevalent despite having been shown to be discriminatory and biased.[40]

From the militarization to the weaponization of AI

There have been joint military–civilian applications of technology in war before now. Nuclear technology is a good example: employed both to generate electricity and to create weapons that kill. This time around the infiltration and diffusion of autonomy and AI have been more rapid and multifaceted, and this affects everyone. The ubiquitous use of AI is already permeating every part of human society (autonomous cars, Facebook algorithms that give you a personalized newsfeed, phone voice assistants, Netflix movie selections); this is different from nuclear technology, which was developed by a few nations and offered a small group the possibility to weaponize it. As Stuart Russell reminds us, "many hands hold AI cards," and so what is happening to the attempts to create global governance for AI today is distinct from what has happened since the use of the nuclear bomb and the subsequent widespread utilization of atomic energy.[41] The UN International Atomic Energy Agency started in 1957 to oversee the safe and beneficial use of nuclear energy. In contrast, AI is accessible ubiquitously and is widely distributed across the individual, public, and private spheres, with dual civilian and military uses at multiple levels. We are talking about something so omnipresent and all-encompassing that it cannot be framed as an "arms race."[42] Therefore, the militarization of AI to achieve strategic superiority is perilous. It will lead to a precarious world and will compound the risks posed by the continuing existence of nuclear arms (Chapter 3).

To reiterate, the use of autonomy and AI computation techniques in military operations is not the problem per se. Instead, what is uncertain, and what raises serious questions, is the inadequacy of human involvement in overseeing the lifecycle stages of weapon systems during system design and during operations. Increased autonomy in weapon systems means that human decisions are made only in the early stages of the mission, and there may consequently be a disconnection from what is actually done at the end. As the International Committee of the Red Cross (ICRC) states:

> It is important to recognize that **not all autonomous weapons incorporate AI and machine learning**: existing weapons with autonomy in their critical functions, such as air-defense systems with autonomous modes, generally use simple, rule-based, control software to select and attack targets. However, **AI and machine-learning software**—specifically of the type developed for "automatic target recognition"—could form the basis for future autonomous systems, bringing a new dimension of unpredictability to these weapons, as well as concerns about the lack of explainability and bias.[43]

It is vital to bear in mind that, on the one hand, not all already deployed autonomous weapons integrate AI, and, on the other hand, some AI-enhanced military robotic systems are not autonomous weapons. They are used for different functions, such as detecting patterns in surveillance or disarming an area of explosive ordinances to protect soldiers and civilians.[44] Some aspects of the militarization of AI are perhaps not as visibly problematic per se—for example: mobility (navigation, take-off and landing), intelligence (detection of explosives, objects, gunfire, data acquisition, map generation, threat assessment), certain levels of interoperability (ability of troops and systems to cooperate with others), and health management (detection of faulty systems, hacking and interference, ability to self-repair and deactivate).[45]

However, other aspects of the militarization of AI are indeed highly contentious and questionable, and are viewed as destabilizing to international security, as well as raising legal and ethical questions. These aspects are tantamount to weaponizing AI: this happens when autonomous systems are increasingly powered by AI for targeting (i.e., identification, tracking, prioritization and selection of targets), image discrimination, and target engagement ("engagement" is a euphemism for killing and destroying). Among all the functions in existing autonomous systems, the Stockholm International Peace Research Institute (SIPRI) has identified "mobility" as the one feature that leads the greatest frequency of use of autonomous functions with which are used, and about 83 out of 381 of these systems were armed when this dataset was first launched in 2017. The second most used autonomous function is "targeting"; about 130 armed systems are already in use.[46] The function of "targeting" is one of the most problematic aspects of the use of autonomous and AI-enabled systems. It is in the "critical functions"—that is, targeting, identification, tracking, prioritization and selection of targets; image discrimination; and target engagement (i.e., killing), as the ICRC calls it—that the dehumanization of war is more pronounced and where the likelihood of nonobservance of current international law is higher. In other words, it is the delegation of decisions to target and to kill to an autonomous system, and to an algorithm that is more likely to contravene moral, ethical, and legal frameworks. The Automated Decision Research confirmed these trends of heightened use of systems for targeting more recently.[47]

It is essential to determine what the acceptable uses of AI are, and more public discussion is needed to understand the extent to which the use of autonomous killing by countries will diminish their ability to live in peace, and to maintain international security and stability. As the United Nations Institute for Disarmament Research (UNIDIR) has pointed out, advancements in the hardware (i.e., the components) and in the software (i.e., AI learning algorithms and use of big data) will enable increased autonomy in weapon systems. Both are taking place at an unprecedented rate. What is hardest to deal with in creating new global governing rules is that autonomy enhances the capacity of different functions and tasks. Autonomy can be deployed to different parts of multiple weapon systems (mobility, navigation, identification and selection).[48] Therefore, according to pioneering projects led by UNIDIR and by the Stockholm International Peace Research Institute (SIPRI), in the creation of new governing mechanisms and principles the focus should be on the autonomy of the weapon systems specifically, not on autonomous systems per se.[49] The "characteristic/attribute" component that AI will add to new systems is different from previous global challenges for existing weapon systems.[50] AI amplifies the attributes already introduced by autonomy. This is what makes this global challenge different from previous attempts to govern and set global rules for weapons proliferation. In other words: in earlier global governance of weapon systems, one could count the systems (one/two/three thousand nuclear weapons/tanks/landmines, so on). At stake in this case is the addition of new autonomous attributes to different parts of diverse systems. It is mostly about the software (not the hardware, as previously). Therefore, the focus of the creation of new global governing rules shall be on the relations between machines and humans. The goal of new norms is to clarify how humans can interact with the enhanced (autonomous or AI) systems whilst remaining compliant with international law and protective of human dignity by not delegating the principal decisions to algorithms.

Ideally, autonomy and AI in weapon systems should aim to approximate the initial assumptions of the weapon users during the initial operation and the final targeting to reduce risks to life and human dignity as well as avoiding violations of existing legal, ethical, and moral constraints.[51] In order to ensure that human control remains present, or at least valid (from the initial assumptions and decisions onwards), and to attain the goal of minimizing harm, each of the lifecycle stages of any weapon system—design, development, testing, deployment, monitoring and operation, maintenance, and disposal—should strive to meet the goal of minimal harm. The observance of this basic goal ensures that systems with increased autonomy and those that use AI remain under the purview of humans and are human centered.[52] In other words, the focus of each stage of the operation of any weapon system must remain on the primacy of human control, and this makes it necessary to examine and scrutinize how the level of human involvement is upheld in the operational context of each mission.

The intensifying utilization of autonomous weapons, as well as those enhanced by AI, signals the loss of our humanity and of effective human control in waging war and in law enforcement situations. One of my concerns is the disintegrating effect on the commonly agreed global norms of international law, especially those relevant to restraining the use of military force in international relations and to the protection of civilians during times of war and in peace. This breakdown of global norms is already evident in conflicts in Yemen, Syria, Libya, and beyond. The world is headed toward an uncertain future of precarious security and fragile peace. The protection of civilian populations must take center stage again. Throughout this book I highlight the need for, and the centrality of, the human element at every stage, which is the only way to ensure that the use of such technologies remains sound, protective of human dignity, and future-proof. By this I mean that a new international agreement should stand the test of time. Even in the light of new technological advancements and discoveries, human dignity should not be infringed upon.

Readers will be informed about how taxpayers' money is being allocated for war and law enforcement guided by algorithms rather than by human reasoning and discretion. I suggest that these vast investments could be channeled toward improving social problems through the beneficial use of technology that AI makes possible. A comparable abuse of power has occurred before, when a few technologically powerful nations invented nuclear technology and weaponized it instead of using it solely for the common good of humanity. They instead amassed vast quantities of nuclear weapons under the guise of preserving "security" and "stability."[53] This kind of irresponsibility and contempt for humanity resulted in the diversion of spectacular financial investments to the production of thousands of nuclear weapons and the creation of a palpable existential threat of nuclear annihilation of humanity; to this day, there are still 13,080 nuclear weapons in existence. The risk of accidents, diversion, and malicious use is high because 3,825 are deployed in high alert.[54] A related concern is that the bulk of the investment in commercial and academic research on AI, especially computer vision and image recognition, as well as other areas, could be applied to the military realm by states or other groups such as criminal networks and terrorists.

The militarization of AI generates concerns about the future and the impact and undesirable effects of AI on human life. Enthusiasm for the potential of AI has rightly increased over the past few years, capturing the public's imagination and the attention of the media. Advancements in AI are a result not only of improvements in software programs and computational techniques, but also of two other factors. One is the emergence of big data generated by billions of Internet users around the world, ubiquitous sensors, and observation information from satellites in record numbers (Chapter 2); the other is the declining cost of the massive processing power of computers. These two factors allow for the unprecedented development and commercialization of machine learning that have enabled many AI discoveries, particularly in image and voice recognition as well as data modeling. There is thus an urgent need to determine the acceptable and nonacceptable uses of AI.

This book will also inform readers about the relevant legal and political frameworks under international law. These are the tools that can address the challenges ahead and confront the perils and obstacles. Readers will appreciate the indispensable role of rules and norms under international law in everyone's lives in this century, and will understand the risk of failing to agree on the necessary rules. They will gain a perspective on the possibilities of, and avenues toward, a nonviolent future global order where peace is predominant. In this world, AI will fulfill its potential to be employed for the common good of humanity.

Key definitions

The utilization of autonomous functions for military applications and the way that this process is progressively heightened by AI raises the following question: To what extent should AI be applied in the military arena, or should it mostly and broadly promote the common good of humanity? To address this, I investigate how AI can be harnessed for the common good of humanity and not be used to kill. Therefore, it is essential to inquire in tandem: Will global norms and the rule of law under existing international law be able to stand the test of time in the face of the militarization and weaponization of AI?

I adopt the definition of international law as "the legal order which is meant to structure the interaction between entities participating in and shaping international relations."[55] This is a broad, more encompassing understanding of international law that does not depend on the state as the primary mover in international relations. Instead, the definition references and takes into account the work and impact of international organizations, scientists, nongovernmental organizations, and other change makers who create rules and norms, and, more recently, do not necessarily act on behalf of any single state. The definition also takes into account how international law has evolved to be a law of coordination and a guiding framework of action for all actors operating in the international system to deal concretely not only with the most prominent global problems of cooperation, but also to steer humanity away from war and violence.

I am interested in the power of humanity, using the rule of law globally agreed by all nations, to create a world equipped to safeguard future generations from the scourge of war. I consider the role of the foundational human right—namely, the right

to dignity. In Chapters 2 and 5 I also highlight several cases where global cooperation has been successful in protecting the people and the planet from environmental
harms, and from the excesses of weapons proliferation, from conventional arms to
nuclear and chemical weapons. Additionally, I use tried and tested foundational principles of international law, such as precaution, the common heritage of humanity,
intergenerational equity, and the broader application and practice of international
law in other areas to prevent the harmful impacts of the weaponization of AI. *Common good governance* will construct an avenue to combat the imminent affront to
human dignity represented by the march toward the weaponization of AI.

AI is an umbrella concept applied to a vast intellectual domain, with many areas
and fields, including computational techniques that use a set of rules that specify how to solve a problem (an algorithm) to accomplish goals, make predictions,
and classify objects (Table I.1). "Machine learning" is a subcategory of AI that has
recently achieved significant breakthroughs in speech recognition, image processing, and other areas.[56] These tasks that had been the sole province of human beings
are now delegated to computers to carry out. Algorithms find data patterns using
large samples of data and ever-increasing computer processing power. Therefore, the
implications of technological advancements as they pertain to the subject of this book
are more about the software and the algorithms than the hardware. It is essential to
make a distinction between narrow AI (single-task performance by a machine, such
as speech and image recognition), general AI (the machine can understand the environment, has situational awareness and the ability to construct a logical sequence;
these features are still in the developmental stage), and super AI (when machines will
surpass human capabilities). This book is situated at the intersection between narrow and general AI to account for the problems of the present and those of the future.
Technological advancement is fast outpacing the slow progress of discussions at the
United Nations. Still, it is essential to clarify that we are not yet at the point where

Table I.1 Definition of artificial intelligence

"Artificial intelligence (AI) systems are software (and possibly also hardware) systems
designed by humans that, given a complex goal, act in the physical or digital dimension
by perceiving their environment through data acquisition, interpreting the collected
structured or unstructured data, reasoning on the knowledge, or processing the
information, derived from this data and deciding the best action(s) to take to achieve the
given goal. AI systems can either use symbolic rules or learn a numeric model, and they
can also adapt their behavior by analyzing how the environment is affected by their
previous actions. As a scientific discipline, AI includes several approaches and
techniques, such as machine learning (of which deep learning and reinforcement
learning are specific examples), machine reasoning (which includes planning,
scheduling, knowledge representation and reasoning, search, and optimization), and
robotics (which includes control, perception, sensors and actuators, as well as the
integration of all other techniques into cyber-physical systems)."

Independent High-Level Expert Group on Artificial Intelligence European Commission (2019).
High-level expert group on artificial intelligence. Ethics guidelines for trustworthy AI.

machines are more capable and possess more abilities than humans. Therefore, "Terminator" analogies (super AI) are not helpful in elucidating the complexity of what I am examining—namely, the existing problems arising from the applications of narrow and general AI.

The application of AI to weapon systems is challenging to regulate globally under rules commonly agreed to by all countries. The technologically powerful countries are reluctant to share information or to be transparent about algorithm-based decision-making to carry out tasks and increased autonomy in operations. Additionally, the militarized major powers ascribe significant importance to achieving a competitive advantage through acquiring a dominant position in AI development. In other words, the major powers, especially China and the United States, are looking to be the AI superpowers of this century.

AI needs to be distinguished from autonomy, but their interaction creates new challenges and raises ethical considerations, especially the new systems that utilize machine learning that, in turn, gives rise to issues of scrutiny and lack of predictability.[57] Autonomy entails the delegation of human authority to machines to perform different tasks. Eventually, therefore, autonomous weapon systems will be able to generate new goals and chart their own paths of algorithmic killing and decision-making. However, the increasing autonomy in weapons at present has been made possible by heightened capabilities in components and operational capacity and power. The limited ability to interrogate the outcomes of machine-learning algorithms—because of how difficult it is to determine how outputs result from data inputs (i.e., how the machine came to its conclusions)—is problematic. If the continuous learning occurs online and after the system has been deployed onto the battlefield, then the possibility of scrutinizing and assessing any outcomes becomes even harder. If a weapon system changes its behavior due to the abilities and capacities provided by machine-learning, and if this occurs mainly with the continuous feeding of online data, then it becomes ever more arduous to exercise human control.[58] It is essential to add a caveat to this affirmation: "machine learning" is not unpredictable per se. However, the decision-making system is like a black box that we do not yet fully understand. Further academic research is needed so that machine-learning systems can be opened up to better understand how they arrive at a decision. Therefore, the challenge is that because we may not understand the underlying model, we can be surprised or even confounded by its decision-making system. In addition, machine learning models are often opaque—a black box wherein we cannot undertake an inspection of the decision-making system. Finally, these machine models can also be "fragile" in the sense that an adversary may manipulate the environment/scene in such a way that the algorithm incorrectly believes it has found a correct pattern.

The following definition of autonomous weapons is illuminating here, because it could encompass systems enhanced by AI:

> a weapon system that, once activated, can select and engage targets without further intervention by a human operator. This includes human-supervised

autonomous weapons systems that are designed to allow human operators to override the operation of the weapon system but can select and engage targets without further human input after activation.[59]

Certain existing weapon systems already possess autonomy, which is a characteristic that can be included in any present and future weapon system. Autonomy enables weapon deployment to occur based upon initial assumptions and decisions about the mission's objectives as well as the time, target, and location. However, the exact final target, timing, and location are determined by a library of algorithms. The final determination often occurs without human control and oversight and does not take into account changed circumstances. Therefore, there is a separation, and a disjunction can occur between the initial assumptions and the actual execution of the mission.

To be clear, any new weapon system is subject to international humanitarian law (IHL)—the branch of international law that sets rules about what is lawful and unlawful conduct during war—as a guiding regulatory framework. Therefore, we cannot say that the use of autonomous weapons is taking place in an international legal vacuum. Not only is IHL a vital source of what all states' legal obligations are, but many other parts of the oldest system of rules and global norms governing international relations, namely international law, may furnish guidance for the ways that states will create limitations and regulations not only relating to autonomous weapons but also to the militarization of AI. In this story, however, it is not only states that are likely to construct forms of governance, but also other entities such as those I examine in my *transnational networked cooperation* analysis, which include scientists, civil society, and international organizations; hence, global governance will clearly be composed of a complex network with a diverse range of actors. In general, restrictions on methods of warfare since the first Hague Summit of nations in 1899—and even before that, when the first Geneva Convention was adopted in 1864[60]—have emerged in two ways: the first is the formulation of general principles and rules that apply to all means of warfare, and the second is through prohibition and regulation treaties (for instance, the 1993 Chemical Weapons Convention or the 1997 Landmines Treaty). The first caveat here is that these laws evolved in the first instance to address wars on an international scale (World Wars I and II, for example), and then applied in more localized civil conflicts (Yemen and Syria, for instance). I explore the legal and political architecture that governs many weapon systems and investigate its role in maintaining peace and security that could illuminate legal pathways toward the regulation of autonomous weapons under international law. Additionally, I inspect other areas where global cooperation worked before to protect humanity and the planet from threats and perils (Chapter 2).

Transnational networked cooperation

I examine the conditions under which *common good governance* could be enacted to safeguard the future of peace and security, in particular the role of *transnational networked cooperation* in the creation of a global public good: that is, no weaponization of AI. I also observe how different change makers are spearheading new norms and new forms of global governance on their own, since some member states at the United Nations—namely, the militarized great powers—may be falling behind in their duty to act as custodians to protect peace. The extent to which new challenges are dealt with in the international system, mainly because new advances are being made more quickly than global governance can take shape, is of great concern. It is not clear how international law will address these emerging challenges, or if the prevailing global norms will be sufficient to deal with them. To understand the range of conditions necessary for *common good governance* to develop, I will assess the relationships between, significance of, and role of the various actors and entities shown in the chronology (Table I.2), starting with the role of scientists and then reviewing the work of the United Nations in this discussion over recent years. I also devote attention to the transnational and interdisciplinary groups of people who founded the international Campaign to Stop Killer Robots. I delve into and investigate the role of private sector actors, as well as weapons producers, Nobel Peace laureates, and the United Nations Secretary-General, among many others involved.

There are noticeably widening gaps between developments in the technology of warfare and the international law regimes to regulate them. Systematic investigation is needed into issues of accountability for violating international law, as well as to understand current attempts at developing satisfactory legal regimes. The rise of the militarization and weaponization of AI marks a fundamental shift in international politics and signals a changing global order at the intersection of the fourth industrial revolution—characterized by autonomous decision-making, cyberspace, AI, and the possibilities of weaponization the new technologies—and the third revolution in warfare.[61] The first revolution was enabled by gunpowder, the second by the invention of nuclear weapons; the third is differentiated from the preceding two by machine autonomy and robotics with enabling AI technologies that will make them increasingly autonomous. The confluence of the fourth industrial revolution and the third revolution in warfare creates opportunities but also heralds the risks created by a shifting global order. There is thus an admonitory dimension to this book.[62] Humanity is entering the fourth industrial revolution, as Klaus Schwab, the President of the World Economic Forum, has noted.[63] In this world, the digital economy will be ubiquitous, breaking the barriers between the biological, digital, and physical realms, and affecting all people on the planet in ways that the previous revolutions did not. The rapid development of AI will be a predominant feature of this new world.

The United Nations has been discussing what do about such new developments and technologies in war since 2014. There is widespread consensus that human control and judgment over decisions should prevail when force is applied and lives are taken. A growing chorus of countries is clamoring for new global governance in the areas of autonomy in war: they would like to see a new international treaty. All 55 countries of the African Union would like it. Thirty countries have requested a preventive prohibition of autonomous weapons. Austria, Brazil, and Chile formally proposed the start of negotiations toward a legally binding treaty that will ensure "meaningful human control" over critical functions (i.e., the ones used to kill) of autonomous weapon systems. The forms of governance emerging to grapple with the

Table I.2 Raising global attention

2009: The International Committee for Robotic Arms Control is founded. The following scientists sounded the alarm regarding robotic systems that are autonomous: Noel Sharkey, Peter Asaro, Jürgen Altmann, Robert Sparrow.

2011: The International Committee of the Red Cross (ICRC) mentions autonomous weapons in a statement for the first time.

2012: The United States is the only country to make autonomy an official component of its national security strategy in the Department of Defense Directive 3000.09.[64]
Human Rights Watch issues a report, *Losing Humanity: The Case against Killer Robots*, arguing against the use of autonomous weapons.

2013: The Campaign to Stop Killer Robots is launched.
The UN Human Rights Council debates the issue. The UN Special Rapporteur on extrajudicial, summary, or arbitrary executions, Christof Heyns, publishes a seminal report. Heyns laments that if the application and widespread use of lethal robotics in war goes unchecked and rapid technological advancement occurs, especially on the heels of the violation of international law through the use of drones, this "could undermine the ability of the international legal system to preserve a minimum of global order."[65] Nobel Peace laureates add their influential voices. The campaign has shown impressive growth since its creation, with more than 100 nongovernmental organizations in over 50 countries participating.

2014: May 13–15. Autonomous weapons and new technologies are discussed for the first time at a historic meeting of the United Nations member states in Geneva.

2015: April 13–17. Second Informal Meeting of Experts at the United Nations, chaired by Ambassador Michael Biontino of Germany.

2016: April 11–15. Second Informal Meeting of Experts at the United Nations, chaired by Ambassador Michael Biontino of Germany. Widespread mention of "meaningful human control." He decides to call for the first formal meeting by establishing a Group of Governmental Experts (GGE).

2017: Ambassador Amandeep Singh Gill of India chaired two formal GGE sessions. For details, Chapter 3. Most countries called for an international treaty, but Germany, Australia, Turkey, the United States, and Israel were opposed to this.

2018: April 9–13. GGE formal meeting chaired by Ambassador Amandeep Singh Gill of India. Thirty countries called for a preventive prohibition treaty.
August 27–31: outcome document—"Possible Guiding Principles" (Chapter 1)
Twelve countries do not support a new treaty (Chapter 3): Australia, Belgium, France, Germany, Israel, Republic of Korea, Russia, Spain, Sweden, Turkey, the United States, and the United Kingdom.

2015–2019: A dense network of change makers calls for different types of global action:

Scientific community
Private sectors (civilian and military)
Transnational advocacy community: The Campaign to Stop Killer Robots
The International Committee of the Red Cross
and the Member states of the United Nations.

2015–2019: The AI Scientists' Letters
The first open letter was published on July 28, 2015. It received sustained widespread attention and publicity from media worldwide.

The letter states: "Autonomous weapons select and engage targets without human intervention"; these weapons exclude drones where humans are in charge of the decision-making on targets. The heart of their call for action is this: "AI technology has reached a point where the deployment of such systems is—practically if not legally—feasible within years, not decades, and the stakes are high: autonomous weapons have been described as the third revolution in warfare, after gunpowder and nuclear arms." They add that these AI weapons will be the future Kalashnikovs because what makes them different from nuclear weapons is that they do not require expensive raw materials and will become omnipresent.[66] They state that the key question for humanity is whether to start a global race to militarize AI or to act preventively. If humanity fails to act, the scientists' warning is stark: "Autonomous weapons are ideal for tasks such as assassinations, destabilizing nations, subduing populations, and selectively killing a particular ethnic group. We, therefore, believe that a military AI arms race would not be beneficial for humanity. There are many ways in which AI can make battlefields safer for humans, especially civilians, without creating new tools for killing people."[67]

Other letters have been published since that have had a significant impact.

2017 and beyond: *The AI for Good Global Movement*
What I call the *AI for Good Global Movement* comprises initiatives that seek ways to use AI for the benefit of humanity (i.e., for the common good). The movement finds ways to use AI for humanitarian purposes to implement the United Nations Sustainable Development Goals (SDGs) and to improve humanitarian relief.

2018: The European Parliament passed a resolution that calls for a ban on autonomous killing. About two dozen Nobel Peace laureates issued a joint statement in favor of a ban. More than 70 prominent faith leaders from around the world released a statement calling for a ban.

2018: Over 200 technology companies and organizations from more than 36 countries and 2,600 individuals issue a pledge committing to "neither participate in nor support the development, manufacture, trade, or use of lethal autonomous weapons"; because of moral, accountability, proliferation, and security-related concerns over fully autonomous weapons, the pledge states that "the decision to take a human life should never be delegated to a machine."[68]

2018: Google makes a historic announcement that it is "not developing AI for use in weapons" and "will not design or deploy AI" for technology that causes "overall harm" or "contravenes widely accepted principles of international law and human rights."

2018: António Guterres, United Nations Secretary-General: "The weaponization of Artificial Intelligence is a growing concern." "The prospect of weapons that can select and attach a target on their own raises multiple alarms and could trigger new arms races." "The prospect of machines with the discretion and power to take human life is morally repugnant."[69]

2018: The ICRC's position is that states must determine limitations on the type and degree of autonomy required for lawful actions under international humanitarian law and international law. Notwithstanding compliance, the ICRC admits its concerns that the heart of the matter remains the discomfort about delegating the authority for the decision to kill to computer algorithms.

2021: The ICRC publishes its new position in May, calling on states to create new global governance through legally binding obligations.

Continued

Table I.2 *Continued*

2018–2021: European Parliament resolution calls for an international treaty on autonomous weapons.

United Nations member states continue meeting in Geneva and fail to reach an agreement on what to do due to opposition from Russia. The majority of states desire an international legally binding agreement.

2022–2025: discussions continue at the United Nations. Costa Rica leads a coalition requesting all countries to call for urgency in establishing a new international treaty on autonomous weapons.

2023: first summit on Responsible AI in the Military Domain (called by the Netherlands and the Republic of Korea). This was the first times a group of countries jointly discusses military AI.

---

challenges are complex, and the actions of states and what is happening at the United Nations, even though notable, are only part of the story. To describe the complexity of the actions on the global stage, I coined the term *transnational networked cooperation*: a discernible mosaic of different change makers trying to cope with global challenges by using authoritative knowledge and drawing on lessons learned from what happened in previous cases of global cooperation.

Common good governance for a shifting global order: A more inclusive and humanistic approach

This book proposes avenues for creating a new global framework to regulate autonomous weapons and govern the military use of AI—a global public good—with renewed ways to operationalize more inclusive cooperation in this complex area of international security. This novel approach includes states and scientists, civil society, philanthropists, private sectors, and activists. In many ways, the new world order will require innovative ways to solve problems, in addition to clear knowledge of existing successful models. I examine the global trend toward militarizing AI and, at the same time, appraise the initiatives that set principles and standards. *Common good governance* is anchored in previous instruments that have established global constraining mechanisms for earlier evolutions and revolutions in warfare, namely those seeking to prohibit chemical warfare, control conventional arms, or limit nuclear arms. It is in this context that I proffer reasons why the world must care. I gauge and assess the instability and insecurity that may arise from the weaponization of AI and, at the same time, review the United Nations' endeavors to maintain peace and sustain hybrid global governance initiatives. In the light of these undertakings, I also evaluate the role of the United States, the European Union, China, and others on the global stage.

The world is up against a completely new challenge because AI-associated technologies will affect every sector of society and will be available to many more people than nuclear or conventional weapons ever could be. Therefore, it is uncertain whether the current forms of global governance under existing international law frameworks will be adequate to address the challenges posed by this new transformation facing humanity, precipitated by advancements in AI that have a great impact on peace and conflict. In terms of weapons controls and disarmament, arms are either regulated (across categories) or prohibited (one category at a time). But we are now up against something substantively different and unusual: this is about software in an ever more ubiquitous technology accessible to many more people than previous technological innovations have been.

My participation in high-level global initiatives on autonomous weapons and applications of AI provides me with first-hand scholarly insider perspectives on—and practical familiarity with—the communities involved in the relevant discussions across the world. Consequently, throughout this book's chapters:

- I offer an in-depth insider explanation of the attempts to create principles and global norms to address the intensification of autonomy in warfare;
- I examine the intricacies of the creation of a new global framework to govern the military use of AI;
- I investigate the challenges to existing international law, and survey the germane and pertinent parts of the political and legal architectures that relate to the matters scrutinized here;
- I give an account of the threats to global security as a consequence of the increasing militarization of AI;
- I reflect on the factors that imperil peace in the world by investigating the inspiring and elucidating examples of previous cases of global cooperation to protect the climate and different parts of the planet, and also attempts to prohibit and regulate different previous technologies of the means and methods of warfare;
- I offer three new concepts: *transnational networked cooperation*, *common good governance*, and *humanity's security* to suggest the way forward in offering more humanistic approaches.

Transnational networked cooperation: this refers to an exceptional mosaic of change makers, emerging from a multi-actor cooperative effort, who spearhead debates about what is legally, morally, and ethically acceptable in shaping the future of humanity. These change makers do not represent any single country and they do not act under the auspices of a particular national leadership in the international arena; instead, they are bound by a belief in securing a humane and just future. Such *transnational networked cooperation* can emerge despite the dearth of state-to-state cooperation and create new blueprints for action and more inclusive change in a way that is informed by scientists, civil society members, the private sector, and some states, including the developing countries that tend to be excluded from high-level discussions on AI. In this book, I advance the idea that there are five requisite criteria for the rise of *transnational networked cooperation* to address ways to prevent autonomous killing: knowledge generation about the problem based upon a common humanity-based discourse; creation of precautionary governing or preventive regulatory frameworks; the presence of at least one epistemic community; the influence of a transnational advocacy network that promotes activism and attempts to persuade; and the formation and cooperation of networks in promoting the sense of urgency to act. I see the same formation of *transnational networked cooperation* that emerged to fight the pandemic and create and distribute vaccines, and to combat climate change. This is a concept that will be useful to fully understand other areas of global governance.

To elaborate on the requisite criteria, I delve into the work of AI scientists, the private sector that mostly generates the technologies in question, the global campaigners, the United Nations, the European Union, and regional organizations. I probe the nature of the collaboration between government and civil society to face a common challenge that requires *common good governance* to be successful. I see *transnational networked cooperation* as a shared enterprise that should include people or representatives from different communities to be transparent and hold leaders accountable for their decisions. It is also an initiative that can directly involve other actors in international law, as well as civic actors such as philanthropists and scientists.

Common good governance: the creation of a global public good that arises from the efforts of several entities (states and others) to advance and drive global processes, as well as combat problems in areas where there are either no global norms or institutional foundations, a lack of political willingness and determination, or, at best, imprecise guidelines for global action. In other words, there is neither certainty nor specific governance in these areas—that is, there are no precise rules administering commonly agreed behaviors among nations. *Common good governance* takes into account the urgency to act by present and future generations and is therefore based upon the already existing principles of precautionary action, the common concerns and heritage of humanity, intergenerational equity, and the need for preventive action.[70] These two related terms will offer novel avenues for further exploration in the literature to fill the ontological lacuna in this area of study within international law and global governance. Here, they are applied specifically to the regulation of the matters under consideration, but can be later used to investigate other areas of global governance where state action is lagging—for example, in tackling the climate crisis, where there are rising philanthropic, financial, and grassroots networks driving the action. The framework the concepts offers makes a persuasive contribution to the discussions on military AI by advancing an innovative perspective on how the debates on military AI might be framed to ensure a humanistic approach to the way that new technologies are used in war. The chief motivation of this type of generation of cooperation is the attainment of the common good for present and future generations.

Notions of the common heritage of humanity, the common concern of humankind, the principle of precaution, the distinction between civilians and combatants, rising principles on AI, and the existing international legal instruments in different areas of global cooperation are the operating pillars guiding the creation of a framework that animates attempts to develop new *common good governance* structures and mechanisms for a shifting global order (Chapters 2 and 5). Containing the unrestrained militarization of AI is a pursuit of global dimensions for the sake of peace and security. As a result, the creation of *common good governance* is shaped by utilizing the successes and failures of previous attempts at global cooperation, along with all relevant sources of legal and political guidance, including the precautionary and intergenerational principles encompassed in international law, as well as all pertinent previous legal and political frameworks that may be applicable or used as inspiration for something made anew.[71] I will investigate the extent to which prevailing ideas and mechanisms to govern global security problems (such as nuclear or chemical weapons, protecting the ozone layer, Antarctica and other areas of the planet) can inform what kind of new governance is needed. I also draw inspiration from the architecture of the "common heritage of humanity," and update and operationalize it to reflect on AI as a "global common" that should be used for the benefit of humankind. "Global commons" are areas and spaces on the planet that cannot be weaponized, but have to be used for peace, and no one can claim jurisdiction over these spaces, such as Antarctica, outer space, the atmosphere, and the high seas. In this regard, my new concept of *common good governance* also draws from several areas of existing international law practice and doctrine, as well as from the principles for the advancement of sustainable development for the betterment of humanity as a whole.

I examine the conditions under which *common good governance* can create global public goods, in particular the role of *transnational networked cooperation*. Accordingly, I observe how different change makers are spearheading new norms and global cooperation on their own, since member states at the United Nations Security Council—the arbiter of peace and security—may be falling behind in their duty to act as custodians of the peace. The extent to which new challenges are governed in the international system, mainly because new advances are being made more quickly than global governance can take shape, is of great concern. It is not clear how international law will address these emerging challenges or if the prevailing global norms will be sufficient to deal with them. Significant gaps are growing between developments in the technology of warfare and the international law regimes to regulate them.

Finally, *humanity's security* is an effort to challenge the outdated notion of national security—with its military focus on what constitutes a threat and a typically insular way to tackle problems—that serves little purpose today where all problems facing humanity necessitate a concerted approach. Humanity's security requires states to pool their resources, capacities, and strengths for the common good of humankind to attain global public goods on a planetary scale. At the center of this new concept is the idea that the security of states is fundamental (national security). However, the safety of individuals, especially vulnerable populations, must also be safeguarded (human security); crucial is the realization that the security and safety of states and individuals in one country are inextricably intertwined with the security and safety of individuals in all countries. The notion of humanity's security emphasizes that the fate and well-being of individuals in one country are tied to and depend upon the welfare of all individuals in all other countries.

The pandemic has proven that no one is safe until everyone is protected, and climate change has shown that there is no place from which stand by and watch from afar. The effects of anthropogenic interference with the climate at calamitous levels are ongoing everywhere. What is different about humanity's security, derived from the concepts of national and human security, is that it attests to the urgent need for solutions that must come from all countries, in collective, preventive action, to respond to the threats by pooling their resources. Additionally, humanity's security calls for a more self-aware and purposeful integration between human beings and their natural environment and ecological systems. Without the realization of this inextricable connection, there will be no easy way out of the conundrum that humans face. Humanity—the partnership between governments, scientists, individuals, aboriginal communities, and international institutions—is at the center of the communal and global changes needed to contain the ongoing planetary mega threats. Instead of privileging only the state as the hub for action, I argue that the state remains essential but is no longer capable of acting alone, so it must rally the necessary strategic partnerships: scientific, collective, and practical. Combined, these three concepts will guide consideration of how to create frameworks to halt the march toward autonomous killing, and a race to the bottom led by the competition to militarize AI.

The global geopolitical context

War among states is again a reality—in a markedly worrying trend since the decline in international wars after 1945. We are in a phase where there is a confluence of new and potentially contending challenges marked by renewed global power rivalry: the fourth industrial revolution (the digital economy), the diffusion of AI that is affecting many aspects of human society, the third revolution in warfare, and a retreat from globalism and from long-held norms of international law. These are daunting challenges and raise difficult questions that need to be answered. I confront such challenges head-on with an examination of the increasing rivalry among the technological superpowers to militarize and weaponize AI. The amounts of money being spent on this are astounding and so, with no global legal framework to govern the military use of AI, the road to the future is fraught with uncertainty.

In order to construct *common good governance*, I address several questions in turn. First, can algorithms meet the obligations and lawful constraints set by international law? Second, can the legal scope of responsibilities in current and prevailing law—for instance, IHL—be codified in computer-controlled processes that will then operate predictably in hardware or in cyberspace? Third, even if this is technologically and legally feasible, should humanity yield its capacity to authorize the decision to kill?[72] In the latter case, I explore whether there are fundamental ethical and moral impediments to granting permission for autonomous killing that are independent of technological prowess and advancement. These constraints would include the need to preserve human dignity as a permanent right from which observance cannot be exempted, and to avoid the breach of responsibility that would occur with the distancing that technology would enable between the humans supervising or monitoring operations and the systems that conduct killings.[73] This breach would be objectionable as the responsibility, or lack thereof, pertains to the thresholds that can be put in place to enable operators to confirm or deny the permissibility of autonomous killing. Likewise, within the legal realm, the law of state responsibility, an old foundational component of international law, would advise that responsibility is inextricably connected to human agency. International law has evolved with human intent as a central precept for its functioning. In this discussion, a simple antipersonnel landmine or a sophisticated AI-enabled weapon would raise the same set of concerns that go above and beyond their technological capabilities to address the humanitarian aspects of their use. Consequently, they can be deemed unacceptable for the conscience of humanity to bear.[74]

As mentioned, autonomy is a characteristic that can be added to any civilian or military components of any current or future system. Such flexibility will add enormous complexity to creating and administering new forms of global governance. Currently, there are highly autonomous components and attributes in systems already being deployed. In terms of prevailing international law frameworks, the inclusion of autonomy is not illegal per se. However, its attributes and features might be linked and programmed in ways that may violate international law prescriptions. There may also be morally and ethically questionable uses that may be intolerable or unlawful under international law. The question here is: will it be ethically acceptable for weapons with AI software to be programmed to independently select and target people to kill? Furthermore, machine learning will occur because of progress in AI, meaning that software with learning capabilities now prompts significant questions about predictability: machine learning systems may be inconsistent and therefore inscrutable, consequently raising the risk that international norms and laws may be violated.[75]

In sum, increased autonomous weapon systems raise ethical and moral questions: will it be right, even if technologically possible, to allow an algorithm to take a human life? Is the contest among the technological superpowers to militarize AI unavoidable? In what ways can the 193 member states of the United Nations prevent it? AI weapons will be cheap and abundant, according to scientists, so how can the international community stop terrorists from acquiring them? What global norms should be in place? What will happen when autonomous cyber weapons become operational? The international community must act preventively to stop the development of AI technologies capable of being utilized for military purposes. The global competition to militarize AI and to develop autonomous arms is underway. If this cannot be stopped—which would be desirable—it must be regulated under international law.

The precedents to autonomous killing

Unmanned aerial vehicles, commonly known as drones, have been weaponized and are increasingly used in warfare and in situations that are not considered to be states of war, with no multilaterally agreed rules under international law. While a human remains in the control loop, the use of drones has lowered the threshold for the use of military force in international relations. Targeted killings have become commonplace. But drones are different from autonomous weapons, AI-enhanced or not. There is still a human in the decision-making control loop who decides to kill. The terrorist attacks against the United States in 2001 prompted the country to start weaponizing its drones. In 2002 the United States was the only country developing armed drones, but now this technological innovation has proliferated. Armed groups are also in possession of such systems.[76] The United States and other countries, including China, France, Germany, India, Israel, Russia, South Korea, and the United Kingdom, are working to increase the autonomy of military systems, and different examples are already in place. Drones are not autonomous weapons, which are qualitatively different because no humans are controlling the use of force.

The use of armed drones in the last few years serves as an indication of what lies ahead. First, armed drones have proliferated rapidly[77] and with this proliferation comes a decline in cost. Thus, more disruptive opportunities arise as more actors have access to the new technology at lower prices.[78] That being said, the decisions that states make on peace and security are profoundly informed by international law.[79] If they disrespect IHL and human rights law, their reputation and prestige may be compromised.[80] For instance, there are heated discussions on the legality and legitimacy of the use of armed drones to conduct extrajudicial killings through extraterritorial targeting (targeted killings).[81] Even though there is nothing inherently illegal in the use of drones and their remote operators may be fully able to comply with the rules of IHL, their current use may disrespect and distort other branches of international law, such as human rights law, as well as the rules on the legality of the use of force that have been responsible for sustaining the long peace among nations since World War II.[82]

A robot world

The benefits of the increased use of robotics in society are significant and groundbreaking.[83] Robots with increasing levels of autonomy are already an integral part of life in this century and will gradually play an ever more significant role in medicine, in the judicial system, and in the entertainment industry. As Stuart Russell says, the future is super intelligent.[84] Especially noteworthy is the new breed of robots, which will be more autonomous and decide independently on their courses of action. Autonomy in robotics will be made even more possible with further progress in AI and the growing availability of data from which AI systems can learn. These phenomena characterize the shifting global order toward full autonomy—characterized in particular by the automation of the use of force—and by an economy that is dominated by digital technology and the digital economy.

A global legal framework governing military AI is of the essence and warrants global cooperation. The weaponization of AI is disruptive; it represents a paradigm shift in the way wars are waged, law enforcement is conducted, and violence in enacted. Autonomous killing is likely to become the dominant aspect of the new AI military race of the 21st century, which is developing fast via the increasing adoption of autonomous weapons, the progressive militarization of AI, and other means of enacting violence. Nonetheless, there is a caveat: this "race" is not like those of the past (e.g. the nuclear arms race), because innovations will not be exclusive to nation states and "autonomous weapons" do not necessarily have to be embodied in an object or hardware (as in previous weapon systems). Many of the autonomous weapon systems we will start to see can be derived from consumer products, modified to become weapons. The crux of the problem is more about the software and the algorithms than the hardware. One consequence is a continued escalation of asymmetric warfare, terrorism, and cyberattacks (in peace time), for instance. An autonomous weapon can be as simple as a mass-produced drone with an explosive payload attached to it. In the future, open-source drone software could enable swarms of low-cost drones to become significant weapons. The new technology of 3D printing and plentiful civilian technology (motors, batteries) would also allow new devices to be created directly, bypassing traditional supply chains and the enforcement of customs regulations. For all these reasons, the weaponization of AI marks a critical shift not only in the nature of warfare but also in international security. The proliferation of autonomous weapons will occur more rapidly, at a lower cost, and in different ways from anything we have experienced in the development of any other conventional weapons or weapons of mass destruction.

The changing relationship between humanity and technology will have profound consequences for peace and security in a way that is already affecting the current global order in unfavorable and detrimental ways.[85] There is a connection between the use of force and the violation of the bodily integrity of people. In terms of the expectations of international law, the use of lethal force is only to be carried out in exceptional cases. The use of force in a nonattributable way increases the risk of war. If it becomes easier to initiate conflict with readily accessible technologies that will permit more states not to have to risk the lives of their soldiers, then more conflicts will take place. In addition, given the capacity for states to develop and use military force incrementally through autonomous systems that are nonattributable, it may be very difficult to determine how the action was initiated. It will therefore not be possible to hold anyone accountable through the existing global governance mechanisms of international law.[86]

At this critical juncture for humanity, the weaponization of AI would divert the world's resources away from attempts to reverse catastrophic climate change. Compounding the challenges ahead, these new technologies all have dual applications: civilian and military. We are talking about applications of technology that will soon be accessible to individuals for legitimate and beneficial purposes in medicine, assisted care, and life in general, but they will also be available to criminals, terrorists, and dictators oppressing their populations. This heightens the need for the creation of *common good governance* for all, thereby achieving prosperity and well-being on a global scale.

The protection of human dignity should guide conduct in war and peace; decisions over life and death shall not be done on the basis of algorithms in software. My premise is that all powerful technologies must serve humanity. *Common good governance* frameworks will be needed to set guidelines and to coordinate global action to attain *humanity's security*. Countries cannot relinquish their international legal, moral, and ethical responsibilities, or their humanity in war and at peace. The quest for peace should be undertaken through cooperative diplomacy for a better world, despite the resistance of the few technologically powerful nations. This is about what kind of future we want for all people living now, and for future generations.

Notes

1. *An Open Letter to the United Nations Convention on Certain Conventional Weapons* (Future of Life Institute, 2017), https://futureoflife.org/2017/08/20/autonomous-weapons-open-letter-2017/.
2. Paul Scharre, *Army of None: Autonomous Weapons and the Future of War* (W. W. Norton & Company, 2018): p. 27; Paul Scharre, "Killer Apps: The Real Dangers of an AI Arms Race," Foreign Affairs (May/June 2019), https://www.foreignaffairs.com/articles/2019-04-16/killer-apps.
3. Toby Walsh, *Autonomous Weapons: An Open Letter from AI & Robotics Researchers* (Future of Life Institute, 2015), https://futureoflife.org/2016/02/09/open-letter-autonomous-weapons-ai-robotics/.
4. Denise Garcia, "Redirect Military Budgets to Tackle Climate Change and Pandemics." *Nature*, vol. 584, no. 7822 (August 2020): pp. 521–523, doi:10.1038/d41586-020-02460-9.
5. António Guterres, United Nations Secretary-General. General Assembly, September 2018.
6. Philip Feldman, Aaron Dant, and Aaron Massey, *Integrating Artificial Intelligence into Weapon Systems* (arXiv, Cornell University, May 10, 2019), https://arxiv.org/abs/1905.03899; Michael C. Horowitz et al., *Artificial Intelligence and International Security* (Center for a New American Security, July 2018), https://www.cnas.org/publications/reports/artificial-intelligence-and-international-security.
7. Vincent Boulanin and Maaike Verbruggen, *Mapping the Development of Autonomy in Weapon Systems* (SIPRI, November 2017): p. 38.
8. Ibid; Scharre, *Army of None: Autonomous Weapons and the Future of War.*
9. Walsh, *Autonomous Weapons: An Open Letter from AI & Robotics Researchers.*
10. Jürgen Altmann and Frank Sauer, "Autonomous Weapon Systems and Strategic Stability." *Survival*, vol. 59, no. 5 (2017): pp. 117–142, doi:10.1080/00396338.2017.1375263.
11. Daniele Amoroso and Guglielmo Tamburrini, "In Search of the 'Human Element': International Debates on Regulating Autonomous Weapons Systems." *The International Spectator*, vol. 56, no. 1 (February 2021): pp. 1–19, doi:10.1080/03932729.2020.1864995.

12. Vincent Boulanin et al., *Limits on Autonomy in Weapons Systems: Identifying Practical Elements of Human Control* (ICRC & SIPRI, June 2020).

13. In appreciation of Frank Sauer's advice.

14. Frank Sauer, "Stepping Back from the Brink: Why Multilateral Regulation of Autonomy in Weapons Systems is Difficult, yet Imperative and Feasible." *International Review of the Red Cross*, vol. 102, no. 913 (April 2020): pp. 235–259. doi:10.1017/S1816383120000466.

15. Michael Boardman and Fiona Butcher, *An Exploration of Maintaining Human Control in AI Enabled Systems and the Challenges of Achieving it* (NATO, 2019), STO-MP-IST-178-07. Elke Schwarz, "Autonomous Weapons Systems, Artificial Intelligence, and the Problem of Meaningful Human Control." *The Philosophical Journal of Conflict and Violence*, vol. 5, no. 1 (2021). doi:10.22618/TP.PJCV.20215.1.139004.

16. Statement by Secretary of Defense Lloyd J. Austin III on the President's Fiscal Year 2024 Budget, Department of Defense Releases the President's Fiscal Year 2024 Defense Budget, US Department of Defense, March 13, 2023.

17. Ronald O'Rourke, *Renewed Great Power Competition: Implications for Defense—Issues for Congress* (Congressional Research Service, 2020), https://sgp.fas.org/crs/natsec/R43838.pdf; The Economist Newspaper Limited, "The Growing Danger of Great-Power Conflict," January 25, 2018, https://www.economist.com/leaders/2018/01/25/the-growing-danger-of-great-power-conflict.

18. Inge Kaul, Isabelle Grunberg, and Marc Stern, *Global Public Goods* (New York-Oxford: Oxford University Press, 1999); Séverine Deneulin and Nicholas Townsend, "Public Goods, Global Public Goods and the Common Good." *International Journal of Social Economics*, vol. 34, no. 1/2 (2007): pp. 19–36.

19. Institute for Economics & Peace, *Global Peace Index 2021: Measuring Peace in a Complex World* (IEP: Sydney, 2021), https://www.visionofhumanity.org/wp-content/uploads/2021/06/GPI-2021-web-1.pdf.

20. Diego Lopes da Silva et al. *Trends in World Military Expenditure* (SIPRI, 2022).

21. Artificial Intelligence in Military Market by Offering (Software, Hardware, Services), Technology (Machine Learning, Computer vision), Application, Installation Type, Platform, Region—Global Forecast to 2025. Markets & Markets, Market Research Report, March 2023.

22. Denise Garcia, "Lethal Artificial Intelligence and Change: The Future of International Peace and Security." *International Studies Review*, vol. 20, no. 2 (May 2018), doi:10.1093/isr/viy029.

23. Ruti Teitel, *Humanity's Law* (Oxford University Press, 2011).

24. Daniel S. Hoadley and Kelley M. Sayler, *Artificial Intelligence and National Security* (Congressional Research Service, January 2019); fas.org/sgp/crs/natsec/R45178.pdf.

25. See the International Panel for the Regulation of Autonomous Weapons reports, available at https://www.ssoar.info/ssoar/discover?query=iPRAW&submit=.

26. I thank Carlos Arriaga Serrano and my Global Governance class of Fall 2020 for our conversations.

27. Capgemini Research Institute, "Climate AI: How Artificial Intelligence can Power your Climate Action Strategy," December 2020, https://www.capgemini.com/wp-content/uploads/2021/05/Report-Climate-AI-4.pdf.

28. Ricardo Vinuesa et al., "The Role of Artificial Intelligence in Achieving the Sustainable Development Goals." *Nature Communications*, vol. 11, no. 233 (2020), doi:10.1038/s41467-019-14108-y.

29. Ibid., 7.
30. Maaike Verbruggen, "The Role of Civilian Innovation in the Development of Lethal Autonomous Weapon Systems." *Global Policy*, vol. 10, no. 3 (2019): pp. 338–342, doi:10.1111/1758-5899.12663.
31. On May 17, 2021, SIPRI's, Vincent Boulanin participated in a virtual United Nations Security Council Arria-formula meeting entitled "The Impact of Emerging Technologies on International Peace and Security."
32. Michael C. Horowitz, "Artificial Intelligence, International Competition, and the Balance of Power." *Texas National Security Review*, vol. 1, no. 3 (May 2018), http://hdl.handle.net/2152/65638.
33. Stuart J. Russell, *Human Compatible Artificial Intelligence and the Problem of Control* (Penguin Books, 2019), p. 113.
34. Stuart J. Russell and Peter Norvig, *Artificial Intelligence: A Modern Approach*, 3rd ed. (Pearson Education, 2003).
35. Isabella Jibilian and Katie Canales, "The US is Readying Sanctions Against Russia Over the SolarWinds Cyber Attack." Business Insider, April 15, 2021. https://www.businessinsider.com/solarwinds-hack-explained-government-agencies-cyber-security-2020-12.
36. Russell, *Human Compatible Artificial Intelligence.*
37. I thank Eugenio V. Garcia for our conversations about this point and for all his advice.
38. Responsible AI in the Military Domain Summit, REAIM, The Hague, The Netherlands, February 15–16, REAIM Call to Action. https://www.government.nl/ministries/ministry-of-foreign-affairs/news/2023/02/16/reaim-2023-call-to-action.
39. Vincent Boulanin and Dustin A. Lewis, "Responsible Reliance Concerning Development and Use of AI in the Military Domain." *Ethics and Information Technology*, vol. 25, no. 8 (2023).
40. Daniel Varona, Yadira Lizama-Mue, and Juan Luis Suárez, "Machine Learning's Limitations in Avoiding Automation of Bias." *AI and Society*, vol. 36, no. 1 (2021): pp. 197–203, doi:10.1007/s00146-020-00996-y.
41. Russell, *Human Compatible Artificial Intelligence*, p. 249; I thank my conversations with the always prescient Benoît Pélopidas.
42. Heather M. Roff, "The Frame Problem: The AI 'Arms Race' Isn't One." *Bulletin of the Atomic Scientists*, vol. 75, no. 3 (2019): pp. 95–98.
43. International Committee of the Red Cross, "Artificial Intelligence and Machine Learning in Armed Conflict: A Human-Centered Approach." *International Review of the Red Cross*, no. 913 (March 2021): p. 4, https://www.icrc.org/en/document/artificial-intelligence-and-machine-learning-armed-conflict-human-centred-approach.
44. Ibid.
45. See SIPRI reports since 2017, https://www.sipri.org/research/armament-and-disarmament/emerging-military-and-security-technologies/artificial-intelligence.
46. Boulanin and Verbruggen, *Mapping the Development of Autonomy in Weapon Systems.*
47. Automated Decision Research, "Artificial Intelligence and Automated Decisions: Shared Challenges in the Civil and Military Spheres," September 2022 Report. Available at: https://automatedresearch.org/news/report/artificial-intelligence-and-automated-decisions-shared-challenges-in-the-civil-and-military-spheres/.
48. According to a database by Heather Roff, formerly available here: https://globalsecurity.asu.edu/robotics-autonomy. [Last accessed December 10, 2018; no longer publicly available.]

49. Kerstin Vignard, *The Weaponization of Increasingly Autonomous Technologies: Consider-ing Ethics and Social Values*, UNIDIR Resources 3 (UNIDIR, 2015), https://unidir.org/files/publications/pdfs/considering-ethics-and-social-values-en-624.pdf; Paul Scharre and Michael C. Horowitz, *An Introduction to Autonomy in Weapon Systems* (Center for a New American Security, 2015), https://www.cnas.org/publications/reports/an-introduction-to-autonomy-in-weapon-systems; Vincent Boulanin, *Mapping The Development of Autonomy in Weapon Systems: A Primer on Autonomy* (SIPRI, 2016).

50. Kerstin Vignard, "The Weaponization of Increasingly Autonomous Technolo-gies: Concerns, Characteristics and Definitional Approaches: A Primer," *UNIDIR Resources* 6 (Geneva: UNIDIR, 2017), https://unidir.org/files/publications/pdfs/the-weaponization-of-increasingly-autonomous-technologies-concerns-characteristics-and-definitional-approaches-en-689.pdf; Boulanin and Verbruggen, *Mapping the Development of Autonomy in Weapon Systems.*

51. International Panel on the Regulation of Autonomous Weapons, *Building Blocks for a Reg-ulation on LAWS and Human Control: Updated Recommendations to the GGE on LAWS* (July 2021), https://www.ssoar.info/ssoar/discover?query=iPRAW&submit=.

52. ICRC, *Artificial Intelligence and Machine Learning in Armed Conflict.*

53. Ray Acheson, *Banning the Bomb, Smashing the Patriarchy* (Rowan and Littlefield, 2021).

54. SIPRI Yearbook, Armaments, Disarmament, and International Security, July 2021. Fed-eration of American Scientists, Status of the World's Nuclear Forces 2021.

55. Samantha Besson, "Theorizing the Sources of International Law." In *The Philosophy of International Law*, ed. Samantha Besson and John Tasioulas (Oxford University Press, 2019), pp. 163–185; see also Rüdiger Wolfrum, "International Law." In *Max Planck Encyclopedia of Public International Law* (Oxford University Press, 2012): p. 1.

56. The most elucidating author who guides my writing is Cassie Kozyrkov, the Chief Deci-sion Intelligence Engineer at Google. See her pieces on Medium at https://kozyrkov.medium.com/. For this part, I am very thankful to software engineer Rebecca Leeper and scientist Robert Mason, a computer engineer and managing founding partner at Argon Ventures for their insights.

57. The Pentagon Defense Innovation Board, *AI Principles: Recommendations on the Ethical Use of Artificial Intelligence by the Department of Defense* (October 2019).

58. Lex Fridman et al., "Arguing Machines: Human Supervision of Black Box AI Sys-tems that Make Life-Critical Decisions." Paper presented at IEEE/CVF Conference on Computer Vision and Pattern Recognition Workshops, Long Beach CA, June 2019, doi:10.1109/CVPRW.2019.00173.

59. US Department of Defense, "DoD Directive 3000.09: Autonomy in Weapon Sys-tems" (Incorporating Change 1, May 8, 2017), November 21, 2012, https://www.esd.whs.mil/portals/54/documents/dd/issuances/dodd/300009p.pdf; The Department of Defense Directive 3000.09, "Autonomy in Weapon Systems," clarifies policies on semi-autonomous and autonomous weapon systems and "allow[s] commanders and operators to exercise appropriate levels of human judgment over the use of force," along with weapons review processes to assess the compliance of any new system with international humanitarian law; I am thankful for pertinent comments by Frank Sauer and Peter Asaro.

60. Convention for the Amelioration of the Condition of the Wounded in Armies in the Field (Geneva Convention of August 22, 1864) (entered into force June 22, 1865); The 1864 Convention gave rise to the International Committee of the Red Cross, which became and remains the guardian of the rules of war and has since assisted all states in reviewing

and implementing the tenets of international humanitarian law that has now produced a densely regulated part of international law with hundreds of treaties.

61. Humanity is entering the fourth industrial revolution, as Klaus Schwab, the President of the World Economic Forum, has described it. In this world, the robot economy will be preponderant, affecting all people in ways that the previous revolutions did not. Klaus Schwab, *Shaping the Fourth Industrial Revolution* (World Economic Forum, 2018). The other revolutions were, respectively, mechanization and steam power, mass assembly-line production after the invention of electricity, and computers and automation; the fourth revolution is now taking place, characterized by the use of autonomous and cyber digital systems.

62. Stuart Russell and John Bohannon, "Artificial Intelligence: Fears of an AI Pioneer." *Science*, vol. 349, no. 6245 (New York, July 2015), p. 252, doi:10.1126/science.349.6245.252.

63. Klaus Schwab, *The Fourth Industrial Revolution* (World Economic Forum, 2016).

64. US Department of Defense, "DoD Directive 3000.09."

65. Christof Heyns, *Report of the Special Rapporteur on Extrajudicial, Summary or Arbitrary Executions to the United Nations Human Rights Council A/HRC/23/47* (United Nations, April 9, 2013): p. 21.

66. I thank Robert Mason and Rebecca Leeper for several comments regarding this topic.

67. Walsh, *Autonomous Weapons: An Open Letter from AI & Robotics Researchers.*

68. Sundar Pichai, *AI at Google: Our principles* (Google, June 7, 2018), https://blog.google/technology/ai/ai-principles/.

69. António Guterres, *Secretary-General's Address to the General Assembly* (United Nations, September 25, 2018), https://www.un.org/sg/en/content/sg/statement/2018-09-25/secretary-generals-address-general-assembly-delivered-trilingual.

70. Ruti Teitel, *Humanity's Law* (Oxford University Press, 2011); Antônio Augusto Cançado Trindade, *International Law for Humankind*, 2nd ed. (The Hague Academy of International Law Monographs and Martinus Nijhoff, 2013); Edith Brown Weiss, "In Fairness to Future Generations and Sustainable Development," *American University International Law Review*, vol. 8, no. 1 (1992): pp. 19–26; Dinah Shelton, "Common Concern of Humanity." *Environmental Law and Policy*, vol. 39, no. 22 (2009): pp. 83–86.

71. I thank Francesca Batault for her thoughtful comments.

72. I am grateful to Kerstin Vignard of UNIDIR for her writings and years of conversations that inspired me to think through these issues in a much more nuanced way.

73. I thank Peter Asaro, a philosopher of science and technology, whose work has inspired me in recent years.

74. The Ottawa Convention or Mine Ban Treaty prohibited landmines; its official title is The Convention on the Prohibition of the Use, Stockpiling, Production and Transfer of Anti-Personnel Mines and on Their Destruction. It was adopted in 1997 and entered into force on March 1, 1999.

75. My thanks go to Robert Mason, a computer engineer, Trustee of the Awesome Foundation, and angel investor.

76. New America, "Who Has What: Countries Developing Armed Drones." https://www.newamerica.org/in-depth/world-of-drones/4-who-has-what-countries-developing-armed-drones/.

77. Denise Garcia, "The Case Against Killer Robots—Why the United States Should Ban Them." *Foreign Affairs* (May 2014), https://www.foreignaffairs.com/articles/united-states/2014-05-10/case-against-killer-robots.

78. Greg Allen and Taniel Chan, *Artificial Intelligence and National Security* (Harvard Kennedy School Belfer Center for Science and International Affairs, July 2017), https://www.belfercenter.org/publication/artificial-intelligence-and-national-security.

79. Cecilia Marcela Bailliet and Kjetil Mujezinovic Larsen eds., *Promoting Peace Through International Law* (Oxford University Press, April 2015), doi:10.1093/acprof:oso/9780198722731.001.0001.

80. Jennifer L. Erickson, *Dangerous Trade: Conventional Arms Exports, Human Rights, and International Reputation* (Columbia University Press, 2015).

81. Nils Melzer, *Targeted Killing in International Law* (Oxford University Press, 2008).

82. Janina Dill, *Legitimate Targets? Social Construction, International Law and US Bombing* (Cambridge University Press, 2014); Jelena Pejic, "Extraterritorial Targeting by Means of Armed Drones: Some Legal Implications." *International Review of the Red Cross*, vol. 96, no. 893 (2014): pp. 67–106; Stuart Casey-Maslen, "Pandora's Box? Drone Strikes Under Jus Ad Bellum, Jus In Bello, and International Human Rights Law." *International Review of the Red Cross*, vol. 94, no. 886 (2012): pp. 597–625.

83. Wendell Wallach, *A Dangerous Master—How to Keep Technologies from Slipping Beyond Our Control* (Basic Books, 2015); Toby Walsh, *Machines that Think: The Future of Artificial Intelligence* (Prometheus Books, 2018).

84. Stuart Russell, "Artificial Intelligence." *Nature*, vol. 548, no. 7669 (August 2017): pp. 520–521, doi:10.1038/548520a.

85. Lyria Bennett Moses, "Why Have a Theory of Law and Technological Change." *Minnesota Journal of Law, Science & Technology*, vol. 8 (2007): p. 589.

86. I thank Francesca Batault and Matthew Kokkinos for their comments.

Chapter 1
Transnational networked cooperation

The AI Military Race. Denise Garcia, Oxford University Press. © Denise Garcia (2023).
DOI: 10.1093/oso/9780192864604.003.0002

PART I

From autonomous weapons to the militarization of artificial intelligence

Artificial intelligence (AI) is not to be trusted when the risks and stakes are high.[1] It is hard to imagine a use of AI where the stakes are higher than applying it to kill people. Autonomy is an attribute that has been used in weapon systems since the 1960s. Nonetheless, the growing advancements in AI are progressively amplifying the scope and reach of autonomous systems, beyond the initial realms of navigation and radar detection, to include data analysis for target acquisition, facial software, swarming, and teaming capacities. In November 2018, the United Nations Secretary-General António Guterres stated: "For me there is a message that is very clear—machines that have the power and the discretion to take human lives are politically unacceptable, are morally repugnant, and should be banned by international law."[2] Such talk of "killer robots" is highly emotive. It conjures up images of the Terminator—a fully autonomous robot as a relentless killing machine.

There is an abundance of sci-fi movies and books depicting a future where robots roam about killing humans. This has become a pervasive subconscious concern. Can this be a possible future? Some say that talking about the problem of "killer robots" in the future may distract from facing the implications of what is already occurring, namely greater autonomy in existing systems. The increasing presence of autonomous features in operational weapon systems raises ethical concerns, the most troubling of which is the employment of computational techniques associated with AI, such as machine learning and other mathematical pattern organizers and identifiers that permit greater autonomy to drive decision-making in several areas. We do not have movie-type Terminators yet, but we are on the road toward more autonomous systems in all areas of society, including the military and warfare, and this journey includes the increasing weaponization of AI, a set of technologies that could potentially be used exclusively for the common good of humanity.

In this book, I explain the broader features of the militarization of AI, focusing specifically on the risk of ever greater reliance on autonomous systems—by which I mean systems or machines that have increasing levels of autonomy to search, destroy, and kill without human input and involvement—features that can also be enabled or enhanced by AI. It is vital to understand that many of the autonomous weapons already deployed do not have integrated AI, and that some AI-enhanced systems are not autonomous weapons. Several facets and uses of the militarization of AI are not problematic per se: for example, navigation, detection of explosive devices, mapping and data generation, and assessing threats. Conversely, some aspects of the militarization of AI are controversial and raise a host of legal, ethical, and strategic challenges, and could be destabilizing to international security, namely weaponizing AI, which includes identification, tracking, selection, and engagement of targets without human involvement, or not allowing sufficient time for humans to intervene appropriately to avert potentially fatal problems.

I start by explaining the circumstances that first highlighted the concerns around autonomous weapons and eventually attracted attention at the highest levels of world politics, and how this high-level focus on autonomous weapons at the United Nations also started to shine a light on the larger phenomenon of the militarization and weaponization of AI. Renewed and heightened competition among the superpowers has driven the pursuit of dominance in AI for military purposes. Scientists, Nobel Peace laureates, civil society peace movements, and others came together to sound the alarm. Many aspects of the militarization of AI are perhaps not as visibly problematic, as I will show; however, it is the weaponization of AI that creates a global problem that could potentially have as great a global impact as climate change or the onset of pandemics, and it is so pressing because it may represent a paradigm shift for humanity. The intensification of the risk of "autonomous killing" through the use of autonomous weapons and the growing militarization of AI signal a fundamental transformation in the nature of warfare. In response to that, what I call *transnational networked cooperation* has emerged and is intensifying; this is characterized by novel global governing cooperation networks attempting to curtail the dangerous side of how technology is reshaping international relations. The concept of *transnational networked cooperation* can also be applied to address climate change, for instance, and other areas where states may be failing to act but other actors are more actively engaged. My focus will be on examining the role of *transnational networked cooperation* in restraining the progression of autonomous killing systems in international relations.

I put forward the term *transnational networked cooperation* to embody the kind of cooperation that can form and be viable even in the absence of sufficient state involvement, especially from the major military powers. This implies that collaboration and coordination can still occur despite a dearth of *international* cooperation between states: norms can emerge and blueprints for action can be formulated with innovative mandates and structures by other movers and shakers in international relations. In other words, in a shifting global order within which we are moving toward declining sustained *international* cooperation at the state level, I see a rise in *transnational* networks *of cooperation* that are formed by five types of groups: scientific and educational organizations (technology workers, scientists, and academics), members of civil society (individuals, nongovernmental organizations, the media, indigenous and religious groups), the private sector (including financial organizations), international and regional organizations, and governments (including some middle and major powers).

This innovative governing architecture, shaping a hybrid form of governance (Chapter 3), is composed of a complex tapestry wherein action is taken by a multiplicity of change makers, beyond the formal state level, in several areas of international relations, from climate to global public health, and even in the domain of security, which is the one I will investigate. Public–private partnerships are an increasingly a dominant feature allowing alliances for change to occur. In the realm of security, however, the transformation of the status quo (i.e., change) occurs slowly, or may even occur only rarely, because power politics is the dominant operating principle preserving national security and there is thus scant motivation for change. However, even in this more impenetrable domain, transformation is taking place and the possibility of a more inclusive multilateral order where many voices are heard is emerging.

Transnational networked cooperation is a practical way of characterizing how such modes of collaboration can materialize to forge *common good governance*: by means of networks, such as those listed in Table 1.1, that link and bind together engaged and concerned individuals from different segments of many countries that would not otherwise have the opportunity to form alliances in a true collective endeavor. Each segment has a strength, and all are mutually complementary. States find solutions to global problems typically by negotiating treaties. However, treaties are no longer the sole form of managing global problems. Each node in the network of cooperation buttresses the others by creating novel forms of global action, heralding a powerful debate about what is ethically and morally acceptable in shaping the future for humanity and charting new courses of action. Change makers can act in the absence of any national leadership in the international arena; they are instead bound by a belief in a humane and just future, free of violence.

I will demonstrate that *transnational networked cooperation* endeavors to create new global public goods by means of *common good governance*. The technologically advanced nations relentlessly pursue attaining an ever higher competitive edge to enhance their own national security and international military standing by introducing greater autonomy into weapon systems and by militarizing AI. A global framework to govern military AI would be an indispensable global public good as this ongoing military competition takes place at the risk of jeopardizing international stability and security, and with scant regard for considerations of ethics, international law, or threats to peace. The use of computation techniques that will enable further autonomy, especially with the rapid progress of such techniques in the realm

Table 1.1 List of change makers relevant to *transnational networked cooperation*

Transnational Networked Cooperation **Inclusive multilateralism**[3]
Change makers Scientific and educational organizations, technology workers Members of civil society: individuals, nongovernmental organizations, the media, indigenous and religious groups The private sector (including financial organizations) International and regional organizations Governments

Table 1.2 Five requisite criteria for *transnational networked cooperation*

Transnational Networked Cooperation
Five requisite criteria
Generation of authoritative knowledge using a humanity-based discourse
Creation of precautionary governing frameworks
Presence of at least one epistemic community
Existence of an activist transnational advocacy network
Cooperation among networks to publicize matter's urgency

of AI in war, may have a destabilizing impact and significantly alter the ability of nations to continue to live at peace under established global norms of international law. Therefore, my contention is that there are five requisite criteria for the formation of *transnational networked cooperation*; they do not necessarily manifest in a linear or causal way and may occur in parallel. These criteria are listed in Table 1.2 and are described after the table.

Authoritative knowledge is initially articulated to raise the alarm regarding a critical issue and suggesting possible courses of action that should be taken in response; this is done by scientists using a common humanity-based discourse or by activists who construct a discourse premised upon universal legal frameworks of human rights and the laws of war, namely human rights law and international humanitarian law. In combination, these two humanity-based branches of international law provide an essential foundation for upholding human dignity and ensuring human survival, and for taking all the necessary precautions to avoid harm. The march toward autonomous killing systems foreshadows the disruption of such respect for human values and breaches the essential tenets of the legal foundation established from the time of the birth of the United Nations that advanced the foundational norms to prevent a third world war and safeguard the basic rights of all.

The search for precautionary action and preventive global governance arrangements reaches the highest level of world politics at the United Nations, with an agenda directing international deliberations. Concerns about the future of humanity's security and the loss of dignity are central features in this agenda. Human rights law and international humanitarian law represent the advancement of international law toward the protection of the individual and "the turn toward humanity in International Law"—as Ruti Teitel and the late International Court of Justice judge Antônio Augusto Cançado Trindade suggest—or a shift toward a legal order centered on human security that has been taking place since the establishment of the United Nations (Chapter 4). The search for competitive dominance in the military realm using AI represents a significant challenge to this order and may in fact put it at risk. However, the constant participation of actors in the evolving *transnational networked cooperation* and in the transnational legal process helps to reconstitute and transform national interests, develop norms, and, eventually, secure compliance with preventive governing frameworks, namely by creating *common good governance*.[4]

Momentum and strength are achieved when a broader array of scientists joins the ranks, bringing authoritative scientific expertise to relieve uncertainty and help all to navigate the technical complexities. The combined moral clout of the scientists and workers who create the technology employed in autonomous killing—including their resistance to the potentially malicious and evil uses of their creation—adds a compelling and overriding impetus to *transnational networked cooperation*. In many ways this cooperation is built upon the existence of epistemic communities and other such communities that share a common set of normative principles and perspectives on the course of action to be adopted.[5] The most widely accepted definition of an epistemic community, by Peter Haas, underpins my concept of *transnational networked cooperation*: an epistemic community is formed by professionals from a variety of disciplines and backgrounds who share a set of normative and principled beliefs that provide a rationale for action and serve as a basis for clarifying the multiple connections between action and outcome. These professionals' pooled methodologies across expertise domains and professional competence are directed to improving human welfare.[6] This means that the shared principled beliefs arise from the combined strength of different methodological and world views that lead to collective engagement. As such, epistemic communities (which are composed not only of natural scientists, but of many other types of professionals too) are conduits for knowledge sharing and the generation of initial principles that act as the guiding posts for the formation of new norms.[7]

Common humanity-based discourse is reinforced when transnational advocacy to elevate human rights and dignity is energized by groups of civil society members with previous experience in related areas who support the cause, which will in turn consolidate the networked cooperation concomitantly with the work of the scientists. Epistemic communities share the ethical standards that arise from the commonly shared, principled approach toward taking action for change. In the case I investigate, scientists perform an essential role in informing the course of the *transnational networked cooperation* in their belief that technology must serve the common good. Characteristically, members of an epistemic community work toward the improvement of the collectivity. This is exactly what the scientists in this instance attempt to do. Their work is enhanced by other overlapping epistemic communities that form a powerful transnational advocacy network. Combined, epistemic communities and advocacy networks produce what I call *transnational networked cooperation* as a result of their collective work of knowledge generation, persuasion, education on the technical aspects of the issue in question, and the generation of policy solutions for the world to embrace. This is arduous work as the powerful support of the major powers may not necessarily be forthcoming.

In sum, my concept of *transnational networked cooperation* builds upon previous ground-building concepts: transnational advocacy networks and epistemic communities. It is important to elucidate how my novel concept contributes to this already existing essential literature. It does so by taking an enlarged pool of players into account in a network. The diffusion of ideas and new norms is not necessarily tied to the agendas of the most prominent actors.[8] I explain, in turn, how the change makers' networked actions contribute to generating novel forms of governance and give rise to forms of "hybrid governance" where multiple types of partnerships abound—for instance, private and public (Chapter 3).

The International Committee of the Red Cross (ICRC) is a highly prominent actor in this realm. It published its definitive position on the matter only in May 2021, a decade after the first alarm bells started ringing to alert the world to the perils of autonomous warfare (Chapter 4). In other words, the salience of an issue stems from a networked mosaic of actors instead of a handful of major powers seeking to impose their views about what matters most for humanity's future. As Martha Finnemore, a leading and influential political scientist, has stated, "states are embedded in dense networks of transnational and international social relations that shape their perceptions and their role in that world."[9] According to Finnemore, it is fair to presume that states might not necessarily know what their initial position on an issue may be, but they can be informed and can learn. So many issues require the attention of state diplomats and officials that not even the most advanced states would be able to adopt positions on each and every one of the issues on the diplomatic agendas at the highest levels; some of them are highly technical, such as the militarization of AI, climate change, and the prevention of pandemics. Margaret Keck and Kathryn Sikkink formulated the seminal concept of transnational advocacy networks and created a guiding framework to understand how these networks emerge.[10] The first transnational networks, such as the abolitionist movement to end slavery, up to those existing today encourage change to occur through persuasion in areas in which transformation may have seemed unthinkable. However, as Keck and Sikkink explain, persuasion does not fully account for the work the networks can carry out, and the typology to properly explain the range of actions includes the ability to disseminate information, to utilize symbolic storytelling to attract attention, and to leverage opportunities for weaker members to exert their influence, as well as accountability politics where promises must be kept. This can be seen, for example, in the negotiations that led to the 2017 Nuclear Ban Treaty, and the Nobel Peace Prize-winning International Campaign to Abolish Nuclear Weapons that laid its foundations (Chapter 5), which is an illustrative example of *common good governance*.

Finally, knowledge is further diffused and publicized by the denser networks of cooperation that address the urgency of precautionary action and examine the possibility of irreversible harm even in the absence of irrefutable scientific certainty (as in the case of the 1987 Montreal Ozone Protocol, considered to be the most successful environmental treaty to date), now drawing on the combined force of different strategies and multidisciplinary expertise. The matter I am examining is still evolving, but I shall address the issue of whether the standards set in the absence of major power involvement will still guide state behavior. It seems to me that the chance of such compliance is higher in the broad area of AI, where much of the creative impetus originates with private actors. This is all the more true in cases where strengthening cooperative networks can produce new modes of resistance and activism by which ideas of *common good governance* can be reinforced in a networked world where nonstate and private actors have acquired greater force and significance.[11]

I offer an approach through which to harness a more fruitful perspective on global governance—one that explains and focuses on the transnational networks that have been cooperating on the issue of autonomous weapons, and the other networks on the broader matter of the weaponization of AI, as a mode of mustering *common good governance*.

Other extraordinary movements for change in the unfathomable and often inscrutable domain of national security have arisen before and many scholars (myself included) have documented them extensively in previous publications. Change was sought by regulating or prohibiting certain weapon systems with the aim of improving human security. A notable example is the century-long movement to ban chemical weapons, as well as the banning of landmines and cluster munitions, which are appallingly inhumane weapons that cannot discriminate between civilians and combatants, and that have harmed communities all over the world during and since the Cold War. More recently, a ban was levied on nuclear weapons in 2017; prior to this, and also notable, was the preventive prohibition of blinding laser weapons in 1995. The regulation of uncontrolled conventional arms and nuclear weapons is the purpose of an extensive web of international treaties under international law (Chapter 5).[12]

Nonetheless, the present situation to address and curb the development of automated weapons and the heightened militarization of AI is qualitatively different. What I observe now has never occurred before because we are not talking about the banning or prohibition of a single weapon system. This is about a whole range of technologies. Previous movements to ban and regulate weapons, to bring about change and improvement to international politics and human security, were extraordinary and involved different groups of change makers (or change agents)[13] who effectively worked persuasively with states to initiate change that benefited communities in postwar and at-peace situations everywhere. Several factors make this instance an exceptional turning point that signals the rise of a new global governing world order as well as opportunities to forge *common good governance*. Militaries of the highly technologically advanced countries are actively pursuing and already deploying AI to enhance their military operations. Projects that seek to enhance "man–machine teaming" or "hybrid intelligence" are in vogue. A startling statement by the former US Vice Chairman of the Joint Chiefs of Staff, General Paul Selva, demonstrates the urgent need to create commonly agreed rules to contain a race that could leave everyone worse off and lead to a more anarchical state of affairs in war: "Wouldn't it be cool if you could shoot somebody in the face at 200 kilometers and they don't even know you're there?"[14] Certainly, the United States would not wish for itself the same fate of being shot in the face, from a distance, by other armies; therefore, it is evident that more international legal rules are necessary to prevent a descent into disorder and chaos due to the lack of global regulations.

Another instance is the Pentagon's Project Maven, which attempts to incorporate AI across all the Department of Defense's operations; this was justified at the outset and framed as necessary to counter a relentless military race between China and the

United States. Military officials have been trained to assume a zero-sum scenario of losers and winners, and one can only win if the other side loses. The major powers' framing of the "imminent threat," first in the suicidal nuclear deterrence mutually assured destruction, then in the war against terror, and now in the notion of endless wars with the continuous use of armed drones in countries the United States is not at war with but engaged in hunting for legitimate targets all justify the militaries seeking more autonomy and further reliance on military AI to contain new threats. As Lucy Suchman notes, the promise of algorithmic warfare is futile because it conflates the speed of operations with the supposedly desired results. Rather than continuing down this path of violence, and notwithstanding the proclamations of the inevitability of an AI race, nations should instead redirect their investments toward diplomacy and social justice. This would enable them to tackle the geopolitical and planetary threats to global security more effectively.[15] Like Suchman, I would caution against the rush to remilitarize or militarize even more intensively by saying that it is imperative to halt an utterly inequitable and unbalanced state of affairs where the technologically dominant countries continue to overmilitarize and to create new Cold Wars in the name of their national security. Meanwhile, the actual threats to global security, which are now predominantly of a nonmilitary nature, remain poorly addressed.[16]

I develop my concepts of *common good governance* (Chapter 2) and *transnational networked cooperation* to demonstrate that, given the critical juncture at which the world currently finds itself, everyone will lose in the relentless pursuit of militarization and the world will become increasingly less safe.[17] To avoid this hopeless fate, and to point the route toward a new approach of multilateralism, *transnational networked cooperation* offers a more inclusive way to look at the solutions for the contemporary problems of global cooperation. In this case, there are three dynamics at play. First, the transnational cooperation examined here is formed by a fascinating mosaic of different groups that have converged around the need to restrain autonomous killing. This matter has acquired great significance on the global agenda and is receiving increasingly sustained attention with every year that goes by. These groups include scientists who create and employ AI, legal scholars, social scientists, the ICRC, the United Nations, think tanks, civilian private sector companies and technology workers, Nobel Peace laureates, and a transnational movement composed of civil society members worldwide. International cooperation, namely between states, seems to be assuming a new form as well, in which the major powers are not intrinsically involved but multiple cooperative alliances between different countries are being forged.

Second, not only has the intensified use of autonomous weapons received sustained attention, but the attempts to set rules and limits have been rigorous. At the highest level of conversations at the United Nations, member states refer to "autonomous weapon systems," "lethal autonomous weapon systems," and "fully autonomous weapon systems." Yet, it has proven difficult to agree on new international law to address the challenges posed by the increased autonomy of weapon systems, or even to agree on what these challenges are. Perhaps the source of the difficulties lies in the fact that global governing mechanisms will have to be sought anew. Some states continue to maintain, deceptively, that existing legal mechanisms will suffice, so they can pay lip service to the urgency of the need for regulation and at the same time disguise their unwillingness to move responsibly and create new legal norms with globally agreed rules of behavior that will withstand the challenge presented by these technologies in warfare and beyond. The added difficulty is that the existing international regulatory architecture will not suffice, and current international law that governs previous bans and regulations of weapons can neither fully account for these new technologies nor serve as a good model for action in the future.[18] This is where *transnational networked cooperation* may serve to drive the necessary development of novel forms of global governance.

Third, the issue at hand is about software and the decision-making algorithms. Rarely has an issue been so challenging to discern precisely and to clarify in commonly agreed terms at the international level. Previous bans and regulatory processes to restrain a weapons system had to do with one weapon or a set of weapons. With the issue at hand, the analogies with arms control will help only to a limited extent. In addition to the complexity of this novel situation, controlling weapons is always a delicate issue to manage on the political spectrum because states often do not want to accept any interference in the way that they manage their weapons. States want to retain the discretion to produce, use, and transfer weapons as they see fit. This issue is at the core of national security. Martha Finnemore points out that it is precisely their control over the use of weapons that states guard most jealously. The development of wide-scale military AI, as such a transformative technology, adds a whole new dimension to this scenario, even beyond the issue of autonomous weapon systems. What are the possibilities of controlling the ongoing weaponization of AI, and what forms of prevention are in place that demonstrate sufficient precautionary vision to avoid a precarious and perilous future? This book explores these possibilities and offers a path for coordinated global action seeking to create global public goods through *common good governance*.

The global investment in the militarization of AI and autonomous killing

Reliable figures for spending on AI and autonomy for weapon systems that increasingly rely on the advances in AI computational techniques are not always readily available publicly, nor are they always trustworthy. However, the launch of the Global Partnership on AI (led by Canada and France, with Australia, Germany, India, Italy, Japan, Mexico, New Zealand, the Republic of Korea, Singapore, Slovenia, the United Kingdom, the United States, and the European Union) and the Organization for Economic Cooperation and Development (OECD) AI Policy Observatory and Network of Experts on AI in 2020 brings more clarity and makes more data available in the civilian realm, even if the data remain sparse on the military realm of AI applications.[19] It is prudent to start by examining what countries' broad-scope plans are for developing AI to gauge where they are.

The United States became the first country to publish a "Political Declaration on Responsible Military Use of Artificial Intelligence and Autonomy," in 2023.[20] The strong points in this declaration include the following: human control should be maintained over nuclear weapons; deployment should occur within the bounds of international law; states should develop AI with auditable methodologies, data sources, and documentation; and, finally, states should develop systems that can detect failures and deactivate those that display unintended behavior. However, the declaration fails to meet the growing calls for strong, legally binding frameworks to prohibit systems that target humans and unpredictable systems that can operate without human control. It is elusive in offering a substantive framework and parameters for what responsible military use of AI means, lacking leadership to move the global matter forward on the diplomatic stage. The US Declaration was launched at the first ever state summit on military AI, which took place in February 2023, hosted by the Netherlands. At the Responsible AI in the Military Summit, more than 60 countries—including the United States and China—endorsed a Call to Action on "responsible AI."[21] Even though the Call to Action thrusts military use of AI onto the international stage, and offers a preliminary contribution to creating new global governance in this area, it does not delineate the scope of "responsible use," and it does not make concrete inroads into developing new international law by providing a tangible legal framework that would assuage the ethical, legal, and moral concerns raised in this book. Responsible use of AI in the military remains elusive.

Canada was the first country to publish its AI strategy, in 2017. Therein, it positions itself as a thought leader in the ethical and legal implications of AI. Also, in 2017 China released a high-level blueprint, deemed to be the most comprehensive plan in the world, which acknowledges that AI has become a new focus of international competition and a tool to protect its national security. At that point, it boasted that it was one of the countries with the highest number of papers on AI, second only to the United States, and the leader in voice and visual recognition technology; it was poised to lead in "hybrid intelligence" where human–machine teams cooperate to optimize information generation and "behavioral strengthening through human-machine smart symbiosis and brain-machine coordination" and swarm intelligence technologies.[22] China's strategy positions it to become the world's leader in AI by 2030 as the primary innovation center. In terms of defense, China plans to develop autonomous intelligence and unmanned systems and to depend on AI as a strong foundation for command, decision-making, and defense innovation. The blueprint commits China to participate in the global governance of AI, and to deepen international cooperation on AI laws and regulations to cope with global challenges. In 2019 the strategy was updated to launch a multistakeholder coalition that included academic institutions and Baidu and Tencent—technology companies that are the equivalent of Google and Yahoo in the United States. It is important to bear in mind that in China the military, defense, and civilian domains, where the inventions and innovations are taking place, are inextricably intertwined. There is a fusion of military and civilian applications, and the AI strategy makes clear that all sectors work to enhance the aspirations set by the central government.[23] In the United States and the European Union, there is much greater separation between and independence of the respective sectors. The United States remains the leader in the development of autonomy in the civilian sector but also in weapon systems. The predominant use of AI is in civilian applications, in large part because of the operations of Amazon, Apple, Facebook, Google, and Microsoft.[24] In the United States, the Pentagon may try to woo the major innovators in the private sector, such as Google, Facebook, and Microsoft, to work on defense projects.[25] Talented engineers and technology professionals in the United States and at the European Union resist working with the defense applications of AI, whereas in China they would have less choice.[26]

The European Union Commission published its long-term strategy on AI in April 2018; it involves Norway and Switzerland (non-EU member states).[27] From the outset, the Union has been clear that its strategy is "human-centric" and will be marshaled toward resolving the most pressing global challenges—from climate change to preventing pandemics. The EU is the most advanced region in terms of creating a comprehensive policy on AI.[28] The European Commission started by establishing a High-Level Expert Group on Artificial Intelligence early in 2018, which formed the basis for all action from then on. At the core is the AI Alliance, which would fit as a form of *transnational networked cooperation*: it is a multistakeholder forum that joins businesses, trade unions, and civil society and engages them in discussion on AI policy while eliciting concrete feedback on the direction of travel. The blueprint recommends that the EU spend 20 billion euros a year. The General Data Protection Regulation (GDPR) precedes the EU blueprint, establishing a foundation for the protection of fundamental human rights as data are generated and used in the development of AI, enhancing its human-centric stance. This sets the EU apart from and ahead of other major powers in their quest for AI superiority. Additionally, the EU's AI strategy recognizes that the use of AI in weapon systems fundamentally transforms the nature of war, which in turn raises significant questions and concerns. The strategy shows that the EU position is that human control must be retained in the use of force and that human rights and international humanitarian law apply. In January 2021 the EU Parliament issued its Guidelines on Military and Non-Military Use of AI and AI in Healthcare and Justice. It is noteworthy that autonomous weapon systems are only lawful if deployed under human control; AI does not replace human judgment and decision-making. In April 2021 the EU published the first ever legal framework, the AI Act, based upon protecting human rights and carrying its human-centric mandate further.[29] The Act categorizes the societal application of AI according to a hierarchy of risks, from minimal risk (most applications), to limited risk (emotion recognition, deep fakes), unacceptable risk (education, employment, immigration assessments), and high risk (facial recognition and other risks to the health and safety or fundamental rights of persons).

The major powers leading investment in AI are China, the European Union, South Korea, Russia, and the United States, followed by India and Israel. The largest arms-producing companies are in the United States, followed by the European Union; China has four weapon manufacturers.[30] All have a clear intention to develop lethal autonomous systems[31] (Chapter 3). Overall, there is little public scrutiny and debate—except within the European Union—or accountability for expenditure, or any indication of how the billions are allocated and spent to advance novel uses of AI technologies as applicable to the military domain in each of these countries. This spending is considered necessary to preserve and protect the core of national security—that is, fighting enemies more efficiently and maintaining secrecy.[32] The European Union includes a few countries that are leading investment in research. For instance, Germany's defense establishment is investing substantially to advance the dual-use industrial development of robotics; France is seeking to make AI a major part of its military strategy; the United Kingdom wants to continue its leadership role as one of the leading arms exporters and wants to maintain its edge in the development of autonomous systems.[33] To attain this goal, it has increased its defense spending to $21.8 billion dollars over the next half a decade to update its AI capacities.[34]

The AI Partnership for Defense includes Australia, Canada, Denmark, Estonia, Finland, France, Israel, Japan, Norway, South Korea, Sweden, the United Kingdom, and the United States. It is hosted by the Pentagon's Joint Artificial Intelligence Center under the American AI Initiative, launched in 2018. The center is expected to convene like-minded states to chart a common course from hardware- to software-centric and data-focused militaries to confront shared threats such as natural disasters together.[35] This is a promising initiative that focuses on nonmilitary threats to security. This is where the energy and resource expenditure should be. However, the initiative is clouded by the fact that details of the Department of Defense's investment in AI were withheld from publication for "national security reasons" and hence are not publicly available. However, the estimate is that the combined American military budget for AI R&D in FY 2021 was $5.0 billion.[36] Surely, the prevailing talk of a new Cold War will prompt all sorts of justifications to spend more on militarizing AI, as was the case with nuclear technology after World War II.[37]

The path toward greater autonomy in warfighting in the United States started in 1983 with a modest $1 billion for "strategic computing," and this figure has since increased. The United States was the first country to weaponize unmanned aerial vehicles, colloquially known as "drones," after 2001 in the aftermath of terrorist attacks against the country. Up until 2015, it spent $2–6 billion each year on improving the lethality and accuracy of drones. The projects that will be at the center of the militarization of AI in the coming years are: 1) Rapid Capability Development and Maturation, by the US Army ($284.2 million); 2) Counter-WMD Technologies and Capabilities Development, by the DoD Threat Reduction Agency ($265.2 million); 3) Algorithmic Warfare Cross-Functional Team (Project Maven), by the Office of the Secretary of Defense ($250.1 million); 4) Joint Artificial Intelligence Center (JAIC), by the Defense Information Systems Agency ($132.1 million); and

5) High-Performance Computing Modernization Program, by the US Army ($99.6 million). Moreover, the Defense Advanced Research Projects Agency (DARPA) has invested $568.4 million in AI R&D annually since 2021.[38] The public expenditure allocated to the Department of Defense already outpaces the next ten agencies by several millions of dollars, and is only expected to grow now that the JAIC has been launched and become central to attempts to increase the use of AI for military purposes. The American AI strategy seeks to maintain the US strategic position and prevail on future battlefields.[39]

At the same time, the market demand for military AI is swiftly intensifying: for unmanned drones it is estimated to reach $16.5 billion, and global military spending on AI is expected to reach about $20 billion by 2025.[40] Drones are ubiquitous and are used for intelligence acquisition, surveillance, and reconnaissance; targeting; communications; and direct attack by militaries around the world.[41] Software and cybernetics are expected to generate the largest market share by 2030, at $8.07 billion dollars. The market for military AI is projected to reach almost $40 billion dollars by 2028; all segments in the military AI market are expected to grow worldwide by 2025, reaching an estimated $11.6 billion dollars.[42] AI-enabled systems already permeate every aspect of the battlefield and are endowed not only with greater speed, scale of operation, and autonomy, but also lethality.[43]

The erosion of the fundamental norms of international law against the use of force, which have prevented the major powers from going to war against one another for almost 80 years, may have even worse consequences in the future (Chapter 4). The lowering of the threshold for what is acceptable in war has already begun with the use of armed drones, with no public accountability in the United States, whereby successive American presidents have taken the decision to use drones for military purposes, but what lies ahead could further imperil global peace.[44]

Autonomy and AI for war

Autonomy refers to a machine's ability to conduct a task without human intervention or input in different environments.[45] I will trace how the international discussion on autonomy has evolved to the point of favoring the "functional approach" in diplomatic discussions toward a new global governance to limit autonomy in weapons (i.e., a focus on the critical functions that kill and destroy). When autonomy is applied to different parts of weapon systems, ascertaining the limit to the autonomy that a weapon system can or should possess, and whether that limit is ethically acceptable or not, or lawful or unlawful, is tied to the answer to the following question: Is it autonomous in its critical functions? After all, there is nothing inherently problematic about autonomous navigation and other functions.[46]

> Increasingly autonomous technologies are a feature of today's world—and touch many aspects of our lives—from the factory floor to the "smart appliances" in our homes to robot-assisted surgery. Whether we realize it or not, we already

rely on machines with considerable autonomy—and this is only going to increase. Advances in robotics, machine learning, AI, computational power, networking, engineering, and other disciplines are driving increasing autonomy in machines and systems. Such technologies promise (or are already delivering) significant benefits to those who have access to them.[47]

It is essential to bear in mind that, on the one hand, not all already deployed autonomous weapons integrate AI, and, on the other hand, some AI-enhanced military robotic systems are not autonomous weapons. They are used for different functions, such as detecting patterns in surveillance or object recognition.[48] Some aspects of the militarization of AI are not problematic per se: mobility (navigation, take-off and landing), intelligence (detection of explosives, objects, gunfire, data acquisition, map generation, threat assessment), certain levels of interoperability (ability of troops and systems to cooperate with others), and health management (detection of faulty systems, hacking and interference, ability to self-repair and deactivate). However, other aspects of militarization are hugely contentious and debatable. They are viewed as destabilizing to international security, as well as raising fundamental legal and ethical questions. These aspects are tantamount to weaponizing AI; such as: the use of autonomous systems, and many of them are increasingly amplified by AI for targeting, i.e., identification, tracking, prioritization and selection of targets, image discrimination and target engagement (i.e., kill or destroy). The different dimensions of autonomy and the way that it can be set out along three concurrent spectrums are indicated in a useful framework developed by Michael Horowitz and Paul Scharre.[49]

At the United Nations, the dimensions along different spectrums of machine sophistication (outlined in Table 1.3) led to three main approaches to the question of definitions, which partly explains the delay and even stalemate in the progress toward shaping new global governance mechanisms. Kerstin Vignard explains that the choice of one of the three approaches, presented in Table 1.4, by different countries has complicated the negotiations. She suggests that

> starting with a human-centric approach allows us to reaffirm human responsibilities and legal frameworks, regardless of the specific new technology. Then, turning to identifying the key critical features or tasks that we have uncertainties or concerns about when autonomy is applied to them will help narrow down the scope of the discussion. Finally, after determining the appropriate and necessary human role, as well as the tasks of concern, one can turn to a tech-centric conversation.[50]

The way to maintain control as the machine's complexity increases is the central question; more specifically, how will these advances change the extent to which humans can exercise control over the use of military force? Let us take the typology above and apply it to existing military systems, some of which have been in use for several decades. Bonnie Docherty from Harvard University, one of the first legal scholars to write about autonomous weapons, explains that there are three categories

Table 1.3 Machine complexity's independent dimensions along different spectrums

---

Machine complexity's independent dimensions along different spectrums

---

Human–Machine Relation & Command-and-Control Relation
Human-in-the-loop: semi-autonomous—human input is needed in different phases
Human-on-the-loop: human-supervised autonomous—machine performs on its own, but human can intervene
Human-out-of-the-loop: autonomous—machine performs and humans cannot Intervene

Machine's Complexity
Automatic: bread toaster, landmine
Automated: rules-based systems: self-driving car, thermostats, many weapon systems
Autonomous: free to select course of action and learn from it and modify course, and sometimes exhibiting human-like level of cognition for narrow tasks: some weapon systems, Alpha Go

Type of Decision to be Automated
Tasks and functions must be specified, and these questions posed:

- Which function, or task, makes a machine autonomous (homing, surveillance, target acquisition)?
- Is a task limited in time?
- Only in determined environments (air, land, sea, cluttered environments, cities)?

---

of unmanned robotic weapons, characterized by the relationship between human involvement and the degree of autonomy:

- Human in the loop: robots select targets and deliver force under human command;
- Human on the loop: robots select targets and deliver force under the control of a human operator, who can override the robots' actions; and
- Human out of the loop: robots can select targets and deliver force without any human input or interaction.[51]

Two widely publicized studies may serve to demonstrate the difficulty of determining the threshold of the amount of autonomy that a weapon system can or should possesses, and whether that threshold is ethically or legally problematic.[52] Autonomy functions in complex applications for different functions and tasks, and the decision-making power that machines will eventually acquire will function along a continuum. The first study was published by the Stockholm International Peace Research Institute (SIPRI) in 2017.[53] It investigated 154 existing unarmed and armed military systems. Of these systems, 50 had a "human in the loop," where a human operator retains the power to decide to engage the target; in the case of 31 systems it was unclear whether a human could intervene in the autonomous engagement of the system; and 49 armed systems had "human on the loop" and "human out

Table 1.4 Different approaches to autonomous weapons

Types of Definitional Approaches to Autonomous Weapons

Technology-centric approach
A few governments prefer the technical definition route in which a physical object is described. This is in line with what has traditionally been done when tackling arms control issues: specific type of weapon, range, payload, and the scope of deployment. The problem is that increased levels of autonomy can be implemented in already existing systems and in different parts of each system (navigation and homing, for example).
A technology-centric definition has two major disadvantages: first, it is unlikely to capture the range of characteristics and variations that can occur between human and machine, or the scope and quality of control; second, it is likely to be outdated by the progress of new technologies.

Human-centered approach (meaningful human control)
This second approach focuses on the human–machine relationship. Systems with increased autonomy are a result of the delegation of authority and control by a human to a part of a machine system, but humans remain "in," "on," or "out" of the loop of command and control. Within this framework, the discussions at the United Nations saw the emergence and consolidation of the concept of "meaningful human control" that emanates from existing legal and political frameworks under international law.

Task/functions approach
This third approach to the definition centers on the tasks or functions that a machine performs autonomously. The ICRC calls these "critical functions": i.e., search, detect, identify, track, and select to apply the use of force without human decision-making. This is the most comprehensive and useful approach because it takes into account the human–machine relationship, and the need for effective control.

---

of the loop" attributes, where the system was able to engage the targets without human supervision (but note that "human on the loop" systems can still have their actions overridden by the human operator). The second study was published by the Future of Life Institute and conducted by Heather Roff and Richard Moyes, influential pioneering observers in the area of autonomy. They differentiated five areas where autonomy is applicable in a range of instances.[54] The amplest use of autonomy is in the area of mobility, followed by, in this order, homing, target acquisition, navigation, and target-image discrimination. Roff usefully traced the steep increase in the degree of greater autonomy in each of these areas or military applications since 1961. Her finding was that the degree of autonomy increased exponentially in each area. Autonomy is a characteristic, an attribute. It can be applied to any weapon system or to any civilian object. It is already being employed in different parts of different systems for positioning, navigating, and targeting. The uses of autonomy in deployed functions are "homing" (offensive and defensive target identification); loitering; autonomous capacity; missile- and rocket-defense weapons; vehicle "active-protection" weapons; antipersonnel "sentry" weapons; sensor-fused munitions, missiles, and loitering munitions; and torpedoes and encapsulated torpedo mines. Many systems are constrained in the tasks they are used for (e.g., defensive rather than offensive operations), the types of targets they attack (vehicles and other objects rather than personnel), the circumstances in which they are used (in simple, relatively predictable, and constrained environments rather than complex, unpredictable environments), and/or the time frame of their autonomous operation. Some are also supervised in real time by a human operator. Generally, these weapons incorporate a radar to detect incoming projectiles or aircraft, and a computer-controlled "fire-control system" to aim and fire the weapon. The weapons system selects an incoming projectile, estimates its trajectory, and then fires interceptor missiles or bullets (depending on the system) to destroy it.

Maintaining human control

A new principle referred to as *meaningful human control* has rapidly gained momentum and achieved widespread recognition. How can meaningful human control be applied over autonomous weapon systems that can select and engage targets without further human intervention once they have been launched?[55] The original conception of the principle appeared in 2015 in the publication *Killing by Machine: Key Issues for Understanding Meaningful Human Control.*[56] The authors (Heather Roff and Richard Moyes) explain that human control must be present in every individual attack. Therefore, in autonomous systems, there are two key aspects: first, the constraints set on the target's limits at the time of programing, along with the types of sensors and algorithms and the way that they are linked to and input the target's limits; second, the delimitation of the geographic area of operation and the time at which the weapon system is disconnected from human control. This understanding encapsulates the ethical and legal concerns that the application of autonomy for military purposes raises because it is based on two premises. The first is that it is inconceivable that a system (robotic, an autonomous weapon, or a software in cyberspace) that uses force can do so without human involvement. The second is the inadmissibility of nonsubstantial human control, or of decisions that are taken solely as a result of inputs from a computer program (software with the rules given by sets of algorithms). In other words, decisions should be informed by human awareness at each step of the process.[57]

To maintain effective control, two components must be in order, according to the thinking of another pioneering scholar in this field, Paul Scharre. The first is the ability of the human operator to predict how the autonomous system will behave, assess the potential failures, and employ it only in situations when it will perform according to initial specifications. The second is the ability of the human operator to intervene and correct.[58] It is unlikely that the human operator will always be able to accurately predict the machine's behavior; the level of risk is high. Additionally, complex systems can interact in ways that are not anticipated and that may cause disaster. It is alarming that more autonomous systems capable of applying force are being developed without the knowledge of the public at large, especially if there is no certainty whether the systems are robust and safe. As Paul Scharre notes: "Given the inevitability of failures over a long enough period of operational use, the military necessity of autonomous weapons must be quite high to warrant accepting the risk of their employment."[59]

SIPRI and UNIDIR conclude that the dominant focus of the discussions at the United Nations should be on human control. A human-centered approach enables the global discussion to capture what is already occurring and what will most likely take place in the future. Another group that scrutinizes the complexities associated with human control and the relationship of such control while operating autonomous systems is the International Panel for the Regulation of Autonomous Weapons (IPRAW). This is a multinational, interdisciplinary panel of experts created in 2017 by the German Ministry of Foreign Affairs and initially led by a physicist, Dr. Marcel Dickow, formerly at the German Institute for International and Security Affairs in Berlin. I have been a member of IPRAW since its inception. We have published several technical advisory reports to inform the deliberations at the United Nations, which are available online.[60] IPRAW takes into account that there are significant legal, moral, and ethical considerations that arise in each step of the weapon system's engagement and targeting cycle that may be hampered or made difficult to discern in the light of the growing autonomy of certain functions. This is the case because increased autonomy profoundly changes the human–machine relationship. In order to maintain the need for precaution and for human dignity to be upheld at all times, as stipulated under international law (Chapter 4), IPRAW's view is that the necessary human control should be exercised and be present at each step of the engagement cycle—not only during the critical phases of targeting and engagement—as the absence of human supervision in any given step may result in cumulative lapses or miscalculations that may lead to erroneous judgments in the final decision to kill and destroy.

Our work and findings indicate that there are specific requirements for human control that should be present in a global governing mechanism to prevent autonomous killing, as outlined here:

1. Control by Design (technical control)
   1.1. Maintain situational understanding through the ability to monitor information about the environment and the system;
   1.2. Human intervention must be possible and required in specific steps of the engagement cycle.
2. Control in Use (operational control)
   2.1. Maintain situational understanding by appropriate monitoring of the system and the operational environment;
   2.2. Capacity to intervene prior to the ultimate use of force should be a default feature: this implies the authority and accountability of human operators and commanders under the rules of international humanitarian law (IHL).

The requirement of the presence and persistence of human control in design and operations should be a foundation for the global governing framework to guard against autonomous killing. Through IPRAW's observations of the deliberations at the United Nations, we notice that most states concur that human control over the use of force must always be present, which affirms a mounting consensus that war is a human activity and should not be waged by robots. We have recommended to member states at the United Nations that there must be universal recognition of human control as the principle upon which new norms of behavior should emerge to regulate the use of autonomous weapons. In sum, we view human control as entailing situational understanding and options for intervention, enabled both by design and in use. Therefore, both the life cycle of a weapon system and the targeting process should be taken into account when implementing and operationalizing human control, with special attention being devoted to the final step of the targeting cycle.

Some find the concept of meaningful human control elusive. One of the keenest observers of the debate on the relation between human control and machines—robotics Professor Mary "Missy" Cummings, a former United States fighter pilot—argues that in future there needs to be "meaningful human certification of autonomous weapons," as increased autonomy would aid human decision-making, especially in environments that are difficult to read and where there is incomplete information.[61] Lucy Suchman—another prominent observer and a member of the International Committee for Robot Arms Control—argues that the feasibility of lawful autonomy is impaired especially if there is an obligation that each action adheres to the rules of IHL. If each action is always context dependent, then it may not be feasible for the algorithms to adapt to and be compliant with existing international law. This stands in contrast to the notion of "rule" in the algorithmic sense (i.e., algorithms are codes, rules). It is therefore unlikely that the necessary discernment that will result in the capacity to discriminate between combatants and civilians (according to international law) can be coded in algorithmic rules.[62] The lack of clarity and uncertainty raised in these arguments warrants new international legal rules and globally accepted norms of behavior.

PART II

Transnational networked cooperation

Transnational network cooperation entails rewriting the rulebook and redesigning the institutions that are needed for governing a nonviolent future where subsequent generations are protected and may benefit from a humane norms-based framework. This will involve mobilizing grassroots or bottom-up connections to change and challenge the unyielding ways of the militarized great powers that maintain their commitment to developing ever-increasing autonomous systems—and, in fact, using AI to assist in this process. The way to achieve global cooperation in the absence of the major military powers is the crux of the issue of *transnational networked cooperation*, which starts to emerge precisely when major power championship for change falters.[63] When I started observing the diplomatic process at the United Nations in 2014, there was ample room for an incisive global treaty to restrain militarization that demanded greater autonomy and application of AI. This window of opportunity has now virtually closed as these systems have been developing rapidly and long-term investments have been made. At the same time, while a handful of major military powers are continuing to attempt to thwart global norm-making at the United Nations, the majority of countries wish to promulgate new international laws to govern the unimpeded militarism of the automation of violence. The window remains open to institute what kinds of action will be deemed unlawful and unacceptable, such as targeting humans, and to formalize the need for human control of the critical functions when the use of force is applied.

I attempt to understand how such grassroots connections help shape new international law by impacting on the high-level discussions at the United Nations. International law is "the legal order which is meant to structure the interaction between entities participating in and shaping international relations."[64] I adopt this wide-ranging definition of international law because it is the one that most accurately reflects the nature of the international legal system today. It includes the state, implicitly, but refers to international organizations, individuals, and many other participants that constitute and help shape international law in the 21st century. More recently, these groups have not necessarily been focusing on advancing action on behalf of any single state, but are moved to act by promoting a cause or addressing a global problem that, if fixed, will assist in the advancement of global public goods by creating *common good governance*. This is especially true in disarmament and the reduction, even prohibition, of weapons—conventional to nuclear—but also in other areas such as climate change and pandemic prevention. *Transnational networked cooperation* creates a space for the protection of human beings and offers a framework to confront existential challenges to individual security and ensure human dignity—the preeminent and foundational human right.[65]

There are five main groups of change makers (or change agents) that advance *transnational networked cooperation* in this case:

- The scientists: the ones who imagine and create AI;
- The private sector;

- Transnational advocacy: civil society;
- The guardian of the laws of war: The International Committee of the Red Cross;
- Member states of the United Nations.

The Scientists: Sounding the alarm first and alerting the world

The first warnings about the uncontrolled use of autonomy, and the development of autonomous weapons in warfare, emerged from a group of scientists: Jürgen Altmann, Peter Asaro, Noel Sharkey and Robert Sparrow.[66] Noel Sharkey sounded the alarm in 2007 about the potentially devastating impact of robot wars and alerted the world to a dangerous development, noting that the first armed battlefield robots had been deployed in Iraq, and that Israel and South Korea were already guarding their borders with armed robots that had high levels of autonomy.[67] In 2009, these scientists formed the International Committee for Robot Arms Control, composed of experts in various areas, including robotics technology, AI, ethics, human rights, and international politics and law.[68] As Noel Sharkey raised the alarm, the American Department of Defense (DoD) published the "Unmanned Systems Roadmap 2007–2032," which planned to start prioritizing robotic weapons:[69]

- The Department will pursue greater autonomy in order to improve the ability of unmanned systems to operate independently, either individually or collaboratively, to execute complex missions in a dynamic environment."
- "Unmanned systems provide autonomous and semi-autonomous capabilities that free warfighters from the dull, dirty, and dangerous missions that might now be better executed robotically and enable entirely new design concepts unlimited by the endurance and performance of human crews. The use of unmanned aerial vehicles in Afghanistan and Iraq is the first step in demonstrating the transformational potential of such an approach."
- "As confidence in system reliability, function, and **targeting algorithms** grows, more autonomous operations with weapons may be considered."[70]

The United States, the largest military power and developer of such technologies, started to deploy greater levels of autonomy in its military operations from 1991 during the first Gulf War in Iraq, but two later wars marked a more decisive shift toward greater autonomy in military systems and robotics: the 2001 Afghanistan conflict (after the attacks against the United States on September 11), and the Second Gulf War in Iraq in 2003; by 2008 this had reached a point where 12,000 robots were deployed in Iraq.[71] It was also after the mission in Afghanistan that the United States started arming its unmanned aerial vehicles, known as drones, which had been used since the wars in the former Yugoslavia. Since then, the United States has continued its quest to enhance performance in war by increasing the autonomy of certain functions of existing weapons as well as by creating new ones. Autonomous killing capability represents a major change in the way war is waged, and it has a significant impact on the existing laws of war and the protection of civilians.

The International Committee for Robot Arms Control compellingly called for global regulations on the development, acquisition, deployment, and use of armed drones and future autonomous robotic weapons, as well as for a global convention that would operationalize the principle of human control over all actions in war; this is because increases in autonomy will only serve to accelerate the tempo of utilization, and the faster pace will increasingly overshadow human decision-making. I joined this group of scientists in 2013, in a meeting organized by Matthew Evangelista of Cornell University on new technologies and the necessary new norms, held in the Italian Alps near Trento. In 2013, I hosted Noel Sharkey at Northeastern University in the first lecture series in the area. Since 2016, I have been one of the vice-chairs on the International Committee for Robot Arms Control, along with Jürgen Altmann and Peter Asaro. We have participated as a delegation in the meetings at the United Nations, in Geneva, since 2014.

From the outset, scientific knowledge has been the basis of *transnational networked cooperation*, and two scholars have been particularly central in helping to initiate the process of raising concerns about the dangers associated with autonomous killing at the highest level of the United Nations Human Rights Council in Geneva: Philip Alston, and the late Christof Heyns, whose untimely death in 2021 we all lament. Heyns and I used to meet in Geneva with our groups of students on annual visits to the United Nations headquarters. We celebrated the 100th anniversary of Nelson Mandela's birth with a moot court including students from around the world, and in 2019 my students met Heyns in a private meeting at the High Commissioner for Human Rights in Geneva. My alumna Francesca Batault, from South Africa, and I moderated a session about increasingly higher levels of autonomy in warfare and law enforcement situations, and the implications of this for international law.

Philip Alston, of the New York University School of Law, served as the United Nations Special Rapporteur on Extrajudicial, Summary or Arbitrary Executions from 2004 until 2010 (preceding Heyns). Alston published the first United Nations report on the issue in 2010.[72] He alerted readers not only to the perils of the rapid advancement of lethal technologies associated with reduced human control, but also of the implications of the lack public knowledge of the issue. He realized that, at first glance, the topic of robotic technology in war seemed not to belong in human rights discussion circles, partly because the information was confined to secretive military circles. However, he was the first to point out that the use of greater autonomy in war (i.e., the use of weapon systems with reduced human oversight) would have implications for the right to life and the right to dignity, arguing that there is no reason why human rights considerations and IHL could not be factored into the design of weapon systems. He called on the human rights community to urgently address (and that was in 2010!) the legal, moral, ethical, and political implications of the development of lethal robotic technology. The United States was the first country to use robotic warfare—increasingly so after the September 11, 2001 terrorist attacks—on the battlegrounds of Afghanistan (2001) and Iraq (2003). The increased implementation of autonomous systems in warfare meant that systems "in the loop" became "on the loop" with a progression that signified the increasing removal of the human dimension from the lethal decision-making process.

Alston points to three areas that have continued to plague international discussions to date.

- **Definitions**: the threshold of autonomy and what constitutes "autonomous"; what, in fact, are robots? The public imagination identifies "fully autonomous weapons" with an image of the Terminator, the brutal robot with humanoid characteristics, but the reality of the development of the technology is more ordinary, and even mundane. "Fire-and-forget" missiles were first developed in the 1970s, but since then technological advancements have made them more autonomous. The same advances enable greater autonomy to be applied to already existing systems. These applications have nothing to do with the image of machines with cognition and AI. Progress in AI techniques such as machine learning and image recognition processing will enable more advanced applications of autonomy.
- **State responsibility and criminal responsibility**: who will be regarded as responsible for violations of human rights law and IHL arising from the application of greater autonomy in lethal decision-making? These branches of international law are premised upon human cognition for responsibility and accountability. If human judgment is progressively turned over to algorithms, then it becomes much harder to determine to whom responsibility should be attributed (Chapter 4).
- **Starting a war is made easier**: the threshold of the use of force (*jus ad bellum*) can be lowered, especially if not all the safeguards and testing procedures are in place before a weapon is deployed. Here, Alston highlights the fundamental question that needs to be addressed: Should lethal force ever be allowed to be autonomous?

Alston's groundbreaking and forward-thinking reports were followed by Christof Heyns' enduring contributions to the debate. Heyns was Professor of Human Rights Law and Director of the Institute for International and Comparative Law in Africa at the University of Pretoria in South Africa, and served as the United Nations Special Rapporteur on Extrajudicial, Summary or Arbitrary Executions from 2010–2016. The combined work of these two scholars was seminal to advancing awareness of the perils of increased autonomy in weapon systems at the highest levels at the United Nations.

Heyns was a towering figure in law in South Africa and made foundational contributions toward the understanding this complex matter. In his seminal report to the United Nations Human Rights Council in April 2013,[73] he starts by saying: "Lethal autonomous robotics are weapon systems that, once activated, can select and engage targets without further human intervention. They raise far-reaching concerns about the protection of life during war and peace." Heyns warned about an erosion of international law that would arise because of disrespect of human rights law and IHL, which are such vital foundations for peace and stability in international relations today. Heyns also examined the development of the increase of autonomous lethality in military robotic systems vis-à-vis the other revolutions in warfare, namely the invention of gunpowder and nuclear weapons. Nuclear weapons were invented and then used in 1945, but the first international treaty created to regulate them was concluded only in 1968 with the Nuclear Non-Proliferation Treaty, followed by the 1996 Comprehensive Test Ban Treaty, and, in 2017, the Nuclear Ban Treaty. For the current revolution in warfare, Heyns called for a proactive approach, in line with what I argue here, that will halt the diversion of financial and human resources to the development of these new systems in the coming years (Chapter 5).

Heyns also advocated limitations of autonomous weapon systems, as I had called for in an article published in *Foreign Affairs* in 2014.[74] Since then, I have come to realize that an outright ban will be untenable, for all the reasons I explained earlier. However, in a situation of armed conflict, it is the qualitative human deliberations vis-à-vis the larger picture, unfolding events, and people's intentions that can save the lives of others. The quantitative capabilities of robotic systems can be useful in many areas, but perhaps not to distill the complex set of judgments that must be made on the battlefield, especially regarding decisions to safeguard life and protect human dignity; such judgments represent a nuanced value- and principles-based appreciation of the world that is beyond the capacity of algorithms.

I align my arguments here with those of Heyns when he offered a trenchant criticism of the argument that new high technologies lead to lower casualties in war. With his usual clarity and insight, he pointed out that such argumentation does not survive closer scrutiny. What is war, then, if it becomes a demonstration of the unrivaled power of the one side that possesses the technology and therefore bears no human responsibility because of its use of advanced technologies? Here Heyns refers poignantly to "riskless wars" or "wars without casualties" in which the lives of those in countries that possess the technologies are regarded as more valuable and worth protecting than the lives of those who are attacked.

In line with my argument in this book, Heyns lamented that rapid technological advancement, especially on the heels of the contestation and nonobservance of international law arising from the use of armed drones, along with the application and widespread use of lethal robotics in war, "could undermine the ability of the international legal system to preserve a minimum of world order." The international efforts to impose some level of control over autonomous killing rose to global attention with meteoric speed; this is perhaps the most rapid rise of international concern I have encountered in the high-level politics of international security. The United Nations Institute for Disarmament Research embraced Heyns' call and spearheaded an expert consultation that resulted in important work to generate knowledge and clarification in the international discussions; this was then led by Kerstin Vignard, whose guiding frameworks are cited here, and whom I met with every year while in Geneva.

The role of scientists in elucidating the complexities and in assisting to chart the right course of action is indispensable in advancing *transnational networked cooperation*. Concerted collaboration is taking place to examine the economic and social impacts of AI for the future and to ensure that that future is more just and equitable.[75] The Institute of Electrical and Electronics Engineers (IEEE) is the world's largest technical professional organization dedicated to advancing technology for the benefit of humanity. I have been involved in the IEEE's Autonomous Weapons Systems Expert Advisory Committee, which aims to become a trusted and highly utilized resource for national and international governments and nongovernmental entities to ensure safe, responsible, and trustworthy policies and technologies related to autonomous weapons. The committee was created in 2020 and led by Ariel Conn, who used to work for the Future of Life Institute. In 2021, after reviewing many AI and AWS principles that various organizations and governments from around the world adhere to, we identified ten categories of challenges associated with applying these principles to AWS, which we outlined in the published paper "Ethical and Technical Challenges in the Development, Use, and Governance of Autonomous Weapons Systems."[76] The challenges we identified are: establishing a common language, enabling effective human control, determining legal obligations, ensuring robustness, testing and evaluation, assessing risk, addressing operational constraints, collecting and curating data, aligning procurement practices, and addressing nonmilitary uses. In essence, we recommended the development of national and international norms regarding the degrees of human control and accountability to reduce risks to life and human dignity, and to ensure compliance with existing legal, ethical, and moral constraints. The committee has now been converted into a research group on Autonomy and AI for Defense Systems, convened by the IEEE.[77]

There is broad consensus from the scientific community that AI is currently developing ever more relentlessly and progressively toward greater breakthroughs.[78] Scientists have also agreed upon research priorities that should guide future developments. Stuart Russell, Daniel Dewey, and Max Tegmark have gathered more than 7,000 signatures in a petition to determine what these priorities should be. The agreement among scientists is that it will be imperative that autonomous AI-based systems behave "robustly"—that is, intended to benefit humanity—whether they be autonomous vehicles, medical systems, or autonomous weapons. In certain critical systems, such as weapons, a human remains *on* or *in* the control loop, along a spectrum from less to more supervision, along with the observance of some parameters discussed by Russell, Dewey, and Tegmark:

- **Verification**: How to prove that a system satisfies certain desired formal properties. (Did I build the system right?)
- **Validity**: How to ensure that a system that meets its formal requirements does not have unwanted behaviors and consequences. (Did I build the right system?)

- **Security**: How to prevent intentional manipulation by unauthorized parties. (What would be ways to prevent intentional manipulation?)
- **Control**: How to enable meaningful human control over an AI system after it begins to operate. (The system is not operating as intended; can I fix it?)[79]

Taken together, the need to provide verification, validity, security, and control may still be faced with two palpable difficulties. First is the possibility of using AI in cyberspace to launch malicious attacks. On the one hand, AI-based attacks in cyberspace may be very effective as scientists predict that machine-learning techniques can be used to perpetrate cyberattacks. On the other hand, AI could make systems less vulnerable. Second, it is still uncertain whether it will be possible to check verification and validity robustly to ascertain whether AI machine-learning systems are aligned with societal values, both ethical and moral, in line with the interpretation of law and legal codes.

The principles of common good and safe AI

Keeping AI beneficial for humanity was first discussed comprehensively at the 2017 Asilomar Conference, which came up with a foundational set of 23 principles led by Massachusetts Institute of Technology (MIT) professor Max Tegmark, the founder of the Future of Life Institute. To date, the principles have been signed by 1,797 AI and robotics researchers, and 3,923 others.[80] I invited Tegmark to give a lecture on these principles at the Future of Life Institute at Northeastern University in the fall of 2018. The ideas discussed with Tegmark further advanced my ideas on *common good governance*. The Asilomar (Future of Life Institute) principles encompass several critical components of the larger role of AI in the world, and, more specifically, the weaponization of AI. The principles could serve as foundational frameworks for *common good governance* of military AI. First, the principles address research priorities. In this realm, AI's research goals should be to attain beneficial, ethical, and human-centered systems that are sufficiently robust to prevent the possibility of interference or hacking (safety first) and malfunctioning. In addition, AI should enhance and expand humanity's prosperity, resources, and aspirations. In this sense, cooperative and transparent synergies should be promoted among members of the different scientific communities, as well as between the scientific and the policy-making communities. Humans should remain in control of overseeing verifiability, accountability, and judicial decisions. Along the same lines, responsibility should be attributable to designers and builders of advanced AI systems, who are stakeholders and, as such, accountable for the moral and ethical implications.

Second, the principle of "Preserving Human Values" is an essential component of the existing international legal architecture of human rights law. According to this principle, AI systems must be compatible with human dignity, rights, freedoms, and cultural diversity, and adaptable to what makes societies thrive. Principles 20 and 21, for instance, state:

- **Importance**: Advanced AI could represent a profound change in the history of life on Earth and should be planned for and managed with commensurate care and resources.
- **Risks**: Risks posed by AI systems, especially catastrophic or existential risks, must be subject to planning and mitigation efforts commensurate with their expected impact.

Third, the principles embody a keen awareness that AI will catalyze profound changes in the history of humanity. Therefore, care should be taken to ensure sufficient resources are available and precautionary measures are in place. Essentially, the scientists conclude that AI should embody a shared aspiration that benefits humankind and allows humanity to prosper on all fronts in terms of health, economics, and social welfare (Chapter 5). This is reiterated in the following principles:

- **Shared Benefit**: AI technologies should benefit and empower as many people as possible.
- **Shared Prosperity**: The economic prosperity created by AI should be shared broadly, to benefit all of humanity.
- **Common Good**: Superintelligence should only be developed in the service of widely shared ethical ideals, and for the benefit of all humanity rather than one state or organization.

This set of principles aligns with my argument for the establishment of common precautionary frameworks to benefit humanity within a system of *common good governance* that creates a global public good (i.e., principled AI). To make all this possible, the Asilomar Principles advise that human beings should remain in control and carefully ponder what kinds of decisions should be delegated to AI systems. Finally, Principle 18 cautions against an arms race in developing lethal autonomy in warfare:

- **AI Arms Race**: An arms race in lethal autonomous weapons should be avoided.

Taken together, the Asilomar Principles signal the growing consensus among scientists on the notion of the common good as well as AI safety. If the algorithms are not robust and safe, then weaponizing them is even more perilous. Indeed, after Asilomar, the AI safety agenda was strengthened and invigorated by the Future of Life Institute granting support for researchers around the world interested in developing such an agenda further.

Since Asilomar, there have been numerous initiatives to create principled AI.[81] The Berkman Klein Center at Harvard published a rich comprehensive global database that draws from all regions of the world to portray the nature of AI principles from states (usually part of a national AI strategy), civil society, and companies. The compilation enabled the identification of points of convergence and emerging norms:

- **Privacy**: respect for individual freedoms: 97% of the documents mention this;
- **Accountability**: mechanisms to ensure responsibility: 97% mention this;
- **Safety and Security**: robust systems that cannot be compromised: 81% mention this;
- **Transparency and Explainability**: possibility of oversight and intelligible outputs: 94% mention this;
- **Fairness and Non-Discrimination**: elimination of bias in algorithm creation, promotion of inclusivity: 100% mention this;
- **Human Control**: humans remain in the loop: 69% mention this;
- **Professional Responsibility**: the creators' integrity and long-term judgment on impacts: 78% mention this;
- **Promotion of Human Values**: humanity's well-being is the end goal: 69% mention this.

The administration of President Barack Obama of the United States convened five workshops to discuss AI. One of the major reports was on AI for Social Good.[82] The reports focus on benefiting the larger population in areas of direct economic benefit: education, safety, health, and the environment, which are deemed not to have benefited from AI thus far. However, the United States does not have a policy on AI in general. Most countries do not have such policies either. Therefore, the greatest challenge for all countries at this critical juncture is twofold: to translate the "social good" to the international level and to prevent harm to the commons— whether in cyberspace, or in avoiding the utilization of AI to cause harm and wage war (Chapter 2).

As mentioned, the IEEE, the world's largest technical professional association, "advances technological innovation and excellence for the benefit of humanity" and has 400,000 members in 160 countries. The IEEE Global Initiative for Ethical Considerations in Artificial Intelligence and Autonomous Systems (The IEEE Global Initiative) was initiated to address the perils of developing AI in the absence of concomitant ethical considerations. I have been a member since 2018 and can confirm that the scientists posit that AI systems may have an impact on the world in the same ways that the agricultural and industrial revolutions did; "Human wellbeing is our metric for progress in the algorithmic age."[83] In many ways, the IEEE's report "Ethically Aligned Design: A Vision for Prioritizing Wellbeing with Artificial Intelligence and Autonomous Systems" is a significant contribution to this debate.[84] The high ethical concerns and general principles guiding it are that all AI Autonomous Systems (AI/AS) should "embody the highest ideals of human rights, prioritize the maximum benefit to humanity and [the] natural environment, [and] mitigate risks and negative impacts as AI/AS evolve as socio-technical systems."[85] The issue at hand is to ensure that AI does not violate human rights and that it is at the same time accountable,

transparent, and not misused. As a corollary, the norms enshrined in the AI/AS algorithms should be compatible. An additional concern is autonomous weapon systems
that may cause physical harm and therefore have additional ethical implications:
higher ethical standards are therefore needed. The recommendation is to ensure
"meaningful human control" because this is beneficial to society. To realize this goal,
audit trails are necessary that ensure human control and that "those creating these
technologies understand the implications of their work, and that professional ethical
codes appropriately address works that are intended to cause harm."[86] A number of
key issues have been identified:

- Professional organization codes of conduct contain manifest ambiguities that
  may fail to hold the technology creators accountable;
- Confusions about definitions and concepts in AI/AS have the effect of creating
  a deadlock in conversations on critical issues;
- Autonomous weapon systems are "by default amenable to covert and nonattributable use."[87]

The IEEE Global Initiative on Ethical Considerations for AI/AS recognizes that
autonomous weapon systems can be compromised, and their impact may not be
foreseeable and comprehensible. Making their use legitimate may lead to imprudent
escalation of tensions and conflict among groups that will most likely include terrorists and other criminals as well (easier access will lead to more rapid proliferation),
along with breaches of human rights law.

- The type of automation in autonomous weapon systems encourages the rapid
  escalation of conflicts.
- There are no standards for design assurance verification of autonomous weapon
  systems.
- Understanding the ethical boundaries of work on autonomous weapon systems
  and semi-autonomous systems can be confusing.[88]

When I was invited to testify on autonomous weapons during the United Nations
deliberations in Geneva in 2016, I argued that an AI military race will have disintegrating effects on the existing international legal structure of peace and security, and
will be particularly destabilizing for regional security.[89] The IEEE also pointed out
that the advent of AI and AWS can aggravate the power differences and imbalances
between developing and developed countries.

The IEEE Global Initiative for Ethical Considerations in Artificial Intelligence
published a second report in 2017.[90] The report recommended that there should
be meaningful human control on autonomous weapon systems, with discernable
human operators, clearly identified, along with audit trails to ensure accountability
and control. Therefore, the design of such systems must align with and meet the obligations of IHL and human rights law, and must apply engineering standards that can
indicate the potential consequences of their use at the global level. Of special concern
to the scientists are miniature autonomous weapons that may not be attributable to

the people who deployed them. Additionally, the lack of clarity about the concept of autonomy is challenging and may be used to block any implementation of new global governance on these matters. The report notes that the relationship between human control and autonomy is highly complex and can be perplexing, because autonomy can be employed for different functions in different systems (searching but not targeting, for instance), and in distinct combinations, pairings, and gradations. This is what the report suggests:

> The term autonomy in the context of autonomous weapons systems (AWS) should be understood and used in the restricted sense of the delegation of decision-making capabilities to a machine. Since different functions within AWS may be delegated to varying extents, and the consequences of such delegation depend on the ability of human operators to forestall negative consequences via the decisions over which they retain effective control, it is important to be precise about the control of specific functions delegated to a given system, as well as the ways in which control over those functions is shared between human operators and AWS.[91]

Importantly, the report aligns itself with the definition of the ICRC—the guardian of international humanitarian law— recommends it as the guideline for engineers: an autonomous weapon system is "any weapon system with autonomy in its critical functions. That is, a weapon system that can select (i.e., search for or detect, identify, track, select) and attack (i.e., use force against, neutralize, damage or destroy) targets without human intervention" (p. 1). [92] As a starting point, engineers who design autonomous weapons should comply with the profession's codes of ethics; however, this may not be sufficient to address all the ethical challenges posed by such systems and therefore the IEEE, the Association for Computer Machinery (ACM), and counterpart organizations in Canada, the United Kingdom, and Japan are revising their codes.[93] These revision procedures will be complex and require knowledge of distinct aspects of international law that are pertinent, such as IHL and human rights law (Chapter 4).

The scientists' letters: Meaning and impact

The moment when the movement to stem the rise of autonomous killing and prevent its worst destabilizing effects became truly global and multifaceted *transnational networked cooperation* was when the AI scientists and then the AI-creating companies lent their moral weight to it by highlighting the knowledge that they can convey together to the world. I was representing the International Committee for Robot Arms Control in a side event at the ongoing deliberations at the United Nations in Geneva (November 13–17, 2017), on the "Rationale for Banning Fully Autonomous Weapons," hosted by the Campaign to Stop Killer Robots.[94] On the same panel was one of the leading AI scholars and computer engineers in the world, Stuart Russell of Berkeley University. He had the idea to produce *Slaughterbots*; this is a short, fictional film that became a viral sensation and won numerous prizes for depicting an enthralling but frightening reality where mini-swarms of autonomous killer robots search and kill selected groups of young people who hold politically combative views. During the panel discussion Russell explained that, "[b]ecause autonomous weapons do not require individual human supervision, they are potentially scalable weapons of mass destruction—unlimited numbers could be launched by a small number of people."

Slaughterbots was a sharp strategy adopted by some scientists to cleverly convey a message to a much broader audience. *Transnational networked cooperation* is intensifying on the basis of knowledge about autonomous weapon systems being spread to much larger concerned audiences. The scientists' first open letter was published on July 28, 2015.[95] Toby Walsh, a computer engineering professor at the University of New South Wales in Australia, who welcomed me to his campus in February 2020, was instrumental in initiating the process. After the publication of the letter, the management of what became a global movement fell under the purview of the Future of Life Institute, headed by the MIT's Max Tegmark. The letter is titled "Autonomous Weapons: An Open Letter from AI & Robotics Researchers." This letter—a somber and stern call for action—received widespread and sustained attention and publicity from the media worldwide. It received conspicuous coverage in *The New York Times* as Elon Musk (then Tesla CEO) and the renowned scientist Stephen Hawking were among the prominent personalities who endorsed the letter.[96]

These personalities have been joined by almost 5,000 AI and robotics researchers and over 30,000 other individuals. If that is not a global movement of concerned individuals, I do not know what is. They start by bluntly defining the core of autonomous killing: "Autonomous weapons select and engage targets without human intervention"; these weapons exclude drones, since humans are in charge of the decision-making regarding the targeting decisions. The heart of their call for action is this: "AI technology has reached a point where the deployment of such systems is—practically if not legally—feasible within years, not decades, and the stakes are high: autonomous weapons have been described as the third revolution in warfare, after gunpowder and nuclear arms." They add that these AI weapons will be the future Kalashnikovs because, as opposed to nuclear weapons, they do not necessitate the acquisition of expensive raw materials and will thus quickly become omnipresent. They state that the key question for humanity is whether to start a global AI race or to act preventively. If humanity fails to act, this the scientists' warning:

> Autonomous weapons are ideal for tasks such as assassinations, destabilizing nations, subduing populations, and selectively killing an ethnic group. We therefore believe that a military AI arms race would not be beneficial for humanity. There are many ways in which AI can make battlefields safer for humans, especially civilians, without creating new tools for killing people.[97]

The most exciting part is their stated kinship with other professionals: for example, chemists and biologists, who are not inclined to develop prohibited chemical and biological weapons, and the physicists who have underwritten the principles of peaceful outer space law. AI researchers have no interest in building AI weapons. The scientists' policy prescription is that AI should be used for the common good of humanity and a military race should be avoided through the creation of a new global governing mechanism that will "ban offensive autonomous weapons beyond meaningful human control."[98] In his persuasive 2018 book, *Machines that Think*, Toby Walsh, who helped initiate the letter-writing process, thought the most important feature was that the letter was signed by many well-known researchers in AI and robotics.

The next iteration of this science-based movement that galvanizes the common humanity-based discourse and makes science work for a human-centered world, where humans are kept out of harm's way from the malicious use of technological advances, took place in July 2018, when almost 2,500 individuals and 150 companies from 90 countries signed a Lethal Autonomous Weapons Pledge.[99] This means that 247 organizations and 3,253 individuals are now involved. Among the companies that underwrote the letter were Google Deepmind, Clearpath Robotics, Silicon Valley Robotics, and Tesla, along with leading AI scholars. They explain that AI is playing an increasingly significant role in military systems, and it is therefore time that the public understands what the acceptable and nonacceptable uses of AI are, arguing as follows:

> The decision to take a human life should never be delegated to a machine. There is a moral component to this position, that we should not allow machines to make life-taking decisions for which others—or nobody—will be culpable. There is also a powerful pragmatic argument: lethal autonomous weapons, selecting and engaging targets without human intervention, would be dangerously destabilizing for every country and individual. Thousands of AI researchers agree that by removing the risk, attributability, and difficulty of taking human lives, lethal autonomous weapons could become powerful instruments of violence and oppression, especially when linked to surveillance and data systems. Moreover, lethal autonomous weapons have characteristics quite different from nuclear, chemical, and biological weapons, and the unilateral actions of a single group could too easily spark an arms race that the international community lacks the technical tools and global governance systems to manage. Stigmatizing and preventing such an arms race should be a high priority for national and global security.

By encapsulating all the pertinent ethical and moral arguments involved in the debate to stem what looks like an inexorable drift toward AI-assisted autonomous killing, the scientists warn that these are very different from previous weapon systems, and the world is not equipped with the right global governing mechanisms to grapple with the challenges. They urge governments to create "a future with strong international norms, regulations, and laws against lethal autonomous weapons." These norms do not yet exist, they explain, and therefore they "opt to hold ourselves to a high standard: we will neither participate in nor support the development, manufacture, trade, or use of lethal autonomous weapons."[100]

This signals the acceleration of the knowledge-based norm against autonomous killing initiated by the scientists, which sets the highest standard. A validation of the rise of this new and necessary norm was evinced when Toby Walsh led an academic boycott, followed by many of the other leading AI researchers, against the Korea Advanced Institute of Science and Technology (KAIST, equivalent in South Korea to MIT in the United States):

> KAIST's President, Sung-Chul Shin, responded to the boycott by affirming in a statement that "KAIST does not have any intention to engage in development of lethal autonomous weapons systems and killer robots." He went further by committing that "KAIST will not conduct any research activities counter to human dignity including autonomous weapons lacking meaningful human control."[101]

This was followed by a revolt by Google employees, mentioned earlier, against the company's decision to initiate a Pentagon-associated "Project Maven" that would intensify the use and application of AI to further advance the autonomy of armed drones. The letter starts by stating that "We believe that Google should not be in the business of war. Therefore, we ask that Project Maven be cancelled, and that Google draft, publicize and enforce a clear policy stating that neither Google nor its contractors will ever build warfare technology."[102] The International Committee for Robot Arms Control, led by Peter Asaro, initiated a petition signed by more than 1,000 academics to support Google's employees' actions.[103]

The scientists' letters represent a profound cautionary tale for the future of humanity: those who understand how to create AI and fully grasp the significance of their applications are sending a warning the world. The inescapable diffusion and permeation of AI in all areas of society is unstoppable. Because of its mostly beneficial uses for peace and the advancement of humankind, AI should be ubiquitous and available to as many people as possible. However, the scientists are looking ahead to what could happen if AI is not properly regulated, and they caution against its most nefarious use: to kill human beings. Therefore, before AI is generally employed for military purposes, there should be clear prudential norms of conduct in place.

Many argue that the employment of AI could create substantial advantages on the battlefield. However, the risks associated with the largely unregulated and uncoordinated deployment of AI in the military domain far outweigh these advantages. Unlike previous technologies in the nuclear, chemical, and biological spheres, computation techniques under what is called "narrow AI" will be more widespread than anything seen to date. Therefore, the major powers will only have the technological edge for a short window of opportunity—the same window that is now open to introduce regulation. This is perhaps the most persuasive argument for the establishment of preventive comprehensive *common good governance* mechanisms to forge global public goods. Here the private sector, especially the major technology giants in the United States and Europe, has a central role to play as they can resolutely decline to allow their AI inventions to be weaponized.

These actions by the scientists prompted the participation of the private sector as an active change maker. Scientists and individuals in the private sector have an essential role to play. The former do not wish to see their inventions being used for harm, while the latter do not want to see their businesses being deceitful. Successful private and public partnerships cooperate in the peaceful uses of outer space and Antarctica, and in the protection of the atmosphere. In the evolving domain of AI, companies will benefit from cooperation. In addition, the joint fruit of their work must be tapped for the higher aims of saving the planet from catastrophic climate change and for the promotion of sustainability and development for all countries. More than in any previous military races, which proved to be rather costly for humanity, it is highly probable that this time the race will be so dispersed and diffused throughout so many sectors of society—adversaries and allies alike, as well as criminals—that avoiding a new futile race in the first place would be in everyone's interests.[104] Combined, these initiatives spearheaded an essential global dialogue, bringing together the most diverse group of change makers, to determine the opportunities created by AI and to ensure that they are used in ways that are beneficial for humanity by setting standards and promoting collaboration across disciplines, advancing the *transnational networked cooperation*.

The private sector

The world is at a critical juncture, a turning point at which humanity can decide on the path that is most appropriate to preserve the dignity of the whole of humankind and benefit not only a few technologically sophisticated countries that are trying to impose an ever more unequal world order. This would be a world with one-sided wars in which the perpetrators suffer no casualties and where the full benefits of technologies that have the potential to improve the future for all are instead diverted to the very few. It is evident that technology companies have a corporate social responsibility not to weaponize any technology that could benefit all human beings, all over the world. Yoshua Bengio, a Turing Award winner (the equivalent of winning the Nobel Prize in Computer Science), has stated that "The use of AI in autonomous weapons hurts my sense of ethics," and adds that the development of autonomous weapons "would be likely to lead to a very dangerous escalation" that "would hurt the further development of AI's good applications."[105]

Boston Dynamics changed its Ethical Principles statement in 2021 to include the following proposition: "We will not weaponize our robots: We will not authorize nor partner with those who wish to use our robots as weapons or autonomous targeting systems. If our products are being used for harm, we will take appropriate measures to mitigate that misuse."[106] The first company to decline to participate in the weaponization of AI was Clearpath, in August 2014, being the first robotics company to announce that it will not be making "killer robots"[107]—that is, it will not manufacture products that will eliminate the human dimension from the decision-making loop and so allowing the robot to take the final decision to kill human beings.[108]

Clearpath also aligned its mission statement with the transnational activist Campaign to Stop Killer Robots. In its critical announcement, Clearpath affirmed that it values ethical principles over potential future revenue. It called on others to act preventively before it is too late. Clearpath Robotics' cofounder and CTO, Ryan Gariepy, became a prominent and important voice in the debates in the United Nations and beyond. I have heard him speak on several occasions and can attest that his contribution and actions are exemplary for other private-sector industry members that should seriously consider following his lead. In the announcement, Gariepy warns that autonomous technologies will not meet the appropriate ethical standards, and may kill indiscriminately and proliferate extensively. He warns of the horrendous consequences of the employment of this technology and calls for stringent preventive regulations, because it is evident that the negative consequences will offset any gains by far. Clearpath maintains that it will continue to develop leading autonomous technology for military use in the areas of logistics, reconnaissance, and search and rescue. Essentially, this is what Gariepy affirms about the technological development of autonomy: there is no need to invent killer robots to develop to maturity the technology in other beneficial areas.

The IEEE Global Initiative, the Asilomar Principles on Common Good and Safe Artificial Intelligence, and Clearpath's action led me to believe that no one is ready to accept unconstrained development toward autonomous killing: technologically, legally, or ethically. There is no persuasive reasoning that can justify or validate the existence of a technological device that is so precarious and unpredictable in its application. Weaponizing AI will not enhance or pave the way for other uses of the technology that are beneficial, such as other ways in which robotic systems can improve human lives: for example, in medicine, agriculture, and transportation. Some of the largest technology giants—Amazon, DeepMind, Facebook, Google, IBM, and Microsoft—created the Partnership on Artificial Intelligence to Benefit People and Society (Partnership on AI); this was set up as a nonprofit organization, initially chaired by Microsoft's Chief Scientific Officer Eric Horvitz and DeepMind cofounder Mustafa Suleyman. These companies endorsed the 2015 scientists' letter mentioned earlier, reiterating that an AI military race would be a bad idea. Two main objectives animate the group: the first is to educate as well as learn from the public, with an inclusive vision of engagement with several interdisciplinary stakeholders. The second is to devise principles of common action based upon best practices, seeking to develop systems that are reliable and robust. Seven thematic pillars guide their work: safety; fairness, transparency, and accountability; human-AI systems collaborations; impacts on labor; impact on society; special initiatives with different stakeholders; and AI for the social good.[109] The focus on safety applies especially in the areas of healthcare and transportation to develop robust systems that align ethical principles with human needs. This multistakeholder group, involving more than 100 organizations, also aims for transparency and accountability in the areas of biomedicine, public health, safety, criminal justice, education, and sustainability, along with addressing the potential major disruptions in economic markets. The vision enshrined in the initiative is for AI to promote the public good.

The year 2018 was a turning point for AI industries to start recognizing the repercussions and probable impacts of the development of the technology and to begin formulating self-imposed limitations and constraints. What prompted this move? What is the impact of setting limits on the creation of new technology? Many people may look at Google's actions with skepticism, but I would say that Google took a much-needed and long-awaited courageous action that is likely to have profound reverberations for the technology industry at large. Clearly, the rise of the Technology Workers Movement in Google's own ranks of engineers who are not willing to have their technological inventions used in war catalyzed the publication of the principles. In June 2018, Google published seven principles of conduct to use AI for the common good.[110] Google's Chief Executive Officer, Sundar Pichai, announced them as concrete standards for the company. It is important to note them carefully as Google is a world leader in AI research and such principles may indicate a basis for the development of global governance for the industry.

The Google Principles

1) Be socially beneficial
2) Avoid creating or reinforcing unfair bias
3) Be built and tested for safety
4) Be accountable to people
5) Incorporate privacy design principles
6) Uphold high standards of scientific excellence
7) Be made available for uses that accord with these principles

Equally important, Google published the AI applications that it will not pursue and stated that this position is the right foundation for its role in the future development of AI:

1) Technologies that cause or are likely to cause overall harm. Where there is a material risk of harm, we will proceed only where we believe that the benefits substantially outweigh the risks and will incorporate appropriate safety constraints;
2) Weapons or other technologies whose principal purpose or implementation is to cause or directly facilitate injury to people;
3) Technologies that gather or use information for surveillance violating internationally accepted norms;
4) Technologies whose purpose contravenes widely accepted principles of international law and human rights.[111]

Furthermore, discussions to stem the rise of increasingly autonomous weapon systems have been in progress on the global stage since 2013. Google's principles come at a moment when people are starting to realize that the big technology companies—ingeniously called the "G-Mafia" by Amy Webb, where G-Mafia stands for: Google, Microsoft, Amazon, Facebook, IBM, and Apple—are mining data freely available from their users worldwide to feed AI to enhance its predictive capabilities, but this practice is not accountable to the consumers, who increasingly experiencing a sense of malaise and are launching a backlash against these companies.[112] The European Union is leading the way in the imposition of limitations on the use of data in order to safeguard privacy. If data gathering is enriching the leaders of these companies, then ways must be found to convert the data collection to serve the common good. Indeed, hopefully data is not the "new oil" and, in contrast to oil, will be used for the benefit of humanity and the planet. Indeed, data can also be advantageous to the world: the more data is collected, the more predictive patterns can be inferred to assist in improving healthcare provision, supporting the delivery of humanitarian assistance in warzones and in the aftermath of human-made and natural disasters, and in preventing the illicit trafficking of guns, drugs, and humans.

All things considered, the significance of the publication of private companies' principles is noteworthy for three reasons. First, it is of paramount importance that the creation of technologies for social good should be explicitly stated as the chief organizing goal, accountable to people, along with a commitment to safety and the creation of robust and unbiased algorithms that do not precipitate disasters and do not discriminate against people on the basis of race, gender, or religion, but are be utilized for the common good of society. Second, other technologies that caused widespread bodily harm, especially among innocent civilians, have been prohibited under international law: for instance, the use of chemicals for warfare, nuclear energy in weapons, and lasers for weapons that can cause blindness. All these malevolent uses of technologies that are otherwise suitable for humanity now face a range of prohibitions and regulations. As a result, there is widespread condemnation of, and a deeply felt opprobrium in response to, the development and use of chemical, nuclear, and laser weapons. It is about time, then, that the technology giants, which will probably still develop the bulk of their inventions in the coming years, put the brakes on the harmful uses of the technologies they develop and not assist in their weaponization. Third, it is a momentous decision by technology companies to align their inventions with universally and widely accepted international law and human rights. This level of compliance is a vital step toward bringing the tech giants into line with the commonly agreed norms of humanity that have now been accepted for almost a century, such as human rights law and the precepts of international law in general, which represent the collection of norms embodying a plan for the betterment of humanity and for saving the planet from the climate crisis and other urgent global cooperation problems.

Transnational advocacy for humanity: The Campaign to Stop Killer Robots

The Campaign to Stop Killer Robots was initiated in October 2012 and launched in London in April 2013. From the outset, the efforts of the campaign to strike a chord resonating decisively with human rights law were carefully orchestrated by Bonny

Docherty from the Harvard International Human Rights Clinic. Her 2012 publication, *Losing Humanity*, was decisive in connecting the high-level development of the initial discussions in the United Nations Human Rights Council and the publication of Christof Heyns' aforementioned report with the wider world of human rights activism. *Losing Humanity* demonstrated the impossibility of the permissible and lawful deployment of autonomous systems and became a reference source for anyone studying this matter.[113] The campaign has shown impressive growth since its creation, with almost 200 participating nongovernmental organizations in 70 countries. Its original intention of achieving a ban on fully autonomous weapons has evolved to become advocacy for retaining meaningful human control over the use of force; in recent years the campaign has been "working for an international legal instrument that prohibits machines that determine whom to kill and requires meaningful human control over the use of force."[114] From the outset, the campaign has called for a moratorium on autonomous weapon systems and the establishment of a group of experts to examine the matter. It had illustrious activists and scientists on its steering committee from the onset, such as Noel Sharkey, Peter Asaro, Nobel laureate Jody Williams, Richard Moyes, and Human Rights Watch director Steve Goose. My observations of the work of the campaign show that it is concerned with three areas that I believe could form the principled basis for the creation of *common good governance* in the shifting world order.

> Preventive prohibition and regulations, as proliferation has been rapid and widespread, and the overall trend toward increasing autonomy of these systems is here to stay. The campaign advocates for "meaningful human control" over individual attacks where lethal force is applied and for a new international treaty to govern autonomous killing where humans will always maintain ultimate control and take responsibility. According to Mary Wareham, the former founding coordinator of the Campaign to Stop Killer Robots, the creation of new international law should be guided by the inclusion of meaningful human control as a foundational principle, because it gives rise to a positive obligation that will stand up against new technological developments and prevent states from becoming entangled in the complex assessments of the threshold of autonomy as well as from time-consuming and difficult technical debates.[115]
> Compliance with IHL and human rights law: based on present and probable future technological developments, guaranteeing that autonomous weapon systems will be used in compliance with international law will present a daunting challenge. For the campaign, autonomous killing transgresses a moral threshold: machines are not suited to make complex ethical choices, and using machines to decide who is killed and who lives is a fundamental violation of human dignity. The United States, China, Israel, South Korea, Russia, and the United Kingdom are engaged in what will increasingly become a risky military AI race, but they have a choice now to make preventive decisions that will steer the world toward peace and stability instead.

Protection of civilians in conflict and beyond: this implies that autonomous killing is primordially a humanitarian issue and not solely an arms control question. The members of the campaign are well placed to apply and advance the humanitarian perspective and focus, because of their previous successes in creating new international law in other pressing areas of international security that advanced human security worldwide. Who would be accountable for errors made by the machines? The accountability gap is disgraceful, and justice would not be satisfied. The negative geopolitical, strategic, and destabilizing humanitarian implications far outweigh the benefits. Systems are already being deployed with evolving degrees of autonomy and this means that we may soon pass the tipping point for preventive prohibition. Autonomy is already being added to different capabilities in positioning, navigating, and targeting. Proliferation is likely to accelerate as it never has before.[116]

World-renowned political scientists Margaret Keck (Johns Hopkins) and Kathryn Sikkink (Harvard) explained in their seminal, epoch-making book, *Activists beyond Borders: Advocacy Networks in International Politics*,[117] that advocacy networks are one of the most powerful sources for new ideas and global norms for change for the world, such as the antislavery movement and the campaign for women's right to vote. Keck and Sikkink recognize that campaigners may fail, but their work is characterized by the centrality of principled ideas and values guiding their advocacy for change.

The model of activism followed by the Campaign to Stop Killer Robots, led by extraordinarily capable people, has nevertheless succeeded twice before: they achieved the prohibition of landmines and cluster munitions in two separate international treaties. A similar campaign, the International Campaign to Abolish Nuclear Weapons, was awarded the Nobel Peace Prize in 2017, and the endeavors of its inspiring leader, Beatrice Fihn, continue to make a difference in leading the world toward the point of nuclear zero. Prior to this, the International Campaign to Ban Landmines was awarded the Nobel Peace Prize in 1997, and its chief, Jody Williams, has lent her moral weight to the international Campaign to Stop Killer Robots. For me, the most exciting and instructive part of any meeting at the United Nations to hear Williams address the member states. Since 2014, Beatrice Fihn has been speaking to students taking my annual course on the Future of Global Governance at the United Nations in Geneva, communicating her powerful conviction that a better future for humanity is possible, wherein there is no place for nuclear weapons (Chapter 2).

A transnational advocacy network, according to Keck and Sikkink, emerges when "political entrepreneurs" or activists believe that networking across borders will advance their cause and create synergies that were not possible with localized action, since they seek to change the equation of what constitutes right and wrong. For instance, in promoting the landmines ban, activists led by Jody Williams sought to alter the calculation of what was perceived to be militarily indispensable. Most counties held landmines in their arsenals and considered them to be useful. It was, in great part, the work of the International Campaign to Ban Landmines that changed this perception. The work of education to cultivate respect for IHL, conducted by the ICRC, was also instrumental in the achievement of that change in perception. The ICRC engaged with militaries all over the world to remind them of their duty to distinguish between civilians and combatants, and that implementing precautionary measures was paramount, as key obligations under IHL. Together, they managed to convince militaries that the terrible humanitarian consequences of disrespect for the law in employing a weapon that does not distinguish between civilians and combatants far outweighs its military utility.

The work of the Campaign to Stop Killer Robots can be explained in terms of the authoritative framework put forward by Keck and Sikkink. First, the Campaign to Stop Killer Robots plays an important role in providing *information* by connecting key experts who contributed to establishing the *transnational networked cooperation* by generating credible and authoritative information, and especially by communicating it strategically. Second, the campaign applies *symbolic* politics by framing the problem in terms of "killer robots" and therefore tapping into a powerful subconscious fear of humanity that leads to repudiation of any form of takeover by autonomous killing machines. Third, the campaign *leverages* the work of states, small and large, on the premise that the combined voices of the mid-sized and small states may counter the power of the major countries. Networks provide international allies to people promoting change within each state that would not have the chance to meet such allies otherwise. Finally, the campaign summons states to be *accountable* for what they have committed themselves to abide by under international law. After examining a wide range of historical and current transnational action networks— such as those that ended slavery and fought successfully for the universal right for women to vote—to understand under what conditions these networks could have exerted their influence, Keck and Sikkink identified that the most effective networks were those that organized around matters that involved causing bodily harm to vulnerable individuals and around issues involving a striving for equal opportunities. They propounded five identifiable stages in the influence these networks exerted to bring about change to the world, as follows:

1) Issue creation and agenda setting by provoking media attention and raised prospects of attaining an international profile (e.g., to be discussed at the highest levels of world politics at the United Nations). After defining the problem, the networks convince target audiences that the problem exists and can be solved, and then offer prescriptions. Networks tend to monitor the evaluation of the implementation, when applicable;
2) Influence on the position adopted by states and international organizations;
3) Effect on institutional procedures;
4) Impact on "target groups," such as multinational corporations and other private entities;
5) Influence on state behavior.

There is no doubt that the Campaign to Stop Killer Robots had garnered significant weight to be able to marshal and rally the international community to start profiling the rise of autonomous killing as a global problem and to act upon this realization. My own close interactions with and observations of the exceptional forces mobilized by the campaign worldwide[118] mean that I can say with certainty that the five stages were evident and are still in progress in a true global movement.[119] In the first stage, the meteoric ascendance of the "issue" propounded by the campaign—namely, to stop the march toward autonomous killing—was astounding. This growing salience of the issue and intensification of attention can be seen in the first meeting of member states at the United Nations in 2014, just one year after the campaign was launched. In almost a decade of concerted action, the following developments are worth highlighting as evidence of *transnational networked cooperation*.

By the end of 2018 the United Nations Secretary-General called for "a ban on autonomous weapons, which are politically unacceptable and morally repugnant."[120] This is in line with the Secretary-General's promotion of "disarmament to save future generations" in his "Securing our Common Future" agenda (Chapter 3).

At the same time, 30 countries made their position explicit: a prohibition on autonomous weapons, and an insistence that meaningful human control over the use of force must be retained. Austria, Brazil, and Chile formally put forward a proposal for an international treaty to guarantee that meaningful human control over the critical functions of weapons remains integral. Additional coalitions have formed, most notably the G13, which evinces the solidarity among countries that do not wish to see autonomous systems developed and tested in their territories. They posit that life and death decisions cannot be minimized to be data points that aggravate social inequities as a result of algorithmic biases.[121]

The European Parliament agreed on a momentous resolution that called for the adoption of an

> EU Common Position on lethal autonomous systems that ensures meaningful human control over the critical functions of weapons systems. Such weapons systems range all the way from missiles capable of selective targeting to learning machines with cognitive skills to decide whom, when and where to fight. Parliament considered that human involvement and oversight are central to the lethal decision-making process.[122]

This is notable because of the call for a "Common Position," which is usually legally binding and signifies the rising consensus amongst the European countries.

In a riveting turn, thousands of technology workers from Google wrote a letter asking the leadership of the company to "stay out of the business of war." They aligned themselves with the campaign's objectives by starting to participate in some of its activities. What prompted the engineers to act was Google's project with the Pentagon, codenamed *Maven*, to use the AI-enabled technique known as facial recognition to enhance the operations of armed drones. The combination of the Tech

Workers Coalition, the Campaign to Stop Killer Robots, and the letter of the International Committee for Robot Arms Control, which had gathered thousands of signatures (led by Peter Asaro of the International Committee for Robot Arms Control), is what prompted Google to turn away from the Pentagon.[123] A week later, Google published its AI ethics principles.[124]

A prominent group of 30 Nobel Peace Prize laureates have expressed regret at the lack of action by the members of the United Nations to impede the unrelenting rise of killing algorithms that will lower the threshold and weaken the norms determining when countries should go to war. Along the same lines, in Germany the industry association, BDI, along with the top AI researchers and scientists, called for their government to lead the international efforts to create a new international treaty.

Even though these developments signify concrete turning points and denote markers in the development of *transnational networked cooperation*, which is unique in its make-up, it is probably not accurate to claim a causal relationship between the actions of the Campaign to Stop Killer Robots and the changing landscape of political action—even if the latter development points to a coalescing of opinions about the impermissibility and undesirability of algorithms programmed to kill. There seems to be mounting evidence, though, of a rising epistemic community of AI researchers in North America, Asia, and Europe who may play a central advocacy role in the ethics and governance of AI—as creators of the inventions and algorithms, and by advocating for change—and who are increasingly averse to the development of autonomous weapons and AI-assisted systems (75% against); they claim they would quit their jobs if asked to create such kill systems (42%). These professionals tend to place more trust in international organizations and scientific institutions in developing AI governance for the common good, while expressing low levels of trust in national military strategies to do this.[125]

Yet, my observations over the years at the United Nations in Geneva and in New York nevertheless suggest that it is undeniable that the campaign has been a significant contributing factor. For me, there are two more decisive factors influencing the process. The first is the United Nations acting as a forum where, over the last five years, a vast array of people can convene to meet and discuss the thorny questions raised by the issue of autonomous killing. Synergies occurred and working networks were created during the formal and informal meetings at the United Nations. The formal part was led by the former Ambassador of India to the United Nations, Amandeep Singh Gill, whom I met a few times and invited to address my students while we were in Geneva in 2017 and 2018. Ambassador Gill, a seasoned negotiator, led the talks in a format that expanded the focus from looking simply at autonomous weapon systems to also examining the role of AI in advancing their development. This meant that the invited delegates and the networks created during these meetings were of a more diverse and wide-ranging nature, bringing together scientists, entrepreneurs, activists, and United Nations member states. This may seem rather routine, but these meetings ultimately played a role not only in creating denser networks for action, but also in forming new ones.

The second factor is the role of the series of letters produced by the group of scientists convened by Toby Walsh of the University of New South Wales, Max Tegmark of the MIT and the Future of Life Institute, and Stuart Russell of Berkeley. After the first letter was published in 2015,[126] the landscape of action was altered ineradicably. Their actions through the letters brought the gravitas and sober conviction that those who create the technology should be heard and taken seriously by the world in addressing this issue. In addition, there was "celebrity clout" associated with many of the signatories, such as Bill Gates, Stephen Hawking, and Elon Musk. This milestone decisively and irreversibly elevated the efforts of the Campaign to Stop Killer Robots. I invited Max Tegmark and Stuart Russell to come to Northeastern University to discuss these letters and all the other questions I examine here. They are uniquely placed to look at the big picture and to situate these matters within a long-term context of the development of AI toward "singularity": the point at which the technology is likely to attain human capabilities of cognition and learned decision-making, and even outstrip human intelligence.

The guardian of the laws of war: The position and significance of the International Committee of the Red Cross

In May 2021, the ICRC published its legal position and called on states to create new, legally binding governing rules on autonomous weapons (which I examine in Chapter 4).[127] A decade earlier, in 2011, the ICRC had referenced autonomous weapons for the first time at the 31st International Conference of the Red Cross and Red Crescent in a report titled "International Humanitarian Law and Challenges to Contemporary Armed Conflicts," which stated: "An autonomous weapon system is one that can learn or adapt its functioning in response to changing circumstances in the environment in which it is deployed."[128] This was the first call for caution issued by the guardian of IHL. Here, the ICRC asks states to conduct a full assessment of the legal and ethical implications of the fielding of such systems and to do so in a manner that would abide by the provisions of IHL. I first heard about the use of autonomy in military operations and "man-out-of-loop robots" a year later during my annual visit to the ICRC in Geneva with my students, when Lou Maresca, an experienced expert from the Arms Division, addressed us.

The ICRC position on autonomous weapons represents a turning point in the advancement of *transnational networked cooperation*. The role of the ICRC as the guardian of IHL, or the laws of war, is unique and means this branch of international law holds an unusual position compared to others. The ICRC maintains neutrality and acts only in response to credible humanitarian challenges in terms of both its mandate and experience. Therefore, the opinion of the ICRC is taken seriously by states because of the universal and customary nature of IHL.

States and other parties to an armed conflict have an obligation to "respect and ensure respect for" IHL "in all circumstances" (Art. 1 common to the Geneva Conventions that form the basis of IHL). They must attempt to prevent and end violations of IHL by all parties taking part in the conflict. However, it is the ICRC that carries out this role most actively most of the time. The ICRC also assists and reminds states that they are treaty-bound to abide by IHL and that it is in their interest to do so. Armies that respect IHL are more efficient as a result of increased unity and consistency. The ICRC functions as a "guardian." This task entails defending IHL from adopting new rules or laws that would weaken or completely undermine its existence. It is important to keep in mind that some of the main rules of IHL, apart from the main precautionary tenets, are:

- Preserve the distinction between civilians and combatants: civilians are protected;
- Maintain proportionality vis-à-vis the military objective;
- The choice of weapon: weapons that do not respect the two other rules are unlawful.

Kathleen Lawand is a seasoned IHL expert with years of field experience and first-hand knowledge of the suffering of civilians in war; I had an opportunity to talk to her a few times in 2014 and 2015, especially during a London meeting of the International Committee of Arms Control. She used to lead the ICRC Arms Unit and considers autonomous weapons as those on one end of a spectrum of incremental automation; she also reminds states of their obligations under IHL to respect its main rules, especially those related to distinction, proportionality, and precautions. In the 2014 meeting of states at the UN in Geneva, the ICRC statement put forward a pioneering concept that came to be viewed as essential to consolidate the international discussions: autonomous weapon systems were defined as weapons that can independently select and attack targets—that is, they have autonomy in the "critical functions" of acquiring, tracking, selecting and attacking targets.[129] The idea of focusing on the "critical functions" substantially clarified what is at stake. The identification of the need to maintain "meaningful human control" over the "critical functions" became an established standard element in international discussions.

Here, the contribution of the ICRC was vitally important and shaped all that happened subsequently. It provided a further basis for the formation of *common good governance*. At that point, in 2014, only the United States and the United Kingdom had published their national policies on autonomous weapons.[130] For the former, "autonomous and semi-autonomous weapon systems shall be designed to allow commanders and operators to exercise appropriate levels of human judgment over the use of force." The ICRC issued a reminder that the development of new systems, including autonomous weapons, is governed by IHL. It was unclear, however, given the nature of these systems, how they could be properly tested. Additionally, many questioned the suitability of IHL to regulate autonomous weapons and proposed a ban on these systems, whereas others claimed that the existing legal framework is sufficient.

In 2015, I was present when the ICRC statement presented to the United Nations First Committee of the General Assembly in New York intensified its call for states to create limits on autonomy in the critical functions of weapon systems and act in accordance with IHL norms. Two years later, the United Nations met formally in Geneva to discuss lethal autonomous systems for the first time. This was in November 2017; the previous discussions and meetings since 2014 were considered "informal." At this stage there was broad consensus that human control must be maintained in the use of force and the decision to kill; however, uncertainty remained as to what human control entails, and at which point it must be present and applied. Here the ICRC called on states to establish limits on autonomy in weapon systems to ensure observance of international law. Specifically, states were required to evaluate what the required degree and type of human control would be. The ICRC also advises on the principled foundations of human control to guarantee observance of IHL: predictability; human supervision that includes the ability to intervene; and multiple operational restrictions such as knowledge of the operating environment, exact time frame, the scope of movement, and the context of deployment (in conflicts or during peacetime).[131] Along the same lines, the ICRC pointed out that moral responsibility for the decision to use military force to kill cannot be delegated to machines because this would relinquish human agency. This is to be observed especially in the light of the rapid advances in AI and their current use in military applications.

In the following year, in 2018, the United Nations member states of the Convention on Certain Conventional Weapons (CCW) met twice more and significant progress was made in the high-level discussions on the option of adopting a human-centered approach. I was present at these meetings. In concrete terms this meant that the path toward the establishment of globally agreed limits on autonomy that meet legal and ethical considerations would be a durable one because the limits will constrain the pace of technological advancement. This highlights the need for positive obligations on human control (type and degree).[132] At the end of 2018 the ICRC asked states to attempt to set "strong, practical, and future-proof limits on autonomy in weapon systems" and to determine what human control means in practice, proceeding from the premise that weapon systems should not be able to make the decision to kill.[133] The ICRC president, Peter Maurer, says that we are at a critical juncture for establishing limits and the appropriate level of human control to meet ethical and legal requirements.[134] Concretely, for the ICRC, human control in practice would take into account:

1) A system that operates autonomously in its critical functions and incorporates a level of supervision that includes the ability to intervene and deactivate;
2) A level of reliability and predictability according to tasks and the operational environment;
3) All other operational constraints: tasks, quality of the environment (populated or not), duration of the operation, and scope of the movement.[135]

The requirements set by the ICRC for what constitutes human control align quite well with those set by IPRAW, as I explained earlier. This leads to enhanced *transnational networked cooperation* and the diffusion of knowledge intensifying and coalescing around a more consensual common humanity-based discourse, where the implicit assumption is that technology should protect and not harm humans.

In advising member states at the United Nations, the ICRC submitted that a number of factors could potentially serve as a basis for setting limits on autonomous systems: the loss of human decision-making as a preponderant factor in the use of force; the difficulty of determining moral responsibility (attributability); and the loss of human dignity.[136] In the light of my examination of all the statements and studies produced by the ICRC and a close analysis of the progression of its position, this submission represented a substantial evolution in the position of the ICRC (Chapter 4 for an analysis of the current ICRC position on AI and autonomous weapons). Under IHL there is a duty to test weapons before they are fielded, according to Article 36 of Additional Protocol 1 to the Geneva Conventions of 1949, the basis of all IHL. The ICRC is rightly concerned about the limited ability to interrogate the outcomes of machine-learning algorithms because of how hard it is to determine how outputs result from inputs (i.e., how the machine came to its conclusions). If the continuous learning occurs online and after the system has been deployed on the battlefield, then the possibility of scrutinizing any outcomes becomes even harder. If a robotic system changes its behavior as a result of the capability provided by machine-learning, and especially if this is occurring with the continuous feeding of big online data, then the validity of the required testing may become null. From the outset, the ICRC had urged states to set internationally agreed limits but without commenting on the nature of the rules: are they legally or politically binding? It advised states on the need for predictability, types of targets, scope and situations of use, and the basic requirement for human supervision.[137]

Previous examples of new international law that promoted human security and increased the safety of people worldwide are the following treaties: blinding laser weapons, landmines, and cluster munitions, and which also regulated conventional arms (the Arms Trade Treaty), as well as nuclear, biological, and chemical weapons. On nuclear weapons, for instance, by launching a global campaign in February 2019 encouraging all states to ratify the 2017 Nuclear Ban Treaty, the ICRC not only calls for states never to use them again, but also for their complete prohibition and elimination. The ICRC played an essential catalyzing role with its unique moral authority as the guardian of the most universal part of international law—namely, IHL, which also holds customary force that binds all humanity to respect the necessary limits to prevent the barbarities of war and further dehumanization.

Member states of the United Nations

The first time the United Nations Secretary-General raised concerns about autonomous weapons was after the Special Rapporteur's reports by Heyns at the end of 2013, even though these weapons "have not been deployed yet":

the use of autonomous weapons systems, or what are known as "killer robots," … once activated, can select and engage targets and operate in dynamic and changing environments without further human intervention. Important concerns have been raised as to the ability of such systems to operate in accordance with International Humanitarian and Human Rights Law. Their potential use provokes other questions of great importance: is it morally acceptable to delegate decisions about the use of lethal force to such systems? If their use results in a war crime or serious human rights violation, who would be legally responsible? If responsibility cannot be determined as required by International Law, is it legal or ethical to deploy such systems? Although autonomous weapons systems as described herein have not yet been deployed and the extent of their development as a military technology remains unclear, discussion of such questions must begin immediately and not once the technology has been developed and proliferated. It must also be inclusive and allow for full engagement by United Nations actors, the International Committee of the Red Cross and civil society.[138]

The forum where states negotiate the regulation of autonomous weapons and discuss broader aspects of AI in the military realm is the CCW. The high-contracting parties started the discussion on autonomous weapons in May 2014.[139] I was present at that first meeting—as part of the delegation from the International Committee for Robot Arms Control—and at several subsequent ones, so I can attest to the fact that this is a framework convention, which means that it set out a general provision and an aspirations map for further action to be taken under international law. The convention aims to regulate or ban certain weapons and "methods of warfare of a nature to cause superfluous injury or unnecessary suffering" (Preamble) to combatants, or that can affect civilians. It is an IHL convention. Part of the credit for taking up the issue of autonomous weapons in the CCW goes to the then French Ambassador to the United Nations in Geneva and chair of the CCW in 2014, Jean-Hugues Simon. After the Heyns report, in which UN rapporteur Christoph Heyns alerted the Human Rights Council to the infringements of human dignity that could be caused by autonomous systems, Simon concluded that the CCW would be the right forum for a more detailed and informed discussion. He convened a group of friends and built up support for the formation of a first informal group of governmental experts, which he chaired. Ambassador Michael Biontino of Germany succeeded him. This marks the beginning of a Franco-German alignment on this issue, and there has been close cooperation throughout the years. I had the privilege of talking to Ambassador Biontino several times about how he viewed all these matters and what was needed for norm-shaping governance on the matter. Both Germany and France are inclined toward a more modest governing option in the form of an initial code of conduct that is only politically binding, instead of a legally binding treaty that prohibits or regulates all aspects of the matter.

The CCW has a few protocols where the actual substantive prohibitions or regulations are specified and codified. Of notable interest is Protocol IV of 1995, which prohibited the development and use of blinding laser weapons. This was the first time that an IHL instrument prohibited the application of a technology (namely laser technology applied to weapon systems with the aim of blinding opponents) before it entered the battle arena. It is remarkable to note the role that the ICRC played here.

The ICRC usually adopts a neutral stance, but in this case it decided to take a stand in support of a movement that wanted to limit the application of a technology that could cause harm and increase the barbarities of war.

Yet despite the valiant initial efforts of Ambassadors Biontino and Simon, the fact that the CCW has embraced the global discussion on autonomous weapons within the United Nations has done more harm than good. Creating new forms of global governance in the CCW is usually limited by the debilitatingly slow pace of the process of achieving consensus. If one country opposes any element, nothing can be adopted. Even though back then Heyns welcomed the CCW's attention, he had cautioned that even though autonomous weapons and autonomous killing are in part a disarmament issue, they have far-reaching human rights implications, and the CCW is not the place where human rights are discussed within the United Nations. The CCW is an IHL forum, and it limits discussion to this ambit. For instance, if we take the usage of armed drones as an example, most of the time the employment of drones takes place outside the scope of armed conflicts, where IHL will thus not be applicable, and therefore autonomous weapons should remain on the agenda of the Council of Human Rights and also be taken up by the United Nations General Assembly. Several years later there is still no palpable and substantive framework for action in the context of the CCW, with its archaic, consensus-based framework wherein all member states need to agree (Chapter 3). The result has been a low common denominator with simply a list of soft law principles to show for their efforts.

The member states of the CCW have been meeting, informally and then formally, since 2014 to discuss the rise of automation and the use of force without human input. Criticism of the CCW as a negotiating forum at the UN arises because of its inability to agree to anything bold and decisive in a timely fashion. This is a forum that works by consensus and therefore any country can block progress. After years of discussing how to prevent the rise of autonomous killing, states agreed on a set of "Possible Guiding Principles" in October 2018, four years after the first discussions at the United Nations. The result was reached by consensus, which is the rule of the CCW as a negotiating forum. Therefore, it was the lowest common denominator that was agreed on. Most countries want strong action and a legally binding path toward new global governance in the form of a new treaty; however, a handful technologically advanced and highly militarized countries, especially the United States and Russia, block any more ambitious developments. This is not an encouraging or action-oriented development. Nevertheless, the most substantive elements within these "Guiding Principles" for the creation of globally agreed governing norms are:

- First, "human responsibility" for decisions on the use of weapons must be maintained, because accountability for actions taken cannot be assigned to machines;
- Second, a responsible chain of human command and control that elicits accountability must exist at the point of creation of new weapon systems, along with safeguards against hacking or spoofing, as well as other cyber security enhancing measures;

- Human–machine interactions take various forms throughout the system's life cycle to ensure that their use is consonant with international law and IHL.[140]

The slow pace of the progress at the United Nations is partly explained by the different approaches that countries have adopted or have been adamant about regarding the definition (Table 1.4). Despite its shortcomings and out-of-date negotiating structure, the CCW played a useful role by providing a "convening forum" where many change makers could meet and interact. This visibly strengthened *transnational networked cooperation* in the development of new norms and in preventing a future characterized by the loss of human control over decisions to kill. But it is highly unlikely that any action toward change of the status quo, by means of the creation of new governing mechanisms under international law, will emanate from the CCW. It is a negotiating body that operates by consensus and attempts to strike a balance between military and humanitarian considerations. The former tends to prevail because, at least initially, the major military powers tend to oppose action that is predominantly motivated by humanitarian concerns. However, years of discussion in this same forum have driven the creation of networks between the many groups interested in the topic and cemented the rise of new norms. Yet, it is unlikely that new international law will emerge from the CCW because of opposition from the United States and Russia, especially.

Most importantly, the CCW as a forum is used to prohibit or regulate the use of physical weapons—for instance, laser weapons. The rise of autonomous and AI-assisted weapon systems precipitates a highly unconventional range and scope of topics that would need novel forms of regulation. The way autonomy is being employed as a feature of war has unlocked something novel and opened an unfamiliar road for the international community to embark upon. Perhaps it has therefore been ill-conceived to count on the CCW as the negotiating forum to initiate any action that could stem the march toward autonomous killing.

The result of the years of deliberation at the United Nations led to most countries in the world calling for strong action through the negotiation of a legally binding international treaty that will prohibit the absence of meaningful human control in decisions to kill in war. More recently, in 2023, there was a historic call for urgent negotiations of a legally binding treaty.[141] Thirty countries explicitly called for an outright preventive prohibition on "fully autonomous weapons." This group includes Argentina, Austria, Brazil, Chile, China, Colombia, Costa Rica, Egypt, the Holy See, Iraq, Mexico, and Pakistan. China calls for a ban only on the use of such systems, so it would be free to develop and produce them. Even though this group frames "fully autonomous weapons" as the object of new international law, they understand that what is at stake is the loss of meaningful human control, and they also appreciate the current questions raised by increased autonomy. Four states opposed negotiating new international law from the outset: Israel, Russia, the United Kingdom, and the United States. In recent years they have been joined in their opposition by Australia, France, Germany, the Republic of Korea, Spain, Sweden, and Turkey. In contrast, Austria, Brazil, and Chile were the first to issue a formal recommendation "to negotiate a legally-binding instrument to ensure meaningful human control over the critical functions" of weapon systems.[142]

Diplomacy at the United Nations is rapidly being outpaced by technological advancements that put the world on course toward a new international military race. More than that, we are witnessing the third revolution in warfare. The reasons for concern about the sluggish progress in the diplomatic front are threefold. First, the existing political and legal architecture under international law that had previously contained threats posed by the proliferation of weapons will not suffice now, as what is at stake is not "a weapon" as such, but technologies that can be applied in different ways to perform different functions within varied environments and in diverse conditions; they do not even need to be "embodied" in hardware, as they can also operate on cyber platforms. Second, there is great difficulty in discerning exactly what it is that needs to be contained. After years of deliberation, several groups have come to the fore to offer explanations and remedies, but the major powers persist in their resistance and opposition to acting upon solutions that would benefit all of humanity. Third, there are billions of dollars of vested interests in a future market that will enrich a few who will develop and sell these systems to supposedly "enhance national security"; this is preventing the taking of action to ensure the common good of humanity.

I view the world at the start of the 21st century as possessing adequate foundational global legal frameworks to protect human security on the basis of a largely "humanity-centered international law" (Chapter 4). It needs updating and reforming, but the foundations are built. Autonomous AI wars threaten to unsettle this legal world order. This is why the world is now going through a transformation—a shifting world order—that is epitomized by a mounting contempt for humanity-based laws and disrespect for the nonuse of force, a world where the primacy of the gains in national security and global competition for prominence is again on the rise. What is encouraging, however, is the rich and diverse tapestry of different change makers who constitute what I call *transnational networked cooperation*, where networks cooperate for change and progress independent of country or nationality. They operate transnationally, even in the absence of the major powers' acquiescence or a declining appetite for *international* cooperation. Instead, a firm humanity-based discourse anchored in human rights and a precautionary concern with the loss of dignity of human beings in future autonomous killing fields created by autonomous weapons is proposed as a reaction to the reluctance of the major powers to address this issue. The mosaic of change makers with influence has gained momentum and strength not only through the involvement and actions of a broader array of scientists with combined moral authority, but also through the responses of those who created the technology and express their revulsion against the evil uses of their creation. This concerted response has intensified *transnational networked cooperation* by adding authoritative voices insisting on the urgency of the need for global precautionary action to contain what might lead to irreversible harm to any attempt to ensure *humanity's security*.

Notes

1. Rodney Brooks, "A Hman in the Loop: AI won't Surpass Human Intelligence Anytime Soon." *IEEE Spectrum*, vol. 58, no. 10 (October 2021): p. 48, doi:10.1109/MSPEC.2021.9563963; Brooks was the director of the MIT Computer Science and AI Lab, and founded several robotics companies.
2. António Guterres, *Machines with Power, Discretion to Take Human Life Politically Unacceptable, Morally Repugnant, Secretary-General Tells Lisbon "Web Summit"* (United Nations, 2018), https://www.un.org/press/en/2018/sgsm19332.doc.htm.
3. António Guterres, *Inclusive, Networked Multilateralism Vital for Better World Governance, Says Secretary-General, at General Assembly's Seventy-Fifth Anniversary Meeting* (United Nations, September 21, 2020), https://www.un.org/press/en/2020/sgsm20264.doc.htm; The United Nations Secretary-General highlighted the need for "networked multilateralism" that is more inclusive of all voices in his speech marking the 75th anniversary of the organization.
4. Harold Hongju Koh, "Why Do Nations Obey International Law?" *Yale Law Journal*, vol. 106, no. 8 (1996): p. 2599, doi:10.2307/797228.
5. Peter M. Haas, "Introduction: Epistemic Communities and International Policy Coordination." *International Organization*, vol. 46, no. 1 (1992): pp. 1–35, doi:10.1017/S0020818300001442; Mai'a K. D. Cross, "Rethinking Epistemic Communities Twenty Years Later." *Review of International Studies*, vol. 39, no. 1 (2013): pp. 137–160.
6. Haas, "Introduction: Epistemic Communities and International Policy Coordination," p. 3.
7. Cross ("Rethinking Epistemic Communities") argues that the more internally cohesive they are, the more effective the networks will be in affecting change in transnational global governance. As Cross states on page 138: "Transnational epistemic communities have the advantage of projecting shared knowledge at the same time as understanding the particular circumstances of the various countries they represent, and being seen as a legitimate voice domestically. As transnational interaction grows, uncertainty abounds, and the role of nonstate actors becomes ever more prominent, the intersection of global governance and expert knowledge should be a significant part of the next generation of epistemic community research." It is where uncertainty is present that the role of transnational epistemic communities becomes all the more central and guiding.
8. R. Charli Carpenter, "Studying Issue (Non)-Adoption in Transnational Advocacy Networks." *International Organization*, vol. 61, no. 3 (2007): pp. 643–667, doi:10.1017/S002081830707021X.
9. Martha Finnemore, *National Interests in International Society* (Cornell University Press, 1996), p. 2.
10. Margaret Keck and Kathryn Sikkink, *Activists beyond Borders: Advocacy Networks in International Politics* (Cornell University Press, 1998).
11. I thank a thoughtful anonymous reviewer for this insight.
12. This refers to, among others, the 1997 Anti-Personnel Mine Ban Convention (the Ottawa Treaty that prohibited all aspects related to landmines development, manufacturing, stockpiling, transfer, and use), the 2008 Cluster Munition Convention, the 1968 Nuclear Non-Proliferation Treaty, the 2014 Arms Trade Treaty, and the 2017 Nuclear Ban Treaty. See Denise Garcia "Humanitarian Security Regimes." *International Affairs*, vol. 91, no.1 (January 2015): pp. 55–75 for further analysis.

13. I thank an anonymous reviewer for this comment.

14. Defense One, *The Race for AI—The Return of Great Power Competition Is Spurring the Quest to Develop Artificial Intelligence for Military Purposes*, Ebook, 2018, p. 7.

15. Lucy Suchman, "Algorithmic Warfare and the Reinvention of Accuracy." *Critical Studies on Security*, vol. 8, no. 2 (2020): pp. 175–187, doi:10.1080/21624887.2020.1760587.

16. Denise Garcia, "Redirect Military Budgets to Tackle Climate Change and Pandemics." *Nature*, vol. 584, no. 7822 (August 2020): pp. 521–523, doi:10.1038/d41586-020-02460-9.

17. Toby Walsh, Machines that Think: The Future of Artificial Intelligence (Prometheus Books, 2018).

18. The work of Rebecca Crootof from Yale is very instructive; in particular, see Rebecca Crootof, "Autonomous Weapon Systems and the Limits of Analogy." *Harvard National Security Journal*, vol. 9 (2018): pp. 51–83.

19. I am grateful to Eugenio V. Garcia.

20. US Department of State, "Political Declaration on Responsible Military Use of Artificial Intelligence and Autonomy, Bureau of Arms Control," Verification and Compliance, February 16, 2023.

21. Responsible AI in the Military domain Summit, The Hague, The Netherlands, 2023, REAIM Call to Action, February 2023.

22. China's State Council, AI Next Generation Artificial Intelligence Development Plan, ed./trans. Rogier Creemers et al. (2017): https://d1y8sb8igg2f8e.cloudfront.net/documents/translation-fulltext-8.1.17.pdf, p. 9.

23. Nik Hynek and Anzhelika Solovyeva, "Operations of Power in Autonomous Weapon Systems: Ethical Conditions and Socio-political Prospects." *AI & Society*, vol. 36, no. 1 (2021): pp. 79–99, doi:10.1007/s00146-020-01048-1.

24. Amy Webb, *The Big Nine: How the Tech Titans and Their Thinking Machines Could Warp Humanity* (Hachette UK: PublicAffairs, 2019).

25. Ibid.

26. Maaike Verbruggen, "The Role of Civilian Innovation in the Development of Lethal Autonomous Weapon Systems." *Global Policy*, vol. 10 (2019): pp. 338–342, doi:10.1111/1758-5899.12663.

27. The European Union, Coordinated Plan on Artificial Intelligence (COM(2018) 795 final) (Brussels, 2018), https://eur-lex.europa.eu/legal-content/EN/TXT/HTML/?uri=CELEX:52018DC0795&rid=3.

28. Eugenio V. Garcia, "Multilateralism and Artificial Intelligence: What Role for the United Nations?" In *The Global Politics of Artificial Intelligence*, ed. Maurizio Tinnirello (2020), http://dx.doi.org/10.2139/ssrn.3779866.

29. The European Union, *Proposal for a Regulation of the European Parliament and of The Council Laying Down Harmonised Rules on Artificial Intelligence (Artificial Intelligence Act) and Amending Certain Union Legislative (COM(2021) 206 final)* (Brussels, 2021), https://eur-lex.europa.eu/resource.html?uri=cellar:e0649735-a372-11eb-9585-01aa75ed71a1.0001.02/DOC_1&format=PDF.

30. SIPRI, "International Arms Transfers and Developments in Arms Production," *SIPRI Yearbook 2021: Armaments, Disarmament and International Security* (2021): pp. 14–15.

31. SIPRI, *Military Expenditure Database* (2020), https://www.sipri.org/databases/milex.

32. Justin Haner and Denise Garcia. "The Artificial Intelligence Arms Race: Trends and World Leaders in Autonomous Weapons Development." *Global Policy*, vol. 10, no. 3 (2019): pp. 331–337; Boulanin and Verbruggen, *Mapping the Development of Autonomy in Weapon Systems*.

33. Boulanin and Verbruggen, *Mapping the Development of Autonomy in Weapon Systems*.
34. Nestor Maslej et al., "The AI Index 2023 Annual Report." AI Index Steering Committee, Institute for Human-Centered AI, Stanford University, Stanford, CA, April 2023.
35. Joint Statement, *AI Partnership for Defense (AI PfD)* (September 15–16, 2020), https://www.ai.mil/docs/AI_PfD_Joint_Statement_09_16_20.pdf.
36. AI Index Steering Committee, p. 18.
37. Denise Garcia, "Stop the Emerging AI Cold War." *Nature*, vol. 593, no. 7858 (2021): p. 169, doi:10.1038/d41586-021-01244-z; Hal Brands and John Lewis Gaddis, "The New Cold War: America, China, and the Echoes of History." Foreign Affairs (December 2021), https://www.foreignaffairs.com/articles/united-states/2021-10-19/new-cold-war.
38. AI Index Steering Committee, p. 19.
39. The American AI Strategy is available at https://media.defense.gov/2019/Feb/12/2002088963/-1/-1/1/SUMMARY-OF-DOD-AI-STRATEGY.PDF.
40. DARPA, *AI Next Campaign*. https://www.darpa.mil/work-with-us/ai-next-campaign
41. Joachim von Braun et al., eds., *Robotics, AI, and Humanity: Science, Ethics, and Policy* (Springer Nature, 2021).
42. Global Military Artificial Intelligence (AI) and Cybernetics Market—Analysis and Forecast, 2019–2024. Accessed via the Statista database. Cross-referenced with Markets & Markets, Artificial Intelligence in Military Market by Offering (Software, Hardware, Services), Technology (Machine Learning, Computer vision), Application, Installation Type, Platform, Region—Global Forecast to 2025. https://www.statista.com/statistics/1238530/worldwide-military-artificial-intelligence-cybernetics-revenue-by-service/
43. von Braun et al., *Robotics, AI, and Humanity*, p. 143.
44. Ingvild Bode and Hendrik Huelss, "Autonomous Weapons Systems and Changing Norms in International Relations." *Review of International Studies*, vol. 44, no. 3 (2018): pp. 393–413, doi:10.1017/S0260210517000614.
45. Paul Scharre and Michael C. Horowitz, Meaningful Human Control in Weapon Systems: A Primer (Center for a New American Security, 2015), https://www.cnas.org/publications/reports/meaningful-human-control-in-weapon-systems-a-primer.
46. I am grateful to Frank Sauer for several conversations.
47. United Nations Institute for Disarmament Research (UNIDIR), "Framing Discussions on the Weaponization of Increasingly Autonomous Technologies." *UNIDIR Resources* 1 (Geneva: UNIDIR, 2014), https://unidir.org/files/publications/pdfs/framing-discussions-on-the-weaponization-of-increasingly-autonomous-technologies-en-606.pdf.
48. ICRC, *Artificial Intelligence and Machine Learning in Armed Conflict*; emphases are in the original ICRC text.
49. Scharre and Horowitz, *An Introduction to Autonomy in Weapon Systems*.
50. Vignard, "The Weaponization of Increasingly Autonomous Technologies: Concerns, Characteristics and Definitional Approaches: A Primer."
51. Bonnie Docherty, *Losing Humanity: The Case against Killer Robots* (Human Rights Watch, 2012).
52. Nicholas Marsh, *Defining the Scope of Autonomy* (PRIO, 2014): p. 2.
53. Boulanin and Verbruggen, *Mapping the Development of Autonomy in Weapon Systems*.
54. Heather Roff and Richard Moyes, *Meaningful Human Control, Artificial Intelligence and Autonomous Weapons* (Future of Life Institute, Article 36, Arizona State University, 2016).
55. Jürgen Altmann et al., "Armed Military Robots: Editorial." Ethics and Information Technology, vol. 15 (2013): pp. 73–76, doi:10.1007/s10676-013-9318-1.

56. The original explanation of the principle appears in Article 36, *Killing by Machine* (2015). For further exploration, see Roff and Moyes, "Meaningful Human Control, Artificial Intelligence and Autonomous Weapons," a briefing paper prepared for the Informal Meeting of Experts on Lethal Autonomous Weapons Systems, UN Convention on Certain Conventional Weapons, April 2016. https://article36.org/wp-content/uploads/2020/12/KILLING_BY_MACHINE_6.4.15.pdf

57. Daniele Amoroso and Guglielmo Tamburrini, "Autonomous Weapons Systems and Meaningful Human Control: Ethical and Legal Issues." *Current Robotics Reports*, vol. 1 (2020): doi:10.1007/s43154-020-00024-3.

58. Paul Scharre, Autonomous Weapons and Operational Risk (Center for a New American Security, 2016), https://www.files.ethz.ch/isn/196288/CNAS_Autonomous-weapons-operational-risk.pdf.

59. Scharre, *Autonomous Weapons and Operational Risk*, p. 48.

60. See IPRAW's published reports, available at https://www.ssoar.info/ssoar/discover?query=iPRAW&submit=.

61. Mary L. Cummings, *Artificial Intelligence and the Future of Warfare* (Royal Institute of International Affairs, 2017). To further explore autonomy from a robotics point of view, see Mary L. Cummings, "Man vs. Machine or Man + Machine?" *IEEE Intelligent Systems*, vol. 29, no. 5 (2014): pp. 62–69. See also Lucy Alice Suchman and Jutta Weber, *Human–Machine Autonomies. Autonomous Weapons Systems: Law, Ethics, Policy* (Cambridge University Press, 2016): pp. 75–102.

62. Lucy Alice Suchman, "Situational Awareness and Adherence to the Principle of Distinction as a Necessary Condition for Lawful Autonomy." In *Lethal Autonomous Weapons Systems*, ed. Robin Geiß (German Federal Foreign Office, 2017): pp. 273–283.

63. Adam Bower, *Norms Without the Great Powers: International Law and Changing Social Standards in World Politics* (Oxford University Press, 2017).

64. Samantha Besson, "Theorizing the Sources of International Law." In Samantha Besson and John Tasioulas (eds), *The Philosophy of International Law* (Oxford University Press, 2019): p. 163–185.

65. Trindade, *International Law for Humankind*.

66. Peter Asaro, "How Just Could a Robot War Be?" In *Current Issues in Computing And Philosophy*, eds. Philip Brey, Adam Briggle, and Katinka Waelbers (2009); Noel Sharkey, "Automated Killers and the Computing Profession." *Computer Journal*, vol. 40, no. 11 (2007): p. 124, doi: 10.1109/MC.2007.372; Noel Sharkey, "Death Strikes from the Sky: The Calculus of Proportionality." *IEEE Technology and Society*, vol. 28 (2009): pp. 16–19; Robert Sparrow, "Robotic Weapons and the Future of War." In *New Wars and New Soldiers: Military Ethics in the Contemporary World*, ed. Jessica Wolfendale and Paolo Tripodi Robert Sparrow (UK: Ashgate Publishing Limited): pp. 117–133. For other initial works with more alternative views, see William H. Boothby, *Weapons and the Law of Armed Conflict*, 2nd edition, (Oxford University Press, 2016);Jason Borenstein, "The Ethics of Autonomous Military Robots," *Studies in Ethics, Law and Technology*, vol. 2, no. 1 (2008); Ronald C. Arkin, "The Case for Ethical Autonomy in Unmanned Systems." *Journal of Military Ethics*, vol. 9, no. 4 (2010): pp. 332–341.

67. Noel Sharkey, "Robot Wars are a Reality." *The Guardian* (2007), https://www.theguardian.com/commentisfree/2007/aug/18/comment.military. I thank Noel Sharkey for the many conversations we have had throughout the years and all his advice, which inspired me to investigate this.

68. Peter Asaro, "On Banning Autonomous Weapon Systems: Human Rights, Automation, and the Dehumanization of Lethal Decision-Making." *International Review of the Red Cross*, vol. 94, no. 886 (2012): pp. 687–709, doi:10.1017/S1816383112000768. Professor Asaro is the first to connect the discussion on rising autonomous killing to international humanitarian law and human rights law. He and I are very like-minded here: see Garcia "Humanitarian Security Regimes." For some of the more recent views of this important thinker, see Peter Asaro, "Jus Nascendi" In *Robot Law*, ed. Ryan Calo, Michael Froomkin, and Ian Kerr (Edward Elgar Publishing, 2016), pp. 367–386 and Peter Asaro, "'Hands up, Don't Shoot!'" *Journal of Human–Robot Interaction*, vol. 5, no. 3 (2016): pp. 55–69.

69. United States Department of Defense, *Unmanned Systems Roadmap* (Office of the Secretary of Defense, 2007).

70. Ibid., pp. 16, 49, 69.

71. Peter Warren Singer, *Wired for War: The Robotics Revolution and Conflict in the 21st century* (Penguin, 2009).

72. Philip Alston, *Interim Report* (United Nations, 2010). For this report Alston usefully gathered the early literature on the topic: Summary of Harvard Executive Session of June 2008, Unmanned and Robotic Warfare: Issues, Options and Futures, at 14 ("2008 Harvard Session"), *IEEE Technology and Society* 28, no. 1 (Spring 2009): 25–29; Patrick Lin, George Bekey, and Keith Abney, *Autonomous Military Robotics: Risk, Ethics, and Design* (Department of the Navy, Office of Naval Research, 2008).

73. United Nations, Human Rights Council, *Report of the Special Rapporteur on Extrajudicial, Summary or Arbitrary Executions*, A/HRC/23/4 (April 9, 2013) available from undocs.org/A/HRC/23/4.

74. Garcia, "The Case Against Killer Robots—-Why the United States Should Ban Them."

75. Kate Crawford and Meredith Whittaker, The AI Now Report (AI Now Institute, 2016).

76. The authors and panel members are Heather Roff Emmanuel Bloch, Ariel Conn, Denise Garcia, Amandeep Gill, Ashley Llorens, and Mart Noorma. https://standards.ieee.org/content/dam/ieee-standards/standards/web/documents/other/ethical-technical-challenges-autonomous-weapons-systems.pdf.

77. IEEE Standards Association, "Research Group on Issues of Autonomy and AI for Defense Systems." https://standards.ieee.org/industry-connections/autonomy-ai-defense.html.

78. Stuart Russell, Daniel Dewey, and Max Tegmark, "Research Priorities." *AI Magazine*, vol. 36, no. 4 (2015): pp. 105–114.

79. Ibid., p. 107.

80. See https://futureoflife.org/ai-principles/. The story of how the Asilomar Principles came into being are told in detail in Max Tegmark, Life 3.0 (Knopf, 2018). Numbers of signatories from January 2022.

81. Jessica Fjeld et al., "Principled Artificial Intelligence: Mapping Consensus in Ethical and Rights-Based Approaches to Principles for AI." *Berkman Klein Center Research Publication*, 2020–1 (2020).

82. Gregory D. Hager et al., *Artificial Intelligence for Social Good* (Association for the Advancement of Artificial Intelligence and Computing Community Consortium, 2017), 15.

83. IEEE, *Ethically Aligned Design: Version 1* (Institute of Electrical and Electronics Engineers, 2016): p. 2.

84. Ibid.

85. Ibid., p. 5.

86. Ibid., p. 8.

87. Ibid.

88. IEEE, *Ethically Aligned Design: Version 2* (Institute of Electrical and Electronics Engineers [IEEE], 2017): p. 9.

89. Denise Garcia's Testimony to the United Nations member states at the meeting of the Convention on Certain Conventional Weapons Meeting of Experts on Lethal Autonomous Weapons Systems in April 2016 at the United Nations in Geneva. I expanded the testimony in an article: Denise Garcia, "Lethal Artificial Intelligence and Change: The Future of International Peace and Security." *International Studies Review*, vol. 20, no. 2 (2018): pp. 334–341.

90. IEEE, *Ethically Aligned Design: Version 2.*

91. Ibid., p. 116

92. International Committee of the Red Cross (ICRC), *Autonomous Weapon Systems: Implications of Increasing Autonomy in the Critical Functions of Weapons* (ICRC, 2016).

93. IEEE, *Ethically Aligned Design: Version 2*, p. 118.

94. I thank Maria Virginia Olano Velasquez for her assistance in helping me to prepare those presentations at the United Nations.

95. Walsh, *Open Letter from AI & Robotics Researchers.*

96. Daniel Victor, "Elon Musk and Stephen Hawking Among Hundreds to Urge Ban on Military Robots." *The New York Times*, July 28, 2015, https://www.nytimes.com/2015/07/28/technology/elon-musk-and-stephen-hawking-among-hundreds-to-urge-ban-on-military-robots.html.

97. Walsh, *Open Letter from AI & Robotics Researchers.*

98. Ibid.

99. Future of Life Institute, *Lethal Autonomous Weapons Pledge* (2018), https://futureoflife.org/lethal-autonomous-weapons-pledge/.

100. Future of Life Institute, *Lethal Autonomous Weapons Pledge.*

101. Ariel Conn, *AI and Robotics Researchers Boycott South Korea Tech Institute Over Development of AI Weapons Technology* (Future of Life Institute, 2018), https://futureoflife.org/2018/04/04/ai-and-robotics-researchers-boycott-kaist/.

102. Scott Shane and Daisuke Wakabayashi, "'The Business of War' Google Employees Protest Work for the Pentagon." The New York Times, April 4, 2018, https://www.nytimes.com/2018/04/04/technology/google-letter-ceo-pentagon-project.html.

103. "Open Letter in Support of Google Employees and Tech Workers." *ICRAC*, https://www.icrac.net/open-letter-in-support-of-google-employees-and-tech-workers (February 21, 2019).

104. I presented on the issue addressed here at the United Nations, Geneva, November 13—17, 2017, First Formal Meeting of States Parties to the Convention on Certain Weapons on the question of Lethal Autonomous Weapons Systems; I was invited to speak by the Geneva Centre for Security Policy and the Swiss Federal Department of Foreign Affairs on "The Use of Artificial Intelligence and the Defence Industry: Legal, Ethical, Strategic and Governance Issues."

105. Frank Slijper et al., *Don't be Evil: A Survey of the Tech Sector's Stance on Lethal Autonomous Weapons* (PAX, August 2019): p. 13, https://paxforpeace.nl/what-we-do/publications/dont-be-evil.

106. Boston Dynamics, "Boston Dynamics Ethical Principles." https://www.bostondynamics.com/ethics.

107. Meghan Hennessey, "Clearpath Robotics Takes Stance Against 'Killer Robots.'" *ClearPath Robotics*, August 13, 2014, https://www.clearpathrobotics.com/blog/2014/08/clearpath-takes-stance-against-killer-robots/.

108. From the Clearpath Robotics website: "a global leader in unmanned vehicle robotics for research and development, is dedicated to automating the world's dullest, dirtiest, and deadliest jobs. The company serves robotics leaders in over 35 countries worldwide in academic, mining, military, agricultural and industrial markets."

109. Partnership on AI, "About Us: Advancing Positive Outcomes for People and Society," https://partnershiponai.org/about/.

110. Google, "Artificial Intelligence at Google: Our Principles," https://ai.google/principles/.

111. https://ai.google/responsibility/principles/.

112. Webb, *The Big Nine*. The G-Mafia group's counterparts, according this clever classification created by Webb, are in China—the BAT: Baidu, Alibaba, and Tencent.

113. Docherty, *Losing Humanity*.

114. Campaign to Stop Killer Robots, "Our Vision and Values." https://www.stopkillerrobots.org/vision-and-values/.

115. Stop Killer Robots, "Statement to the CCW GGE on LAWS Delivered by Mary Wareham." March 29, 2019. https://www.stopkillerrobots.org/wp-content/uploads/2019/04/KRC_Statement_29March_DELIVERED.pdf.

116. For a gripping account of the details about the robotic systems already deployed, and a tour de force on the specifics of weapon systems, their evolution, and their deployment on the battlefield, see Paul Scharre, *Army of None* (W. W. Norton & Company, 2018). A former US Army Ranger who served in Iraq and Afghanistan, Scharre is a seasoned inside observer in this debate and has testified to the United Nations as well. His book is an essential one also for the understanding of autonomy and the role of AI.

117. Keck and Sikkink, *Activists Beyond Borders*.

118. I thank Steve Goose of Human Rights Watch and Nobel Peace Prize laureate Jody Williams, who always devote their time so generously to researchers like me, excited to get their visionary insights. Most recently, my conversations with Ousman Noor have been most inspiring to me.

119. Mary Wareham and Stephen Goose, "The Growing International Movement Against Killer Robots," *Harvard International Review*, January 2017.

120. "Secretary-General's Address to the Paris Peace Forum." *United Nations*, November 11, 2018, https://www.un.org/sg/en/content/sg/statement/2018-11-11/allocution-du-secr%C3%A9taire-g%C3%A9n%C3%A9ral-au-forum-de-paris-sur-la-paix.

121. The G13 countries are: Costa Rica, Ecuador, El Salvador, Guatemala, Palestine, Phillipines, Kazakhstan, Nigeria, Panama, Peru, Sierra Leone, Uruguay, and Argentina. For the G13 statement, see https://reachingcriticalwill.org/images/documents/Disarmament-fora/ccw/2021/RevCon/statements/17Dec_G13.pdf.

122. The European Parliament Resolution on autonomous weapon systems, 2018/2752(RSP) on September, 12, 2018, by 566 votes (47 negative and 73 abstentions).

123. "Open Letter in Support of Google Employees and Tech Workers."

124. Amr Gaber, "Transcript of UN Remarks by Amr Gaber at CCW 2018/28/8" (Statement to The UN Convention on Conventional Weapons), August 28, 2018, Geneva, https://www.stopkillerrobots.org/wp-content/uploads/2018/11/Amr-Gaber-UN-remarks-2018-28-8-1.pdf.

125. This is a landmark study and comprehensive survey across the world: Baobao Zhang, et al., "Ethics and Governance of Artificial Intelligence: Evidence from a Survey of Machine Learning Researchers." *Journal of Artificial Intelligence Research*, vol. 71 (2021): pp. 591–666.

126. Walsh, *Open Letter from AI & Robotics Researchers*.

127. ICRC, "ICRC Position on Autonomous Weapon Systems." Geneva, 2021, https://www.icrc.org/en/document/icrc-position-autonomous-weapon-systems.

128. ICRC, "International Humanitarian Law (IHL) and the Challenges of Contemporary Armed Conflicts" (International Conference of the Red Cross and Red Crescent, 2011): p. 39.

129. ICRC, "Statement of the International Committee of the Red Cross." *Convention on Certain Conventional Weapons (CCW) Meeting of Experts on Lethal Autonomous Weapons Systems (LAWS)*, May 13–16, 2014, *Geneva*, https://reachingcriticalwill.org/images/documents/Disarmament-fora/ccw/2014/statements/13May_ICRC.pdf.

130. US Department of Defense, "DoD Directive 3000.09"; "Joint Doctrine Note 2/11: The UK Approach to Unmanned Aircraft Systems" (UK Ministry of Defence, 2011).

131. ICRC (2017a), "Weapons: ICRC Statement to the UN, 2017." *International Committee of the Red Cross*, https://www.icrc.org/en/document/weapons-statement-icrc-united-nations-unag–2017; ICRC (2017b), "Statement of the ICRC to the CCW Group of Governmental Experts." https://docs-library.unoda.org/Convention_on_Certain_Conventional_Weapons_-_Group_of_Governmental_Experts_(2017)/2017_GGE%2BLAWS_Statement_ICRC.pdf.

132. ICRC (2018a), "Statement of the ICRC to the CCW GGE on LAWS," http://reaching criticalwill.org/images/documents/Disarmament-fora/ccw/2018/gge/statements/9Ap-ril_ICRC.pdf; ICRC (2018b), *Ethics and Autonomous Weapon Systems: An Ethical Basis for Human Control?*, CCW/GGE.1/2018/WP.5 (March 29, 2018), available from undocs.org/CCW/GGE.1/2018/WP.5; ICRC (2018c) "Weapons, ICRC Statement to the UN, 2018." https://www.icrc.org/en/document/general-debate-all-disarmament-and-international-security-agenda-items#:~:text=The%20ICRC%20firmly%20condemns%20any,CWC%20to%20uphold%20this%20prohibition.

133. Marie-Servane Desjonquères, "Autonomous Weapons: States Must Agree on What Human Control Means in Practice." *ICRC*, 2018, https://www.icrc.org/en/document/autonomous-weapons-states-must-agree-what-human-control-means-practice; Boulanin and Verbruggen, *Mapping the Development of Autonomy in Weapon Systems*.

134. Desjonquères, "Autonomous Weapons: States Must Agree on What Human Control Means in Practice."

135. Ibid; ICRC, "The Element of Human Control," working paper submitted at the Meeting of High Contracting Parties to the CCW, Geneva, November 21–23, 2018, CCW/MSP/2018/WP.3; CRC (2018b), *Ethics and Autonomous Weapon Systems*; ICRC, "Autonomous Weapon Systems: Implications of Increasing Autonomy in the Critical Functions of Weapons," March 2016; ICRC, "Autonomous Weapon Systems: Technical, Military, Legal and Humanitarian Aspects," March 2014.

136. ICRC, *Ethics and Autonomous Weapon Systems: An Ethical Basis for Human Control?*, CCW/GGE.1/2018/WP.5 (March 29, 2018), available from https://reachingcriticalwill.org/disarmament-fora/ccw/2018/laws/documents. This is the best written and most

illuminating report issued on the years of deliberation at the United Nations—essential reading for anyone interested in the questions examined here.

137. ICRC, "Statement of the ICRC to the UN CCW GGE on Lethal Autonomous Weapons Systems," September 21–25, 2020, Geneva; ICRC, "ICRC Commentary on the 'Guiding Principles' of the CCW GGE on 'Lethal Autonomous Weapons Systems,'" July 2020; Vincent Boulanin et al., *Limits on Autonomy in Weapons Systems*; ICRC, *Autonomy, Artificial Intelligence and Robotics: Technical Aspects of Human Control*, August 2019; ICRC, *Statements of the ICRC to the UN CCW GGE on Lethal Autonomous Weapons Systems*, March 25–29, 2019, Geneva; ICRC.

138. United Nations, Security Council, *Report of the Secretary-General on the Protection of Civilians in Armed Conflict*, S/2013/689 (November 22, 2013), available from undocs.org/S/2013/689.

139. The 1980 Convention on Prohibitions or Restrictions on the Use of Certain Conventional Weapons Which May Be Deemed to Be Excessively Injurious or to Have Indiscriminate Effects (CCW) is usually referred to as the Convention on Certain Conventional Weapons. It is also known as the Inhumane Weapons Convention.

140. United Nations, High Contracting Parties to the CCW, *Report of the 2018 Session of the Group of Governmental Experts on Emerging Technologies in the Area of Lethal Autonomous Weapons Systems*, CCW/GGE.1/2018/3 (October 23, 2018), available from https://reachingcriticalwill.org/disarmament-fora/ccw/2018/laws/documents.

141. Comunicado de la Ribera de Belen, Costa Rica, Conferencia Latinoamericana y del Caribe sobre el Impacto Social y Humanitario de las Armas Autonomas, February 24, 2023.

142. Austria, Brazil, and Chile, *Proposal for a Mandate to Negotiate a Legally Binding Instrument that Addresses the Legal, Humanitarian and Ethical Concerns posed by Emerging Technologies in the Area of Lethal Autonomous Weapons Systems (LAWS)*, CCW/GGE.2/2018/WP.7 (August 30, 2018), available from undocs.org/CCW/GGE.2/2018/WP.7.

Chapter 2
Common good governance

The AI Military Race. Denise Garcia, Oxford University Press. © Denise Garcia (2023).
DOI: 10.1093/oso/9780192864604.003.0003

PART I

Humanity's security

The world is in the throes of confronting global problems that affect everyone; only global solutions can solve them, and a truly commonly agreed blueprint is needed not only to face ongoing threats, but also to avoid the worst to come in the near future. Staving off the vilest effects of climate change, preventing nuclear war and conflict, impeding continuous iterations of the current pandemic, and averting the next major global concern are essential, but require decisive joint action in the interests of all humanity. In the light of the stark losses incurred by the world economy as a consequence of the pandemic, a new conceptualization of security must be embraced: *humanity's security*. This is a call for action that requires states to pool their resources, capacities, and strengths for the common good of humanity to attain global public goods on a planetary scale.

> In a historical moment like the present one, of somber recrudescence of indiscriminate use of force, in which it regrettably appears again trivial to speak of war, there is a pressing need to face the new threats to international peace and security within the framework of the United Nations Charter, and to insist on the realization of justice at the international level.[1]

At the center of this new concept is the idea that the security of states is fundamental (national security). However, the safety of individuals, especially vulnerable populations, must also be safeguarded (human security). Crucial is the realization that the security and safety of states and individuals in one country are inextricably intertwined with the security and safety of individuals in all countries. My notion of *humanity's security* emphasizes that the fate and well-being of individuals in one country are tied to and depend upon the welfare of all individuals in all other countries.

The COVID-19 pandemic proved that no one is safe until everyone is protected, and climate change has shown that there is no place from which to stand by and watch from afar. The effects of anthropogenic interference with the climate at calamitous levels are ongoing everywhere. What is different about *humanity's security*, derived from the concepts of national and human security, is that it attests to the urgent need for solutions that must come from all countries, in collective preventive action, to respond to the threats by pooling their resources. Additionally, *humanity's security* calls for a more self-aware and purposeful integration between human beings and their natural environment and ecological systems. Without the realization of this inextricable connection, there will be no easy way out of the multiple problems that confront humanity.

Humanity—the partnership between governments, scientists, individuals, aboriginal communities, and international institutions—is at the center of the communal and global changes needed to contain the ongoing planetary mega threats.[2] Instead of privileging only the state as the hub for action, I would say the state remains essential but is not capable of acting alone, so it must muster the necessary strategic partnerships: scientific, collective, and practical.

Climate change is generally viewed as humanity's greatest contemporary challenge.[3] The Nobel Peace Prize laureate global group of scientists that was established in 1998, the Intergovernmental Panel on Climate Change (IPCC), released a harrowing report in February 2022 and then its final report on 2023, detailing the latest scientific evidence on the irreversible damage humanity has inflicted on the climate.[4] The report admonishes the world to act to avoid catastrophic consequences from "widespread, rapid, and intensifying climate change."[5] The landmark reports are the most definitive collection of scientific evidence to date. With data gathered from more than 14,000 studies, it presents irrefutable, robust, and empirical evidence of a changing climate based on real-life observations.[6] In 2014, the IPCC found that climate change will progressively threaten human security by undermining livelihoods, compromising culture and identity, intensifying migration, and undercutting states' ability to provide the conditions for human security to be achieved.[7]

Humanity's security is a valuable concept by which to evaluate the impact of non-military threats on national security, such as infectious diseases or climate change, and to determine the best way to marshal the forces for action.[8] Nonmilitary challenges threaten all human beings worldwide. For instance, climate-induced natural disasters displaced 24 million people in 2019; in contrast, 7 million people were displaced by armed conflict.[9] By 2040, a total of 5.4 billion people—more than half of the world's projected population—will live in the 59 countries experiencing high or extreme water stress, including India and China. The global economic impact of violence was $14.96 trillion in 2020, equivalent to 11.6% of global gross domestic product (GDP), and this includes military expenditure, expenditure on internal security, violent crime, conflict, and other variables.[10] The Institute for Economics and Peace, which offers authoritative measures for achieving peace, states that if the world were to decrease its levels of violence by 10%, $1.5 trillion could be targeted at other activities.

Nevertheless, the key question is this: What makes us, human beings, secure? Governments have their priorities wrong when it comes to aiming to create a "secure" world. The continued privileging solely of the military aspects of security weakens individual security.[11] Heightened human security enhances the quality of life for all and improves national security too.[12] The COVID-19 pandemic has cast an urgent light on this, in stark contrast to the old, officially ordained ways of viewing security. There were no effective multilateral structures in place to prevent the pandemic, and even the advanced democracies were hit hard. The pandemic has shown the true meaning of what a lack of preparedness can mean for the stability of the international system: no military, not even the mightiest, could contain the virus.[13] In the current, postpandemic world order, it is imperative to maintain the integrity of nature and the environment as mutually enforcing platforms to avoid future, large-scale harm to human security.[14] The scale of the threats requires a shift in the way we view security toward an all-inclusive approach that prioritizes sustaining the conditions of life on the planet.[15]

From national to human to humanity's security

To embark on an examination of how to secure the well-being of humanity, we must first understand the concept of security to determine whether the existing global governing mechanisms suffice and whether a more holistic approach is needed.

What does security mean? Most of the time security was understood as the absence of war between the major powers and an absence of military threats and challenges from one clearly defined enemy. As a result, one view would be that security involves protection from the threat of armed violence. Another view advances the notion that security is tied to guarding individual well-being. Is security primarily about asserting the primacy of the state, or is it about protecting the individual? Traditionally, the scholarship on security has viewed the answer to this question as conceiving the notion of security vis-à-vis a referent object—that is, a specific source of threat or danger. In this light, the state or the individual could become the referent object to be secured against the identified threat.[16] In the realist school, the initial approaches claimed that the state was the sole referent object of security, and nothing else mattered. Taking into account the realist view that prioritizes the national interest, there are three recognizable dimensions to security that presuppose the state as the only referent object of security: the way states prepare to wage war, the protection of the national territory against external military threats, and the protection of the state against defined external enemies. Arising from this approach, at the core of the pursuit of security is the procurement of arms to protect the national territory against these perceived military threats.[17]

The concept of security has been gradually evolving to be a common good rather than solely a matter of national interest. The United Nations' global norms represent a remarkable collective achievement. It is time now for them to be strengthened and updated to carry out *humanity's security* to enhance the common good. The United Nations Sustainable Development Goals (SDGs) provide a concrete global map to do so. Examples of the common good would be creating and distributing vaccines, combating climate change, avoiding war, and eliminating nuclear weapons, leading to the better living conditions that those commitments would entail. The emergence of the idea of "human security" by the mid-1990s consolidates the trend toward viewing security as a common good, where the understanding of security must transcend the focus on national security and include the ideas of "freedom from fear" and "freedom from want."[18] *Humanity's security* furthers the attempt to elevate the notion of security to encompass the fundamental challenges posed to the individual by global conflict, infectious diseases that become pandemics, and climate change on a planetary scale.[19]

In 2012, the UN General Assembly adopted a resolution on human security by consensus for the first time.[20] The resolution represented a milestone, because it harmonized the understanding of human security across the UN by helping the member states identify preventive and people-centered responses to problems and address widespread challenges. The newfound common understanding of human security is composed of three central elements. The first is a person's right to live in freedom and dignity, free from poverty and despair, and with equal opportunities to enjoy all their rights and fully develop their human potential. The second element recognizes the interlinkages between peace, development, and human rights, and equally takes into account civil, political, economic, social, and cultural rights. The third is that human security does not replace state security and recognizes that human security varies significantly across and within countries. The notion of *humanity's security* builds upon the gains won by the concept of human security, decisively going above and beyond its achievements to underscore the necessity for collective action in a concerted way.

Some view ecosystems as one of the central objects of security: ecological security.[21] Many cultures operate in a way that is inextricably intertwined with, and honors, nature. In the West, nature is perceived as occupying a place outside of the human realm, which allows for overexploitation and for the assumption that ecosystems need not be a central factor in making economies grow.[22] Thus far, the separation of humans from their environment has been obstructive in advancing new long-term policies to protect the climate and biodiversity.[23] The contemporary politics of climate and security are falling short of effectively suppressing the threat posed to humanity by climate change.

Matt McDonald recognizes four discourses that focus on different referent objects: the state, people, international society, and ecological security.[24] The latter ensures that the temporal separation between current and future generations is bridged. Additionally, McDonald's view provides a framework for giving expression to the unrepresented in the predominant security discourses (the natural world and all nonhuman living beings). It also moves the analysis away from the unhelpful dichotomy of anthropocentric versus eco-centric by establishing the profound linkages between them. The appearance of human security marks the first broadening of the concept of security and represents the dissatisfaction with, and an insufficiency stemming from, the state-centric focus of security issues.[25] This first redefinition of security places the state as the protector and enabler of governance structures that maintain and sustain human beings by providing them with the safety and freedom to pursue longer-term aspirations.

The wide-ranging evolving framework introduced by the notion of human security compels states to view and practice the attainment of security in a more sweeping and inclusive way. The United Nations Charter mandates states to maintain peace through the regulation of armaments. By the same token, the charter charges the Security Council to act by overseeing the regulation of arms worldwide. With these international legal tools in hand, demilitarizing security in the 21st century is even more pressing with a degraded security environment. In "Securing our Common Future: An Agenda for Disarmament," the United Nations Secretary-General states that, during the Cold War, arms control was integral to security in an environment that included constant communication and negotiations, despite the geopolitical tensions.[26] The UN Secretary-General calls for the continuing evolution of the concept of human security to achieve an end goal: establishing a credible vision for sustainable security to contribute to the attainment of human security in this century.[27]

Getting security wrong and leaving people everywhere vulnerable

Despite the ascendance of the vital concept of human security, most governments continue to get security wrong by misplacing their focus on inapposite priorities. The notion of *humanity's security* builds upon the gains won by the concept of human security, decisively going above and beyond its achievements to underscore the necessity for collective action in everyone's interests. Political, societal instability and unrest are steadily rising, which results in increases in the global economic cost of violence. This cost tends to be around 11% of the global GDP. This means about $15 trillion a year go toward preparing for war and managing the consequences of violence and unrest in societies. To illustrate, Syria, South Sudan, and Afghanistan suffered the highest relative economic cost of violence, equivalent to 81.7, 42.1, and 40.3% of their GDPs, respectively.[28]

Global military spending continues to rise, to annual records of $2 trillion.[29] Cross-border conflicts still occur but are in decline, and when they do take place they provoke widespread condemnation (as with the invasion of Ukraine). Political and societal instability and unrest are steadily rising. During the Cold War, the drive to stay ahead in military expenditure to fuel the arms race led to the accumulation of 70,000 very costly and impracticable nuclear weapons, 13,080 of which are still in existence.[30] This led to extortionate maintenance costs, such as a yearly global maintenance fee of $70 billion, not to mention the horrific humanitarian and ecological toll in the places where they were tested, such as in the islands of the Pacific, in a way that magnifies inequities and disparities of power and capabilities.[31]

Humanity's security, the second expansion of the concept of security from human security, should occur now. Two factors have accelerated this call for action. The first is the ability of humankind to alter the environment on a planetary scale. This points to the risk of humanity exceeding the boundaries of the planetary ecosystem—the limits within which humanity can live safely on the planet.[32] The planetary boundaries framework was devised in 2009 and establishes nine boundaries that should not be breached to sustain life on the planet: these include ozone depletion, biodiversity loss, ocean acidification, and climate change. This framework, like *humanity's security*, calls for the integration of humans and their ecosystems. The second factor is the pandemic, which has accelerated the realization that the security of every population living in every country is connected and inextricably intertwined with everybody's safety. Even though protecting human beings along with nature and their environment is a pressing priority, states continue to prepare for war by forming larger armies and building arsenals.

What is more, both climate change and pandemics are threat multipliers that complicate development efforts and the necessary provisions for safety.[33] Therefore, they should be viewed as the main sources of menace to security everywhere. Data from the Institute for Economics and Peace show that the United States and China are highly vulnerable to climate change and would benefit from preventive public investment at the highest level of national security considerations to avert the worst of these threats. Climate change as a threat multiplier triggers, accelerates, and deepens current instabilities as well.[34] The pandemic has demonstrated that no one is secure until everybody is secure. As the United Nations Secretary-General António Guterres said, "The fury of the virus shows the folly of war." Defense would have to be progressively reoriented to prevent the worst effects of a changing climate, as the IPCC warns.

The notion of *humanity's security* challenges the high circles of countries' security strategists to direct the practice of security toward protecting humans from the actual threats that afflict them, the preservation of ecosystems, but also with the well-being of future generations. *Humanity's security* is about making the national interest coincide with the shared global interest—a common good built to protect everyone.

The reality is that climate change and pandemics are anthropogenic existential threats to the survival of humanity that radically transform the way we should view and practice security. Nathan A. Sears, a scholar whose work straddles security and existential risk studies, warns that this new material context lays bare the growing paradox of the relationship between what is threatening humanity and continuing traditional security that will not help to tackle the existential threats.[35] Yet the meaning and practice of security, despite the emergence of the concept of human security, remain resistant to change, as Sears notes. This exposes the perpetuation of customs and traditions belonging to an era where the sole existential threat was warfare. Now, more existential threats have been added to the material conditions of international relations. The notion of *humanity's security* takes into account this transformation of the concept of security, which seems to be ignored in the high circles of most countries' security strategists, and integrates it not only with the preservation of ecosystems,[36] but also with the well-being of future generations.[37] I concur with Sears's contention that there is a discrepancy between the heightened mega threats of the contemporary world and the outdated modes of protection: assertive defense, military force, and a balance of geopolitical power. Sears's concept of existential security is the most persuasive in establishing that humanity is the referent object and should therefore be the focus of the pursuit of security.[38] His work sits among an eye-opening body of literature from a few security scholars that has been emerging on the existential risks facing humanity, warning that we are at a crossroads and need new concepts and action frameworks to preserve our security.[39] As such, Sears and I are like-minded in realizing that the security literature and, most disturbingly, the practice of security today lack a theoretical and policy framework to comprehensively address the existential threats to humanity.

Putting *humanity's security* at the center of the practice of states' security today involves acknowledging that most states lack the full range of technical means and financial capacity, to cope with the sort of mega perils and trends discussed here. Fundamentally, states would have to collectively develop specific skills and reinforce and create new regional and international cooperative frameworks to contain threats that affect all. The shared burden that lies in collective action may assist states in moving forward with addressing threats more meaningfully and leaving every state better off. One can see that in the relationships in the Arctic, for instance; despite the promise of riches and untold potential for wealth in minerals, oil, and access to lucrative routes, cooperation rather than conflict has prevailed in that region. Peaceful collaboration has been the predominant feature of relations among the eight Arctic states.[40] These guarantors of governance are imbued with the principled and shared purpose of guarding the region's rich human heritage and environment, and protecting human security.[41]

Given the animating premise of the concept that the state is increasingly less capable of tackling problems of a global nature, the consistent and systematic pooling of resources seems to be a prudent way to break the cycle of ineffectiveness at the global level.[42] The most visible example of regional pooling of resources today is the European Union with its 27 members, each with different strengths, capacities, and technical skills. They form the most advanced form of cooperative collective action and represent a moral force and a compass-leading effort on data protection, human rights, and disarmament, and play a prominent role in addressing climate change and transitioning to the green economy.[43] Another, albeit less prominent, example is the Economic Community of Western African States (ECOWAS). This group of 15 countries has been successful in resolving conflicts, peacefully settling disputes among its members, and preventing the spread of Ebola.[44]

Humanity's security has to do with transcending the limited notion of survival of the unit—the state—at the national level. This notion has scant relevance today in a highly threat-interdependent world where the security of all depends on the safety of each one. The current pandemic caused by COVID-19 illustrates how countries must sharpen their security policies by starting to redirect their security expenditure from purely military preparations to investing in prevention against other kinds of menace that affect all human beings.[45] All the existential risks to humanity today are beyond the control of any one state. The concept of security needs to be reconceptualized and further integrated into security policies toward achieving the common good. International relations are hard to change but are not immutable or unalterable, and the persistent efforts of activists, an informed civil society, and scientists may bring change through new ideas and rising norms. As I argue, dealing with existential risks often exceeds the operational, financial, technical, and political capacities of states and global governance institutions to an alarming degree. When the United Nations was founded, the planet had fewer than 2.5 billion people. By the time of the United Nations Millennium Goals, there were 6 billion, and now we are at some 8 billion people. People will seek the benefits of knowledge, political stability, and economic growth, which are increasingly vital yet remain unevenly shared. The growing disparities and inequalities are likely to grow ever more acute in the face of the present inability of global institutions to offer practical and innovative solutions which enable the flourishing of and justice for all. Therefore, the need to achieve *humanity's security* is pressing.

PART II

Common good governance

I define *common good governance* as the processes that create new global public goods in areas where there are either no global norms and institutional mechanisms under international law or, at best, unclear and insufficient frameworks for coordinated global action to confront large-scale risks. In other words, in these areas there is neither certainty nor specific governance—that is, no precise rules administering commonly agreed behavior to prevent wide-scale harm and avert risk. *Common good governance* represents a strategy to curtail uncertainty, harness solidarity, and protect future generations. Global public goods benefit everyone's well-being, promote prosperity, increase international security, and can only be attained by global cooperation.[46]

The accelerated pace of AI technological breakthroughs has the potential to be largely advantageous, but the prospect of weaponizing such advancements holds great peril for the future of peaceful relations. Even though existing international law serves as a foundational springboard, there is uncertainty about how to apply it to the challenges posed by the widespread use of AI in warfare. As it is, international law will not suffice to maintain peace and safeguard future generations. We must, however, learn from what works to foster cooperation under the rules of international law. Therefore, the creation of *common good governance* is imperative and urgent. *Common good governance* promotes a better and more peaceful planet for humanity that that will also protect future generations in the age of militarized AI. The intensification of great power military competition for AI dominance is one of the most foreboding portents of the potentially malevolent use of AI.

The principles of *common good governance* represent a greater narrative that connects people, intensifies solidarity, and creates a sense of common good to amplify human values based upon scientific evidence to ensure the prevention of human harm. It is time to act collectively and globally to reverse the existential risks that humanity faces with ambitious goals that engage all entities across all sectors of societies.[47] *Common good governance* is about the creation of global public goods— that is, finding solutions to the current realities of world politics characterized by the inability of states to act collectively and effectively to tackle existential risks to humanity.[48] Therefore, a radical shift is needed to address the incapacity or unwillingness of states to act toward achieving the kinds of change that will improve the fate of billions in the planet. This is why I investigate the energizing *transnational networked cooperation* by concerned members of civil society as well as scientists, working toward the formulation of a new form of global governance to respond to the imminent disruptions in the global order created by the weaponization of AI. Thus, *common good governance* becomes a reality when diverse networks act collectively to combat a challenge to achieving the creation of a global public good. A multitude of actors—states and other entities—forging a *transnational networked cooperation* can promote action and bring about change. These change makers are concerned not only with what should be legally possible, but also with what is morally and ethically adequate to protect human dignity and safeguard future generations from harm.

Instead of reinventing the wheel, I seek to explore the great ideas that nations and leaders in the past applied to avert catastrophe, all-consuming wars, and overexploitation of the common areas of the planet, and by limiting the means and methods of warfare to reduce the risks of war and harm to civilians (addressed in Chapter 5). I draw lessons from previous triumphs of global cooperation, as well as what was done at moments when previous technological advancements outpaced diplomatic efforts. In this chapter, I seek to identify legal and political guidelines on the basis of what worked in different areas of international relations: from protecting the global commons to repairing the ozone layer, from protecting Antarctica to prohibiting nuclear testing. By examining these varied frameworks, I can infer a fuller picture of what else will be needed to maintain peace and security. In Chapter 5, I examine the kind of global cooperation that restrained and prohibited the means and methods of warfare that, if left unconstrained, would have meant great peril for humanity, especially the use of nuclear weapons.

We live in a time when leaders lack a sound vision for the peaceful future of humanity and hence get security-related issues wrong. They keep investing in ever more powerful weapon systems to kill and destroy ever more efficiently. The wars of the present—in Syria, Afghanistan, Yemen, and Ukraine—and the widespread insecurity that prevails in several parts of the world show that heightened militarism and war generate untold suffering and insecurity for millions of people around the world.[49] These leaders are driven by myopic and simplistic nationalistic perspectives that divide and create more distrust. Therefore, it is time to recognize and acknowledge what is available in the current legal and political global frameworks, which represent a platform to move forward in finding solutions and creating a vision for the planet, which is now facing yet another existential threat—namely, the weaponization of AI.[50] Once we understand the lessons of successful global cooperation stories from the past, we can gauge to what extent they can contribute to the solutions we require, and what must be added or created anew. The rise of autonomous killing systems, many of which will utilize AI to an ever greater degree, provides a stark yardstick for estimating what lies ahead in terms of the threats and challenges to the survival of humankind.[51] In the light of current catastrophic global risks—from the climate crisis, to pandemics, to nuclear war[52]—it is evident that there can be no common good use of AI unless this usage benefits the whole of humanity and protects the human rights and dignity of not only present but also future generations. The protection of fundamental rights has to be center stage and is the ultimate aim of the legal order, both national and international. The implication of this assertion is that every single person must be respected because they belong to the whole of humanity.[53] The rights of human beings must take precedence to ensure the survival of humankind as a whole, and this principle transcends the pursuit of national security:[54]

> There is no point, in our times, for states to keep on by-passing the search of the common good in the pursuance of their own individual advantages (at the cost of others); there is no point for them to keep on replacing reason by their "will" for

more political power and accumulation of wealth—to the satisfaction of the so-called political "realists"—amidst senseless competition.[55]

If I had to select one sentence to describe the state of the world, I would say we are in a world in which global challenges are more and more integrated, and the responses are more and more fragmented, and if this is not reversed, it's a recipe for disaster.[56]

Common good governance seeks to integrate, rather than fragment, the responses to the challenges created by the militarization of AI. It is primarily anchored within prevailing norms and principles to safeguard and protect humanity, such as the existing international law treaty frameworks that were formed to confront global problems like repairing the ozone layer, banning nuclear testing, protecting the oceans, and prohibiting chemical warfare (Chapters 2 and 4). It also draws on some of the associated time-honored principles, such as a belief in the common heritage of humanity, common concern of humanity, precaution, and intergenerational equity, which animate the formation of governing structures and ordering mechanisms for global cooperation that have a bearing on humanity as whole. Such principles, especially the first two—common heritage of humanity and common concern—rise above and go beyond purely interstate relations. They are focused instead on humankind's needs and goals in general, as well as taking into account not only the present but also future generations.[57] Herein lies the importance of my proposal, which aligns with my understanding of the role of international law in steering the direction of humankind in this shifting world order.

The term "common" in both concepts of common heritage of humanity and common concern has brought to the fore the notion of obligation *erga omnes*, engaging all countries and societies, and all peoples within them; the term "concern" has suggested a primary focus on the causes of problems and conflicts.[58]

The principles I adopt here therefore embody collective solidarity and the responsibility that stems from the dictates of public conscience. These qualities transcend those narrower state interests expressed in reckless military competition. These principles therefore act as mechanisms for the attainment of solutions to global problems and, ultimately, *humanity's security*. They reinforce each other in their guiding capacities, and they acknowledge concrete legal obligations and institutions that would bring about compliance with international commitments to realize humanity's aspirations in solidarity.[59]

The goals for *common good governance* are inspired by the need to establish measurable global public goods or deliverables to further humanity's well-being—that is, to ensure that as many people as possible should be able to live dignified lives in security and peace, not only free from the affront of weaponized AI, but also able to benefit from the uses of AI for good. Let me preface my explanation of these deliverables by saying that for the first time in history the international community has a common language to identify the world's problems, namely the United Nations SDGs (Chapters 1 and 3). Let us start nonetheless by identifying what these goods or deliverables are. The literature on global governance in international relations is vast. Even though I reference a number of authors, it is not at all my intention here to survey this whole body of literature, as others have already done so masterfully.[60] My framework for addressing the militarization of AI and the already occurring deployment of autonomous weapons finds its inspiration in the idea of good governance. It bears noting that in the vast body of the literature on global governance, Robert I. Rotberg came up with measurable goals and concrete indicators of progress in the deliverance of good governance. I am inspired by Rotberg's work to develop my proposal for *humanity's security* in concrete terms. He and I met in 2003 when I was working on his team at the World Peace Foundation at Harvard. At the time he was entrusted by Harvard to create one of the first global governance indexes to measure quantifiable progress on good governance in Africa.[61] I was part of the team as a contributor tasked with investigating the ease of access to arms as a destabilizing factor that undermines security. Our work was based on five categories of essential political goods in terms of which each country is evaluated and compared with reference to 58 individual measures in striving to reach concrete goals of progress in development and human well-being. The categories are outlined in the following paragraphs.[62]

- **Safety and Security**: Security is the overriding factor in enabling the achievement of all the other political goods. The indicators are: national security, public safety, government involvement in battle deaths in armed conflicts, internally displaced persons, ease of access to small arms and light weapons, violent crime, and arms imports and exports;
- **Rule of Law, Transparency, and Corruption**: Striving to ensure security is closely aligned to the maintenance of the rule of law: a comprehensive code, usually the constitution, promotes justice to all in society, including minorities. The indicators are: ratification of critical legal norms (core international treaties on human rights), existence of an independent judiciary, public corruption levels, efficiency of the courts, number of days to settle a contract dispute, and other mechanisms to bring justice to the aggrieved;
- **Political Participation and Respect for Human Rights**: Assesses whether citizens are at liberty to participate in the democratic process. The indicators are: participation in elections that are free, fair, and competitive, respect for civil and political rights (including physical integrity, for instance), social and economic rights (press freedom, where the "media is fearless and un-self-censored,"[63] for instance), absence of gender discrimination;
- **Sustainable Economic Opportunity**: Achieved within an enabling environment where prosperity is a possibility for as many as possible, or for all ideally, and individuals can thrive enabled by macroeconomic stability and financial integrity, which are the arteries of commerce; protection of the hardwired elements of the economy: electricity and power for all, roads, ports, airports, and highways that enable commerce and people to flow; and environmental

sensitivity. The objectives can be measured by GDP per capita growth and wealth generation, inflation, reliability of financial institutions, road network, electricity capacity, telephone subscribers, Internet usage, and environmental performance;

- **Human Development**: The reduction of poverty and improvement of health, sanitation, and education are at the heart of the promotion of human development. The indicators are: poverty rate (number of dollars per person per day), life expectancy at birth, child and maternal mortality, undernourishment, immunization, HIV prevalence, access to drinking water, adult literacy, and primary and secondary education, among others.

When Professor Robert Rotberg initiated this groundbreaking approach to examining and measuring good governance, the onus was mostly on states to deliver these goods. Nowadays, it seems that the responsibility rests on everyone: the private sector and individuals as well. Everybody must make a difference and pull their weight, not only states. Everyone is responsible for forging the common good. We are at a critical juncture between the fourth industrial revolution (or the digital revolution) and the third revolution in warfare. My contention is that at this intersection we are witnessing a fundamental shift in the world order.

AI is already playing an essential role in amplifying the benefits of the digital transformation for as many people as possible, so that all can attain the global public goods mentioned and described herein, and each country can measure its success in achieving *common good governance* in concrete terms. However, because of the inability or unwillingness of many governments to deliver these public goods to everyone at scale (as a result of corruption,[64] chronic underdevelopment, or absence of a sustained vision for the future), other groups in society need to assume a leadership role, especially the private sector, in contributing toward enhanced governance and, ultimately, humanity's security. In the light of the challenges and bearing in mind the new opportunities that AI will bring, it is all the more necessary that the private sector, especially the largest companies creating AI, should sustain its important role in scaling up the advantages for the largest number of people possible. In other words, the way to assess *humanity's security* is by measuring the progress made in each of the political goods described. Within the larger global context of the SDGs, humankind has for the first time a common, all-inclusive springboard from which all can strive for equality, security, rule of law, health, and so forth.

This understanding of what is required when shaping *common good governance* is aligned with the recent change in the normative foundations of the international legal order from being purely state-centric to also being oriented toward *humanity's security*.[65] This shift is manifested in international law in the enhanced legal personality of the individual, who now has rights and duties and can be liable for wrongdoing. The consolidation of human rights law, international humanitarian law, and criminal law places the central focus of the search for justice and remedy on their benefits for the individual and not exclusively for the state. It is a process of the humanization of international law, which becomes focused on humankind:

international law for humankind, as described by my former professor and mentor at the University of Brasilia, Antônio Augusto Cançado Trindade, in his work as a judge at the International Court of Justice.[66] This is a paradigmatic transformation of international law and has been framed as "a humanity-centered global turn."[67] This shift in the international legal order means that human beings also emerged as a subject of international law along with states. In other words, states can no longer give primacy to their national interests as the sole driving force to create new mechanisms and frameworks under international law.[68] Historically, and as seen in the cases I discuss in this chapter, it was when the pursuit of humanity's goals prevailed that the greater good was achieved for all. The five categories of political goods examined (security, rule of law, political participation, sustainable economic opportunity, and human development) provide us with the mechanism to properly determine whether *humanity's security* will be achieved and sustained. They also align appropriately with the present-day United Nations SDGs and their 169 targets and 244 indicators.[69]

The horrors of World Wars I and II ushered in a new period of development for international law: from furthering and emphasizing the security of states—namely, addressing external military threats, protection of national territory against invasion and conquest, and the quest to preserve their sovereignty—to focusing on the protection of the individual and human security. The strictly interstate dimension of international law was overwhelmed by the revulsion felt in the aftermath of World War II, which opened up the way to a new era to guarantee that the worst crimes against humanity were indicted and to ensure that those horrors were not repeated. These predicaments meant that not only states but also individuals had to be prosecuted for their actions, and individual security and justice had to be re-established. The postwar period was focused predominantly on the need for ensuring justice to humans, not to states, and on the formation of frameworks whereby grievances and infringements could be met with restitution and reparations.[70] Despite this evolutionary progress in the prevailing legal and political frameworks that now also privilege the human being—such as human rights norms—a vast amount of inequality, suffering in wars, and degradation of the environment continues unabated—but now they continue with the unprecedented risks that the Earth's planetary boundaries are being strained and its threatened biodiversity is reaching a point of no return.[71]

International law serves to establish desirable norms and rules for conduct for relations that have a global scope and international ramifications. The discussion about the application of AI for good is still at an incipient stage—there are no rules and norms specifically for the governance of AI under international law. What we have are germane legal regimes that can be used, and also some existing and some evolving domestic legislation (Chapter 4). There are no commonly agreed frameworks under international law for what lies ahead. Member states at the United Nations are having trouble finding common ground in trying to create a system of global governance to address the rise of autonomous killing, yet they haven't even started to confront the perils posed by the weaponization of AI.

New governance rules under international law to address the weaponization of AI are a global public good need to be based upon *common good governance* to seek to achieve *humanity's security*. Let us first examine the existing foundations upon which this new framework will rest. To complement the top-down governance model favored throughout much of history, my proposal for *common good governance* provides a basis for prevention of harm and for confronting risks that amounts to "a reassertion of the universalist outlook of the law of nations."[72] Let us look at instances of global cooperation and examine how *common good governance* could borrow elements of previous successes in global cooperation, and consider what the implications and significance of this would be. In all the cases to be examined here, there is a need to update the prevailing forms of governance in response to the new challenges facing a shrinking planet. The governance structures that were created have now reached a point where new challenges and threats must be met with renewed vigor through finding new common good solutions. These time-honored cases are nevertheless important so we can derive elements for *common good governance* to create a framework to regulate military AI.

My aim is to take stock of what has worked in harmonizing relations among states, finding solutions to major obstacles to cooperation, and devising ways to attain *humanity's security* by applying current international law regimes (i.e., groups of treaties and other international instruments with their respective norms, principles, and rules) in ways that will seek to clarify or open up fresh avenues for creating new international law.

Start with what protects the planet: The global commons

Planet Earth's traditional "global commons"—the high seas (including the resources on the deep seabed), outer space, the Moon and other celestial bodies, Antarctica, and the atmosphere (including the ozone layer and the climate system)—provide a rich laboratory to study the prospects for peace and the possibilities for global cooperation in the shifting global order. This is essential where emerging technologies play a role in the dynamic of behavior, especially now that there is once again greater competition among the major powers that threatens peace and stability. To ensure the common good use of all the global commons, it is best to seek to anchor the actions, management, cooperation mechanisms, and strategies in already existing international cooperation frameworks that have provided guidance for the international community for decades.

The global commons provide subsistence for humankind and ensure the planet's survival. Safeguarding the global commons for the benefit of humanity thus becomes essential. In an era when there are attempts by the technologically advanced countries to weaponize AI to carry out more advanced forms of autonomous killing, it is all the more urgent that we draw on the knowledge embedded in earlier time-honored frameworks that have served humanity well thus far, and then improve on and expand them by creating more up-to-date solutions.

On November 1, 1967, Arvid Pardo, a diplomat from the small state of Malta, proposed in a groundbreaking speech to the United Nations General Assembly that the same intellectual basis of the common heritage of humanity that already prevented outer space from becoming a battlefield should be extended to the oceans.[73] Pardo's speech marked the start of many years of debate that led to the United Nations Convention on the Law of the Sea (UNCLOS) and created a new global governance structure that aimed to maintain peace on the oceans. The convention defies traditional notions of sovereignty because it incorporates concepts of distributive justice by including the developing countries' views and aspirations. This newfound manifestation of justice represented a platform for the newly decolonized and emancipated UN member states who were just breaking out of their bonds of colonization and moving toward the freedom of giving expression to their own sovereignty.[74]

The steady cooperation in outer space since the first satellites were launched has been a unifying factor, a driver of international cooperation, mostly because of the inherent principles that enshrine global cooperation and solidarity.[75] To ascribe certain areas and domains a distinct legal status that is intended to benefit all of humanity on an equitable basis will mean that these areas shall not be the object of exploitation by any country for the self-interest of its own nationals, corporations, or entities. Instead, all humanity will derive an advantage that must be exploited within a communality of interests. Kemal Baslar's seminal book on the concept of the common heritage of humanity advances the view that this is one of the most extraordinary developments in international law and a radical concept that is inherently about justice.[76] Trindade contends that the concept of the common heritage of humanity created a new paradigm in international law in which "humankind" acquires legal personality and is therefore entitled to protections resulting from international distributive justice. Such a new paradigm takes into account the rights of those countries that are neither rich nor technologically endowed. This is all the more important in the light of the advancements of AI in recent years and the fundamental transformation of humanity's relationship with technology at the intersection of the fourth industrial revolution and the third revolution in warfare that is shaping the new world order.

Baslar and others advance the view that the technological advancements of the 20th century and their consequences—the widening gap between rich and poor countries, and the former's attempts to exploit the riches of the latter for themselves exclusively—were the basic motivating factors driving the formation of the notion of the common heritage of humanity.[77] The technological capacity of the wealthy nations to exploit such areas made their resources accessible only to those nations. This placed the less technologically endowed nations at an enormous disadvantage.[78] The common heritage of humanity is thus a mechanism that addresses the need for averting a planetary catastrophe, something which has now become all the more urgent with the development of AI.[79] As a consequence, the idea of the common heritage of humanity serves as a solid basis for *common good governance*.

AI as a global common

I propose considering AI and cyberspace as the first human-made global commons, not only because they are highly dependent on each other (i.e., AI may function in cyberspace), but also because of their connectivity and their common uses to benefit all of humanity. Recent breakthroughs in AI and its increased influence on human life are the result of a couple of factors that explain why I hold it should be considered a global common—and therefore a foremost global public good that all can benefit from and that would increase predictability and international security: the increase in computing and processing power at lower cost, and "big data" produced by billions of people that can be used to generate the unprecedented development and commercialization of a set of computational techniques such as machine learning.[80] In other words, it is the data generated by people all over the world that is partly enabling the advancements in AI. Therefore, the gains should revert back to the people.[81]

AI needs to be a shared resource—a public domain for the common good—along with cyberspace.[82] There are significant physical differences between the Earth's global commons and the human-made commons. Even though the challenges presented by the latter are different, what they share are the benefits and advantages they endow upon humanity: protecting the planet's common areas and enabling connectivity and representation in the digital revolution. Cyberspace, for instance, is at present partly owned by private entities and governments that can impose restrictions on the flow of information.[83] Additionally, AI exists on the basis of its reliance on data generated by millions of users across the globe. The infrastructure to sustain AI needs minerals and resources that may deplete the planet, as Kate Crawford explains in her *Atlas of AI*.[84] AI is a technology that requires extraction of planetary and human resources, including lithium, rare minerals, human labor, and the electrical power grids. It is not only about cloud-based algorithms and code. Therefore, viewing it as global common—even if human-made—seems reasonable because more equitable rules and norms that take into account climate, human, and planetary protection are needed. Otherwise, the use of AI will eventually become unsustainable because it is exceedingly energy intensive. Data-processing centers are gargantuan consumers of energy from the grid.[85]

> AI is born from the salt lakes in Bolivia and mines in Congo, constructed from crowdworker-labeled datasets that seek to classify human actions, emotions, and identities. It is used to navigate drones over Yemen, direct immigration police in the United States, and modulate credit scores of human value and risk across the world. A wide-angle, multiscale perspective on AI is needed to contend with these overlapping regimes.[86]

My proposal for global cooperation by implementing a *common good governance*-based framework on military AI and achieving *humanity's security* highlights how AI can be used in the service of humanity, and with a view of protecting future generations. All the commons—human and Earth's—must be safeguarded from human exploitation and the perpetuation of inequality whereby the technologically advanced countries benefit without regard to sustainability and fairness. As Kate Crawford says, the climate crisis, the gap between the wealthiest and the poorest, racial discrimination, labor exploitation, and widespread surveillance of populations need to be reversed, not heightened, by AI.[87] I contend that there are two related attributes between the human-made commons and the Earth's global commons. The first is the common use that humanity derives from being able to relish and benefit from them. For instance, all humankind needs an uncluttered realm of outer space, where satellites can operate in an orderly and accident-free environment to enable the resources and capacity for global communication and navigation. In another global common, the high seas, global cooperation must ensure that they remain free and safe for navigation and also to preserve fisheries and other life-sustaining functions that the oceans perform for humanity, such as carbon absorption.[88] Even if vast swathes of humankind do not yet have access, all of humankind is becoming progressively connected in cyberspace. More and more people have recourse to the connectivity provided by the Internet, which now seems increasingly inseparable from sustaining life on the planet itself: electricity grids, agriculture, and weather forecasts depend on the Internet, along with satellite connectivity. The commons allow human livelihoods to thrive.

Little by little, this pervasive connectivity is also occurring in the realm of AI. It already permeates many aspects of human life and will do so more ubiquitously and intensely as greater progress is made through innovations in AI and higher levels of scaling up to more people are achieved. The second attribute is human responsibility to conserve the global commons. Not only does humanity bear responsibility for the conservation of the Earth's global commons, I contend that the same applies to the human-made commons; otherwise, life on the planet will surely be endangered more than it already is. The uses for good across all commons should be the preponderant form of behavior, with transparent, commonly agreed rules and norms. The establishment of a progressive, all-encompassing agreement on how to make the Internet accessible for all is essential, and the same goes for AI. AI technologies should advance and empower as many people as possible.

My argument is in line with and resonates with two prominent interrelated developments at the United Nations. The first is the creation of an "AI Commons," an initiative conceived in 2017, at the United Nations AI for Good Global Summits (Chapter 1). AI Commons aim to collectively generate solutions to tackle the world's most pressing global problems through using AI. It is also a repository of projects that utilize AI for the common good, especially to implement and achieve the United Nations SDGs. The ultimate objective is to safely harvest data for the common good to ensure that everyone can access the benefits of doing so. The creators of AI work in conjunction with communities of developers, entrepreneurs, users, and organizations to determine and enable broader applications in response to real needs. The founding members are distinguished roboticists and computer engineers: Yoshua Bengio, professor at Université de Montréal, Department of Computer Science and

Operations Research, winner of the 2018 Turing Award (equivalent to the Nobel Prize in the field of computer technology) for his pioneering work with colleagues on deep learning; Stuart Russell, Professor of Computer Science and the Smith-Zadeh Professor in Engineering, University of California Berkeley; Francesca Rossi, IBM AI Ethics Global Leader, IBM T.J. Watson Research Centre; and Amir Banifatemi, General Manager, Innovation and Growth, XPrize Foundation.

The second development is the establishment of the High-level Panel on Digital Cooperation convened by the United Nations Secretary-General to advance global dialogue to fulfill the potential of digital technologies to promote human well-being, while mitigating their risks (Chapter 3). The panel's report was published in 2019.[89] The report proposes a "digital commons architecture," where characteristics of the digital domain, such as common Internet protocols, share features of the Earth's global commons.

Considering that the global commons have a special place in international relations, as I will explain, and in the light of their different status in the international legal system, it is important to bear in mind three initial guiding global principles that emanate from the notion of the Earth's global commons in international law:[90] no country can claim jurisdiction over such areas; no country can weaponize them; and collective cooperation toward managing the global commons should occur.[91] All three points combined could supply an initial framework to regulate military AI and prevent its widespread weaponization. Taken together, these practices provide a constructive framework to consider and deal with AI to benefit the whole of humanity and therefore create the *common good governance* frameworks initially needed to stem the heightened use of autonomous killing and malevolent uses of AI in general.

AI will not be beneficial if it does not safeguard and advance human dignity. Its impact will be detrimental if the algorithms are not diverse or are not developed by an inclusive and transparent labor force. The creation of AI must occur according to values that are clearly articulated in order to protect human beings—for instance, a prohibition on the weaponization of AI, or clear restrictive measures on facial recognition algorithms. With these ideas as premises, AI can be considered as a global common for three reasons. The first is that the "big data" that is supplied to enable breakthroughs and progress in AI is derived from the billions of people who live on the planet and their activities in cyberspace. Therefore, all these billions of people should be able to enjoy the benefits arising from AI. The large-scale application of AI will affect everyone in ways that previous societal scientific revolutions did not because of its pervasiveness and omnipresence. Abuse of this development is therefore a matter of concern for the whole of humankind and needs to be confronted in humanity-wide frameworks.

Second, software runs most aspects of interconnected modern life. What enables this interconnectedness is a digital infrastructure that relies on publicly available code—namely, an "open source" code which forms a digital infrastructure that is a public good and which is maintained by communities of developers who do so voluntarily.[92] There are 193 countries in the physical world that are members of the United Nations, but billions of networks are connected through the Internet, and AI will only accelerate this trend toward interconnectivity. Most software depends on the unpaid labor of communities of developers who power and maintain much of the web (digital infrastructure needs preservation as much as physical infrastructure); vast quantities of our data are powering data-driven technologies, such as machine learning. Much of today's digital tech has the potential to deliver common public goods; for example, 78% of the United Nations SDGs' targets could be advanced by applying AI.[93] The private sector can help deliver the value of these goods at scale. It is worth clarifying in more detail what kind of AI I am taking about. There are many AI algorithms that do not depend on data where intellectual property rights should rightfully belong to the inventor, but in this case I am interested in making data-driven algorithms a public good, especially when the data are derived from people "for free." Jennifer Shkabatur[94] states that data should be considered a global common, managed cooperatively, due to its public value, and not managed solely by private entities seeking commercial gain. Many data-driven algorithms do require significant computing power to store and make sense of the massive amounts of accumulated data. This means that even though the data have been provided "for free" by people, the large tech companies do the upkeep and maintenance of the data.[95] Anyone who uses the Internet today gains from and enjoys open-source software that many consider more secure and stable than proprietary software and that allows open access, heralding a world that is open for all to reap the benefits of connectivity, and especially to elevate those who are disempowered.[96]

Third, the power of ordinary people in much of the software industry should be highlighted here as this influences and structures my notion of the Internet and AI as commons for all humanity to take advantage of; the implication is that people who build the Internet are incredibly powerful in influencing the direction of travel for technology today. All the apps that we use today depend on public codes to function and the world runs on software, as I heard Jean Phillipe Courtois of Microsoft say at the AI for Good Global Summit at the United Nations in Geneva in May 2019. The essence of the success of the Internet is collaboration across borders, creating a good that is available to all. Even with all this openness and massive access that is enabled worldwide, the Internet itself is guided by two major governing institutions that set the standards: the Internet Engineering Task Force (IETF) and the World Wide Web Consortium (W3C). The former develops and sets standards, such as identifying each person's computer by means of a unique IP address to connect to the Internet. The IETF is run by volunteers, and since 1993 anyone has been able to join. The W3C has been setting standards for the World Wide Web since 1994—for example, by stipulating that every webpage uses HTML.[97] This management of the Internet as a public good for humanity and the models of governance it utilizes are what make it a common domain in the sense that I propose, adapted from the notion of the global commons. The participation of people to accelerate identification of solutions across multiple datasets and disciplines is at work here, and this will play an ever more pronounced role with the need to deal with the "big data" needed to run AI. Another expression of what I am discussing here is the fact that both NASA and its European counterpart, the European Space Agency (which has one of the biggest budgets to observe the planet), are the largest providers of free and globally available data collected from satellites—one more instance where people generate the data, enablers collect and share, and everyone benefits. With the rise of "big data" from billions of consumers using the Internet, the challenge will be to harvest the data for the public good. The creation of ethical and privacy frameworks will be the underpinning foundations that will enable a more just edifice for *humanity's security*.

The stewardship of the global commons falls under the principles of the "common heritage of humanity," common concern, intergenerational equity, and the precautionary principle—the main tenets can be extrapolated from and harnessed for the human-made commons (as we have seen with the Internet, where this is already happening).[98] The notion of the common heritage of humanity emerged in the 1960s, even though that was a time of great distrust among nations.[99] It is now a legitimate principle of treaty law, but it has since given rise to controversy and scholarly debate as it is at the heart of attempts to address resource exploitation and territorial acquisition.[100] From the main tenets of a common heritage of humanity, we can infer initial formulations and apply them to create a *common good governance*-based global framework to regulate the rapid militarization of AI as a global public good:

1) The global commons are beyond any country's jurisdiction. Therefore, no one can claim jurisdiction: no state, no nation, and no corporation. This restriction set up by these principles of the common heritage of humanity renders ownership legally absent;[101]
2) All states are expected to support efforts toward achieving cooperation within a regime of international management;
3) Benefit sharing (a putative future basis for regulating military AI): the exploitation of these areas shall be pursued to further the interests of all of humanity. Therefore, if economic profits should materialize, they are to be shared under a common mandate and authority which is tasked with the equitable distribution of rights and duties, along with serving as a forum for peaceful settlement of disputes;
4) Common areas are to be used exclusively for peaceful purposes. These areas are not to be weaponized;[102]
5) An international organization can be the site for cooperative scientific research that has to be undertaken in a manner that does not harm its environment. The findings are to be shared to further advance all of humanity.[103]

The perspectives we can garner from the common heritage of humanity, common concern, intergenerational equity, and the precautionary principle are all the more urgent given that, on the one hand, AI-related technologies will enhance already existing technologies that will make possible the exploration and exploitation of the global commons, which can have possible harmful consequences. The most notable example here would be overfishing in the high seas enabled by harnessing technology to detect highly migratory lucrative fish stocks.[104] On the other hand, such technologies will have both life-saving and protective advantages. Take the ocean seabed in the high seas, for example; this was an area considered in the past to be impenetrable for exploration and only tentative partial probes were attempted. In 1874, on the routes between Hawaii and Tahiti, the crew of the British research vessel HMS *Challenger*, who undertook the first great oceanographic expedition of modern times, discovered the first known deposits of manganese nodules in the depths of the seabed.[105] However, large-scale exploration was not possible at that time.

In this century, the situation has changed: we have moved on from the high seas being regarded as opaque and impenetrable to the possibility of open exploitation.[106] This means that even the most traditionally remote spaces and areas of the Earth, such as the Arctic, are now open to exploration—and exploitation. AI-based technologies will only make such utilization of these regions more expedient and more lucrative. This is therefore another reason not only to consider the Earth's global commons as well as human-made domains as global commons for all humanity to gain from, but also to take on the common responsibility for their management and protection.

For all the aforementioned reasons, I therefore propose that the frameworks that protect the global commons be applied to the human-made commons. By doing so, we could extend the underlying guiding idea of the global commons for the good and benefit of all humankind to other realms that are now of concern as well, and, if improperly managed, are likely to have an impact on all humanity; these realms include cyberspace (the first human-made commons) and now also AI (the second human-made commons). The overexploitation, misuse, and lack of global coordination of these human-made realms also have broad repercussions for all of humanity, just as was the case with the global commons in the past and present.[107]

The management of the global commons has become an urgent and challenging task for humanity as a result of the acceleration of the harmful processes of climate change, including melting glaciers and ocean acidification, and in parallel with this the management of the human-made commons has become urgent because of the widespread rise of new technologies. These technologies and those within the remit of AI are increasingly providing new opportunities for humanity. In various areas, such as medicine, agriculture, disaster management, war, and law enforcement, the use of AI is becoming increasingly prevalent. Some of these areas have been the subject of intense research and discussion at the United Nations so far, but one lesser explored domain of the new possibilities created by AI is its impact on the Earth's global commons. Preventive governance in the human-made commons is crucially important for the future peace and security of life on Earth.

Cooperation to protect the life-sustaining domains: Global commons law

Global cooperation to protect the global commons that evolved throughout the 20th century could inspire a framework to regulate the militarization of AI.[108] It was during that period that the rise of international regimes to set norms and rules of behavior for certain domains of the planet occurred.[109] These areas include the high seas (in particular their living resources in the deep seabed), outer space (including the Moon and other celestial bodies), Antarctica, and the atmosphere (which comprises the ozone layer).[110] Certain areas of the globe are meant to belong to all of humanity.

> The obligation to co-operate is established for Antarctica and outer space, as well as the management, exploration, and exploitation of the deep seabed ("the Area"), each of these having been declared the common heritage of mankind. Under these legal regimes the duty to co-operate always entails procedural and substantive obligations, and sometimes includes institutional obligations.[111]

In an article published in 2021, I coined the term "global commons law" to refer to the combined legal regimes protecting all the global commons: namely Antarctica, the atmosphere, the high seas, and outer space (see Table 2.1).[112] I argue that this is a distinct branch of international law with its own set of guiding principles, treaties, and norms of behavior, as well as status. I demonstrate that it is an uncommon realm within current international law, because it serves the distinctive purpose of ensuring the survival of the planet and humankind. Some guiding propositions provide the basis for this reasoning, which will further inform the creation of a regulatory framework on military AI based upon *common good governance*.

The formation of the legal and political frameworks to protect the global commons in the 1960s paved the way for later concepts such as "human security" that emerged in the 1990s.[113] These in turn contributed to a major transformation in international law, namely an international legal order that had once been shaped by a purely state-centric approach but is now also constituted by attributes focused on human security. The state is still preeminent and coexists with other entities that have acquired legal personality, such as international and nongovernmental organizations.

The underpinning principles of global commons law, especially the common heritage of humanity, paved the way for an enhanced and heightened legal personality for the individual in every country, developed or not. Here the foundation is constituted by notions of "international distributive justice" and humankind as a whole becomes entitled to protections (against the applications of AI for malicious and evil purposes, for example). The understanding of the concept of distributive justice serves to level the field between developed and developing countries, thus striking a balance between the technologically advanced, the disadvantaged, and the destitute.

The mechanisms set in place by global commons law serve two functions for international relations in the 21st century. The first is that it provides the tools for averting catastrophe on the planet and hence furnishes a framework for sustaining a livable planet for the future. The second is that it gives humanity the apparatus to confront the challenges posed by an unruly cyberspace and the obstructive threats posed by the malicious uses of AI. The other branches of international law, such as state responsibility, diplomatic law, human rights law, and international criminal law, for instance, serve the objectives of clarifying the scope and nature of state relationships, rights and duties, or the protection of the individual in the international system. With its different focus, global commons law is the only part of international law that ascribes protections to domains or areas of the planet that are critical to the very essence of preserving humanity. In other words, the state and the individual are not the prime subjects, and their rights and duties are not the main object of protection. What is the object of protection is what underpins the survival of humanity: the global commons, and now also AI and cyberspace. The other branches of the law directly provide for protections, exemptions, rights, and corresponding duties to safeguard the individual or the sovereignty of the state. Global commons law provides frameworks to protect the areas and domains of the planet and its surroundings (outer space) that are essential for everyone's survival and for the durability of the ecosystems of the planet as well.

The idea of the global commons is based upon common custodianship in a communality of interests, and it views nations as the guardians of the domain for future generations. Qualifications were set out for the joint management of the commons, in addition to a qualitative evolution in the scope of protection and the role of states as guardians instead of being only users and beneficiaries. Examples of these commons are enumerated in Table 2.1.

Taken together, the regimes that govern each of the commons form a sophisticated tapestry of norms and rules that represent one of the unique aspects of international relations today. This part of international law is innovative because it institutionalized protections by creating forms of governance that supersede national sovereignty for areas that are nonnational and for which no state can claim jurisdiction.[114] Technological advancements that put the existence of the commons in peril and life in the planet in jeopardy were the driving force in the creation of global commons law.[115] Therefore, the leadership of the technologically advanced countries remains essential and they must not abdicate their responsibility of acting as custodians.

When there is an absence of leadership from the technologically powerful and the renunciation of their common responsibility, the significance of *transnational networked cooperation* emerges and is all the more pressing. The duty of custodianship is reinforced by pressure from the developing world which, even though it does not possess the scientific clout necessary for maintaining the management of these domains, can indeed offer the moral and equity elements that are needed for the regimes to subsist.

As it is, AI is ungoverned under international law. Extending to AI the legal and political frameworks that protect the global commons would be beneficial in initiating common rules of behavior. The use of AI will affect everyone in often unseen ways. Its widespread use will impact on the ability to govern the life-sustaining domains of the planet, thereby promoting or hindering effective governance. This is the case especially in the light of the threat of weaponization of AI and the ongoing attempts to carry out attacks in cyberspace.[116] All these perils are already starting to impact on current generations and will also affect the conditions for sustaining life in future generations.

Table 2.1 Example of natural and human-made global commons

Global Commons	Existence of International Legal Frameworks & Institutions	Global Commons Law: Level of Successes & Challenges Faced	Guiding Principles	Institutionalized Scientific presence
Earth's Global Commons				
The High Seas (2/3 of the oceans)	The Convention on the High Seas 1958 (12 NM) UNCLOS 1982 Commission on the Limits of the Continental Shelf (NY) International Seabed Authority (UNCLOS)	Moderate Success Needs updating: Ongoing negotiations toward a new treaty: create marine protected areas—regions that are off limits to at least some kinds of commercial activity. Boost biodiversity in previously decimated regions Needs updating: stressors such as plastic pollution, overfishing, destruction of the reefs.	Common Heritage of Humanity	n/a
Outer Space	*Legal Framework*: The "Outer Space Treaty" 1967 Rescue Agreement 1968 The Moon Agreement 1979 *Institutions*: Committee on the Peaceful Uses of Outer Space (NY) United Nations Office for Outer Space Affairs (Vienna)	Success (but needs updating due to rising threats): Debris Commercial space exploration Increasing rivalry and attempts to weaponize outer space	Common Heritage of Humanity Common Concern of Humanity	The Committee on the Peaceful Uses of Outer Space

Continued

Table 2.1 *Continued*

Global Commons	Existence of International Legal Frameworks & Institutions	Global Commons Law Level of Successes & Challenges Faced	Guiding Principles	Institutionalized Scientific presence
Atmosphere (includes ozone layer)	The Montreal Protocol on Ozone 1987 United Nations Framework Convention on Climate Change 1992 Kyoto Protocol 1997 Paris Agreements 2015 UNFCCC Secretariat Bonn	Atmosphere: Needs urgent implementation Success vis-a-vis the Montreal protocol: it is universal, all countries are parties to this treaty (the Montreal Protocol) Paris Agreements on Climate Change: Ongoing implementation	Common Heritage of Humanity Common Concern of Humanity Intergenerational Equity	Intergovernmental Panel on Climate Change (IPCC)
Antarctica	The 1959 Antarctic Treaty The 1972 Convention for the Conservation of Antarctic Seals The 1980 Convention on the Conservation of Antarctic Marine Living Resources The 1991 Protocol on Environmental Protection to the Antarctic Treaty	Success	Common Heritage of Humanity	International Research Stations

The Arctic	The Arctic Council Agreement on Cooperation on Aeronautical and Maritime Search and Rescue in the Arctic 2011 Agreement on Cooperation on Marine Oil Pollution Preparedness and Response in the Arctic 2013 Agreement to Prevent Unregulated High Seas Fisheries in the Central Arctic Ocean 2018	Success	Agreement on Enhancing International Arctic Scientific Cooperation (signed 2017)
Human-Made Commons			
Cyberspace	No	Some new emerging norms *Jus nascendi*	Internet Engineering Task Force (IETF) World Wide Web Consortium (W3C)
Artificial Intelligence	No	No global rules	n/a

Ensuring intergenerational equity

Intergenerational equity: I undertake a separate consideration of this important principle of international law because it is not often discussed in the high-level deliberations at the United Nations to stem autonomous killing, and it is not being explicitly considered when creating new frameworks to govern military AI. The legal principle of intergenerational equity has an essential role to play not only in containing the threat of autonomous weapons, but also in creating a framework for ensuring peace in the age of military AI for future generations.

All around the world, children as young as 10 years of age have started a movement for action on climate change, most notably Greta Thunberg's history-making, inspiring action that motivated millions worldwide.[117] These activists have taken to the streets to demand change. This is the most vivid example of the striving for intergenerational equity in decades. No matter who you are, act now to reap the benefits decades later.[118] It is essential to examine the central elements of intergenerational equity, which could become part of my framework of *common good governance* to drive the creation of a global framework to govern the military use of AI.

In the striving to protect current and future generations, the interrelated concepts of the "common heritage of humanity" and "common concern" rose to prominence; they both represent a call for global cooperation that includes addressing the rights and duties of present and future generations. Take the notion of the common heritage of humanity. The word "heritage" implies that the current generation is the steward of the commons for future generations.[119] The prevention of environmental degradation is therefore a central component of the shared custodianship of the commons for the achievement of *humanity's security*.

In 1988, United Nations General Assembly Resolution 43/53 declared that "climate change is a common concern of mankind, since climate is an essential condition which sustains life on Earth."[120] Then, during the Earth Summit in Rio de Janeiro in 1992, both the Convention on Biodiversity and the United Nations Framework Convention on Climate Change (UNFCCC) adopted the notion of "common concern." The Preamble of the Biodiversity Convention reads[121]: "Affirming that the conservation of biological diversity is a common concern of humankind." The Preamble of the UNFCCC[122] notes: "Acknowledging that change in the Earth's climate and its adverse effects are a common concern of humankind." The application of the notion of "common concern" brings the common heritage of humanity fully into operation with its inherent embrace of present and future generations. According to ICJ Judge Antônio Augusto Cançado Trindade, it transcends strict interstate relations and emphasizes the aspirations of all humankind by highlighting equitable burden-sharing in common stewardship, universal solidarity, and future protection, instead of simply focusing on the acquisition of benefits resulting from natural resource exploitation. Both concepts aim at implementing "superior common values shared by the international community as a whole, over the interests of an individual state or small group of states, the technologically more advanced ones. Both concepts have been constructed to respond to the needs and aspirations of humankind."[123]

Both concepts, according to Trindade, bear witness to the evolution of international law away from being purely state-centric and toward having a greater bearing on humankind. Judge Trindade identifies six elements of the concept of common concern:[124]

1) It serves to guide the true common questions for all humankind by universally shared values;
2) It engages everybody in each society;
3) The intergenerational dimension is definitive and comprises both current and future generations;
4) The emphasis is on protection and not interstate relations and interests;
5) Consideration is given to the causes of the problems, for the sake of prevention;
6) There must be equitable sharing of responsibilities and transmission to future generations.

The fact that, over the course of time, the concepts and norms of international law have attained universal acceptance (in such domains as international humanitarian law, the law of treaties, and diplomatic and consular law), independently of the multicultural composition of the international community, reveals the evolution of international law toward universalization.[125]

Intergenerational equity is a principle that evolved within international environmental law from the beginning of modern environmental diplomacy. The first ever summit on the environment was held in 1972 in Stockholm with the theme "Human Environment," and it produced a declaration with 26 principles.[126] They represent the first pronouncements on stewardship of the environment in human history. At that moment, humankind became the official custodians of the planet. Within the remit of this new custodianship lies a responsibility to future generations. Principle 1 of the Stockholm Declaration seeks to promote an environment to protect and improve the life of present and future generations. This objective is reiterated in Principle 2, along with the aspiration to achieve shared benefits for all humankind. These statements are preceded by a preamble that emphatically promotes the novel idea of the improvement of the human environment for present and future generations as an imperative that is to serve as the basis for social and economic development.

Intergenerational equity implies the rights and responsibilities of the current generations as trustees, while ascribing entitlements to future generations. Living humans are the temporary custodians of nature and the planet and have a duty to transfer the custodianship of nature in a condition that enables the fulfillment of a dignified life to those not yet born. The search for equity would then necessitate meeting the basic human needs of food, water, and shelter for all current custodians and future ones. This would imply the need for all countries to cooperate to ensure these resources are available for all across the planet.[127] Thus, the principles of intergenerational equity provide a manifesto in the light of which to scrutinize decisions taken today based upon the impact they will have on future generations and on the planet.

Realizing one's obligations to future generations is an arduous undertaking. When tackling the climate crisis, for instance, there is a temporal separation between costs and benefits. Take the task of repairing the ozone layer: it started in 1987 with the Ozone Protocol and, if all goes to plan, it will be completed in 2067. Political institutions, especially in democratic countries, are not usually equipped to undertake such long-term thinking and politicians tend to selfishly think in terms of their own few years in office. One way, conceptualized long ago, to make people devise a long-term strategy was the 1987 Gro Brundtland Report, *Our Common Future*, which links sustainable development and intergenerational equity in its definition of the former notion:

> Humanity has the ability to make development sustainable to ensure that it meets the needs of the present without compromising the ability of future generations to meet their own needs. The concept of sustainable development does imply limits—not absolute limits but limitations imposed by the present state of technology and social organization on environmental resources and by the ability of the biosphere to absorb the effects of human activities. But technology and social organization can be both managed and improved to make way for a new era of economic growth.[128]

Sustainable development is a definitive manifestation of intergenerational equity,[129] which found firmer expression in the 1992 UNFCCC. Article 3 of the convention states the principles guiding it and is a sound reaffirmation of intergenerational equity, where present and future generations shall benefit from the protection of the climate. The United Nations SDGs and their achievement aim of 2030 also represent a map for long-term thinking and changing the world for the better for future generations (Chapter 3). It is worth further exploring these and other precedents of global cooperation that have benefited humanity in the search for elements to create a framework to regulate military AI that must be protective of future generations too.

Global cooperation that benefits humanity

States are not the sole players and change makers in the mission to protect the global commons. A vast tapestry of groups of concerned people make up the relevant components for sustaining peace and assuring the viability of the commons for future generations: indigenous peoples (about 10 million live in the Arctic region), scientists, environmental activists, and people concerned about the planet. I will examine six case studies to demonstrate how the creation of global public goods can be created and forged collectively and can protect human beings everywhere, promote predictability and prosperity, mitigate conflict, and stimulate long-lasting global cooperation.

The protection of the oceans: The United Nations Law of the Sea Convention (UNCLOS) is comprehensive legal and political framework that was devised at a time of great distrust among nations and increasing rivalry in exploring the riches of the oceans. It succeeded in creating one of the most important dimensions of international relations, including some essential principles, such as common heritage of humanity. UNCLOS is a peace, logistics, and coordination treaty that is considered a constitution for the oceans.[130]

Cooperation in outer space: It is important to study this case as a model for the regulation of complex global challenges posed by the militarization of AI. The story of the governance of outer space is one about the creation of a sphere of peace and unremitting cooperation during a period of distrust at the height of the Cold War. It is about hope in the light of the newest technological breakthroughs with the launching of the first satellites. These discoveries could have led to war, but instead generated decades of international collaboration even among rivals.

Protection of the ozone layer: This is one of the most successful cases of global commons management in history, namely the protection of the ozone layer by an international treaty that is now universally ratified, respected, and followed by every country, all members of industry, and all scientists. This case demonstrates the concrete application of the principle of precaution in international relations and international law and its role as a tool for averting catastrophe.

Antarctica as a zone of peace: This case represents the first time that an entire region of the planet has been turned into a zone of peace where no jurisdictional claims are acceptable and only cooperation can occur.

The Arctic—cooperation and innovation: This case demonstrates complete defiance of the predictions of conflict and war, as it has instead remained a place of peace despite the promise of untold riches as a result of the discovery of oil and gas. It is important to take it into account as an instance of regional cooperation that, when properly curated, can induce mutual confidence among supposed rivals.

Prohibition of nuclear tests (monitored and enforceable): Nuclear tests serve as the precursor for a nuclear arms race. Prohibiting testing is the sure path to fewer weapons and a nuclear-weapon-free world. The idea of a ban on nuclear tests was proposed in 1957 by India. In the same year, discussions began in earnest between the United States and the former Soviet Union. Four decades later, the negotiations on the Comprehensive Nuclear Test Ban Treaty (CTBT) were completed. During these four decades more than 2,000 tests were conducted, victimizing about 100,000 people who perished from the fallout.[131] The treaty has not yet come into force, but it has established a robust norm against testing, including a unique global verification and inspection regime.

The protection of the oceans

When UNCLOS was finalized in 1982 after years of complex negotiations, global environmental diplomacy was only ten years old.[132] The negotiations that led to UNCLOS were marked by a profound restructuring of the international system with a dramatic rise in United Nations membership by newly independent countries in

Africa and Asia, as well as growing rivalry between the two superpowers (the United States and the Soviet Union), a sense of impending doom over declining fish stocks, offshore oil-drilling accidents, and pollution. Nonetheless, in a pioneering new way of codifying law, UNCLOS designated the seabed, ocean floor, and subsoil beyond the limits of national jurisdiction ("the Area") as the common heritage of humanity. This was the demand from most countries that joined the ranks of the United Nations as sovereign nations. They clamored to find ways to start balancing the international system where their voice would have equal weight and their coastal resources be explored by them and not by the technologically powerful nations with large merchant fleets. The beginning of the negotiations coincided with a call by the Non-Aligned Movement (at the time numbering 120 countries) for a new economic order and more egalitarian international relations.[133] Bearing in mind that the achievement of these goals would contribute to the realization of a just and equitable international economic order which considers the interests and needs of humankind as a whole. In particular, this new order ushered in by UNCLOS took into account the special interests and needs of developing countries, whether coastal or landlocked.[134]

It is important that we understand how UNCLOS works, and understand its significance, because it represents an extraordinary development paving the way to achieve *humanity's security*. UNCLOS represents a constitution for the oceans.[135] Along with the United Nations Charter, it is a momentous international legal instrument of the 20th century as it is a peace, coordination, environmental, and logistics agreement of great magnitude. It is almost universal and even countries that have not ratified it, such as the United States, follow it closely.

The significance and impact of UNCLOS on international relations can hardly be overstated. It serves as a comprehensive model framework for addressing other major issues where urgent cooperation is needed from multiple countries with disparate interests. Therefore, it is a useful model to examine in the search for concrete elements of *common good governance*. UNCLOS's significance lies in three areas:

1) It creates a distributive justice framework for relations between developed and developing countries. The latter, recently decolonized, were trying to reshape the international system to acknowledge their perspectives as well.[136] This was very important during the Cold War, when frameworks for peace were sorely needed;

2) It sets out the first comprehensive set of rules for the oceans that came to complement the already existing, less strong frameworks for the oceans established in 1958. These rules, it bears noting, were created to align the diverging positions of different states. There was intense bargaining between developed and developing nations, where all the competing interests were subject to discussion to find common ground for future action;

3) It sets a foundation for peace in international relations. Most commerce and trade takes place by way of the oceans. Therefore, this area of the planet needed to be freed of, and protected from, conflict; hence, concrete compulsory

mechanisms were put in place to resolve disputes and conflicts, including the International Seabed Authority, the International Tribunal of the Law of the Sea, the Commission on the Limits of the Continental Shelf, and the meeting of the state parties to the convention. This is a breakthrough in international law. No other convention before this has had such a robust and detailed conflict-solving, dispute-settlement set of mechanisms. Finally, crimes that would threaten the stability of the oceans, such as piracy, were criminalized under UNCLOS.

UNCLOS codifies new ideas about shared human benefits and global cooperation. According to the convention, "the Area" (article 136) is the part of the ocean beyond each coastal state's Exclusive Economic Zone (EEZ), which is defined by UNCLOS as the offshore zone 200 nautical miles along the coastline where each coastal state can exploit oil, gas, fish stocks, mineral mining, and laying of cables for their exclusive benefit or, if they choose, in cooperation with other states. The "Area" is what is known as the "High Seas," beyond the EEZ. An "authority" to control and organize the activities in "the Area" was constituted by UNCLOS as the International Seabed Authority, which sits in Jamaica. This mechanism was set up in consonance with UNCLOS's unique built-in mechanism for the peaceful settlement of disputes: the International Tribunal for the Law of the Sea (located in Hamburg, Germany). Yet, the technologically advanced states that have the means to explore the seabed (most prominently the United States) resist the common heritage of humanity principle. However, if it is properly implemented, it can be beneficial for all, not only the technologically advanced.

UNCLOS provides a legal order for the seas and reaffirms the principle of the common heritage of humanity; it represents a defining moment and a watershed for international relations for three reasons.[137] First, the international community relinquished their respective countries' individual and exclusive claim to the riches that were already known to exist. Instead, countries agreed to explore the resources within the purview of an international organization, the International Seabed Authority, which is vested instead in humankind as a whole. States, coastal or landlocked, developed and underdeveloped, were to be the beneficiaries. One of the reasons for this renunciation of potential riches, which would otherwise have fallen under the sole purview of the developed countries for their exclusive advantage, was that at this moment in international relations the membership of the United Nations had increased with the addition of recently decolonized countries that aspired to and yearned for recognition and equality. Many of them had just emerged from, or were going through, liberation struggles. The Non-Aligned Movement, formed by developing countries that did not want to align with the Cold War superpowers, was definitely a new force in world politics, and their voices were heard and their priorities acknowledged.[138]

Second, the establishment of a supranational "authority" was exceptional in that this was the first time since the formulation of the United Nations Charter that an international treaty incorporated such an oversight system that would advance the

interests of all and not simply of a few technologically advanced nations. This is especially the case in the lucrative area of deep-sea mining. The principle of the common
heritage of humanity serves to create equity in assessing and utilizing the wealth
embedded in the deep sea.

Third, there is a reaffirmation of the principles of peaceful use, already contained
in the provisions of outer space law. UNCLOS represents a universal framework that
everyone respects and further reaffirms *common good governance* that aims to ensure
equality between developed and developing countries, the technologically advan-
taged and the disadvantaged.[139] UNCLOS has been an equalizer in international
relations. It makes clear that the world's resources are not only there for the most
powerful countries to enjoy but form a global public good.

Cooperation in outer space

Over the years, space has captivated the global imagination and helped unite the
world towards common goals. Despite political differences on Earth, countries
have worked together for progress in outer space, leading to great scientific and
technological achievements. We must ensure that everyone can access and benefit from frontier technologies. Let us harness this spirit of cooperation to advance
sustainable development and build a better world for all.[140]

The launch of Sputnik, the first man-made satellite, by the Soviets in 1957 and a
few months later the placing of a second satellite, the Explorer, into orbit by the Americans necessitated supplementary international law to regulate these new activities in
outer space. The main governance mechanism is the 1967 Treaty on Principles Governing the Activities of States in the Exploration and Use of Outer Space (The Outer
Space Treaty), which highlights in its preamble "the common interest of all mankind
in the progress of the exploration and use of outer space for peaceful purposes."[141]
This was a major achievement for international cooperation at a time of multiple
Cold War crises and heralded an era of sustained international cooperation that has
only strengthened throughout the years to the present day. The International Space
Station is a contemporary affirmation of the resilience of the possibilities of global
cooperation. The treaty is based upon the historic Declaration of Legal Principles
Governing the Activities of States in the Exploration and Use of Outer Space, adopted
unanimously by the General Assembly in 1963. Its importance lies in the fact that it
explicitly affirms, for the first time, guiding principles of conduct based upon the idea
of the common heritage of humanity, which were then reaffirmed with legally binding force in the 1967 Outer Space Treaty.[142] This treaty created the first framework
for international space law and sets out a number of global norms:

1) The exploration of outer space (which includes the Moon and other celestial bodies) is to be pursued on an equitable basis to benefit all countries'
   interests, regardless of their status as developed or developing, and "shall

be the province of all mankind." This also extends to unrestrained scientific freedom, which was intended to encourage international cooperation (Article 1).

2) No one can claim jurisdiction over, establish sovereignty for, or occupy any celestial body or any part of outer space (Article 2).

3) Exploration activities in outer space are to be carried out to maintain peace and security, and toward the promotion of global cooperation in alignment with the United Nations Charter (Article 3).

4) The weaponization of outer space is illegal and its use shall be exclusively peaceful. Therefore, states may not place weapons of mass destruction or test them in outer space. Article 4 states: "The testing of any type of weapons and the conduct of military maneuvers on celestial bodies shall be forbidden."

5) Astronauts are envoys of humanity and all states shall cooperate to protect them.

6) States bear international responsibility for activities in outer space carried out by governmental and nongovernmental entities.

7) State parties are responsible for, and may be deemed liable for, damage resulting from objects, or their parts, launched into outer space.

8) The underlying principles that guide conduct in outer space are cooperation and assistance. All activities shall be carried out in consultation with and in the interests of all states and to avoid any harm.

The common heritage of humanity is codified in outer space law by recognizing the common interest of all mankind in the progress of the exploration and use of outer space for peaceful purposes. These norms contributed to the evolution of the law protecting the commons.[143] Additionally, the principles that serve as the basis for the common heritage of humanity form the cornerstone of peaceful relations in outer space and have given rise to international cooperation projects such as the International Space Station, which involves the United States, Russia, Europe, Japan, and Canada.[144] The continuation of these relations of peace and trust, and observance of these aforementioned norms, are essential for the continued maintenance of global security in outer space. The norms of cooperation, scientific advancement, and nonweaponization have kept relations in outer space peaceful and free of conflict.[145] They serve as a robust basis for creating a framework to govern military AI, based upon *common good governance*.

Protection of the atmosphere and the ozone layer: Precautionary action

The atmosphere, including the ozone layer, is considered a global common and is the common concern of humanity. Without it, there is no possibility of life on Earth.[146] The idea of common concern and the necessity to protect the atmosphere and restrain pollution through the emission of greenhouse gases rose to marked prominence in the 1992 United Nations Conference on Environment and Development at the time of the negotiation of the UNFCCC and the Convention on Biological Diversity.[147] The notion of common concern, as applicable to the global commons, might find more support from a broader constituency of actors, because it does not directly involve considerations of sovereignty as the common heritage of humanity. Rather, it entails protection of aspects of the environment that, by reason of their importance and magnitude, the values at stake, and the need for collective action, are commonly recognized globally: for instance, biodiversity, forests, and marine conservation, including the high seas.[148] A comprehensive framework for environmental conservation was developed during the 1992 conference based on the common concern of humankind. This was a milestone in the advancement of international environmental law, as reiterated in the 2015 Paris Agreement on Climate Change. Taken together, the concepts of the common heritage of humanity and common concern provide an appropriate basis for *common good governance*, in turn providing a sound foundation for *humanity's security*. This is especially appropriate because, as Dinah Shelton explains, the notion of common concern reflects a global set of values and interests that is independent of the interests of states.[149]

To summarize, the common heritage of humanity applies to spaces and areas (such as Antarctica or outer space) as well as to resources, whereas common concern applies to specific issues (climate change, deforestation, and now, I contend, AI). Common concern provides a foundational basis for concerted action, as the associated issues can only be resolved if all collaborate.[150] This is regardless of countries' positions or action on any particular issue. The overriding concern is with the whole of humanity and what safeguards it. In this case, the global commons uphold humanity and must be urgently protected. This is essential for *common good governance* because, as I explained in Chapter 1, the attempts to stop the militarization of AI and the already prevailing usage of autonomous weapons will necessitate the engagement of all the different change makers I indicated: civil society (including the international Campaign to Stop Killer Robots), member states of the United Nations, scientists, and the International Committee of the Red Cross.

The UNFCCC represents the international community's first attempt to set up a regime for the protection of all the layers of the atmosphere, which are under threat from high concentrations of carbon dioxide, within a framework of common but differentiated responsibilities.[151] Added to the problem of harm to the atmosphere was the concentration of chlorofluorocarbons in the upper atmosphere that created the hole in the ozone layer. To address this problem, the UNFCCC was preceded by the 1987 Montreal Protocol on Substances that Deplete the Ozone Layer and the 1985 Vienna Convention on Ozone.[152]

To repair the hole in the ozone layer, which was endangering life on the planet, the precautionary principle was at work at the 1987 Montreal Protocol. Even with a lack of unequivocal scientific evidence, the protocol codified the precautionary principle. The protocol is today considered the most successful environmental treaty to date and an unrivaled example of global cooperation and management of one of

the Earth's global commons.[153] This international treaty has been universally ratified by 197 High-Contracting Parties, which is emblematic of its remarkable success
and the result of the joint application of science, innovation, diplomacy, and treaty-
making.[154] The protocol's preamble makes the point that states are determined to
take precautionary measures to protect the ozone layer. It is worth highlighting five
reasons that make this an unprecedently efficacious global cooperation achievement.
These reasons make it a model case to operationalize *common good governance* to
confront current problems posed by the militarization of AI.

First, at the point when negotiations were successful and led to the protocol, there
was no conclusive scientific evidence on the causal link between human-made emissions of harmful substances and the deterioration of the ozone layer. Therefore, states
acted in terms of the precautionary principle: they took action to establish a legal and
political framework back in 1987, and the ozone layer is predicted to heal by 2067.[155]
Second, the United States was the champion state in coalition with a few members of
the European Union, who acted in consonance after listening to the scientists. Third,
the legal framework created set up a fund in conjunction with a flexible mechanism
that allowed states to phase out the production of the harmful gases and were given
an appropriate time frame to do so. This phasing-out approach has paid off as it will
result in an estimated $1.8 trillion in global health benefits, including prevention of
skin cancer, and almost $460 billion in prevented damages that would have been
caused by the depletion of the ozone layer.[156]

Fourth, the treaty text is future-proof; it has stood the test of time because of its
flexible structure, and it incorporated new technological breakthroughs as time went
by, which also allowed for more countries to join (as mentioned, the treaty is now
universal).[157] Finally, the treaty served as the model for managing the other global
commons because it established a cooperative compliance system where the input of
scientists constantly adds to and assists in the implementation of the treaty and its
progress, which is essential for developing countries.[158]

The determination to apply the precautionary principle to environmental problems was reiterated in the 1992 UNFCCC. Article 3 of the convention states the
principles that guide it and prescribes that states must take precautionary measures to

anticipate, prevent or minimize the causes of climate change and mitigate its
adverse effects. Where there are threats of serious or irreversible damage, lack of
full scientific certainty should not be used as a reason for postponing such measures, taking into account that policies and measures to deal with climate change
should be cost-effective so as to ensure global benefits at the lowest possible
cost."

It is essential to bear in mind that the precautionary principle has three components. The first is the threshold of harm that is required to invoke it, which can vary
from negligible to irreversible harm. The second component is scientific uncertainty,
and here the knowledge-generating capacity that can be put in place by those wishing

to invoke the principle could stimulate more scientific investigation. The third component is shifting the burden of proof onto the proponents of the supposedly harmful activity.[159]

The origins of the precautionary principle lie in environmental law, but it has now been extended to other fields of scientific and global cooperation, such as nanotechnology, disarmament, and health. The precautionary principle affords a valuable framework to confront the problems created by the rapid militarization of AI and autonomous killing, the magnitude of which is still uncertain, but this is why the principle is so important in this discussion. Its two interrelated foundational pillars are the assessment and quantification of risks and scientific inputs. In general, action in international relations tends to be more reactive than preventive. Along the same lines, there is not much in international law to confront uncertainty beyond the precautionary principle, which is why my concept of *common good governance* is helpful.

The principle can be invoked if there is a possibility of harm and damage, even in the absence of scientific certainty. It is desirable that AI should be used only for good, but it is highly likely that it will be used for evil purposes, and this is what will create incalculable uncertainty for humankind. The likelihood of harm is considered as a central tenet of the principle, which takes into account that, in most cases, the causal link between action and effect has not been fully established.[160] Not only could the use of insufficiently robust algorithms and the employment of unsafe methods lead to problematic outcomes and a probable high risk of danger, so too could the deliberate application of AI for malicious purposes, such as "deepfake" videos that use AI to produce convincing but counterfeit representations as well as voice impersonations.

The Earth's global commons and the human-made commons lay the basis for sustained and prosperous human life and consequently must be protected by global cooperation. Therefore, the precautionary principle can be invoked when human activities could result in damage. The estimation of such damage must be based upon scientific evidence, even if this is indeterminate, if this can prevent danger to life, irreversible damage, or injustice to future generations. The principle can also take into account harm that is morally unacceptable to present and future generations. Finally, the need to act now stems from the realization that postponing action could make dealing with the consequences at a later stage much costlier and even, in some cases, ineffective.

Already existing concrete applications of the precautionary principle are illuminating. According to the European Commission, recourse to the precautionary principle may be invoked when a "phenomenon, product, or process may have a dangerous effect, identified by a scientific and objective evaluation, if this evaluation does not allow the risk to be determined with sufficient certainty."[161] Therefore, it is necessary to resort to a precautionary framework of risk analysis when three conditions are met: the identification of potentially adverse effects, the evaluation of the scientific data available, and the extent of scientific uncertainty.

The principle has been codified in the Treaty on the Functioning of the European Union (Article 191) to ensure a higher degree of environmental protection through preventive decision-making.[162] Implementing the precautionary principle may mean that it is necessary to generate more information about an activity that could cause harm, which is always welcome anyway. The European Commission has integrated the precautionary principle into its practice when dealing with risks, and invokes it when three preliminary conditions are met:

- identification of potentially adverse effects and assessment of risk of inaction,
- evaluation of the scientific data available, and
- the extent and degree of scientific uncertainty.

The European Union's framework application of the principle could serve as a basis for action by which to regulate military AI. All things considered, it is a positive step that the member states of the European Union have adopted the precautionary principle, as it adds to its cogency in international law in general and as a basis for *common good governance*.[163]

Protection of Antarctica

Antarctica is the only place on Earth that is completely devoted to peaceful scientific exchange for the common good of humanity—a result of the public participation of scientists from across the planet. Antarctica is the object of a densely regulated global protection regime composed of a set of treaties, agreements, annual meetings, and scientific exchanges, and it is internationally governed by what is called the Antarctic Treaty System, which effectively promotes ongoing cooperation on the various environmental and peaceful scientific exploration matters.[164] At the time of the negotiations, there was no explicit attempt to find a solution to the territorial claims that existed prior to the onset of the negotiations. This enabled negotiators to focus on the broader matters of concern, no weaponization, and scientific cooperation and exchange of information, and progressively formed the Antarctic Treaty System:[165]

- The 1959 Antarctic Treaty;
- The 1972 Convention for the Conservation of Antarctic Seals;
- The 1980 Convention on the Conservation of Antarctic Marine Living Resources;
- The 1991 Protocol on Environmental Protection to the Antarctic Treaty.

The first treaty to protect Antarctica was the historic 1959 Antarctic Treaty, deemed to be one of the most successful treaties ever concluded.[166] It provided the basis for a sophisticated commons regime that gave rise to new treaties in related areas of marine protection, conservation, and environmental management. Initially, the treaty set out to promote peaceful relations by managing common issues, such as ecological protection, instead of attempting to solve the territorial disputes and claims that existed at the time. Progressively, as more ancillary treaties were concluded, powerful norms of peace came to fruition: the territory is to be used only for peaceful purposes, which in turn renders militarization and weapons testing illegal. This was strengthened by an inspection system, with observers permitted to visit the region.[167] Antarctica has subsequently been used for transparent public scientific investigation instead. These new norms stemmed the territorial claims, while cooperation flourished among the member states.

Combined, these treaties gave rise to stable and lasting international governance. They have proved to be a powerful symbol of global cooperation, which also establishes Antarctica as a nuclear weapon-free, nonmilitarized, and peaceful zone.[168] This in turn inspires the striving to create a framework to regulate military AI, because it demonstrates the value of nonmilitarization, maintained as a preventive collective responsibility among member states as a tool to avoid conflict. Antarctica has achieved peaceful coexistence and is successful for three reasons. First, the Antarctica Treaty System codifies a norm of demilitarization and no weaponization. The Antarctic global cooperation regime places the highest priority on cooperation and it remains an example of nonmilitarization through concerted diplomacy. Second, jurisdictional claims are illegitimate and, as a result, member states can focus on the other pressing matters of environmental degradation and melting ice caps. Third, as a consequence, cooperative scientific research is the dominant motivation in relationships, making it possible for all states to mutually benefit from the enterprise. The transparent and public exchange of scientific information is what enabled a deep understanding of the facts about the hole in the ozone layer, over the Antarctica, and the processes underlying the melting of glaciers.[169]

Antarctica became a territory for scientific endeavor as a result of the Antarctica Treaty System, which is an efficacious global cooperation mechanism under international law that ordered the relationships of states to favor scientific interactions for the common good. By organizing states to work toward the common good—namely, scientific progress through cooperation—the Antarctica Treaty System achieved keeping the continent free from the pressures of competition and rivalry among the militarized powers. The Antarctica protection norms evolved concomitantly with the consolidation of other new realities in international relations. One is the nonterritorial annexation norm established by the United Nations Charter. The other is the institutionalization of other global common spaces—outer space, the high seas, and the atmosphere—while making the idea of territorial claims intolerable over areas that are viewed as for all humanity to benefit.[170]

The Arctic: Comity for peace

The political and legal framework in the Arctic is not as evolved under international law, and does not form such a robust set of governing mechanisms as in Antarctica. However, the inclusive diplomatic dynamics in the Arctic Council, the central governance mechanism, which includes the voices of indigenous Arctic communities, and other diplomatic dynamics that foster peace are worth observing.[171] It is important to bear in mind that the only part of the Arctic, which is a vast, diverse region, that is incontrovertibly considered a global common is its high seas.[172]

The Arctic is not the subject of a governance system that frees it from the forces of globalization, as is the case in Antarctica, where commercial activity was prohibited along with an intolerance of claims to sovereignty. Therefore, understanding how peace is forged among the Arctic countries is critical to the well-being of its states and peoples, and serves as a good example of how regional approaches may be more effective to promote cooperation in adversarial areas or on issues and domains that can result in conflict, such as the weaponization of AI.

The Arctic has thus far been a region of peace in great part because of the governing institution (i.e., the Arctic Council), the absence of weaponization, and ongoing cooperation between Russia and the Western states in the region.[173] The Arctic Council is not only comprised principally of the eight countries bordering the Arctic; most importantly, the indigenous populations have a voice in participatory decision-making. The lifelong work of Nobel Prize laureate Elinor Ostrom posits that effective governance stems from the participatory decision-making of the stakeholders involved.[174] She rejects the traditional assumption of the tragedy of the commons, and her reasons are convincing.[175] The tragedy of the commons model assumes the actors' fixed preferences, which are dictated from above, whereas she privileges the power and agency of the individual and local policies. According to Ostrom, for governance of the commons to be successful, five conditions must ideally be in place. When they are not, it is necessary to create institutional arrangements that set up these conditions:[176]

1) Resources and their use are monitored and verified at low cost;
2) The scale of change in resources, users, technology, and economic conditions is moderate (supply);
3) Rule-compliance mechanisms are social-capital based (i.e., frequent communications between the stakeholders to increase trust and make monitoring easier [credibility]);
4) Outsiders can be kept at bay and are not permitted to use the resources;
5) The users themselves work toward the monitoring and enforcement of the rules (mutual monitoring).

In the case of the other commons, as Ostrom and her colleagues have noted, the temporal separation between the causes and the outcomes of the problems that the commons are encountering (climate change, for instance), and the fact that large-scale economic pressures and global markets are not necessarily aligned with local conditions and realities, make it much harder to manage them. Polycentric adaptive governance is at the heart of what is needed, according to Ostrom. Taking care of the commons requires heeding a multiplicity of views, from local to international, so that adaptive, flexible institutions may be designed together. In this model, the government is only one actor that generates governance—and not the only or even the central one. Along the same lines, Beverly Crawford argues that the Arctic is governed by networks of overlapping local regimes using traditional aboriginal ecological knowledge. These networks are characterized by participative governance that generates trust.[177]

My concept of *common good governance* aligns with Crawford's and Ostrom's models and presupposes the communality of interests among several groups (states, indigenous communities, scientists, etc.) and many distinct ways to approach the problem from multiple perspectives and create a variety of platforms for action.

I argued back in 2015,[178] and then again in 2021,[179] that, despite the promise of untold riches, the Arctic is a region of peace for three reasons. The first is that all countries play by the rules, which are a combination of legally binding and soft norms within a workable institution, namely the Arctic Council, the only such group that has membership open to indigenous peoples.[180] Second, member states of the Arctic Council are largely secure nations that for the most part score highly according to the rankings of the Global Peace Index (see Table 2.2). That is, they are mostly (but not all) peacemakers rather than troublemakers in the Arctic region. There are thus many incentives for cooperation, and member states have therefore favored joint action rather than conflict. The NATO membership of seven of the Arctic nations (except for Russia) shifts the balance of power toward the West. This means that Russia has less incentive to behave poorly vis-à-vis its counterparts in the Arctic Council. Nor does Russia have the military power to compete in the Arctic against the NATO countries; it does not have sufficient economic or political power to match all of these countries combined. Russia also cares about access to potential Arctic resources, which would be jeopardized by tense relations with its Arctic neighbors and colleagues. The third reason is that the other international law framework beyond the peace-generating governance by the Arctic Council, the UNCLOS, provides the basis for

Table 2.2 Arctic Council members' proclivity toward peace

Member Country	Arctic Council members' proclivity toward peace					
	Global Peace Index	GPI score	Positive Peace Index*	PPI score	Good relations with neighbors	Relations score
Norway	14th	1.438	4th	1.27	11th	1.59
Canada	10th	1.330	7th	1.37	2nd	1.37
Denmark	3rd	1.256	2nd	1.24	3rd	1.37
Finland	13th	1.402	3rd	1.26	15th	1.74
Iceland	1st	1.100	13th	1.54	44th	2.63
Russia	154th	2.993	71st	3.09	68th	3.22
Sweden	15th	1.460	1st	1.23	7th	1.49
US	122nd	2.337	24th	1.95	23rd	1.81

(*Source:* Global Peace Index, 2022)

* Global Peace Index 2021: Measuring Peace in a Complex World. – Sydney: Institute for Economics and Peace, 2022. https://www.visionofhumanity.org/wp-content/uploads/2022/06/GPI-2022-web.pdf

the peaceful settlement of disputes; most conflicts were settled using this overarching legal framework.

This case of peace prevailing among supposedly rival nations tells us what is possible at the regional level: eight countries listed in Table 2.2 are influenced by the native and aboriginal communities, as well as the scientists. The model of governance in the Arctic Council is inclusive and participatory, because it includes a permanent participant category by means of which the indigenous communities have a voice in every meeting.[181] Conflicts have been dealt with thus far using peaceful dispute-settlement methods within the UNCLOS framework that is applicable here. It is unclear that this will remain the case when superpower rivalries are amplified by more anonymous technologies such as autonomous weapons, especially in the cyber domain. This could change the Arctic Council's creative configuration for peace with different actors (not only the eight Arctic states), which is conducive to peaceful settlement of disputes.[182] The inclusive gains in peace and collaboration shown by the Arctic Council could potentially withstand the deteriorating geopolitical environment of the shifting world order. The danger remains, however, that an increasingly acrimonious environment can alter and weaken the gains made through peaceful collaboration. Some states may opt for more diplomatic approaches and some for more militarized tactics.[183] The risk is that the militarized countries will use their technological superiority to explore the Arctic for their own interests, but for now it seems that a proclivity of most of its members toward peace is the prevailing behavior.

Prohibition on nuclear testing

The prohibition of nuclear testing benefits humanity, the environment, and the planet as a whole. It is one of the most consequential bans in international law because it interdicts explosions anywhere on Earth, including the atmosphere. It also represents a shining example of global cooperation at its best, achieved by the 1996 CTBT, negotiated at the United Nations in Geneva. With no testing permitted, states cannot improve existing or develop new nuclear weapons. No testing also means no damage by radioactivity to human beings, wildlife, and flora. Before the CTBT, 2,000 nuclear tests had been conducted, causing indescribable harm to populations and ecosystems where the tests took place.[184] The CTBT is a critical pillar of strategic stability.[185]

The treaty generated a widely respected norm against the testing of nuclear weapons, even though it is yet to come into force. All countries ceased testing except for North Korea. The CTBT Organization (CTBTO) is located in Vienna and ensures the universalization of the treaty (getting more countries to join) and verification mechanism. The CTBT has been signed by 185 states and ratified by 170, which makes its norms almost universal. Ratification is what commits states to the legally binding provisions of an international law instrument such as the CTBT. However, it will only enter into force when it is ratified by 44 specific countries that are members of the Conference on Disarmament, which is the forum where the CTBT was negotiated in Geneva. The specific countries include the five original nuclear weapon states: China, France, Russia, the United Kingdom, and the United States. Ratifications are also required from India, Israel, North Korea, and Pakistan, which all also possess nuclear arsenals. The ratification for entry into force is still required from the following eight states: China, India, Pakistan, North Korea, Israel, Iran, Egypt, and the United States.[186]

What is exceptional about the CTBT is its enforcement mechanism: the International Monitoring System (IMS). The IMS is a complex combination of seismic (monitors shockwaves including earthquakes), hydroacoustic (listens to ocean waves), infrasound (ultra-low frequency sound waves), and radionuclide (measures the atmosphere for radioactive particles) detectors and sensors all connected by satellite. The International Data Centre at the CTBTO in Vienna receives information collected every day from 337 facilities and stations across the planet.[187] North Korea's nuclear tests were detected via this method, as well as earthquake and tsunami early warnings.

Professor Stuart Russell and Dr. Nimar Arora created the NETVISA global seismic monitoring algorithm. They utilized data processing by the International Data Centre, verification and monitoring, and machine learning methods that enhance the ability to localize an event.[188] Their work complements decades of research by leading seismologists and geophysicists to build this extraordinarily complex system's scope and reach across the planet. NETVISA is exemplar of the possibilities of *transnational networked cooperation*, in this case among member states, scientists within the data centre and outside, and the diplomats at the CTBTO. The CTBT and its enhanced monitoring and enforcement mechanism promote greater predictability and security for current and future generations.

Notes

1. Antônio Augusto Cançado Trindade, *International Law for Humankind: Towards a New Jus Gentium* (Brill Nijhoff, 2013): p. 93; Professor Trindade is one of the judges at the International Court of Justice.
2. Denise Garcia, "Global Commons Law: Norms to Safeguard the Planet and Humanity's Heritage." *International Relations*, vol. 35, no. 3 (2021): pp. 422–445.
3. Nina von Uexkull and Halvard Buhaug, "Security Implications of Climate Change: A Decade of Scientific Progress." *Journal of Peace Research*, vol. 58, no. 1 (2021): 3–17.
4. IPCC, 2023: AR6 Synthesis Report Climate Change 2023.
5. Masson-Delmotte, Valérie, Panmao Zhai, Anna Pirani, Sarah L. Connors, Clotilde Péan, Sophie Berger, Nada Caud et al. "Climate Change 2021: The Physical Science Basis." Contribution of working group I to the sixth assessment report of the intergovernmental panel on climate change 2 (2021).
6. For the list of scientists, see: https://archive.ipcc.ch/report/authors/report.authors.php?q=35&p=&p.
7. Adger, W Neil; Juan M Pulhin et al. "Human Security." In C. B, Field and V. R. Barros, eds., *Climate Change 2014: Impacts, Adaptation, and Vulnerability. Part A: Global and Sectoral Aspects. Contribution of Working Group II to the Fifth Assessment Report*

of the Intergovernmental Panel of Climate Change (Cambridge University Press, 2014), pp. 755–791.

8. Craig Albert, Amado Baez, and Joshua Rutland, "Human Security as Biosecurity: Reconceptualizing National Security Threats in the Time of COVID-19." *Politics and the Life Sciences*, vol. 40, no. 1 (2021): pp. 83–105.

9. See Institute for Economics and Peace (IEP) Ecological Threat Register Dataset (p. 4): IEP dataset: https://www.visionofhumanity.org/wp-content/uploads/2020/10/ETR_2020_web-1.pdf.

10. Institute for Economics and Peace. *Global Peace Index 2021: Measuring Peace in a Complex World* (IEP, 2021).

11. Matt McDonald, "Human Security and the Construction of Security." *Global Society*, vol. 16, no. 3 (2002): pp. 277–295.

12. Ramesh Thakur, "From National to Human Security." In S. Harris and A. Mack eds., *Asia Pacific Security: The Economics Political Nexus* (Allen & Unwin, 1997): pp. 52–80.

13. Carlos R. S. Milani "COVID-19 Between Global Human Security and Ramping Authoritarian Nationalisms." *Geopolítica*, vol. 11 (2020): pp. 141–151.

14. Anne Peters, "Novel Practice of the Security Council: Wildlife Poaching and Trafficking as a Threat to the Peace," *EJIL: Talk!*, February 12, 2014. https://www.ejiltalk.org/novel-practice-of-the-security-council-wildlife-poaching-and-trafficking-as-a-threat-to-the-peace/

15. McDonald, "Human Security and the Construction of Security," p. 174.

16. Barry Buzan and Lene Hansen. *The Evolution of International Security Studies* (Cambridge University Press, 2009).

17. Stephen M. Walt, "Realism and Security." The International Studies Encyclopedia. Ed. Robert A. Denemark. Wiley-Blackwell, (2010).

18. Gerd Oberleitner, "Human Security." In *Encyclopedia of Human Rights* (Oxford University Press, 2009): pp. 289–304.

19. Albert, Baez, and Rutland, "Human Security as Biosecurity," p. 83; Miriam Bradley, *Protecting Civilians in War: The ICRC, UNHCR, and their Limitations in Internal Armed Conflicts* (Oxford University Press, 2016).

20. United Nations General Assembly, A/RES/66/290 Resolution adopted by the General Assembly on September 10, 2012, as a follow-up to paragraph 143 on human security of the 2005 World Summit Outcome.

21. Matt McDonald, *Ecological Security: Climate Change and the Construction of Security* (Cambridge University Press, 2021).

22. Augusto López-Claros, Arthur L. Dahl, and Maja Groff, *Global Governance and the Emergence of Global Institutions for the 21st Century* (Cambridge University Press, 2020).

23. McDonald, "Human Security and the Construction of Security."

24. Matt McDonald, "Climate Change and Security: Towards Ecological Security?" *International Theory*, vol. 10, no. 2 (2018): pp. 153–180.

25. Keith Krause and Michael C. Williams. "Broadening the Agenda of Security Studies: Politics and Methods." *Mershon International Studies Review*, vol. 40 (1996): pp. 229–254.

26. United Nations Secretary-General, "Securing our Common Future: An Agenda for Disarmament" (Office for Disarmament Affairs New York, 2018).

27. United Nations Secretary-General, "Securing our Common Future," p. 12.

28. Institute for Economics and Peace. Global Peace Index 2021: Measuring Peace in a Complex World, Sydney, June 2021. Available from http://visionofhumanity.org/reports.

29. Diego Lopes da Silva, Nan Tian, and Alexandra Marksteiner, Trends in World Military Expenditure (SIPRI, 2021).

30. SIPRI Yearbook, Armaments, Disarmament, and International Security, July 2021. Federation of American Scientists, Status of the World's Nuclear Forces 2021.

31. The data is produced by the International Campaign to Abolish Nuclear Weapons (ICAN), which received the Nobel Peace Prize in 2017: https://www.icanw.org/report_73_billion_nuclear_weapons_spending_2020.

32. William Steffen, et al., "Planetary Boundaries: Guiding Human Development on a Changing Planet." *Science*, vol. 347, no. 6223 (2015).

33. Manu Lekunze, "The Environment of Security in Africa: A Threat Multiplier." In *Inherent and Contemporary Challenges to African Security* (Palgrave Macmillan, 2020): pp. 143–166.

34. Andrea J. Nightingale, "Power and Politics in Climate Change Adaptation Efforts: Struggles over Authority and Recognition in the Context of Political Instability." *Geoforum*, vol. 84 (2017): pp. 11–20.

35. Nathan Alexander Sears, "International Politics in the Age of Existential Threats." *Journal of Global Security Studies*, vol. 6, no. 3 (2021).

36. McDonald, "Climate Change and Security."

37. Garcia, "Global Commons Law."

38. Nathan Alexander Sears, "Existential Security: Towards a Security Framework for the Survival of Humanity." *Global Policy*, vol. 11, no. 2 (2016): pp. 255–66.

39. Martin Rees, *Our Final Hour: A Scientist's Warning: How Terror, Error, and Environmental Disaster Threaten Humankind's Future in this Century—On Earth and Beyond* (Basic Books, 2003); Martin Rees, *On the Future: Prospects for Humanity* (Princeton University Press 2018); Des Gasper, "Securing Humanity: Situating 'Human Security' as Concept and Discourse." *Journal of Human Development*, vol. 6, no. 2 (2005): pp. 221–245; Anthony Burke, Stefanie Fishel, Audra Mitchell, Simon Dalby, and Daniel J. Levine "Planet Politics: A Manifesto from the End of IR." *Millennium*, vol. 44, no. 3 (2016): pp. 499–523.

40. Marianne Riddervold and Akasemi Newsome, "Introduction: Cooperation, Conflict, and Interaction in the Global Commons." *International Relations*, vol. 35, no. 3 (2021): pp. 365–383.

41. Beverly Kay Crawford, "Explaining Arctic Peace: A Human Heritage Perspective." *International Relations*, vol. 35, no. 3 (2021): pp. 469–488.

42. Phil Torres, *Morality, Foresight and Human Flourishing: An Introduction to Existential Risks* (Pitchstone Publishing, 2017); Daniel Deudney "Turbo Change: Accelerating Technological Disruption, Planetary Geopolitics, and Architectonic Metaphors." *International Studies Review*, vol. 20, no. 2 (2018): pp. 223–231.

43. Maïa. K. Davis Cross, "The EU Global Strategy and Diplomacy." *Contemporary Security Policy*, vol. 37, no. 3 (2016): pp. 402–413.

44. Gille Olakounle Yabi, "The role of ECOWAS in managing political crisis and conflict." *FES Peace and Security Series* (2010). https://library.fes.de/pdf-files/bueros/nigeria/07448.pdf

45. Denise Garcia, "Redirect Military Budgets to Tackle Climate Change and Pandemics." *Nature*, vol. 584 (2020): pp. 521–523.

46. Inge Kaul, Isabelle Grunberg, and Marc Stern, *Global Public Goods* (New York-Oxford: Oxford University Press, 1999); Séverine Deneulin and Nicholas Townsend, "Public

Goods, Global Public Goods and the Common Good." *International Journal of Social Economics*, vol. 34, no. 1/2 (2007): pp. 19–36.

47. Rees, *On the Future: Prospects for Humanity*.

48. López-Claros, Dahl, and Groff, *Global Governance and the Emergence of Global Institutions for the 21st Century*.

49. Anna Stavrianakis and Maria Stern, "Militarism and Security: Dialogue, Possibilities and Limits." *Security Dialogue*, vol. 49, no. 1–2 (2018): pp. 3–18.

50. Sears, "Existential Security."

51. Nick Bostrom, "Existential Risks." *Journal of Evolution and Technology*, vol. 9, no. 1 (2002): pp. 1–31.

52. Nick Bostrom and Milan M. Cirkovic, eds. *Global Catastrophic Risks* (Oxford University Press, 2011).

53. Trindade, *The Construction of a Humanized International Law: A Collection of Individual Opinions* (Hotei Publishing, 2014).

54. Trindade, *The Construction of a Humanized International Law*.

55. Trindade, *The Construction of a Humanized International Law*, p. 13.

56. Speech by the United Nations Secretary-General António Guterres at the annual meeting of the World Economic Forum, Davos, Switzerland, January 24, 2019.

57. Originally called "common heritage of mankind." Some observers now call it common heritage of humankind and some view it differently from common heritage of humanity. I will call it as the latter from now onwards.

58. Cançado Trindade, *International Law for Humankind*, p. 347.

59. Cançado Trindade, *International Law for Humankind*.

60. Thomas G. Weiss and Rorden Wilkinson, eds., *International Organization and Global Governance* (Routledge, 2018); López-Claros, Dahl, and Groff, *Global Governance and the Emergence of Global Institutions for the 21st Century*.

61. Robert I. Rotberg and Rachel M. Gisselquist, "Ibrahim Index of African Governance: Results and Rankings." The Kennedy School of Government, Harvard University and the World Peace Foundation (2008); See also: https://www.belfercenter.org/publication/ibrahim-index-african-governance.

62. Rotberg and Gisselquist, "Ibrahim Index of African Governance: Results and Rankings."

63. Robert I. Rotberg, ed., "On Governance, What it Is, What if Measures, and Its Policy Uses." *Center for International Governance Innovation* (June 1, 2015): p. 17.

64. Rotberg, "On Governance, What it Is, What if Measures, and Its Policy Uses." "In cases where a ruling family or clan arrogates most of the available sources of economic growth and tightly restricts profit-making opportunities to a select group of cronies and sycophants, a permissive and positive framework is falsified and political patrimony readily displaces the possibility of widespread prosperity." A contrasting example that I always discuss with my students, of a case of two countries that are very wealthy in natural resources and have the most antagonistic and contrasting social economic condition, is that of Norway and the Democratic Republic of the Congo (DRC). Where Norway has consistently made sure that all the natural wealth it gains is invested for future generations, the DRC ruling elites have pillaged and stolen from the people for decades, making it one of the worst governed countries in the world, in absolute contrast to Norway, one of most well-governed countries.

65. Ruti Teitel, *Humanity's Law* (Oxford University Press, 2011).

66. Antônio Augusto Cançado Trindade, *A Humanização do Direito Internacional*, 2nd ed. (Del Rey, 2015), pp. 3–789; Cançado Trindade, La Humanización del Derecho Internacional Contemporáneo (Porrúa/ IMDPC, 2013), pp. 1–324; Cançado Trindade, *Los Tribunales Internacionales Contemporáneos y la Humanización del Derecho Internacional* (Ad-Hoc, 2013), pp. 7–185; Cançado Trindade, *Le Droit international pour la personne humaine*, (Pédone, 2012), pp. 45–368.
67. Teitel, *Humanity's Law*, p. 14.
68. Antônio Augusto Cançado Trindade, "The Principle of Humanity and the Safeguard of the Human Person" (2016): http://ibdh.org.br/wp-content/uploads/2016/02/THE-PRINCIPLE-OF-HUMANITY-AND-THE-SAFEGUARD-OF-THE-HUMAN-PERSON.pdf
69. Steffen Fritz et al., "Citizen Science and the United Nations Sustainable Development Goals." *Nature Sustainability*, vol. 2, no. 10 (2019): pp. 922–930.
70. Cançado Trindade, *International Law for Humankind*; Teitel, *Humanity's Law*.
71. Steffen et al., "Planetary Boundaries"; Johan Rockström et al., "Planetary Boundaries: Exploring the Safe Operating Space for Humanity." *Ecology and Society* vol. 14, no. 2 (2009).
72. Cançado Trindade, *International Law for Humankind*, p. 13.
73. UNGA First Committee, 1515th meeting, Wednesday November 1, 1967 (Official Records, A 22nd session, UN Doc A/C.1/PV 1515, 1967.
74. Chukwumerije Okereke, "Equity Norms in Global Environmental Governance." *Global Environmental Politics*, vol. 8, no. 3 (2008): pp. 25–50.
75. Mai'A. K. Davis Cross, "Outer Space and the Idea of the Global Commons." *International Relations*, vol. 35, no. 3 (2021): pp. 384–402.
76. Kemal Baslar, *The Concept of the Common Heritage of Mankind in International Law* (Martinus Nijhoff, 1998); Antônio Augusto Cançado Trindade, "International Law for Humankind towards a New Jus Gentium." *Recueil Des Cours*, vol. 316 (2005): pp. 365–396; Beatriz Garcia, *The Amazon from an International Law Perspective* (Cambridge University Press, 2011).
77. Bradley Larschan and Bonnie C. B. Brennan "The Common Heritage of Mankind Principle in International Law." *Columbia Journal of Transnational Law*, vol. 21 (1983): pp. 305–33; Mohammed Bedjaou, *Towards a New International Economic Order* (UNESCO, 1979); Nagendra Singh, "Right to Environment and Sustainable Development as a Principle of International Law." *Studia Diplomatica*, vol. 41, no. 1 (1988): pp. 45–61.
78. Lubos Perek. "Interaction between Space Technology and Space Law." *Journal of Space Law*, vol. 18, no. 1 (1990): pp. 19–29.
79. Surabhi Ranganathan, "Global Commons." *European Journal of International Law*, vol. 27, no. 3 (2016): pp. 693–717.
80. Kate Crawford, *The Atlas of AI* (Yale University Press, 2021).
81. Jennifer Shkabatur, "The Global Commons of Data." *Stanford Technology Law Review*, vol. 22 (2019): p. 354; Shkabatur considers that data should be viewed as a "global common."
82. The AI Commons, "Introducing 'AI Commons': A framework for collaboration to achieve global impact." https://aiforgood.itu.int/introducing-ai-commons-a-framework-for-collaboration-to-achieve-global-impact/.

83. Nicholas Tsagourias, "The Legal Status of Cyberspace." In *Research Handbook on International Law and Cyberspace* (Edward Elgar Publishing, 2015): pp. 13–29.

84. Crawford, *The Atlas of AI*.

85. Crawford, *The Atlas of AI*, p. 41–45.

86. Crawford, *The Atlas of AI*, p. 218.

87. Crawford, *The Atlas of AI*, p. 225.

88. Emma L. Cavan and Simeon L. Hill, "Commercial Fishery Disturbance of the Global Ocean Biological Carbon Sink." *Global Change Biology*, vol. 28, no. 4 (2022): pp. 1212–1221. Christopher L. Sabine, et al., "The Oceanic Sink for Anthropogenic CO_2." *Science*, vol. 305, no. 5682 (2004): pp. 367–371.

89. Available online: https://www.un.org/en/pdfs/HLP%20on%20Digital%20Cooperation%20Report%20Executive%20Summary%20-%20ENG.pdf.

90. Garcia, "Global Commons Law."

91. Brigham Daniels and James Salzman, "Our Global Commons." *Brigham Young University Law Review*, vol. 6 (2014): pp. 1251–1256.

92. Nadia Eghbal, *Roads and Bridges: The Unseen Labor Behind our Digital Infrastructure* (Ford Foundation, 2016).

93. Eghbal, *Roads and Bridges*; Ricardo Vinuesa, et al., "The Role of Artificial Intelligence in Achieving the Sustainable Development Goals." *Nature Communications*, vol. 11, no. 1 (2020): pp. 1–10.

94. Jennifer Shkabatur, "The Global Commons of Data." *Stan. Tech. L. Rev*, vol. 22 (2019): p. 354.

95. I am grateful to the conversations and advice from McGill University professor Ajung Moon, a roboticist and engineer, Director of the Open Roboethics Institute, and a fellow member of the International Panel for the Regulation of Autonomous Weapons.

96. Eghbal, *Roads and Bridges*, p. 90,

97. Eghbal, *Roads and Bridges*, pp. 90, 43–50.

98. Scott J. Shackelford, "Common Heritage of Humanity." In *Essential Concepts of Global Environmental Governance*, ed. Morin, Jean-Frédéric, and Amandine Orsini (Routledge, 2020): pp. 44–46.

99. Kristi Govella, "Technology and Tensions in the Global Commons," *Fletcher Security Review*, vol. 6, no. 1 (2019): pp. 38–44.

100. Christopher C. Joyner, "Legal Implications of the Concept of the Common Heritage of Mankind," *International and Comparative Law Quarterly*, vol. 3, no. 190 (1986): pp. 190–199; Christopher C. Joyner, "The Concept of the Common Heritage of Mankind in International Law," *Emory International Law Review*, vol. 13, no: 2 (1999): pp. 615–628.

101. Scott Jasper eds., *Conflict and Cooperation in the Global Commons: A Comprehensive Approach for International Security* (Georgetown University Press, 2012).

102. In a previous article I termed this the "law of the commons": Denise Garcia, "Future Arms, Technologies, and International Law: Preventive Security Governance." *European Journal of International Security*, vol.1, no. 1 (2016), pp. 94–111.

103. Garcia, "Global Commons Law."

104. Enric Sala, et al., "The Economics of Fishing the High Seas." *Science Advances*, vol. 4, no. 6 (2018).

105. Albert Günther, "II.—Preliminary Notices of Deep-Sea Fishes Collected During the Voyage of HMS 'Challenger.'" *Journal of Natural History*, vol. 2, no. 7 (1878): pp. 17–28.
106. Jessica F. Green and Bryce Rudyk, "Closing the High Seas to Fishing: A Club Approach." *Marine Policy*, vol. 115 (2020): 103855.
107. Riddervold and Newsome, "Introduction: Cooperation, Conflict, and Interaction in the Global Commons"; Garcia, "Global Commons Law."
108. Riddervold and Newsome, "Introduction: Cooperation, Conflict, and Interaction in the Global Commons."
109. Edward Guntrip, "The Common Heritage of Mankind: An Adequate Regime for Managing the Deep Seabed." *Melbourne Journal of Internationl Law*, vol. 4, no. 376 (2003): pp. 376–405.
110. Nico Schrijver, "Managing the Global Commons: Common Good or Common Sink?" *Third World Quarterly*, vol. 31, no. 7 (2016): p. 1255.
111. Rüdiger Wolfrum, *International Law, Max Planck Encyclopedia of Public International Law* (Oxford University Press, 2012): p. 7.
112. Garcia, "Global Commons Law."
113. Denise Garcia, *Disarmament Diplomacy and Human Security. Regimes, Norms and Moral Progress in International Relations* (Routledge, 2011).
114. Riddervold and Newsome, "Introduction: Cooperation, Conflict, and Interaction in the Global Commons."
115. Joyner, "Legal Implications of the Concept of the Common Heritage of Mankind."
116. Rebecca Crootof, "International Cybertorts: Expanding State Accountability in Cyberspace." *Cornell Law Review*, vol 103, no. 3 (2018): pp. 565–644.
117. Greta Thunberg, *No One is Too Small to Make a Difference* (Penguin, 2019).
118. Marianne Takle, "Common Concern for the Global Ecological Commons: Solidarity with Future Generations?" *International Relations*, vol. 35, no. 3 (2021): pp. 403–421.
119. Edith Brown Weiss, "In Fairness To Future Generations and Sustainable Development." *American University International Law Review*, vol. 8, no. 1 (1992): pp. 19–26.
120. UNGA Res. 43/53, December 6, 1988, on the Protection of Global Climate for Present and Future Generations.
121. The United Nations Convention on Biological Diversity of 5 June 1992 (1760 U.N.T.S. 69).
122. United Nations Framework Convention on Climate Change, May 9, 1992, S. Treaty Doc No. 102-38, 1771 U.N.T.S. 107.
123. Cançado Trindade, *International Law for Humankind*, p. 348.
124. Cançado Trindade, *International Law for Humankind*, p. 351.
125. Cançado Trindade, *International Law for Humankind*, p. 17.
126. Problems of the Human Environment, GA Res. 2398 (XXIII), UN GAOR, 23rd session (1968). This resolution decides to convene the first ever meeting on the environment, held in Sweden: Stockholm Declaration of the United Nations Conference on the Human Environment, June 16, 1972, UN Doc. A/CONF.48/14/Rev.l, online: United Nations Environment Program (UNEP).
127. Brown Weiss, "In Fairness To Future Generations and Sustainable Development," p. 22.
128. *Our Common Future* (Oxford University Press, 1987): p. 16.
129. Brown Weiss, "In Fairness To Future Generations and Sustainable Development," p. 116.
130. Shirley V. Scott, "The LOS Convention as a Constitutional Regime for the Oceans." In *Stability and Change in the Law of the Sea: The Role of the LOS Convention* (Brill Nijhoff, 2005): pp. 9–38.

131. Ola Dahlman, et al., "The Inside Story of the Group of Scientific Experts and its Key Role in Developing the CTBT Verification Regime." *The Nonproliferation Review*, vol. 27, no. 1–3 (2020): pp. 181–200.

132. The United Nations Convention on the Law of the Sea was adopted by the Third United Nations Conference on the Law of the Sea and opened for signature, together with the Final Act of the Conference, at Montego Bay, Jamaica, on December 10, 1982. The conference was convened pursuant to resolution 3067 (XXVIII) Official Records of the General Assembly, Twenty Eighth Session, Supplement No. 30 (A/9030), vol. 1. The Final Act was signed on December 10, 1982.

133. 3201 (S-VI). Declaration on the Establishment of a New International Economic Order: UN General Assembly, *3201 (S-VI). Declaration on the Establishment of a New International Economic Order*, May 1, 1974, A/RES/3201(S-VI).

134. Preamble, UNCLOS, adopted on December 10, 1982. 1833 UNTS. 397.

135. See opinion by Tullio Treves, Judge of the International Tribunal for the Law of the Sea, Professor at the University of Milan, Italy, United Nations Audiovisual Library of International Law, 2008; Lilian Del Castillo, ed. *The Law of the Sea, from Grotius to the International Tribunal for the Law of the Sea, Liber Amicorum Judge Hugo Caminos* (Brill Nijhoff, 2015); Yoshifumi Tanaka, *The International Law of the Sea* (Cambridge University Press, 2015).

136. Jutta Brunnée, "Common Areas, Common Heritage, and Common Concern." The Oxford Handbook of International Environmental Law (Oxford University Press, 2007), Part V, chapter 23.

137. Joyner, "Legal Implications of the Concept of the Common Heritage of Mankind," pp. 190–199.

138. Rudolph Preston Arnold. "The Common Heritage of Mankind as a Legal Concept." *International Lawyer*, vol. 9 (1975): pp. 153–158.

139. Douglas Yarn, "The Transfer of Technology and UNCLOS III." *Georgia Journal of International and Comparative Law,* vol. 14 (1984): p. 121.

140. United Nations Secretary-General António Guterres' video message for the UNISPACE+50 high-level segment held in Vienna, June 20–21, 2018: Harness Spirit of Cooperation in Using Space Science, Technology to Advance Sustainable Development, Secretary-General Tells UNISPACE+50 Event.

141. Treaty on Principles Governing the Activities of States in the Exploration and Use of Outer Space, including the Moon and Other Celestial Bodies, adopted by the General Assembly in its resolution 2222 (XXI), opened for signature on January 27, 1967, entered into force on October 10, 1967.

142. A/RES/18/1962 (XVIII) Declaration of Legal Principles Governing the Activities of States in the Exploration and Use of Outer Space.

143. Cançado Trindade, *International Law for Humankind*.

144. Kenneth S. Pedersen, "The Changing Face of International Space Cooperation: One View of NASA." *Space Policy*, vol. 2, no. 2 (1986): pp. 120–137.

145. Davis Cross, "Outer Space and the Idea of the Global Commons."

146. Jack George Calvert, et al., *The Mechanisms of Reactions Influencing Atmospheric Ozone* (Oxford University Press, 2015).

147. Frederiech Soltau, "Common Concern of Humankind." In The Oxford Handbook of International Climate Change Law, vol. 14, no. 2 (Oxford University Press, 2016): p. 202.

148. Alexandre Kiss, "The Common Concern of Mankind." *Environmental Policy & Law*, vol. 27 (1997): p. 244.

149. See the eminent international legal environmental scholar: Dinah Shelton, "Common Concern of Humanity." *Environmental Law and Policy*, vol. 39, no. 2 (2009): p. 83.

150. Shelton, "Common Concern of Humanity."

151. Jutta Brunnée and Charlotte Streck, "The UNFCCC as a Negotiation Forum: Towards Common but more Differentiated Responsibilities." *Climate Policy*, vol. 13, no. 5 (2013): pp. 589–607.

152. Jack Williams, "The Ozone Hole: A Story of Healing and Hope." *Weatherwise*, vol. 71, no. 1 (2018): pp. 12–17.

153. Williams, "The Ozone Hole."

154. Tina Birmpili, "Montreal Protocol at 30: The Governance Structure, the Evolution, and the Kigali Amendment." *Comptes Rendus Geoscience*, vol. 350, no. 7 (2018): pp. 425–431.

155. Susan Solomon, et al., "Emergence of Healing in the Antarctic Ozone Layer." *Science*, vol. 353, no. 6296 (2016): pp. 269–274.

156. Birmpili, "Montreal Protocol at 30," p. 426; Paul A. Newman, "The Way Forward for Montreal Protocol Science." *Comptes Rendus Geoscience*, vol. 350, no. 7 (2018): pp. 442–447.

157. J. A. Mäder, et al., "Evidence for the Effectiveness of the Montreal Protocol to Protect the Ozone Layer." *Atmospheric Chemistry and Physics*, vol. 10 (2010): pp. 12161–1271.

158. Graham Epstein, et al., "Governing the Invisible Commons: Ozone Regulation and the Montreal Protocol." *International Journal of the Commons*, vol. 8, no. 2 (2014): pp. 337–360.

159. Lesley Wexler, "Limiting the Precautionary Principle: Weapons Regulation in the Face of Scientific Uncertainty." *UC Davis Law Review*, vol. 39 (2005): p. 459.

160. John Weckert and James Moor, "The Precautionary Principle in Nanotechnology." *International Journal of Applied Philosophy*, vol. 20, no. 2 (2006): pp. 191–204.

161. Communication from the Commission on the precautionary principle (COM(2000) 1 final of 2 February 2000).

162. Ibid.

163. Science for Environment Policy, "The Precautionary Principle: Decision Making under Uncertainty," Future Brief no. 18 (2017). Produced for the European Commission DG Environment by the Science Communication Unit, UWE, Bristol. Available at: http://ec.europa.eu/science-environment-policy.

164. Thomas Lord, "The Antarctic Treaty System and the Peaceful Governance of Antarctica: The Role of the ATS in Promoting Peace at the Margins of the World." *The Polar Journal*, vol. 10, no. 1 (2020): pp. 3–21.

165. Gillian Triggs, "The Antarctic Treaty System: A Model of Legal Creativity and Cooperation." In Science Diplomacy: Antarctica, Science, and the Governance of International Spaces, ed. P. A. Berkman, et al. (Smithsonian, 2011): pp. 39–49.

166. Neil Gilbert, "A Continent for Peace and Science." In Exploring the Last Continent: An Introduction to Antarctica, ed. Liggett, Daniela, Bryan Storey, and Yvonne Cook (Springer International Publishing, 2015): pp. 327–359.

167. Christopher C. Joyner, "Nonmilitarization of the Antarctic: The Interplay of Law and Geopolitics." *Naval War College Review*, vol. 42, no. 4 (1989): pp. 83–104.

168. Joyner, "Nonmilitarization of the Antarctic."

169. Triggs, "The Antarctic Treaty System," p. 40.

170. Triggs, "The Antarctic Treaty System," p. 40.

171. Crawford, "Explaining Arctic Peace."

172. Yen-Chiang Chang and Mehran Idris Khan, "May China Fish in the Arctic Ocean?" *Sustainability*, vol. 13 (2021): p. 11875.

173. Michael Byers, "Arctic Security and Outer Space." *Scandinavian Journal of Military Studies*, vol. 3, no. 1 (2020): pp. 183–196.

174. Elinor Ostrom, *Governing the Commons: The Evolution of Institutions for Collective Action* (Cambridge University Press, 1990).

175. Garrett Hardin, "Extensions of the Tragedy of the Commons." *Science*, vol. 280, no. 5364 (1998): pp. 682–683.

176. Thomas Dietz, Elinor Ostrom, and Paul C. Stern, "The Struggle to Govern the Commons." *Science*, vol. 302, no. 5652 (2003): pp. 1907–1912.

177. Crawford, "Explaining Arctic Peace."

178. Denise Garcia, "Generating Successful Global Governance: Creating Comity in the Arctic." In *On Governance*, ed. Robert Rotberg (McGill-Queen's University Press, CIGI Press, 2015): pp. 135–150.

179. Garcia, "Global Commons Law."

180. Crawford, "Explaining Arctic Peace."

181. Thomas S. Axworthy and Ryan Dean, "Changing the Arctic Paradigm from Cold War to Cooperation: How Canada's Indigenous Leaders Shaped the Arctic Council." *The Yearbook of Polar Law Online*, vol. 5, no. 1 (2013): pp. 7–43.

182. Crawford, "Explaining Arctic Peace."

183. Michael Williams Wiper, *Geopolitics in the Arctic: Why Do Some Nations Have a Militarized Strategic Emphasis while Others Diplomatic?* (PhD Diss. 2020).

184. Comprehensive Test Ban Treaty Organization database: https://www.ctbto.org/specials/who-we-are/.

185. Lisa Tabassi, "The Nuclear Test Ban: Lex Lata or de Lege Ferenda?" *Journal of Conflict and Security Law*, vol. 14 (2009): p. 309.

186. Comprehensive Test Ban Treaty Organization database, "Text of the Treaty." https://www.ctbto.org/the-treaty/status-of-signature-and-ratification/.

187. Tabassi, "The Nuclear Test Ban: Lex Lata or de Lege Ferenda?"

188. Nimar S. Arora, Stuart Russell, and Erik Sudderth. "NET-VISA: Network Processing Vertically Integrated Seismic Analysis." *Bulletin of the Seismological Society of America*, vol. 103, no. 2A (2013): pp. 709–729.

Chapter 3
The dynamics of international diplomacy

High-stakes diplomacy at the United Nations

The diplomatic process on autonomous weapons that started at the United Nations in 2014 preceded the full embrace by most major powers of AI into their militaries. It was in 2017, with the publication of the first national AI strategies by Canada, and then by China in the same year, that a more public inclusion of the discourse on AI in the military realm started in earnest. However, there has been reluctance to extend the scope of the diplomatic talks in Geneva from autonomous weapons to the broader field of the militarization of AI and, within that realm, the weaponization of AI. The diplomacy in Geneva has nonetheless shone a bright light on the need to reflect on the broader aspects of the militarization of AI, and has already brought into clearer focus the uncertainty and peril created by AI-enabled autonomous weapon systems. Additionally, negotiations in Geneva have demonstrated how countries view the responsible uses of military AI.[1] My proposal for a *common good governance-*based military framework on military AI, as a global public good, is a fitting way forward.

On the United Nations stage, the diplomatic dynamics attempting to set limits on autonomy in warfare have been thorny and complex. It all started in 2010 with the first reports to the Human Rights Council by rapporteurs Philip Alston and the late Christof Heyns (Chapter 1). They warned that autonomous weapons would pave the way toward a dehumanization of warfare where humans would be removed from the decision-making process and killing machines would decide whom to kill and what to destroy. AI-assisted autonomous weapon systems were not yet on the horizon. Then, due to a Franco-German diplomatic initiative, diplomacy moved from the Human Rights Council to a negotiating forum known as the Convention on Certain Conventional Weapons (CCW). The last notable moment for the CCW had been the successful negotiation of an international treaty that prohibited blinding laser weapons back in 1995.[2] This is why many were skeptical when, in 2014, at the United Nations in Geneva, deliberations on autonomous weapons started in earnest; the CCW had not proved effective in anything since the treaty banning blinding weapons. Hence, there was controversy about whether this was the most suitable forum. The archaic negotiation rule of consensus presides over the procedures, which means that even one dissenting country can block progress, as consensus is viewed not as a useful diplomatic tool but rather as full unanimity. The CCW became known

The AI Military Race. Denise Garcia, Oxford University Press. © Denise Garcia (2023).
DOI: 10.1093/oso/9780192864604.003.0004

as a breeding ground for stalemates and where good intentions went to perish. A *common good governance* framework would be a way to move the diplomatic process in an inclusive way.

Despite years of concerted activist work by the Campaign to Stop Killer Robots, growing international public opinion against autonomous killing machines, and most AI scientists, along with the United Nations Secretary-General and Nobel Peace laureates, standing against them, diplomatic negotiations have been plagued by discordant exchanges between the militarized major powers and the rest of the countries in the negotiating room. The positions of the former were in large part determined by their continued desire to develop autonomous systems and increase their use of AI to assist them in achieving military superiority in a world of intensifying geopolitical rivalry. The latter group consisted of most countries in the world. They wished to have strict limits on what is being called the dehumanization of warfare in the face of increasingly autonomous machines that kill without human oversight. In their view, automating violence further means an increasingly more insecure and precarious future. In this scenario, international law will be further eroded, and the global norms of peace and security will not be respected.

Back in 2010, Philip Alston, the first United Nations rapporteur on extrajudicial, summary, or arbitrary executions, alerted the Human Rights Council to the notion that greater autonomy in warfare by using systems with less human oversight and control would impinge upon the protections afforded by human rights law. As a result, the right to dignity and to life would be in jeopardy. Back then he called upon the Council to address the legal, moral, ethical, and political implications of this worrying development. Alston's pioneering work was followed by that of Christof Heyns. Heyns, who passed away in March 2021, made an ineradicable mark on the discussions and influenced countries to think about the centrality of the right to dignity in the diplomatic discussions.[3] Heyns, who was always the tallest person in the room, was also a towering legal figure, highly regarded by everyone as affable and thoughtful. His untimely death left all despondent. Being from South Africa, he was keen to think from a developing world perspective. His position in the first seminal report published in 2013[4] was that the autonomous weapons race was diverting essential resources to yet another arms race that would weaken peace and security. Arms do not provide greater security, they promote human suffering. His trenchant criticism was directed at the militarized countries that protect the lives of their soldiers by conducting wars that further remove the human dimension from the battlefield. Are victorious wars about technological superiority, then? Heyns said the arguments posed by the superpowers did not stand up to scrutiny: the quest for wars without casualties represents a failure of moral standards by the powerful over the technologically dispossessed.

A nuanced and principled appreciation of the world derives from human intuition, not from algorithms. The main questions raised by Alston and Heyns were about the march toward the dehumanization of war, and subsequently about responsibility and criminal accountability for future atrocities that arise from waging autonomous wars. Additionally, as international legal scholars of renown, they were all the more aware of the framework that makes most wars unlawful in international relations. The threshold for initiating war since the adoption of the United Nations Charter in 1945 is set very high (Chapter 4): Wars can only be waged in self-defense or when the Security Council authorizes them. This international norm against territorial annexation has thus far prevented World War III.[5] Alston and Heyns warned that the continuing automation of weapon systems would create "riskless wars" for the superpowers. Riskless wars would contribute to a world where wars occur more frequently as there is lower risk of casualties for the technologically advanced military powers.

The diplomatic negotiations in Geneva did not allay the concerns Alston and Heyns raised a decade earlier. A new innovative treaty would have created novel global governance setting the limits on autonomy in war. Instead, the will of most states in the world was disgracefully suppressed by the few countries that wanted to continue pursuing the development of autonomous systems.[6] These are the technologically advanced countries and the ones who also wish to attain dominance in the domain of AI technologies (especially represented by Russia, the United States, Israel, and India during the last round of diplomacy). These countries rejected the presence of "human control" and a new legally binding instrument in the final text. Their views are that current international humanitarian law (IHL) would suffice to tackle the challenges presented by the use of autonomous systems. The diplomatic failure and inability to reach any agreement happened despite the fact that in the last two years of a decade of negotiations there was a growing chorus of consensus about the shape and nature of the new form of global governance through international law. It should be legally binding and would be comprised of some prohibitions (proscriptions) and some regulations. This would mean that certain modes of autonomy devoid of human control and predictability would be prohibited. Additionally, some systems that target humans would also be made unlawful. The regulations—also legally binding—would apply to various other aspects of the use of autonomous systems, such as fail-safes, duration and context of operations, and the possibility of deactivation to avoid errors.

The coalescence of opinions on the shape and nature of the new global governing rules within a new international treaty became even clearer when the International Committee of the Red Cross (ICRC), the guardian and custodian of IHL, announced its position in May 2021. This was a watershed moment that was intended to galvanize the opinion of most states (Chapter 4). The ICRC called on states to enact new international law—namely, legally binding prohibitions and regulations to limit the increasing levels of autonomy and use of AI in warfare. The ICRC also stated that existing IHL will not suffice to address the challenges posed by AI-assisted autonomous systems. As a result of the high moral ground set by the ICRC position, a sense of renewed hope and an expectation of a breakthrough grew more intense. However, the ICRC's clearly expressed opinion did not quite move the major powers, who remained unyielding and held their recalcitrant positions, to the frustration of all other countries. This was a raw display of power politics by a handful of powerful countries, contrasting sharply with the informed and enthusiastic view of the majority, who clamored for change. Most countries also thought that there was an abuse of the time-honored rule of consensus. Many regarded it as a diplomatic tool to include more opinions and reach higher ground, not as a stratagem to be used to derail and obstruct progress. There was a sense of loss of legitimacy in that most countries felt betrayed by the lack of good faith among the minority of countries that sought to impose their devalued worldview.

In this latter view, the minority seeks to continue to add gains to its weapons industries and privilege a vision of the world in which more arms mean more security. But what exactly do we mean when we think of "security"? Let us answer this question by examining it in the light of other world events. After the current pandemic, and with the unequivocal scientific certainty that the world has only a few more years left to act decisively to avert the worst of the climate crisis, it is irresponsible to continue supporting a framework of threats to security as totally military in nature. According to Nathan A. Sears—a scholar on the nature of existential risks—there has been a noticeable material transformation in international politics.[7] The main factors underlying this transformation are the existential threats—namely, nuclear war and climate change—that loom over the future of humanity. However, this shift has not been matched by a change in the practice of security. States continue to rely on the balance of power, self-help, and the use of military force, none of which is appropriate to confront these risks. Consequently, there is a misalignment between what threatens states and people, and the way they seek protection from these threats. Security should entail finding ways to withstand the existential threats and not solely continuing to fight wars by military means. A *common good governance* framework would be inclusive of all these views.

The dynamics of the negotiations at the United Nations over the past few years have been delayed by the global public health pandemic that started in 2020 with the appearance of the novel Severe Acute Respiratory Syndrome Coronavirus 2 (SARS-CoV-2) that causes the coronavirus disease of 2019 (COVID-19). The pandemic showed that the most heavily armed countries did not perform better at protecting their citizens against death from the disease caused by the virus.[8] On the contrary, most of the heavily militarized nations fared worse than others (especially India, Russia, and the United States). The worldview that the continuing acquisition of expensive weapons creates a more robust form of national security could be on its way to falling out of favor. It is becoming unjustifiable to accumulate so much armament. At this critical juncture for humanity, countries must privilege spending on what really matters: tackling the climate crisis and preventing the next pandemic.[9] My alumna Paula Domit said in a class discussion one day during the worst phase of the pandemic: "Do you feel safe about your country weaponizing AI or amassing nuclear weapons, or would you perhaps feel more assured by your country taking all measures necessary to prevent the next inevitable pandemic?" The idea of *common good governance* I present here presupposes a recognition that most threats to national security today are not of a military nature; rather, they are economic, societal, and planetary in scope.[10]

Instability and insecurity

The major military powers have been redefining their national security in terms of their pursuit of superiority in the realm of AI. Many countries have already announced their national plans to do just this. The Chinese have termed the search for AI-assisted weapon systems as *"intelligentized* warfare," which represents a military revolution characterized by ubiquitous data-rich networks of autonomous and sensor-based intelligent systems.[11] The advent of the fourth industrial revolution creates incentives for states to include not only AI but also quantum, nanotechnology, biotechnology, and other forms of technology into their military spheres.[12] The fourth industrial revolution is qualitatively differently from the preceding ones by rapidly fusing the biological, digital, and physical domains of life on Earth. The technologies that fall under the umbrella term "AI" feature prominently. Indeed, the Chinese approach to *"intelligentized* warfare" epitomizes the third revolution in warfare. The confluence of the fourth industrial revolution and the third revolution in warfare may create some opportunities, but also harbingers risks.

The militarization and the weaponization of AI are both underway and this phenomenon will impact on international peace and security in appreciable ways. It is already creating a renewed sense of rivalry and competition that is manifesting in the quest to develop more weapon systems. The allocation of funds devoted to AI systems has also been on the rise (Chapter 1).[13] Will this march toward including AI lead to a redistribution of power and a sense that world security and stability are threatened? Along with other scholars, I contend that the impact of AI will be disruptive of the prevailing, yet volatile, balance of power.[14] The need to preserve strategic stability is where there may be some common ground: self-interested states always work toward maintaining their own national security. In principle, all countries want to maintain international stability to carry on commerce, trade, and other human activities. It is worth noting that "strategic stability" is a concept related to nuclear stability, the centrality of the notion of deterrence, and the absence of incentives to use nuclear weapons first. The concept then came to encompass more widely the reliance on conventional weapons, cyber security, and emerging technologies. However, it continues to be based on the idea that the international system is changeable and precarious.[15] This perpetuates the view that more arms mean greater security. A more appropriate view would be to regard strategic stability as the consequence of a global security environment wherein states can maintain peaceful and harmonious international relations.[16]

The major military powers see AI as a critical magnifier of their present and future nuclear capabilities. Most of the countries seeking to militarize AI also possess nuclear weapons. According to the authoritative assessment by the Stockholm International Peace Research Institute (SIPRI), machine learning algorithms are already unpredictable and lack transparency (i.e., it is hard to understand how the machine arrives at the outcome). Therefore, command and control of nuclear systems are too critical to international security to be left to algorithms. This signals an agreement not to integrate machine learning and autonomy into the command-and-control systems of nuclear weapons.[17] Nonetheless, the nuclear states do see AI as a vital amplifier of their future military capabilities.[18] The risks are not trivial, though. The use of AI may heighten the risk of inadvertent use and, as a result, an escalation that could be magnified because of the loss of human control. The unpredictability and unreliability of AI could make for a precarious international system.[19]

The costs and benefits of the use of AI must be considered against the background of the broader geopolitical landscape, and how they may cause instability. Altmann and Sauer warn that the perils of operating machine-learning weapons reside in the inability to accurately foresee all outcomes in advance.[20] This is especially the case when different countries' algorithms interact with each other during operations. This lack of capacity to predict outcomes hampers the ability of humans to act as overseers in case things go wrong. Machine learning—succinctly defined by Sauer as the use of algorithms and advanced statistical models to improve task performance—is still limited to an extremely narrow set of tasks. Machine learning is "greedy (i.e., hungry for immense amounts of data), brittle (i.e., failing when confronted with a task that differs slightly from what it was trained for), and opaque (i.e., generating unexplainable outputs, essentially rendering it a black box that is impossible to debug)."[21]

It is worth bearing in mind the two dimensions of instability: the first is arms proliferation and a horizontal and vertical arms race.[22] This refers, firstly, to proliferation beyond militarized countries and, secondly, to destabilizing accumulations by key military powers that would exacerbate the security dilemma. Autonomous systems are easier to build than nuclear weapons, which require extensive apparatus such as centrifuges, high-speed fuses, and controlled use of rare raw materials. Autonomous systems are likely to become available to a wider range of actors, including nonstate actors, because their implementation is more about the software. The implication of this is that a potentially destabilizing military race is already taking place. The centrality of software in autonomous systems makes them less reliant on traditional, quantitative, weapons-counting arms control. The software can be more readily duplicated and interfered with by manipulating computer network operations. On the battlefield, characterized by a dearth of data, this means that unpredictability and vulnerability compound uncertainty.

The second dimension of instability is escalation due to accidents or lack of communication.[23] Three factors are relevant here: casualty avoidance, cost reduction, and the implications of weapon swarming (the use of small or miniaturized systems operating together); this explains why it is likely that countries would more often resort to autonomous systems in surprise attacks that could lead to crises. Casualty avoidance is prompted by the attempt to keep soldiers out of harm's way and reduce political risks, especially in democracies. Autonomous systems may lead to cost reductions as 3D printing becomes increasingly common. Autonomy can bring military advantages but creates vulnerabilities that create risks because it removes the human as the overseer. The costs of the deployment of autonomous weapon systems far outweigh the benefits. Global security will be harmed as more actors, many not accountable to legal frameworks under international law, start to play a more prominent role by using these systems. The interaction of different-origin algorithms increases the likelihood of the precipitous escalation of a crisis into violent conflict.[24]

For all these reasons, AI may not reach the levels of reliability and trustworthiness required by many military applications where life is at stake. What is certain is that the pursuit of the weaponization of AI is indeed leading to a greater risk of military races.[25] Furthermore, the premature application of AI in the military may reduce and not enhance compliance with IHL. In sum, new global governance is the guardrail needed to foster prudence to avert a reckless AI military race toward the promised yet unfulfilled role of AI technologies.

Because of the military significance ascribed to autonomy and AI-assisted autonomy by the militarized great powers, the creation of global governing norms will be arduous. If we zoom in and examine autonomous weapons as a yardstick, new global governance will not codify a prohibition on a category of weapons; instead, it will create a positive obligation to retain meaningful human control over the use of force. This is qualitatively different from previous attempts to regulate powerful technologies, such as that needed to generate nuclear energy.[26] In other words, this form of governance is not about a specific category of weapons, but entails figuring out when a machine or a human being should make a particular decision or perform a function, particularly in the last two stages of the targeting cycle, which are the critical functions. States must create global governance norms to limit autonomy in critical functions. Unrestricted action will bring short-term military advantages that will quickly be dwarfed by calamitous long-term strategic and ethical risks. During the new paradigm-shifting transformation forged by the delegation of decision-making in war to machines, Frank Sauer was the first to pose the question succinctly: Who or what—human or machine—is deciding what, when, and where when deadly force is applied?[27]

In 2018, the Institute of Electrical and Electronics Engineers (IEEE) Global Initiative—the largest professional association of engineers—published a report on the ethics of "Autonomous and Intelligent Systems" entitled "Ethically Aligned Design: A Vision for Prioritizing Human Well-being with Autonomous and Intelligent Systems." The report was drafted in consultation with 250 global thought leaders and experts in related areas. They affirmed that development and adoption of autonomous weapons will be widespread and therefore an AI military race will take place. Several issues that were noted in this groundbreaking report are worth highlighting. First, the deployment of autonomous weapons will lead to geopolitical instability as a result of arms races. As a key recommendation, the report states:

> It is unethical to design, develop, or engineer autonomous weapon systems without ensuring that they remain reliably subject to meaningful human control. Systems created to act outside of the boundaries of "appropriate human judgment,"

"effective human control," or "meaningful human control," violate fundamental human rights and undermine legal accountability for weapons use.

Consequently, widespread abuses of human rights are probable. Upholding dignity, the foundational human right, remains paramount.[28] Second, the deployment of systems with automated reactions is likely to lead to a rapid escalation that is so fast that humans will be left unable to intervene in a timely fashion. As a result, accountability can be jeopardized. Systems already in use that would highlight the complexities of human intervention after activation are the C-RAM, the Iron Dome, and the Phalanx. By the same token, it is probable that autonomous weapons will be used for covert attacks that can be virtually nonattributable. Attacks in general may be hard to attribute to the source, and machine learning systems will make it all the more difficult to determine the source. The report suggests, along with the ICRC, that the deployment of unpredictable systems should be deemed illegal. As Eugenio Garcia has noted: "dehumanizing warfare will increase the likelihood that political leaders will authorize resort to force to settle disputes, since their own troops would be 'safe.'"[29]

Global AI militarization

The area of military AI is vast due to the distributed nature of the technology. This means that there are several technologies that fall under the umbrella term AI, including machine learning, deep learning, image recognition, process automation, and speech translation, among others.[30] Most of these technologies are created by and used in the civilian realm. But militaries are increasingly trying to militarize many of their aspects and weaponize them by attracting investments.[31] The discussions at the United Nations only deal with one related aspect of autonomy in weapon systems, and touch upon the uses of AI to enable and enhance such systems. However, they fail to address the broader aspects of the militarization of AI.

It is important to bear in mind that, in the United States, important technical breakthroughs in recent decades have been associated with the Department of Defense (DoD), which has been leading priorities and funding research.[32] The DoD's Defense Advanced Research Projects Agency (DARPA) announced a $2 billion, 5-year investment plan on AI in 2018 in addition to the already ongoing investments in research and development.[33] However, it is in the civilian realm where most of the creative energy and investments are to be found.

The United States' Defense Innovation Board—tasked by the Department of Defense—has adopted pioneering ethical principles for the use of AI in 2020, after a broad process of consultation with experts and civil society. The board sees the United States as being in an AI competition with authoritarian military powers that are not pursuing applications based upon legal, ethical, and moral norms. Ethical uses of AI must be responsible (human judgment in all phases), equitable (avoid biases), traceable (transparent and auditable), reliable (robust and across the entire life cycle), and governable (avoid harm and ensure deactivation is possible).

It is also in the United States where the most vibrant landscape in the private sector, and the most conducive atmosphere for the continuing development of AI, is thriving, even if China is progressing rapidly.[34] Given its central position in the development of AI, the United States could position itself to lead international diplomatic efforts with other powers aspiring to develop AI capabilities. The more agreed global rules there are, the greater the predictability and stability. Even though there is an inclination internationally to discuss initiatives within the AI civilian domain (as indicated in Chapter 1), this does not translate to a comprehensive effort in the military realm. In reality, there is a reluctance to coordinate developments in the military realm, while the growing competition to attain supremacy in the field of AI is marked by suspicion and a lack of trust.

The position of the nuclear-armed powers during the meetings at the United Nations is an indicator of their inclination vis-à-vis the broader aspects of the militarization of AI. They are all seeking to preserve their ability not to enter into any agreement that would constrain their quest for superiority. The nuclear powers seek to do so without the constraints of new global governing rules under international law. This is the case for China, but in an even more pronounced way for Russia and the United States, in particular. Israel, India, and the United Kingdom also hold dubious positions that most of the time set up roadblocks to any progress in the diplomatic talks. As the talks stall, their efforts to continue the militarization of AI progress swiftly.[35] What these nuclear powers are abandoning is the opportunity to create greater predictability and stability by forming new global norms. Without their participation, a descent into a more unstable and war-prone world becomes all the more certain.

The prevailing nuclear geopolitical reality is worrisome. The addition of AI to the military landscape is not a judicious choice. The nuclear-armed states' arsenals currently number 13,080 nuclear weapons. Listed according to the size of their arsenal, the nuclear states are: the United States, Russia, the United Kingdom, France, China, India, Pakistan, Israel, and the Democratic People's Republic of Korea (North Korea). Ninety percent of the 13,080 existing weapons are American and Russian; of these, 3,825 are currently deployed on the level of high operational alert; this is an increase from 3,720 previously. Compounding this trend, Russia has increased its stockpile by 180 warheads, despite the fact that it has also been dismantling retired warheads, as the United States has been doing too. Nonetheless, all nuclear-armed states have announced plans to modernize or create new systems.[36] This move to build more nuclear weapons is in clear violation of the international legal obligations that states agreed to comply with when they ratified the 1968 Nuclear Non-Proliferation Treaty (NPT). This landmark treaty is a cornerstone of the stability of the international system. According to Article 6 of the treaty, the high-contracting parties agreed to completely disarm their arsenals and eventually reduce to zero nuclear weapons. In total, 191 countries are high-contracting parties to the NPT—that is, they have ratified it and are legally bound to comply with its global norms. Some countries—South

Sudan, India, Pakistan, and Israel—have never signed the NPT but everyone else did. Signature, an initial commitment, is the first step toward ratification. North Korea joined the NPT in 1985, but withdrew in 2003.[37] All the nuclear powers now embrace the pursuit of military AI as vital for their national security.[38]

In the United States, the Congressional Budget Office is mandated to estimate the decade-long costs for nuclear weapons every two years. The projection for the period up to 2030 is $634 billion to modernize the current American nuclear arsenal, which represents a 28% increase from the previous recorded period. Most systems are reaching the end of their life cycle.[39] Therefore, the American Congress could still decide not to spend the estimated amount, and could even decide to reallocate it to more pressing areas in national security, such as tackling the climate emergency or preparing for the next pandemic. Countries seeking to modernize their nuclear stocks are tied to a narrow view of national security: nuclear weapons provide security and prestige.[40] This is a posture that was increasingly endorsed after World War II, when the primacy of national security precluded considerations of the global common good. Furthermore, it is a posture that views threats to national security as being only of a military nature, such as war. Therefore, arming themselves with nuclear weapons is a continuation of old and enshrined ways to protect national security. This outdated framework must be replaced with an appreciation of the fact that nuclear weapons do not provide security.[41] They are extremely dangerous systems that could imperil life on Earth. In the wake of the COVID-19 pandemic, it is irresponsible to continue to maintain a framework of threats to security as exclusively military in nature. Even in the United States, the richest country in the world, hospitals were overwhelmed on several occasions during the pandemic, and the same happened in other nuclear nations that continue to privilege a view of the world where security emanates from the possession of weapons. A wiser allocation of treasury resources away from the accumulation of weapons seems both judicious and far-sighted. More enlightened and humanistic views of international security are required even in the light of the current wars, such as in Ukraine. Such views are necessary to shift the focus away from allocating financial resources to nuclear renewal and toward addressing threats of a nonmilitary nature. This shift could pave the way for more goodwill among nations and the prevention of war.

Global governance action: Champions and detractors

Creating global governance related to AI will be one of this century's main challenges.[42] A daunting part of this enterprise will be establishing *common good governance* for applications of AI in the military realm. The formidable task of forging agreed global norms that would constitute a governing framework faces two main hindrances. The first is the military value that the major powers, especially the nuclear-armed states, ascribe to AI. The second is the nature of AI itself. AI is an enabling technology that may amplify areas of human endeavor by enhancing or imperiling them. In other words, AI is an umbrella term that encompasses several technologies or computation techniques with a vast range of applications, including machine learning, recommendation tools, image recognition, and speech translation, among others. In many ways, AI is more analogous to electricity.[43] The stumbling blocks encountered in the process of establishing new global norms under international law for autonomous weapons—one critical aspect of the militarization of AI—serve as an indicator of how arduous it will be to set up governance norms in the broader area of military AI.[44]

Instances of past successes in international cooperation that shaped the creation of innovative global governance counted on the leadership of champion states. These embrace new causes and spearhead them across the international political spectrum.[45] In the case of the most successful environmental treaty to date, the landmark 1987 Montreal Protocol on Substances that Deplete the Ozone Layer, the United States was the champion state and backed the international negotiating process.[46] By working closely with scientists and Mostafa Tolba, the then director of the United Nations Environmental Program and the chairperson of the negotiations, nations constructed a set of global governance rules that effectively engaged in the largest ever planetary repair mission: restoration of the ozone layer.[47] The Montreal Protocol has been ratified by all countries; it is universal and remains able to adapt to and include new technological developments.[48] In general, the creation of new global governance has become more complex in the last decade. The last two major examples of breakthrough in global cooperation took place in 2015 with the United Nations Sustainable Development Goals and the Paris Agreement to tackle climate change. These are two concrete global maps directing multisectoral action at the local and international levels. These achievements are deemed to be pathbreaking in devising solutions to the most pressing problems facing humanity.[49]

I attribute the rising complexity of global governance creation to five factors. The first is the upsurge of populism in several countries that drive their leaders to look inward and not toward conceiving concerted global solutions to problems—for instance, the example set by the United States during the presidency of Donald Trump. The supposed "leader of the free world" behaved obscenely and coarsely in abandoning the observance of time-honored norms of international law. He contributed to the erosion of many previously vital international frameworks for peace and stability. This contempt for international civic duty gave license to others to do the same and for totalitarian rulers to become more assertive of their own power (Brazil, China, India, Turkey, and Hungary are some examples).[50] On the United Nations diplomatic scene, this means there is now much arduous work to be done to reach a compromise and to find solutions to a number of issues on the agenda of nations. In many ways, the world was dispossessed of a shining example: a champion state that could advance causes leading to the betterment of humanity. The European Union could take up that position, but it has been too reserved in its actions.

The second factor is a multiplicity of converging global crises, all in need of rigorous global action, as highlighted by leading scientists: biodiversity loss, the climate emergency and the prevention of the next pandemic are examples of intersecting crises.[51] The third is the dispersed nature of power throughout the international system of nations. This means that many more countries have become prominent economically and therefore feel they can exert power on the global stage as well (examples here are China and India).[52] They see the tragic withdrawal of the United States as opening an opportunity for them to become more forceful, but they lack a well-defined vision for forging *common good governance*. The fourth is an inability of current leaders to think in long-term perspectives. In many ways they are squandering the opportunity to work on building a restored world, even though the science is unequivocal: the world only has a few years left to avert the worst of the climate crises.[53] The fifth is renewed rising rivalry among the major powers that is occurring partly as a result of some of the factors mentioned herein, but also because of a mounting climate of suspicion and lack of trust in each other. The resulting circumstances are tragic for the world: most countries are not focusing on what they should be doing and keep diverting their resources, investmentstreasure, and time to matters that will do little to repair the planet or ensure its health and safeguard that of its people. This imperative need for repair work has been expressed with great urgency by scientists all over the world, who have established beyond any doubt the scientific links between climate and health.[54]

The matter examined in this book—the march toward autonomous killing, and the associated context of the use of AI and how this will change the international order—is a looming global problem that could exacerbate the tribulations the world is already currently facing, but especially accelerate the slide to states of war and conflict. In the light of this, it is worth asking: What do champion states do? How could they influence the creation of new global norms? Champion states can perform several functions. The first function is constituency building, where the champion states exert peer-to-peer pressure to convince other states to embrace the relevant cause. They do so by first creating a coalition of like-minded states from several parts of the world that work with them toward achieving a goal. The second function is momentum building. Typically, a champion state is motivated to come onto the world stage to lead a cause when there are already previously built avenues for action as a result of persuasion through *transnational networked cooperation* by a multitude of other actors and entities that helped to elevate the matter to prominence (Chapter 5). Then, the champion state builds deeper links with scientists and civil society alike to build momentum toward negotiations. The third function the champion state carries out is the consolidation of emerging norms through new treaties or other forms of agreement. These will not only cement the otherwise dispersed attention to the issue, but also pave the way toward concrete outcomes.

Transnational networked cooperation is advanced and managed to elevate and maintain the momentum of resistance to autonomous killing on the international agenda (Chapter 1). It also lead to a widespread recognition that unpredictable systems that "cannot be used in compliance with international law are de facto outlawed and their use must be prevented." These are the words that appeared in the position statement by a group of 16 countries that formed at the end of the discussions in 2021 at the United Nations in Geneva: Austria, Belgium, Brazil, Chile, Finland, Germany, Ireland, Italy, Luxemburg, Mexico, the Netherlands, New Zealand, Norway, South Africa, Sweden, and Switzerland.[55]

However, there is no explicit champion state. Instead, there are supporters and detractors, which complicates the creation of novel global governance. This has happened before. Previous global cases of cooperation to restrict or prohibit the means and methods of war reached stalemate. This happened because of the consensus-bound nature of the negotiating forum, whereby the possibilities for any breakthroughs were stifled by a minority of detractors (Chapter 5). As a result, negotiations moved outside the United Nations, to the General Assembly, where the rules of procedure follow the precept of two-thirds majority. It is worth examining the role of a few prominent states to see how they position themselves within the global governance creation process. The background to keep in mind is the pursuit of global supremacy in AI. Both China and the United States played pioneering roles by publishing their positions on the various aspects of the militarization of AI from the outset, before the international debate started in earnest in 2012–2013, at the United Nations Human Rights Council.

The quest for hegemony in AI is evident in the plans pursued by China, which are characterized by a fusion of the military and the civilian spheres. The separation between innovations in the civilian and the military realms is hard to distinguish.[56] The Chinese are preparing for a future where warfare is *"intelligentized,"* a concept that captures the accelerating integration of AI into military innovations.[57] This goal became a nationwide priority in 2017 with the publication of the New Generation Artificial Intelligence Development Plan.[58] The goal of achieving military superiority in AI is to be reached by 2035.[59] As Elsa Kania explains, as early as 2011 the Chinese coined a definition of an "AI weapon" as "a weapon that utilizes AI to pursue, distinguish, and destroy enemy targets automatically."[60] With the upper hand in addressing the issues nationally, in 2013 China supported the beginning of the discussions in Geneva at the Human Rights Council.[61] China alerted participants to the potential of autonomous systems to jeopardize the international strategic balance. When the discussions moved to another negotiating forum at the United Nations in Geneva, the CCW, China recognized the difficulties in autonomous systems complying with IHL and called for preventive measures.[62] In 2018, China called for a ban on the use of "fully autonomous weapons," but not on development and production.[63] At the end of 2021, China affirmed that it would be amenable to a future legally binding treaty, but doubted whether this was the appropriate time.

The United States spearheaded the debate when it became the first country to publish its position on autonomy in weapon systems in 2012, and then updated it as a directive in 2017. The publication offered the first definition of autonomous weapons as a weapon system that, once activated, can select and engage targets without further intervention by a human operator. Essentially, the directive includes an affirmation that "the system design incorporates the necessary capabilities to allow commanders and operators to exercise *appropriate levels of human judgment* in the use of force."[64] The United States delegation at the United Nations always insisted on the terminology that it had introduced—*appropriate levels of human judgment*—much to the annoyance of civil society groups that preferred the formulation *meaningful human control* instead. However, the directive provides useful steps for the creation of a form of global governance. It includes five criteria that a system must meet before being approved for deployment:

1) By design, systems should include options for operators to exercise appropriate levels of human judgment;
2) The system should complete the engagement in a timeframe that is consistent with the commander and the operator's plans. Otherwise, operation termination is an option;
3) Fail-safe and override capacities should be in place to minimize failure or unintended engagements;
4) Systems must be reliable;
5) Legal review by the general counsel of the DoD must be in place.

Expert views have signaled that these criteria would not necessarily impede the approval of certain systems that could in fact be worrisome, while others insist that as long as there are weapon reviews that follow these steps, this would ensure that they comply with IHL.[65] This latter view was espoused by Michael Meier, Attorney-Adviser at the Office of the Legal Adviser, Political-Military Affairs of the United States Department of State. He was the brilliant head of the United States delegation to the discussions on autonomous weapons in Geneva in their first years. I once went to lunch with him at the Pentagon, and I also invited him to speak at Northeastern University. In these first years of the discussions in Geneva, the United States was adamant about the fact that as long as there were weapons reviews, there could be safe deployment of autonomy. Meier and I discussed the obligation that states are under in terms of IHL to carry out legal reviews before the deployment of any weapon system.[66]

Two pillars upheld the American diplomatic view. The first is that weapons reviews would suffice to assuage legal and operational concerns. Many would argue that that insistence masked a few problems. The first is that most states are not transparent about their reviews, and many do not have the capacity to conduct such technical reviews. The second problem is that the legal review would have to establish whether there would be sufficient predictability and reliability.[67] If we add machine learning systems, the inability to be certain about the system's behavior would be more glaring. Therefore, weapons reviews are no panacea and should not serve as a basis for the creation of global governance. It is an insufficient foundation. The second pillar underpinning the United States' diplomatic position rests on the idea that more autonomation would save lives and lower the risk of collateral damage because of the greater precision it enables.[68] The American delegation contended that "smart" weapons with autonomous functions can be more precise and have been shown to reduce risks of harm to civilians and civilian objects.[69] The "New Pentagon Papers" released in December 2021 seem to prove the contrary, and show evidence of decades of harm rather than safety brought about by "smart" weapons, including civilian casualties and lack of accountability.[70]

The European Union adopts a more humane attitude to military AI, distinguishing itself from the positions outlined here. However, the approach is not unified. Despite the progressive and continuing action by the European Parliament since 2018 calling for a prohibition on the use of autonomous systems without human control,[71] and the European Defense Fund (EDF) declaration that "the development of 'lethal autonomous weapons without the possibility for meaningful human control over the selection and engagement decisions when carrying out strikes against humans' shall be excluded from any EDF funding,"[72] the European Union has not yet presented a joint position in the negotiations in Geneva. Instead, some of its members are more prominent in expressing their own differing national views, especially France, Germany, and Austria. France and Germany would like to see a political agreement analogous to a nonbinding code of conduct, while Austria advocates for a legally binding prohibition. The ideal would be for the EU to put forward what is called at the EU level a "Common Position," which would be legally binding upon all member states.[73]

In January 2021, the EU Parliament issued guidelines that military AI should not replace human decisions. In April 2021, the EU Commission published the first ever international legal framework for making AI secure and ethical. The EU's pioneering global norm-shaping regulatory framework to establish secure and ethical AI places the EU in a position to lead the way in increasing cooperation globally and shape much-needed commonly agreed rules. The EU regulations address high-risk AI systems—even though the regulations do not apply to AI systems developed or used exclusively for military purposes—and call for mandatory human oversight throughout the AI systems' lifecycle in high-risk systems (Article 14) and consider the climate and health as high-impact sectors. The EU Parliament recently issued guidelines for the military use of AI to be human-centered and directed toward the service of humanity and the common good. Taken together, these instruments pave the way toward a human-security-focused approach that serves as a fruitful foundation for building up *common good governance*, in line with my concept of *humanity's security* that embraces a more inclusive and humanistic perspective of national security.

The United Nations and peace

The United Nations plays a role in convening the actors who create novel global governance and in summoning member states to conduct diplomacy at the highest level. One of the United Nations' main functions is to help advance international law through the creation of new norms of behavior for the member states. It is therefore essential to examine its role, as the future of the United Nations is indubitably associated with the formation of *common good governance* on AI.[74] The United Nations is also the only forum—a world assembly—where all 193 states can have a voice. In the still embryonic discussions on the governance of AI, most regions of the world remain largely excluded, most notably Latin America, Africa, South-East Asia, and the Middle East. The creation of global governance principles in the United Nations is a way to address this imbalance.

In May 2021, the United Nations Security Council met for the first time to discuss the role of emerging technologies, including AI, in peace and security. In the following month, also for the first time, the Security Council met to discuss how to keep the peace in cyberspace, advancing the topic of emerging technologies to the highest level of diplomatic efforts at the United Nations.[75] According to the United Nations Charter, the council has custodianship of the decisions on peace, security, the protection of civilians, and the use of force in international relations. The focus on emerging technologies and cyberspace as a novel domain of international relations marks a noteworthy evolution of the role of the Security Council in promoting much-needed norms for common behavior in these areas, which could originally not have been anticipated by the drafters of the charter. Member states spent $1 trillion in 2020 to restore networks that had been breached or to combat malicious uses.[76] The need to create a global cooperative framework on cyberspace, where states can pool their capacities and assist those who lack them, is critical. However, this discussion is beyond the scope of this book.

The role of the UN Secretary-General António Guterres has been central in leading the discussions internationally. He created a High-Level Panel for Digital Cooperation, which met in 2018–2019. In March 2019, the Secretary-General addressed the High-Level Panel with an ardent call for a prohibition against autonomous weapons:

Machines with the power and discretion to take lives without human involvement are politically unacceptable, morally repugnant and should be prohibited by international law.[77]

Based upon the panel's recommendations, after consultations with several different communities, from academia, the private sector, and governments to civil society, Guterres recommended a Road Map for Digital Cooperation in time for the United Nations' 75th anniversary.[78] This map aims to bridge the digital divide between developing and developed countries, to create transparency by curbing the spread of misinformation, to protect critical digital infrastructure, and to protect people's dignity. His Road Map for Digital Cooperation also seeks to restrain the weaponization of emerging technologies in general, and instead use such technologies solely for the common good of humanity. The creation of an AI advisory body could pave the way for the United Nations to serve as a clearing-house, a hub of knowledge that is inclusive of all member states, especially those with little or no technical capacity or technological advancements.

The proactive, action-oriented role that the UN Secretary-General assumed has firmly positioned the United Nations as the cornerstone for global action in emerging technologies.[79] For Guterres, four significant threats to global security today may endanger the future of humanity: mounting geopolitical tensions, the climate crisis, global mistrust, and applying the dark side of technology to commit abuses and crimes, spread hate and misinformation, and oppress people in an increasing number of countries. Technological advancements are fast outpacing diplomatic efforts, and the world is not prepared for the impact of the fourth industrial revolution. In the high-level segment of the United Nations General Assembly in September 2021, Guterres launched the Common Agenda, a comprehensive path forward to tackle the four main threats to humanity, utilizing the already existing platform of the United Nations Sustainable Development Goals. The Common Agenda is the result of a two-year-long crowd-sourcing consultation with thousands of people worldwide and represents a pivot toward protecting future generations, including the youth.[80] Admittedly, there is much work to be done to enact the Road Map for Digital Cooperation, especially in the areas of misinformation, the spread of hate speech, and the digital divide between poor and rich countries.

The Secretary-General of the United Nations has twice before played an important role in advancing the limits on the means and methods of warfare as a tool for the preservation of international peace and security. The first time was in 1995, with the publication of the "Agenda for Peace," where the then Secretary-General Boutros Boutros-Ghali called for "micro-disarmament"—that is, getting rid of small arms and light weapons that were the actual weapons of mass destruction in countries in conflict, in the aftermath of conflict, and in countries at peace but with high homicide rates. This call from the Secretary-General spearheaded a vigorous process of creation of new norms and international treaties to stem the illicit trafficking of small arms and also led to the 2012 Arms Trade Treaty, which was the first to regulate the international trade in conventional arms.

The second time was in 2018, with United Nations Secretary-General António Guterres' agenda for disarmament, "Securing our Common Future" (which I discuss later in this chapter). Guterres is concerned by a deteriorating international security environment, where a new Cold War is emerging within a highly complex world order that is marked by eroding respect for commonly agreed global norms of conduct and erosion of long-standing institutional commitments. He is also alarmed by the human and economic cost of militarization, and by the increasing risks from new weapon technologies. In this troubling new reality, the United Nations can use disarmament as tool for the maintenance of peace and security, and use it to foster the principles of humanity that aim to protect civilians and promote *common good governance.*

The AI for Good Global Movement

What I call the AI for Good Global Movement is comprised of initiatives that seek ways to use AI for the benefit of humanity—that is, for the common good in general, and specifically to find ways to use AI for humanitarian purposes, particularly but not limited to implementing the United Nations Sustainable Development Goals (SDGs) and to improving humanitarian relief.[81] The ideas presented in this section represent one of the foundations of my *common good governance* framework.

Reviewing again my five criteria for the rise of *transnational networked cooperation* (Chapter 1), change makers attempt to create precautionary arrangements to avoid future harm. They try to influence the highest level on the United Nations agenda to gain traction in international discussion. Momentum and strength will develop when a broader array of scientists joins the ranks of those who first raised the alarm against the perils of algorithmic wars where humans lose control. The combined moral authority of the scientists who create the technology adopted for algorithmic killing and the way they express their revolt against the malicious and evil uses of their creation add a compelling and overriding dimension to *transnational networked cooperation*. The common, humanity-based vocabulary is reinforced when the transnational advocacy for humanity is energized by groups of civil society members with previous experience in related areas who support the cause and consolidate the networked cooperation in concurrence with the scientists.

The AI for Good Global Movement epitomizes these aforementioned criteria. The SDGs are currently the foremost comprehensive global map for action on development and sustainability, in that for the first time, for developing and developed countries alike, they offer a common language to tackle the world's problems. They follow on from the Millennium Development Goals (MDGs), which garnered impressive achievements in poverty reduction and alleviation for millions of people worldwide. The MDGs were a map for actions directed especially at poverty reduction and they were largely aimed at developing countries. In reading the final report on the implementation of the MDGs,[82] one realizes that they represent the most successful movement against poverty in history; here are the most impressive achievements:

- More than half of the total number of people living in extreme poverty were lifted out of this condition by 2015, which was the deadline for meeting the goals;
- The number of undernourished people dropped by almost half from 1990;
- Enrollment of children in primary school doubled;
- The mortality rate for infants and mothers was cut by half;
- The incidence of malaria was dramatically reduced;
- Improved sanitation became available to 2 billion people;
- 147 countries met the MDG drinking water target, 95 countries met the MDG sanitation target, and 77 countries met both targets.

The United Nations Sustainable Development Goals

The SDGs represent an all-inclusive endeavor to follow up the MDGs and include the 193 countries of the United Nations that all underwrote the negotiations that led to the 17 new goals, which are to be implemented by 2030. They represent a truly universal agenda covering development, sustainability, environmental security, rule of law, security, and peace. No political agenda has ever been so comprehensive, and it is underpinned by 169 measurable targets and 232 indicators.[83] The road to implementation is uncertain, but the technology is now available to meet the challenge, and AI will play an enabling role in bringing them to fruition.[84] The goals epitomize attempts to create *common good governance*, and are as follows:

1) No Poverty: end poverty in all its forms, everywhere.
2) Zero Hunger: end hunger, achieve food security and improved nutrition; promotion of sustainable agriculture.
3) Good Health and Well-being: ensure healthy lives and promote well-being for all at all ages.
4) Quality Education: ensure inclusive and equitable quality education and promote lifelong learning opportunities for all.
5) Gender Equality: achieve gender equality and empower all.
6) Clean Water and Sanitation: ensure availability and sustainable management of water and sanitation for all.
7) Affordable and Clean Energy: ensure access to affordable, reliable, sustainable, and modern energy for all.
8) Decent Work and Economic Growth: promote sustained, inclusive, and sustainable economic growth, full and productive employment, and decent work for all.
9) Industry, Innovation, and Infrastructure: build resilient infrastructure, promote inclusive and sustainable industrialization and foster innovation.
10) Reduced Inequalities: reduce inequality within and among communities.
11) Sustainable Cities and Communities: make cities and human settlements inclusive, safe, resilient, and sustainable.
12) Responsible Consumption and Production: ensure sustainable consumption and production patterns.
13) Climate Action: take urgent action to combat climate change and its impacts.
14) Life Below Water: conserve and sustainably use the oceans, seas, and marine resources for sustainable development.
15) Life on Land: protect, restore, and promote sustainable use of terrestrial ecosystems, sustainably manage forests, combat desertification and halt and reverse land degradation, and halt biodiversity loss.
16) Peace, Justice, and Strong Institutions: promote peaceful and inclusive societies for sustainable development, provide access to justice for all and build effective, accountable, and inclusive institutions at all levels.
17) Partnerships for the Goals: strengthen the means of implementation and revitalize the global partnership for sustainable development.

Goal 16: AI and its role in the promotion of peace and security

Each goal has measurable targets and indicators. For instance, Goal 16, closely linked to the themes of peace, security, and world order discussed in this book, includes these targets:

- Significantly reduce all forms of violence and related death rates everywhere;
- End abuse, exploitation, trafficking, and all forms of violence against and torture of children;
- Promote the rule of law at the national and international levels, and ensure equal access to justice for all;
- Broaden and strengthen the participation of developing countries in the institutions of global governance;
- Ensure public access to information and protect fundamental freedoms, in accordance with national legislation and international agreements;
- Strengthen relevant national institutions, including through international cooperation, for building capacity at all levels, in particular in developing countries, to prevent violence and combat terrorism and crime.

The targets provide a concrete way to determine how the goals can be achieved and how technology will play a role, especially AI. In the case of the Goal 16 targets, the objective would be for AI to be a factor in the reduction, not in the augmentation, of violence. However, if more groups, including armed nonstate groups and terrorists, have access to the possibility of weaponizing AI, then we may see an amplification of violence. AI can be used to identify the trafficking routes that enable the flow of guns and drugs, as well as human trafficking.[85] However, the shortcoming is that the criminal gangs that conduct these felonies will also have access to the use of AI because it is ubiquitous across societal levels.

AI has the potential to be an equalizer and to assist developing countries to play a greater role in the world, and in the institutions of global governance. However, thus far most of the developing world has been left out. If AI is not employed according to the rules and norms agreed by all states, it has the potential to enlarge the gap between the developed countries and the developing countries of the world. AI can be used to protect fundamental rights and freedoms, but it can also be used to curtail them, as is already happening in certain countries where the technologies enabled by AI, such as image recognition, promote greater surveillance and promote the instruments of population repression and erosion of democracy.[86] Along the same lines, AI can assist in the combating of terrorism and crime through the analysis of big data that breaks down patterns and trends that would facilitate the identification of criminals. For instance, AI techniques of big data analysis from satellite data are already able to track deforestation in major rain forests around the world, thereby paving the way toward enacting policies to contain deforestation.[87]

The SDGs represent an all-encompassing action blueprint to enact *common good governance* broadly. They also inspire states to think beyond a narrow focus on national security and attain *humanity's security*. They were adopted by all states and involve each member state of the United Nations. Under international law, the SDGs are a politically binding mechanism—that is, states will not have to ratify them to be bound to them, as in an international treaty. However, the platform for their implementation is the High-Level Political Forum on Sustainable Development, which meets at the United Nations in New York every year. Here countries check on each other for cooperation and for options to foster the implementation of the goals.

The United Nations AI for Good Global Summit series

There are three preliminary initiatives and organizations involved in the AI for Good Movement. I can trace the birth of this movement to 2017, when the International Telecommunication Union (ITU) hosted the first AI for Good Global Summit at the United Nations in Geneva. The ITU is one of the oldest international organizations, founded in 1865, with headquarters in Geneva, and is a member of the United Nations family of organizations. It has an illustrious history of acting as a facilitator and enabler of communication between nations since the invention of the telegraph. That technological advancement changed the way nations communicated. Consequently, the ITU was created to set rules and norms, commonly agreed by states, for the best use of emerging new technologies. All 193 member states of the United Nations are members of the ITU, but so too are 700 private entities.

More often than not, when the media reports on global governance and the role of the United Nations, they focus on its failings rather than its successes. Nonetheless, international organizations provide essential coordinating mechanisms and services for all states to coordinate their actions: for example, in air space, postal service across borders, and open sea lanes for commerce. Most of the time the global governance and new international laws generated by such institutions work quietly, and their work of facilitating the logistics of life in international relations goes unreported (Chapter 4).

The ITU is one such example of an essential institution of global governance. Since its founding, business transactions between states have grown enormously as greater coordination between them is better than conflict. The ITU adapted with the passage of time to coordinate new technologies and their impact on states' international relations: the telephone, radio, the Internet—and now AI. The inaugural summit in 2017 initiated the first global dialogue on the beneficial uses of AI beyond the exclusively scientific realm. The organizers stated that the goal was to advance the

development and democratization of AI solutions that can address global challenges related to, among others, poverty, hunger, health, education, the environment. A special focus will be placed on leveraging AI to help achieve the United
Nations SDGs. The event provided a neutral platform for government officials, UN
agencies, NGOs, industry leaders and AI experts to discuss the technical, societal,
policy and ethical issues related to AI, offer guidance and promote international
dialogue and cooperation in support of AI innovation.[88]

The 2018 AI for Good Global Summit was aimed at accelerating progress toward
meeting the SDGs and it became the leading platform for dialogue on AI, because
it involved not only many of the other family institutions of the United Nations, but
also the private sector (companies) and scientists, and it was organized in partnership
with the Association for Computing Machinery.[89] I attended the 2018 and 2019 summits with a former student, a computer engineer and international security expert,
Rebecca Leeper, and we both observed the extraordinary network of different change
makers who were brought together.

As a result of the first two AI for Good summits, the ITU launched the Global
Artificial Intelligence Repository, open to the public and searchable by SDG. It has
the potential to galvanize the AI for Good Movement, because it aims to connect
the different projects and communities involved. As Eugenio Garcia explains, the
AI for Good Summit is the flagship platform for global dialogue with the wider
public.[90] As a result of the AI for Good summits, the Global Data Commons was
forged as a way to use the large quantities of data associated with AI development
to continue to pave the way for implementing the United Nations SDGs. The stewardship of the data is undertaken collectively to avoid bias, algorithm maximization
that may encourage violence, and other abuses, while enabling the passing on of the
advantages to the broader public, instead of to only those few tech firms that collect the data.[91] In other words, the users of social platforms generate data for tech
firms such as Google, Facebook, Twitter, etc., but do not get to reap the benefits of
the use of the collected data. The Global Data Commons is a governance mechanism to channel the use of data for the common good—namely, back to benefit the
users.

A second initiative is a leading project that will have far-reaching impacts as
it incorporates the efforts of the IEEE Global Initiative on Ethics of Autonomous
and Intelligent Systems (A/IS) launched in 2016 (mentioned earlier) with the aim
of aligning technological advances with the ethical values of promoting human
well-being: it measures testable levels of transparency and compliance that can be
determined objectively and within specified parameters to avoid biases in algorithms.
This project will be highly influential because it is "the most comprehensive, crowd-
sourced global treatise regarding the Ethics of Autonomous and Intelligent Systems
available today."[92] IEEE has almost half a million members in 160 countries and it
is an "association dedicated to advancing innovation and technological excellence

for the benefit of humanity"; as such, it is "the world's largest technical professional society."[93]

The IEEE 2017 report argues that A/IS have been identified as the key technologies to enable the implementation of the United Nations SDGs.[94] The IEEE also recognizes that "A/IS for the common good" is becoming ever present, with its "human-centered" accountable and inclusive foundational framework. The disparity of wealth between developed and developing countries has grown wider with the recent growth of high technologies. But the largest companies in the world are high-tech ones that tend to concentrate the gains in the hands of a few. We live in a world where eight of the most powerful men earn a higher income than three billion people combined.[95] The challenge will be to create global governing frameworks that harness A/IS for a more equitable world. This could be achieved by enforcing greater tax responsibility, more job creation equity, and higher accountability for investments. Furthermore, less politically contentious aspects of AI technologies include the use of big data for good—for example, the use of geographic information systems for disaster prevention, building resilience, energy production, and traffic control in the increasingly unlivable big cities of the developing world. At this critical juncture, in which the utilization of AI technologies remains largely unregulated globally, the probability that they will be used in ways that will exacerbate inequalities is high. This is one more powerful reason to create *common good governance* for A/IS with a preventive purpose, as an equalizing force for all humans, and not as yet one more technological advance that will not be scaled up to benefit the largest number of people.

Finally, the United Nations Secretary-General, António Guterres, has published a foundational work for future governance on AI: "Securing our Common Future," which is a new map for building peace avenues; as such, he is playing a leading and prominent role in advancing the AI for Good Movement. He calls on countries to increase peace and security through disarmament to save humanity (eliminating weapons of mass destruction), disarmament to save lives (conventional weapons control and regulation), and disarmament for future generations (grappling with emerging means of warfare). He also calls on states to employ new technologies for the common benefit of humankind. He also commits to working with scientists and industries to foster responsible innovation for peaceful objectives. The conviction of roboticists and scientists of the need to sound the alarm against the weaponization of AI and their commitment to develop technology for peace are praised in *Securing our Common Future*. They represent the moral compass needed to ensure that technologies are developed with the goal of serving humanity. International stability will depend upon the enactment of new global governing mechanisms of a preventive nature. Guterres calls on states to avoid the temptation to reinterpret international law in the light of the uses of new technologies. *Securing our Common Future* endeavors to bridge the false dichotomy between national security and humanitarian concerns. It is historic because it highlights that the new order we are entering demands the integration of the pursuit of national security with respect for humanitarian concerns; these two aspects can no longer be separated. This is inextricably aligned with my concept of *humanity's security* that views security through a broader perspective toward the common good. Therefore, new technological advances should be used to accelerate the achievement of sustainable development. Essentially, the Secretary-General states that when use of force takes place, humans must remain in control—in other words, that humans retain ultimate control of weapons and AI.

Steps to *common good governance* under international law

Progressively, discussions on limiting autonomy in weapon systems at the United Nations started reflecting the desire of most states for a new international legal instrument that limits autonomy in weapon systems and restrains the dehumanization of warfare. There was also a rising consensus about the shape and nature of the new agreement. It became clear that most states wished for a combination of prohibitions and regulations. Bonnie Docherty, of Harvard University and Human Rights Watch, and one of the key international legal advisers on the issue from the beginning, had been steering advice in this direction of travel.[96] Additionally, there was widespread agreement that human control should be present, and some countries specifically mentioned human control over the critical functions (targeting and engagement, i.e., decision to kill or destroy).[97] Another way to interpret this and to make a new treaty stand the test of time is to establish control over the use of force—that is, to focus on conduct rather than on specific systems.[98] Whenever force is applied, human oversight must be paramount. As Docherty argues, managing the "use of force," as a form of human conduct reflecting human agency and intention, is enshrined in IHL and in human rights law which makes observance compelling.

The International Panel for the Regulation of Autonomous Weapons (IPRAW) has been advising on the process at the United Nations since 2017. As a member of IPRAW, I was part of the creation of our recommendation to maintain human control in each phase of the targeting process to avoid the impact of cumulative errors. Prior to the targeting process, there is the design of the system, and then the preparation for the attack. Therefore, human control needs to be present during the design and in the action of use (i.e., during the mission execution).[99] For IPRAW, this is about defining the necessary type and level of human control during the interaction between the human and the machine. It is then necessary to take into account the environment in which the operation will take place: Is it a densely populated city, for instance? Will the operation target a military installation? Are there civilians present? To answer these questions, the operator must take into account what the target parameters are and how long it will take to find the target and make the decision. These are aspects of spatial and temporal consideration that are essential for compliance with IHL. It is useful to retain a "functional" approach. This is not about one weapon system, but rather about functions, in particular autonomous functionality in military systems, already existing or yet to be invented. One can discern distinct types of weapons in nuclear, chemical, and conventional weapons. It is possible to count them. However, with autonomous systems, we are talking about adding autonomy to different functions. If it happens to be the "critical functions" of selection and engagement, or target and attack (focus to kill or destroy), then the concern is whether human oversight is maintained during the performance of the function. Therefore, in autonomous systems, a qualitative analysis rather than a quantitative one is essential in the technical and operational aspects, as Table 3.1 indicates.

The regulation of conduct during the use of force would be an innovative pillar in a potential new international treaty. Previous regulations on methods and means of warfare focused on specific systems and their quantities. If a particular state was accumulating inordinate amounts of certain systems, that could be deemed to be destabilizing to international security. Any new treaty would consequently seek to curb quantities or prohibit certain weapon systems all together (Chapter 5). As Bonnie Docherty explains in her influential work, which is in line with IPRAW's conceptions mentioned earlier, the regulation of conduct along the spectrum of the targeting process is appropriate for accounting for how algorithmic decision-making takes place. A treaty must therefore be broad enough to encompass all present and future systems that select and engage sensor-based targets. In other words, every time the target has been identified by sensors and not human observation, the firmest prohibition would be on eliminating the permission to target people.[100] Therefore the strictest exclusion would be placed on eradicating antipersonnel systems.[101] The Figure 3.1 table below illustrates what the nature and scope of a new treaty would look like, based upon the decade-long work of Docherty and the ICRC.[102]

As Figure 3.1 shows, the foundational underpinning of the novel treaty would be the positive obligation to maintain human control throughout all phases and stages of the design and operations. A positive obligation strengthens a more preventive stance in the promotion of human well-being. A purely negative, obligations-based treaty would not necessarily put in place the conditions for long-term comprehensive ways

Table 3.1 IPRAW's concept of minimum requirement for human control

	Situational Understanding	Intervention
Control by Design (Technical Control)	Ability to monitor information about environment and system	Modes of operation that allow human intervention and require them in specific steps of the targeting cycle
Control in Use (Operational Control)	Appropriate monitoring of the system and the operational environment	Authority and accountability of human operators, teammates, and commanders; abide by IHL

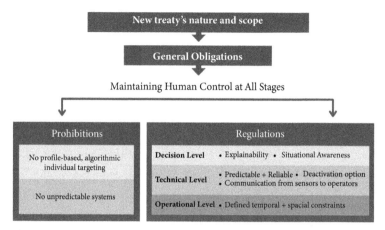

Figure 3.1 New treaty's nature and scope

to keep the treaty relevant, in the light of further technological advancements. An illustrative analogy would be the definition of peace. A definition of peace in terms of only negative obligation would be "the absence of war." Instead, a positive definition of peace would include not only the absence of war, but also the conditions, attitudes, and institutions that create and sustain peaceful societies.[103] A positive obligation to maintain human control would imprint a markedly human-centered tenor on the treaty.

Previous human-centered legal frameworks entailed the responsibility to look after the victims of weapons use, while shifting the burden of proof to the users by highlighting the victim's plight and codifying means of providing reparations. Furthermore, some treaties have pioneered new normative ground by requiring states not only to refrain from initiating harm through the deployment of weapons, but also building the conditions for maintaining peace and human security.[104] For instance, in the 2017 Nuclear Ban Treaty, the main positive obligations are related to victim assistance and environmental remediation. This is groundbreaking because the obligations of the legal framework highlight the unacceptable harm caused by nuclear weapons to people and the environment instead of perpetuating the elusive and futile notion of deterrence.[105] The entry into force of the Nuclear Ban Treaty on January 22, 2021 brought to reality the positive legal obligations to assist the victims of nuclear testing and remediate harms to the environment.[106] Additionally, the light shone on the need to look after the victims and the environment shows the extent of the threat that nuclear weapons pose to *humanity's security*. Hence, the idea that nuclear weapons provide security and enhance the national prestige is weakened further.

The positive obligations in a new treaty on autonomous weapons that would generate a norm to maintain human control were championed by most states at the negotiations. Additionally, regulations would also be needed in three areas.[107] The first is in the realm of decision-making, which must incorporate explainability and situational awareness. This means that the decision maker must understand how the system works and consider rapidly evolving scenarios in conflict situations. This would include an appraisal, for instance, of whether civilians have moved into the area close to the target, thereby imperiling their lives. The second area is in the realm of the technical components of the system to ensure that it preserves human control. Technically, the system must meet three specifications: 1) predictability and reliability; 2) effective communication between sensor and the human operator; and 3) the possibility to intervene and deactivate. The third area incorporates the operational components. There must be temporal and spatial constraints that make the operation time- and space-bound so it respects the original intentions set by the human operator. The goal is to approximate the initial assumptions and the final targeting to reduce risks to life and human dignity. The operation must not jeopardize existing legal, ethical, and moral constraints. In order to ensure that human control remains present, or at least valid (from the initial assumptions and decisions onwards), and to attain the goal of minimizing harm in each of the lifecycle stages of any weapon system—design, development, testing, deployment, monitoring and operation, maintenance, and disposal. Systems with increased autonomy and those that use AI shall remain under the purview of humans in the operational context of each mission.[108]

In sum, the positive obligation to maintain human control would be complemented by a set of legally binding prohibitions and a few regulations. There are two prohibitions: the first is that profile-based individual targeting is unlawful. This means that there is a ban on profiling individuals to be killed based upon sensor information. The second is a prohibition on systems that may be deemed unpredictable and that may produce arbitrary results. The main concern here is about the impact of machine learning-based systems. Due to the system's ongoing acquisition of information and assessment of potential outcomes, the operator would be unable to scrutinize what actually happened.

The negotiations at the United Nations reached a point where states increasingly coalesced around the idea that IHL undoubtedly applies to autonomous systems. However, clarification, and even novel regulations and prohibitions, are needed to deal with the uncertainty created by AI systems. Most states also wished to achieve new international treaty law.[109] Most states are set to formulate a new treaty to eliminate any ambiguity in the current international legal and political framework. In my view, the best course of action will be for states to initiate a treaty process within the United Nations General Assembly, where the rules of procedure call for a two-thirds majority instead of full consensus. As my work on the first legally binding treaty on conventional weapons—the Arms Trade Treaty—shows, the General Assembly is a fruitful and inclusive route for diplomacy.[110] The success in finalizing the Arms Trade Treaty was possible with a powerful champion state, the United Kingdom. As one of the largest weapons manufacturers in the world, as well as a member of the United Nations Security Council, it held significant sway.[111] The chief British diplomats leading the process worked with a like-minded group of states: Australia, Argentina, Costa Rica, Finland, Kenya, and Japan. Together, these countries proposed a handful of well-thought-out resolutions at the General Assembly in 2006, 2008, and 2009. The last one called for the start of negotiations.[112]

I observed the negotiations in New York and Geneva that led to the adoption of the Arms Trade Treaty and its meteoric entry into force in December 2014. In that successful diplomatic process, there are a few similar elements to the diplomatic process currently underway—most importantly, the support of the majority of states. In the diplomatic process addressing the issue of autonomous weapons one can also discern a palpable sense of urgency, and the support of the majority of states. There is an intensifying revulsion among AI researchers in North America, Asia, and Europe at the development of autonomous weapons and AI-assisted systems. A recent landmark study assessed that 75% of AI researchers are against them.[113] The failure to reach a negotiated deal on autonomous weapons thus far is due to a handful of countries that opposes it and abuses the consensus rule, and that does not show good faith by recognizing the will of the majority. However, the presence of concerted *transnational networked cooperation* gives future attempts to create new global governance more robustness and momentum, where many emerging and deepening networks of action are developing across multiple sectors worldwide (Chapter 1). For all these reasons, it is time to start diplomacy anew, where "entering agreements in good faith," a time-honored principle of international law, can be pursued again to create *common good governance* to prevent the digital dehumanization of warfare.

Notes

1. Vincent Boulanin, et al., "Artificial Intelligence, Strategic Stability and Nuclear Risk," *SIPRI* (June 2020).
2. The Protocol on Blinding Laser Weapons was adopted on October 13, 1995, at the First Review Conference of the 1980 Convention on Certain Conventional Weapons (CCW) in Vienna, Austria, and was annexed to the CCW as Protocol IV. The protocol entered into force on July 30, 1998.
3. Christof Heyns, "Autonomous Weapons in Armed Conflict and the Right to a Dignified Life: An African Perspective." *South African Journal on Human Rights*, vol. 33, no. 1 (2017): pp. 46–71.
4. United Nations Human Rights Council, *Report of the Special Rapporteur on Extrajudicial, Summary or Arbitrary Executions*, A/HRC/23/4 (April 2013).
5. Stanley Meisler, *United Nations: A History* (Grove Press, 2011).
6. For an illuminating view of the last stages of the negotiations, see the Stop Killer Robots Campaign final statement: https://reachingcriticalwill.org/images/documents/Disarmament-fora/ccw/2021/RevCon/statements/17Dec_SKR.pdf.
7. Nathan A. Sears. "International Politics in the Age of Existential Threats." *Journal of Global Security Studies*, vol. 6, no. 3 (2021).
8. Mario Coccia "Preparedness of Countries to Face COVID-19 Pandemic Crisis: Strategic Positioning and Factors Supporting Effective Strategies of Prevention of Pandemic Threats." *Environmental Research*, 203 (2022): p. 111678.

9. Denise Garcia, "Redirect Military Budgets to Tackle Climate Change and Pandemics." *Nature*, vol. 584 (2020): pp. 521–523.

10. Denise Garcia, "Stop the Emerging AI Cold War." *Nature*, vol. 593, no. 858 (2021): p. 169.

11. Ryan Fedasiuk et al., "Harnessed Lighting – How the Chinese Military is Adopting Artificial Intelligence." *Center for Security and Emerging Technology* (2021). https://doi.org/10.51593/20200089.

12. Klaus Schwab, *The Fourth Industrial Revolution* (World Economic Forum, 2016).

13. Ngor Luong, et al., "Mapping the AI Investment Activities of Top Global Defense Companies," *Center for Security and Emerging Technology* (October 2021). https://doi.org/10.51593/20210015.

14. Kareem Ayoub and Kenneth Payne, "Strategy in the Age of Artificial Intelligence." *The Journal of Strategic Studies* 39/5-6 (2015): pp. 793–819.

15. Heather Williams "Strategic Stability, Uncertainty and the Future of Arms Control." *Survival*, vol. 60, no. 2 (2018): pp. 45–54.

16. James Acton, "Reclaiming Strategic Stability," in *Strategic Stability: Contending Interpretations*, ed. Elbridge A. Colby and Michael S. Gerson (US Army War College Press, 2013): p. 117.

17. Boulanin, et al., "Artificial Intelligence, Strategic Stability and Nuclear Risk."

18. Boulanin, et al., "Artificial Intelligence, Strategic Stability and Nuclear Risk."

19. Boulanin, et al., "Artificial Intelligence, Strategic Stability and Nuclear Risk," figure on p. 124.

20. The critical pieces in this area of scholarship are Jürgen Altmann and Frank Sauer, "Autonomous Weapon Systems and Strategic Stability." *Survival*, vol.59, no. 5, (2017): pp. 117–142. Michael C. Horowitz, "When Speed Kills: Lethal Autonomous Weapon Systems, Deterrence and Stability ." *Journal of Strategic Studies*, vol.42, no. 6, (2019): pp. 764–788. Ayoub and Payne, "Strategy in the Age of Artificial Intelligence,"

21. Frank Sauer, "Military Applications of Artificial Intelligence: Nuclear Risk Redux," *SIPRI* (2019): pp. 154.

22. Altmann and Sauer, "Autonomous Weapon Systems and Strategic Stability."

23. Altmann and Sauer, "Autonomous Weapon Systems and Strategic Stability."

24. Horowitz, "When Speed Kills." Horowitz is of the view that AI capabilities' impact on military behavior, especially when initiating international wars, is likely to be low due to the limitations of current technological advancements.

25. Allan Dafoe, "AI Governance: A Research Agenda." *Governance of AI Program, Future of Humanity Institute, University of Oxford* 1442 (2018): p. 54.

26. Waqar Zaidi and Allan Dafoe. "International Control of Powerful Technology: Lessons from the Baruch Plan for Nuclear Weapons." *Future of Humanity Institute, University of Oxford* (2021): p. 72.

27. Frank Sauer, "Stepping Back from the Brink: Why Multilateral Regulation of Autonomy in Weapons Systems is Difficult, yet Imperative and Feasible." *International Review of the Red Cross*, vol. 102, no. 913 (2020): pp. 235–259.

28. The IEEE Global Initiative on Ethics of Autonomous and Intelligent Systems, "Ethically Aligned Design: A Vision for Prioritizing Human Well-being with Autonomous and Intelligent Systems." *IEEE* (2018): pp. 121, 125. https://standards.ieee.org/content/ieee-standards/en/industry-connections/ec/autonomous-systems.html.

29. Eugenio V. Garcia, "The Militarization of Artificial Intelligence: A Wake-up Call for the Global South." *SSRN Electronic Journal* (2019): p. 15.

30. Ryan Calo, "Artificial Intelligence Policy: A Primer and Roadmap." *University of California, Davis, Law Review*, vol. 51 (2017).

31. Shaza Arif, "Militarization of Artificial Intelligence: Progress and Implications." In *Towards an International Political Economy of Artificial Intelligence*, ed. Tugrul Keskin, Ryan David Kiggins (Palgrave Macmillan, 2021): pp. 219–239.

32. Boulanin, et al., "Artificial Intelligence, Strategic Stability and Nuclear Risk."

33. Boulanin, et al., "Artificial Intelligence, Strategic Stability and Nuclear Risk."

34. Neil Savage, "The Race to the Top Among the World's Leaders in Artificial Intelligence." *Nature*, vol. 588, no. 7837 (2020): S102–S102.

35. A comprehensive and data-rich survey of the nuclear powers' embrace of military AI was done by Boulanin, et al., "Artificial Intelligence, Strategic Stability and Nuclear Risk."

36. SIPRI Yearbook, Armaments, Disarmament, and International Security, July 2021. Federation of American Scientists, Status of the World's Nuclear Forces 2021.

37. For the NPT database at the United Nations which functions as the repository, see: https://www.un.org/disarmament/wmd/nuclear/npt/.

38. Boulanin, et al., "Artificial Intelligence, Strategic Stability and Nuclear Risk.".

39. Congressional Budget Office, Projected Costs of US Nuclear Forces, 2021–2030, May 2021.

40. John Borrie and Tim Caughley, eds. *Viewing Nuclear Weapons Through a Humanitarian Lens* (United Nations Institute for Disarmament Research, 2013).

41. Bonnie Docherty, "A 'Light for all Humanity': The Treaty on the Prohibition of Nuclear Weapons and the Progress of Humanitarian Disarmament." *Global Change, Peace & Security*, vol. 30, no. 2 (2018): pp. 163–186.

42. Allan Dafoe, a prominent observer at The Governance of Artificial Intelligence (AI) Program at the University of Oxford's Future of Humanity Institute: Allan Dafoe, "Global Politics and the Governance of Artificial Intelligence." *Journal of International Affairs*, vol. 72, no. 1 (2018): pp. 121–126.

43. As noted by another prominent observer, Michael C. Horowitz, "Artificial Intelligence, International Competition, and the Balance of Power," *Texas National Security Review* 1, no. 3 (May 2018), http://hdl.handle.net/2152/65638.

44. Niklas Masuhr, "AI in Military Enabling Applications." *CSS Analyses in Security Policy*, vol. 251 (2019).

45. Denise Garcia, *Disarmament Diplomacy and Human Security: Regimes, Norms and Moral Progress in International Relations* (Routledge, 2011).

46. Tina Birmpili, "Montreal Protocol at 30: The Governance Structure, the Evolution, and the Kigali Amendment." *Comptes Rendus Geoscience*, vol. 350, no. 7 (2018): pp. 425–431.

47. David Leonard Downie, "UNEP and the Montreal Protocol." *Contributions in Political Science*, vol. 355 (1995): pp. 171–186.

48. See the treaty's database at the United Nations, which serves as the repository: https://treaties.un.org/Pages/ViewDetails.aspx?src=IND&mtdsg_no=XXVII-2-a&chapter=27&clang=_en.

49. Augusto López-Claros, Arthur L. Dahl, and Maja Groff, *Global Governance and the Emergence of Global Institutions for the 21st Century* (Cambridge University Press, 2020).

50. Maxwell Pearson, "The Rising Tide of Populism and Its Implications to Global Governance in the 21st Century: A Modern Discourse on an Age-Old Issue in Politics." *Analyzing Current and Future Global Trends in Populism* (IGI Global, 2022): pp. 28–48.

51. Nick Watts, et al., "The Lancet Countdown: Tracking Progress on Health and Climate Change." *The Lancet*, vol. 389, no. 10074 (2017): pp. 1151–1164.

52. Carl J. Dahlman, "China and India: Emerging Technological Powers." *Issues in Science and Technology*, vol. 23, no. 3 (2007): pp. 45–53.

53. H. U. Ting and S. U. N. Ying, "Interpretation of IPCC AR6 on Human Influence on the Climate System." *Advances in Climate Change Research*, vol. 17, no. 6 (2021): p. 644.

54. Marina Romanello, "The 2021 Report of the Lancet Countdown on Health and Climate Change: Code Red for a Healthy Future." *The Lancet* (2021): https://doi.org/10.1016/S0140-6736(21)01787-6.

55. Joint statement by Switzerland on behalf of the Group of 16, CCW, United Nations, December 17, 2021.

56. Maaike Verbruggen, "The Role of Civilian Innovation in the Development of Lethal Autonomous Weapon Systems." *Global Policy*, vol. 10, no. 3 (2019): pp. 338–342.

57. Elsa B. Kania, "Chinese Military Innovation in Artificial Intelligence." *Testimony to the US-China Economic and Security Review Commission* (2019), 2: "intelligentized" (智能化).

58. China's State Council, AI Next Generation Artificial Intelligence Development Plan, July 20, 2017.

59. Kania, "Chinese Military Innovation."

60. Kania, "Chinese Military Innovation."

61. Government of China, Statement to the UN Human Rights Council, May 30, 2013, by compilation: "Country Positions on Killer Robots," *Human Rights Watch*, 2020: http://stopkillerrobots.org/wp-content/uploads/2013/05/HRC_China_09_30May2013.pdf.

62. Government of China, "Country Positions on Killer Robots"; Government of China, Working Paper submitted to the Convention on Conventional Weapons Fifth Review Conference, December 2016.

63. Government of China, "Country Positions on Killer Robots"; Government of China, Working Paper submitted to the Convention on Conventional Weapons Group of Governmental Experts on lethal autonomous weapons systems, April 11, 2018.

64. The United States Department of Defense Directive. 3000.09, Autonomy in Weapon Systems (Nov. 21, 2012), was updated on May 8, 2017: https://www.esd.whs.mil/portals/54/documents/dd/issuances/dodd/300009p.pdf. Emphasis mine.

65. These views are, respectively: Michael W. Meier, "Lethal Autonomous Weapons Systems (LAWS): Conducting a Comprehensive Weapons Review." *Temple International & Comparative Law Journal*, vol. 30 (2016): p. 119; and Paul Scharre, *Army of None: Autonomous Weapons and the Future of War* (W. W. Norton & Company, 2018).

66. "A Guide to the Legal Review of New Weapons, Means and Methods of Warfare: Measures to Implement Article 36 of Additional Protocol I of 1977" *International Committee for the Red Cross* (Geneva, 2006).

67. Neil Davison, "A Legal Perspective: Autonomous Weapon Systems under International Humanitarian Law." United Nations Office of Disarmament Affairs (UNODA) Occasional Papers (2018): pp. 5–18. https://doi.org/10.18356/29a571ba-en.

68. The American delegation at the United Nations in Geneva delivered this paper in 2018: "Humanitarian Benefits of Emerging Technologies in the Area of Lethal Autonomous Weapon Systems," CCW/GGE.1/2018/WP.4.

69. Davison, "A Legal Perspective," para. 5.

70. The American Civil Liberties Union called on the Pentagon to confront past civilian casu-
    alties, promote accountability, and reform. The union issued a letter to the public and is
    gathering momentum.

71. European Parliament resolution of September 12, 2018, on autonomous weapon systems
    (2018/2752(RSP)).

72. European Defense Fund, Directorate General for External Policies of the Union PE
    653.638, May 2021, p. 16.

73. A. Dahlmann and M. Dickow, "Preventive Regulation of Autonomous Weapon Systems:
    Need for Action by Germany at Various Levels." (SWP Research Paper, 3/2019). *Berlin:
    Stiftung Wissenschaft und Politik -SWP- Deutsches Institut für Internationale Politik und
    Sicherheit* (Berlin: 2019). https://doi.org/10.18449/2019RP03.

74. Eugenio V. Garcia, "Multilateralism and Artificial Intelligence: What Role for the United
    Nations?" (2020). Available at SSRN 3779866.

75. "Arria-formula Meeting on the Impact of Emerging Technologies on International Peace
    and Security." https://www.securitycouncilreport.org/whatsinblue/2021/05/arria-for
    mula-meeting-on-the-impact-of-emerging-technologies-on-international-peace-and-
    security.php.

76. United Nations Security Council, SC/14563, June 29, 2021. "'Explosive' Growth of Digi-
    tal Technologies Creating New Potential for Conflict, Disarmament Chief Tells Security
    Council in First-Ever Debate on Cyberthreats."

77. Secretary-General's Message to Meeting of the Group of Governmental Experts on
    Emerging Technologies in the Area of Lethal Autonomous Weapons Systems, March 25,
    2019.

78. UN Secretary-General's Strategy on New Technologies, New York, September 2018,
    pp. 3–5, https://www.un.org/en/newtechnologies/images/pdf/SGs-Strategy-on-New-
    Technologies.pdf.

79. Eugenio V. Garcia, "Multilateralism and Artificial Intelligence."

80. Resolution adopted by the General Assembly on November 15, 2021, A/RES/76/6,
    Seventy-six session, agenda item 124.

81. United Nations, "Sustainable Development Goals," https://www.un.org/sustainable
    development/sustainable-development-goals/.

82. United Nations, General Assembly, *The Millennium Development Goals Report* (2015):
    https://www.un.org/millenniumgoals/2015_MDG_Report/pdf/MDG%202015%
    20rev%20(July%201).pdf.

83. United Nations, "Sustainable Development Goals."

84. Ricardo Vinuesa, et al., "The Role of Artificial Intelligence in Achieving the Sustainable
    Development Goals." *Nature Communications*, vol. 11, no. 1 (2020): pp. 1–10.

85. Reza Montasari and Hamid Jahankhani. "The Application of Technology in Combating
    Human Trafficking." In *Cybersecurity, Privacy and Freedom Protection in the Connected
    World*, ed. Hamid Jahankhani, Arshad Jamal, and Shaun Lawson (Springer, 2021):
    pp. 149–156.

86. Karl Manheim and Lyric Kaplan. "Artificial Intelligence: Risks to Privacy and Democ-
    racy." *Yale Journal of Law & Technology*, vol. 21 (2019): pp. 106.

87. Jeremy Irvin, et al., "Forestnet: Classifying Drivers of Deforestation in Indonesia using
    Deep Larning on Satellite Imagery." arXiv preprint arXiv:2011.05479 (2020).

88. "AI for Good Global Summit 2017," International Telecommunications Union, https://
    www.itu.int/en/ITU-T/AI/Pages/201706-default.aspx.

89. James Butcher and Irakli Beridze, "What is the State of Artificial Intelligence Governance Globally?" *The RUSI Journal*, vol. 164, no. 5–6 (2019): pp. 88–96.

90. Garcia, "The Militarization of Artificial Intelligence."

91. https://www.unglobalpulse.org/wp-content/uploads/2023/06/annual-report-2022-4.pdf

92. IEEE, *Ethically Aligned Design: Version 1* (Institute of Electrical and Electronics Engineers, 2016).

93. IEEE, "Mission and Vision," https://www.ieee.org/about/vision-mission.html.

94. IEEE, *Ethically Aligned Design: Version 2* (Institute of Electrical and Electronics Engineers, 2017).

95. "Just 8 Men Own Same Wealth as Half the World." *Oxfam International*. https://www.oxfam.org/en/press-releases/just-8-men-own-same-wealth-half-world.

96. Bonnie Docherty, "Areas of Alignment: Common Visions for a Killer Robots Treaty." In *Human Rights Watch and Harvard Law School International Human Rights Clinic* (IHRC, 2021): pp. 1–17.

97. Docherty's team engaged in a thorough assessment and examination of all countries' statements during the 2020 meetings at the United Nations. See Docherty, "Areas of Alignment."

98. Docherty, "Areas of Alignment."

99. IPRAW, *Focus on Human Control*, (2019). https://www.ssoar.info/ssoar/discover?query=iPRAW&submit=.

100. Bonnie Docherty, "Crunch Time on Killer Robots: Why New Law is Needed and How It Can Be Achieved." *Human Rights Watch and Harvard Law School's International Human Rights Clinic* (2021). https://www.hrw.org/sites/default/files/media_2021/11/Crunch%20Time%20on%20Killer%20Robots_final.pdf.

101. Ronald Arkin, et al., "A Path Towards Reasonable Autonomous Weapons Regulation." *IEEE Spectrum: Technology, Engineering, and Science News*, 21 (October 2019).

102. Table designed by Emerson Victoria Johnston and Sebastian Chavez.

103. See Institute for Economics and Peace. *Positive Peace Report 2022: Analysing the Factors that Build, Predict and Sustain Peace* (Sydney, January 2022). Available from: http://visionofhumanity.org/resources.

104. Dinah Shelton and Ariel Gould, "Positive and Negative Obligations." In *The Oxford Handbook of International Human Rights Law*, ed. Dinah Sheldon (Oxford University Press, 2015): pp. 562–583.

105. Matthew Bolton, *The Nuclear Weapons Ban and Human Security for All: Assessing the Draft Convention on the Prohibition of Nuclear Weapons from a Human Security Perspective* (Friedrich-Ebert-Stiftung, 2017).

106. Bonnie Docherty, "A Singular Opportunity: Setting Standards for Victim Assistance under the Treaty on the Prohibition of Nuclear Weapons." *Global Policy*, vol. 12 (2021): p. 126–130.

107. Docherty, "Areas of Alignment"; IPRAW, *Focus on Human Control*; Rebecca Crootof, "A Meaningful Floor for 'Meaningful Human Control'." *Temple International & Comparative Law Journal*, vol. 30, no. 1 (2016): pp. 53–62.

108. Emmanuel Bloch, et al., *Ethical and Technical Challenges in the Development, Use, and Governance of Autonomous Weapons Systems* (The Institute of Electrical and Electronics Engineers, June 2021): pp. 1–25.

109. As well documented and explained by Docherty, "Areas of Alignment."

110. Garcia, *Disarmament Diplomacy and Human Security*.
111. Denise Garcia, "Global Norms on Arms: The Significance of the Arms Trade Treaty for Global Security in World Politics." *Global Policy*, vol. 5, no. 4 (2014): pp. 425–432.
112. Denise Garcia, "Disarming the Lords of War, A New International Treaty to Regulate the Arms Trade," *Foreign Affairs* (December 2014).
113. This is a landmark study and comprehensive survey across the world: B. Zhang, et al., "Ethics and Governance of Artificial Intelligence: Evidence from a Survey of Machine Learning Researchers." *Journal of Artificial Intelligence Research*, vol. 71 (2021): pp. 591–666.

Chapter 4
Legal and political frameworks

What is international law, and what is its role in forming common good governance?

"International law is the legal order which is meant to structure the interaction between entities participating in and shaping international relations." (p. 2)[1] I use this broad definition of international law because it is the one that most accurately reflects its nature today, with its expanded legal scope of international concern. This definition does not include the state explicitly, but makes reference to international organizations, individuals, and other entities and change makers that constitute international law in the 21st century. All these actors are engaged in *transnational networked cooperation* to create *common good governance*. More recently, they have not necessarily been acting on behalf of any single state, but associate themselves with a global cause or problem; this is the case with those entities examined here, who are trying to halt the march toward a world where robots kill, and also those in the global AI for Good Movement, who seek ways to create *common good governance* in the application of the technology to be used for the common benefit of humanity. The definition also takes into account how international law has evolved to be not solely a law of coordination, but a guiding framework of action for all operating in the international system to tackle the main problems of global cooperation that affect not only humanity in general, but also our everyday affairs.[2] Therefore, my approach to international law aligns with my concepts of *common good governance* and *transnational networked cooperation* in endeavoring to create global public goods. These concepts concur with the altered normative foundations of the international legal order that, in the decades since the creation of the United Nations, have shifted from being purely state-centric to being aligned with human security interests.[3] In this human-centric international legal order, more voices are included in making new global norms, not only states.[4]

> It is beyond dispute that the baseline for what constitutes responsible military use of AI in armed conflict is compliance with international law, including IHL. This is the case for all means and methods of warfare.[5]

The world is at a point of deep interconnectedness, and no country can solve on its own any of the most pressing global cooperation problems and existential risks, such as nuclear warfare, climate change, the prevention of pandemics, ocean acidification,

The AI Military Race. Denise Garcia, Oxford University Press. © Denise Garcia (2023).
DOI: 10.1093/oso/9780192864604.003.0005

and the loss of biodiversity, all of which threaten life on Earth. The need for an effective, operational, and highly honored system of international rules and norms that guides and coordinates everyone's actions on the planet has become all the more pressing[6]—hence, the need to understand and appreciate the value of international law in creating *common good governance* in military AI as a global public good. Some observers nowadays see it as going through a process of fragmentation (i.e., different silos with their own treaties, and international organizations with specific functions and roles). Most areas of international relations interactions have been codified, as indicated in Table 4.1, and there are an almost infinite variety of treaties and regimes for almost every area of international law.[7] I view international law metaphorically as a tree, and not as a collection of fragmented parts.[8]

International law is the oldest system of rules and norms coordinating the actions of countries, international organizations, civil society and scientists, and humanity as a whole.[9] From the beginnings of humanity's ever denser global networks of commerce and trade in the 16th century, international law started to play a coordinating role. In a marked departure from what had been common practice since the 16th century, international law has evolved over recent decades to include and privilege the individual (rather than the state) as a subject with rights and obligations. Individuals can appear in international courts and can be held accountable for their behavior or claim compensation for wrongdoing.[10] The individual has progressively gained a legal personality, and this means a different legal order is applicable—in contrast to what came beforehand, when only states had a legal personality (rights and duties). This development signifies a departure from the origins of international law, which is premised on the view of the state as the sole actor and the only subject, doer, and creator of global rules and norms.[11] International law regimes have promoted the formation of commonly agreed global norms of behavior among states through customs, formal treaty-making, and other avenues, called soft law.[12] Some behaviors that were once considered normal—such as piracy, torture, slavery, and territorial annexation by recourse to the use of force—are now prohibited under international law.[13]

The origins of the norms of international law can be associated with the need to regulate the initial interactions between states.[14] The first legal frameworks were created in three areas of international life: the first is to set the elementary, embryonic rules for the coordination of activity on the oceans. The publication of *The Freedom of the Seas* in 1608 by the founding thinker of international law, Hugo Grotius, marks the beginning of a new era wherein pioneering ideas for the supranational coordination of the behavior of nations emerged.[15] Grotius' seminal work that came to define international law advocated for the seas to be free for navigation and commerce for all sea-faring nations, unencumbered by jurisdictional claims made by the most powerful naval powers of the time. Therefore, the first regulations regarding freedom of the seas formulated during the 17th century had a markedly egalitarian character, whereby all should benefit from the riches derived from unbound freedom of navigation, independent of the imperial desire to control among the major powers.[16]

Table 4.1 International law at work and how it affects everyday life

Examples of branches or parts	International institutions and places	Area of international life	How it affects your life as a citizen in the world
States' Responsibility and Recognition of each other	International Law Commission (Geneva and New York) International Court of Justice	Reparations, liability for wrongdoing Disputes between states	Examples: Prevents air crashes, civil aviation disasters, and organizes restitution Pollution of river waters Behavior of states (use of force, diplomacy) Emission of passports, visas
Law on the Use of Force *Jus ad bellum*	United Nations (New York) United Nations Security Council	Prevention of war on an international scale, such as World War III	Sustained peace and the unlikelihood of international war
International Humanitarian Law *Jus in bello*	International Committee of the Red Cross (Geneva) Regulates international and internal conflicts such as in Syria, Yemen, etc.	Limiting degree of suffering in war, i.e.: Dignity of treatment of prisoners of war No torture during war Families can communicate and be traced during war No odious weapons used (chemical weapons) No targeting humanitarian services during war	Prohibition of: Targeting of civilians, chemical warfare, torture, rape, mutilation. Such behaviors constitute violations of the set norms and spark outrage.
International Human Rights Law (includes Refugee Protection Law)	United Nations High Commissioner for Human Rights and Human Rights Council (Geneva) United Nations High Commissioner for Refugees	Universal Declaration of Human Rights is the basic document that laid the foundation. Civil and political rights Social and economic rights Other Examples: United Nations Convention against Genocide	Right to life, to dignity, to a fair trial, to freedom and security Right to work, to food, to a fair wage Genocide is prohibited; when it occurs it sparks an outcry and condemnation

International Criminal Law	International Criminal Court (The Hague)	Universal criminalization of the prohibited activities (*jus cogens*): slavery, genocide, and crimes against humanity are now prohibited	More humane international society where no one should be enslaved, killed arbitrarily, or go unpunished for the above crimes
	Other courts include:		
	The International Criminal Tribunal for Rwanda		
	The Extraordinary Chambers in the Courts of Cambodia		
	The International Criminal Tribunal for the Former Yugoslavia		
Global Commons Law	Many, for example:	Outer space regulations	Freedom to navigate the oceans
	Civil Aviation Organization (Montreal): sets global norms to coordinate 100,000 daily flights	No weapons on the Moon	Trade and commerce are assured
		Maritime disputes	Fewer, if any, civil aviation crashes
	International Tribunal for the Law of the Sea	Regulations on the atmosphere	
		High seas should be free for navigation	
		Repair of the ozone layer	

The second area where the first international rules and norms appeared in international law emerged with the founding of the International Committee of the Red Cross (ICRC) in 1864 in the city of Geneva. This is the first organization of an international character to oversee the creation of the first multilateral constraints on the waging of war, known as international humanitarian law (IHL), or the rules of war—one of the oldest and most important branches of international law (*jus in bello*).[17] The initial convention of IHL was agreed in the same year (1864) and created the first rules for the amelioration of the condition of wounded combatants in war, regardless of nationality, along with the neutrality of humanitarian medical personnel: the Convention for the Amelioration of the Condition of the Wounded in Armies in the Field, Geneva, August 22, 1864. The 1864 Geneva Convention fulfills an aspiration and an aim to set up standards of behavior during war aimed at reducing the horrors of conflict: care of sick and wounded military personnel, regardless of nationality, and recognition of the neutrality of medical personnel, hospitals, and ambulances.[18]

The third area where international law started to emerge is the regulation of long-distance communication after the revolutionary invention of the telegraph in 1844. Multilateral regulations vis-à-vis the global governance of telecommunications and postal services appeared in 1865 with the formation of the International Telecommunications Union in Geneva, which was the second international organization created at the time. These historic developments mark the establishment of a new era when international relations become coordinated by means of rules and norms shaped in international organizations.[19] The appearance of the third international organization in another area of communications, namely the Universal Postal Union in 1874, also in Switzerland, cemented the trend toward multilateralism negotiated in international organizations. In sum: from the start, international law was created and applied to promote an environment to enable commerce across the oceans, to set limits to the barbarities of war, and to meet the growing demand arising from the technological innovations that gave rise to the need to coordinate movement and the flow of communications.

These modest original "coordination" functions of international law were advanced and taken to higher levels of activity and vigor, with expanded scope for action, almost a century later with the creation of the United Nations in 1945.[20] This decisive moment in the history of humanity created the essential framework for peace and security that generated new global norms imposing further restrictions on war, and establishing a branch of international law known as the law on the use of force, *jus ad bellum*, governing the resort to force. If international wars and battles for territorial conquest had been common occurrences in international relations before this, now they were prohibited.[21] The prohibition of war stands as a central pillar in the current architecture of peace and has had a civilizing effect in international relations.[22] Currently, international warfare is illegal and wars among nations have declined dramatically.[23] Wars of conquest and annexation are no longer the primary tools of foreign policy; normal multilateral practice is to resort to peaceful settlement of disputes through supranational courts and other means.[24] Intrastate conflicts, known as civil wars, still abound, but World War III has been averted as a result of the development in international law prohibiting the resort to force as a prime tool of foreign policy.[25]

The United Nations Charter, the foundational treaty in international law, contains the first explicit and systematic codification of "human rights" in international law. With the United Nations Charter, human rights is an idea whose time had come.[26] The charter sets the first outline, at the international level, for the humane treatment of human beings.[27] The United Nations Charter therefore contains some of the most fundamental new norms: the prohibition of the use of force; the Security Council as the chief arbiter of peace and security (transforming international relations from being purely a matter of coordination to acquiring a subordinate nature, whereby a few countries, namely the veto-wielding Security Council members, decide on peace and security); and the initial contours for the protection of the dignity of the human being as a basis for peace and prosperity in the world.[28] This new legal framework gave rise to the 1948 Universal Declaration of Human Rights (UDHR) and the four 1949 Geneva Conventions of IHL that further created limits for behavior during war and hostilities. These developments heralded a new era for humanity, now under the greater certainty and predictability of international law, where human dignity has a normative space and has started to occupy a central place in international relations. It is noteworthy how the further refinements in IHL brought about by the Geneva Conventions coincided with the consolidation of the importance of the protection of human rights as a normative framework.[29] It is worth exploring what this means and what the significance of these contemporaneous developments is, especially in the light of the potentially destabilizing effects of the militarization of Artificial intelligence (AI) and the accelerated pace of use of autonomous weapons for fully autonomous killing.

A few years later, the 1966 International Covenant on Civil and Political Rights and the International Covenant on Economic, Social and Cultural Rights furnished the legal codification of all human rights initially contained in the UDHR, which had only hortatory force at first.[30] The Vietnam War provided the horrific shock necessary for further political action. A conference convened in Tehran, under the auspices of the United Nations in 1968, furnished the impetus for further regulation of IHL in internal conflicts with a resolution titled "Human Rights in Armed Conflicts," which requested that the General Assembly examine concrete ways to apply the Geneva Conventions to all armed conflicts. As a result, the General Assembly adopted Resolution 2444 (XXIII) on "Respect for Human Rights in Armed Conflicts." The combination of IHL and human rights law concerns paved the way for diplomatic conferences under the sponsorship of the ICRC that led to the 1977 Protocols. This contributed to further regulation of the protection of civilians in war that used Article 3 of the Geneva Conventions as its basis.[31]

These two comprehensive legal frameworks—human rights law and IHL—represent the foundational platform for protecting individual human dignity in international law.[32] The Security Council played an essential role in advancing IHL, and also in its relationship with human rights law, a fact that is not often noted.[33] It did so in two ways: 1) by addressing large-scale human rights violations and resulting humanitarian tragedies as threats to peace and security through the adoption of legally binding resolutions;[34] 2) by establishing two ad hoc tribunals: the International Criminal Tribunal for the Former Yugoslavia (ICTY) and the International Criminal Tribunal for Rwanda. The United Nations has also been involved with the Special Court for Sierra Leone and the Extraordinary Chambers in the Courts of Cambodia, amongst others. The Security Council's first resolution, no. 688, adopted in 1991 with regard to the Kurds in Northern Iraq, referred explicitly to the destabilization caused by flows of refugees as threats to international peace and security.[35] The council's second resolution (no. 770) was issued on August 13, 1992, in relation to the deteriorating situation in Bosnia-Herzegovina, based upon Chapter VII,[36] and called upon all states to facilitate the delivery of humanitarian aid. Several similar resolutions followed on Somalia, Kosovo, Rwanda, Haiti, and Albania. Those relating to East Timor and Sierra Leone in 1999 authorized the use of force for humanitarian purposes.[37]

More than seven decades into this post–World War II normative order, with its intense codification of global norms, urgent challenges and complexities remain that need to be addressed in the light of the dangers posed by, among other threats, climate change, pandemics, loss of biodiversity, and the march toward autonomous killing (with autonomous weapons and the militarization of AI) in the new world order that is now unfolding. Of primary concern is finding ways to best protect the dignity of the individual against atrocities and to respond to the disrespect of global norms of humanity. It is uncertain whether or not states can tackle the problems and challenges of this shifting world order by means of the historical treaty-making approach; whether they will also opt for informal governance methods to create new rules and norms—such as soft law—to tackle problems; or whether they will privilege new forms of governance in certain areas and interpret these alongside existing law and incorporate other branches of international law.

My preoccupation is with what will happen to the stability of international relations if international law is eroded and unravels. The human-centered systems that humanity has in place to comply with the law are at risk in the age of increased autonomy in weapons and militarized AI. In the framework of IHL, for instance, the balance between humanitarian considerations and military necessity may be upset; given the nature of rising autonomous technologies, military necessity will occupy a more dominant position in instances where lethal operations are carried out by autonomous systems. The risk is consequently that humanitarian considerations will be overshadowed. International law, IHL in particular, is conceived and structured on the assumption that humans are present in the battlefield instead of robots.

The origins of the discussions on autonomous killing on the international agenda can be traced back to the Human Rights Council at the United Nations in Geneva. These initial examinations and framing of the issue privileged and favored the language of the protection of human rights, and in particular human rights law. As I explain in Chapter 1, the international discussion moved to another forum known as the Convention on Certain Conventional Weapons (CCW), and the matter gained prominence globally. The CCW is where the 1980 Convention on Certain

Conventional Weapons was negotiated and is implemented. The 1980 convention is considered an IHL treaty: it regulates behavior during conflict, and limits or prohibits the use of certain weapons. This meant that the discussion shifted from a human rights law perspective and was instead confined solely to IHL. In terms of developing new international law, this was limiting: not only for the maturity of the global discussion, bogged down in unproductive technical considerations that arose in the CCW; it was also constraining—and, indeed, counter-productive—when it came to the expansion of the scope of protections to civilians. The threat of autonomous killing and the weaponization of AI are human security issues and, consequently, the primary concern should be humanitarian considerations and the preservation of human dignity (the foundational human right).

International law has expanded considerably throughout the 20th century to protect human dignity, and it is now also about safeguarding human security and even the security of humanity as a whole (*humanity's security*). It is no longer only a law addressing the coordination of practical matters such as telecommunications and international transport among states. The concepts of "International Law for Humankind" or "Humanity's Law" formulated by Antônio Augusto Cançado Trindade and Ruti Teitel, respectively, encompass the paradigmatic changes that have occurred over the last 75 years, when international law became applicable to all who live on the planet. International law is a tool for addressing problems of global cooperation with mechanisms to advance sustainable development and human security, and is most definitely no longer intended only to protect the interests of states, even if the major powers sometimes continue to understand and use international law in that way.[38] It took international law centuries to get to where it is today, with frameworks that protect human beings, such as human rights law and the prohibition of the recourse to military force and international wars. The parts of international law that privilege the security of the individual and the protection of civilians in war are at risk now, and are about to unravel for a number of reasons, including the ongoing militarization of the AI race to achieve the most advanced means of conducting warfare led by the major powers, and the rise of leaders who disregard the common rules of behavior that are beneficial for all humanity. Let us examine the circumstances of this turning point.

Is existing international law enough? How the weaponization of AI disrupts international law

It is important to recognize that **not all autonomous weapons incorporate AI and machine learning**: existing weapons with autonomy in their critical functions, such as air-defense systems with autonomous modes, generally use simple, rule-based, control software to select and attack targets. However, **AI and machine-learning software**—specifically of the type developed for "automatic target recognition"—could form the basis for future autonomous systems, bringing a new dimension of unpredictability to these weapons, as well as concerns about lack of explainability and bias.[39]

Machines with the power and discretion to take lives without human involvement are politically unacceptable, morally repugnant and should be prohibited by international law.[40]

It seems reasonable at this stage to determine what kinds of risks and perils arise for humanity and the ordering system of the global rule of law that is represented by international law. It is important to realize that this organizing system is in danger of unraveling under the pressures of the shifting world order in this age of the rapid militarization of autonomous technologies and presently also of AI, including the weaponization of its techniques, that is underway among technologically powerful countries.[41]

International law is a rules-based world system that was strengthened and made more attentive to the need to protect human dignity after 1945. As Theodor Meron has argued, at that point, the "humanization of international law" began.[42] It is now under threat from renewed competition between the great powers, the threat of nuclear war, a rising disdain for international norms by many countries, and the emergence of militarized AI, which will make it easier to initiate war and also to maintain a constant state of aggression, including through cyber-attacks. Therefore, the role of *transnational networked cooperation* attempting to establish *common good governance* is all the more pressing. Great power conflict is possible again between China, the United States, and Russia; in the age of autonomous weapons and the precipitous militarization of AI this could happen more speedily and with greater magnitude than in the past. The multilateral channels for conflict resolution proposed in the United Nations Charter and put into practice over recent decades are in danger of falling out of favor. As a result, new ideas are required to develop a novel form of global governance that will give the common good the highest priority. But what form will the disruption of international law take? What frameworks will be undermined, disrupted, or abandoned?[43]

When new technologies emerge and threaten to unsettle peace and security, as well as undermine the existing legal systems that regulate relations in the international arena, a number of questions arise:[44] What is the role of international law and how can it assist the international community to address the challenges posed in our current age by the utilization of autonomous killing and the greater weaponization of AI? Is the existing international law global framework adequate to address the challenges posed by the development of new autonomous weapons and technologies? Who will be held responsible for autonomous killing? Does international law permit the replacement of human decision-making with algorithmic control and responses? Should it permit this? What parts of international law should apply, or should it be only IHL (i.e., the laws of war)? How will the response to unforeseen circumstances be accounted for? What are the consequences of autonomous killing by autonomous weapons, or other types of killing stemming from the weaponization of AI, for the shifting world order in the absence of new international law to govern it?

By posing these questions, I highlight not only my essential concerns but also those that permeate the literature, especially in the light of the discussions taking place at the highest level of the United Nations and among observers who are examining issues around the intensification of algorithmic killing and the weaponization of AI. Most ask whether existing international law is up to the task of addressing the challenges. Should preventive bans or prohibitions be in place or not?[45] Will technological developments within the realm of AI be able to comply with existing laws? And, within this framework, these commentators and observers tend to focus on that part of international law which sets the rules to limit the barbarities of war—namely, IHL or the laws of war.

While these analyses have been essential in steering the international debate, we are at a point where a more probing examination of all the relevant aspects of international law is in order. This is a matter of some urgency, along with addressing another key question: How will such transformative technological advancements in the employment of autonomous systems and also those within the ambit of AI affect the purpose and scope of the rules and norms of global governance that have been set by international law for decades? International law, I contend, will be profoundly disrupted for three reasons.

1) The new technologies of autonomy and AI as they are currently being employed already circumvent the global rules and norms of peace, such as the nonuse of force in international relations and the peaceful settlement of disputes (countries already employ armed drones against entities with whom they are not at war instead of seeking avenues for peaceful resolution).[46] Restraints on the use of force and the practice of peaceful settlement of disputes through negotiation, mediation, and other means are the two main pillars upon which the entire edifice of the United Nations Charter on global governance rests.

2) The part of global governance that protects human beings' dignity, and is unequivocally underpinned by international law, is human-centered (human rights law, in particular). International law has indeed been constructed on the basis of the human being as the creator, adjudicator, benefactor, and beneficiary. If decisions were to be delegated and entrusted to algorithms and robots as their executors, then what would happen to the existing legal structures?[47] They will most likely be evaded in the name of the expediency provided by the technological convenience of acting more rapidly or in the secrecy of cyberspace. The purpose of common human action as the basis of international law will wither into irrelevance and become peripheral.

3) International law was initially created to benefit and serve states' aspirations to expand their commercial activities, facilitate cooperation, and maintain their sovereign domains and rules. It took centuries and two calamitous world wars for international law to become gradually humanized and emphasize human beings and the concomitant protections as significant principles.[48]

But technological advancements and the rapid pace at which states are already disrespecting the tenor of the purpose and objectives of the current international rule of law-based global governance are astounding and should be of great concern. This development should alert the whole of humankind that it is on a dangerous path toward a potentially precarious and uncertain future with more wars and no universally agreed norms, where the rule of the technologically powerful might prevail.[49] This disruption may set international relations back to the point where states' national interests had primacy over the protections afforded to human beings: there will be a shift away from human security-centered law (that now coexists with states' national interests) and back to an exclusive focus on national security interests, regardless of the human cost. International law took centuries to become humanized.[50] This perverse disrespect for the global rule of law, which may be further intensified by the expeditious use of a seductive technological advantage offered by autonomous weapons, may portend what lies ahead with the weaponization of AI. The ongoing deployment of greater autonomy in weapons is already having a disintegrating effect on the most important norms of conduct that maintain global peace.

My premise for the construction of a new form of global governance to forge new global public goods, namely *common good governance*, to stem the rise of algorithmic killing and the rapid of weaponization of AI is that human beings need to oversee—and dare not relinquish—the decision-making process to kill. Systems that are autonomous in the functions designed to kill—the so-called "critical functions"—must be placed under the scrutiny of international law. This will pave the way toward creating governing restrictions at the global level that will also slow the pace of the weaponization of AI.

A bird's eye view of all the pertinent international law that could be applicable can help form the basis for the creation of what I call *common good governance* and will assist us with designing new mechanisms for averting a perilous future. This is especially so because, in the case of autonomous systems, the currently prevailing legal frameworks that regulated or prohibited other kinds of weapons (such as nuclear or chemical weapons) will provide some guidance, but they will not be entirely useful or applicable (Chapter 5). This is because we are not necessarily talking about one concrete object: autonomous systems are mostly software algorithms that can be placed in networked structures, parts, or functions of different systems.[51] Current legal regimes prevented, prohibited, or regulated an object or entity (one weapon or a few categories of weapons, as demonstrated in the Annex to Chapter 5). Nonetheless, autonomous technologies are taking the implementation of long-standing global governance rules into risky and uncharted territory.

***

Zooming in on the challenges presented by autonomous killing in particular, and the use of military AI even if algorithms are eventually designed to be ethical and comply with IHL (which I and many others find unlikely), autonomous systems and AI-enabled ones will undermine international law.[52] The principles and fundamental norms enshrined in the United Nations Charter may be at stake: sovereign equality, peaceful settlement of disputes (by negotiation, mediation, arbitration, and other methods), nonuse of force to acquire territory and further national interests, and the prohibition of war.[53]

It bears noting again that not all autonomous weapons (including the ones already deployed) use AI and machine learning. Notwithstanding this clarification, the difficulty with the creation of new regulatory global governance frameworks for already existing autonomous weapons and AI-based autonomous systems is that autonomy can be applied separately to each of the several functions of weapon systems (see Introduction and Chapter 1). When machine learning, an AI technique that represents a real leap in the domain's technological advancement, is fully incorporated into weapon systems, then the perils of complete loss of human control will become a reality. When applied in the cyber realm, the weaponization of AI will change not only the capability to defend against a cyberattack, but also to detect an imminent attack.[54] If the use of force is made unproblematic and expeditious (with certain functions deployed in an autonomous manner), international peace and security are likely to fray and unravel because states will have fewer incentives to talk or negotiate. They may instead attack in cyberspace, or deploy autonomous robotic system soldiers without consulting their national publics. Historically, unlawful military action and interference by force have generated great instability and animosity, as seen in the two World Wars. The principles and purposes of the United Nations Charter are predicated upon the quest for geopolitical stability for the sake of and led by humans.[55]

In the shifting paradigm of world order that is currently under way, it is essential to understand which rules of global cooperation will need to be updated and which will require new international law and form *common good governance*. Many of the global governance frameworks—on trade, disarmament, protecting the oceans, the atmosphere—were initially devised decades ago. It is clear, therefore, that the existing global frameworks need updating. With a shifting world order unfolding before our eyes, it will be necessary to understand at least two pressing matters:

- What updates will be needed in existing global legal and political structures? For instance, the global international law framework that governs the oceans was created when ocean acidification and the problem of plastics contamination were not problems yet. What new forms of international law will be needed to address such issues?
- What will be the impact of technologies in the realm of AI that facilitate, modify, and alter behaviors and realities in all areas? The scope of these profound changes is beginning to be grasped now, but humanity is most certainly in uncharted territory.

We can probably borrow elements of existing regulatory and prohibition frameworks (as examined in Chapter 5), but their utility as analogous frameworks will be limited. Existing regulatory contexts will open up new avenues, but they should not obscure the difficulties and limitations involved.

As technology is fast outpacing the ability of member states of the United Nations to forge new global governance mechanisms and apply existing international law, states and the private sector alike may opt for "faster" approaches to global rule making, such as engaging informal legal remedies rather than formal mechanisms, especially in areas which entail reaching consensus. Many of the new complexities also necessitate the involvement of new actors, such as scientists and civil society. It is critical to determine how existing branches of international law apply to protect civilians from harm,[56] and whether regulations which currently exist are sufficient to address the challenges ahead. Some authors claim that the existing frameworks are sufficient in principle.[57] Furthermore, the fact that a particular means or method of warfare is not specifically regulated does not mean that it can be used without restriction.[58] However, this does not, in turn, mean that laws cannot be strengthened or that new laws do not need to be created in order to address future weapons developments and new technologies.[59] Yet the question of how to create governance frameworks which sufficiently take into account new technological developments within the domain of warfare, formal or informal, is not without complexity.

There are three major challenges that I contend are worth addressing in order to initially understand why states may turn to informal instruments of governance to confront the growth of autonomous killing. The first challenge relates to the idea that international law may be insufficient to address the issues because it is not adapting fast enough to new problems. In this regard, two questions arise: Is existing international law up to the task of protecting civilians within the current dizzyingly dynamic mosaic of various intrastate conflicts, where fewer IHL rules apply than rules to address international armed conflict? Are existing IHL and human rights law sufficient to address new challenges and new actors participating in conflicts and that use new technologies not yet explicitly regulated by international law? This sense of "insufficiency" around the existing law may lead states to turn to informal instruments in attempting to remedy mounting problems.[60]

The second challenge: in today's conflicts, nonstate armed groups operate in densely populated civilian areas. Governments and nonstate groups often target civilians with arguably excessive force (sometimes including the use of prohibited weapons) and without proper observance of the rules of proportionality (as demonstrated in the Syrian conflict).[61] Such actions hinder the ability to provide humanitarian relief and gain access to vulnerable populations caught up in the conflict. Given the increasing number of situations where such challenges occur, states may turn to informal arrangements to remedy humanitarian emergencies and to counter the reality that international law is currently failing to protect civilians. Such situations will be exacerbated in a future with autonomous weapons.[62]

The third challenge that may generate new hybrid forms of global governance (as my concept of *transnational networked cooperation* illustrates), initiated not only by states but especially by others such as the private sector, is the sense that the use of new technologies in the realm of AI, many operated in the cyber domain, is outpacing the capacity of international law and IHL to set rules of behavior. Are new rules needed here? It is not yet clear how international law will apply to these emerging threats, especially the militarization of AI and its consequent weaponization, or whether existing global governance structures will be sufficient. While some say that these interconnected issues have not created a gaping legal hole or a new legal crisis, and that existing international law may well suffice to deal with such situations, there are certainly questions that still need to be addressed and the law will at least need to be clarified. Cyberspace is digitized, which allows for greater anonymity, thus complicating issues of accountability. The ability to enforce international law depends on attribution of responsibility, so if a perpetrator cannot be identified, it is not clear how existing rules can be applied.[63] Thus, an understanding must be reached regarding the level of attribution needed under the law. It is not clear who can be held responsible for attacks by robots, for example, as one cannot hold a robot itself responsible. The programming of the algorithms raises concerns, as there needs to be agreement regarding the types of data they receive. The data have to allow for fair and equitable outcomes and restrict discriminatory ones. Remote-controlled weapons and cyberwarfare raise legal questions around who would be considered the attacker in such circumstances, and what constitutes a battlefield. And what would be the position and legal standing of any conflict when no war has been formally declared?

The phenomenon of autonomous killing gives rise to numerous legal and ethical concerns that need to be addressed and clarified by clear new global governance mechanisms that create global public goods—through the formation of *common good governance*—and by new institutions to assist not only states but all of humankind to cope. The international community additionally needs to decide if existing laws allow for the replacement of human discretion in the decision to kill with programmed responses, and, if so, under what circumstances.[64] Mary Ellen O'Connell, whom I have had the opportunity to meet a few times, affirms that there is a legal and ethical requirement that humans make lethal decisions; she was one of the first to argue for the banning of autonomous killing in terms of an affirmative treaty that prohibits algorithmic killing.[65]

***

Noel Sharkey, roboticist and Emeritus Professor at the University of Sheffield, first alerted the world to the perils of algorithmic killing.[66] Back in 2009 he argued against sacrificing and stretching IHL for the sake of an elusive accuracy on a far-away battlefield in a war engaged in illegally by an attacker that is a technologically superior power utilizing morally disengaged fighters that commit targeted killings which are generally illegal under international law.[67] As I explained in Chapter 1, in 2009 Sharkey created the International Committee for Robot Arms Control to alert the world to the perils of a future when robots kill. I am now a cochair, along with founders Professors Juergen Altmann and Peter Asaro. Back in 2011, O'Connell and Sharkey started writing about the advantages of a preventive legal remedy to pre-empt autonomous killing instead of waiting until the technology has proliferated. O'Connell argued that the essential new core norm that must be forged is a "ban on removing humans too far from the kill chain."[68] Even without a treaty, O'Connell contends, the negotiations at the United Nations could pave the way to the formation of a principle of customary international law that prohibits autonomous killing. Almost a decade after these seminal opinions were expressed, many questions remain. What would be the remaining pathways to build a novel treaty limiting the dehumanization of warfare and common good governance for military AI in general? Is there an emerging core norm that outlaws the removal of human control from the kill chain? To answer these questions, an overview is necessary of the germane parts of international law that are possibly useful to create new *common good governance* to safeguard humanity, preventing war and preserving peace for future generations.

As international law remains the foundational tool to create new global public goods in all areas of common human endeavor, let us explore this.

Relevant applicable branches of international law

With the ongoing militarization of AI in international relations and the prevailing use of autonomy in weapons, it is essential to ask what law is applicable to restrain autonomous killing, and whether existing international law will be sufficient to address the challenges. Observers who try to grapple with these questions tend to focus on IHL, which is indeed a significant and essential source constraining states during hostilities and guiding their actions.

> Any new technology of warfare must be used, and must be capable of being used, in compliance with existing rules of IHL. This is a minimum requirement. However, the unique characteristics of new technologies of warfare, the intended and expected circumstances of their use, and their foreseeable humanitarian consequences may raise questions of whether existing rules are sufficient or need to be clarified or supplemented, in light of their foreseeable impact. What is clear is that military applications of new and emerging technologies are not inevitable. They are choices made by states, which must be within the bounds of existing rules, and take into account potential humanitarian consequences for civilians and for combatants no longer taking part in hostilities, as well as broader considerations of "humanity" and "public conscience."[69]

Other parts (or branches) of international law will be instructive for the creation of new *common good governance*.[70] Algorithmic killing raises legal issues that international law will have to grapple with, such as the attribution of responsibility to a software program and the uncertainty and unpredictability of decision-making by machine-learning algorithms. This section intends, therefore, to provide a wide-ranging overview of potentially pertinent sources that could guide the formation of new global public goods (i.e., my framework of *common good governance*). It is critical to bear in mind that autonomous killing by autonomous weapon systems and AI-assisted algorithmic killing are not exclusively an IHL matter, and that they raise profound ethical questions.[71] This phenomenon goes far beyond the ambit of IHL, because this part of international law applies only once conflict has started. IHL governs conduct during hostilities.[72] Many applications of AI-assisted algorithmic killing (current and future) could occur in nebulous circumstances between nations in a state of war and no-war, where no war has been declared, and also in cyberspace, where the question of attributability is particularly problematic. The difficulty, however, is that the international discussions have focused mostly on IHL, within the CCW, which proceeds slowly and by consensus, to the detriment of the advancement of the cause of protecting humanity and finding a solution to the threat.[73]

In international law, custom (or customary law) and treaties generate legal obligations. The principal challenge is that there is no treaty or custom that explicitly deals with autonomous weapons, nor with military AI, even though the march toward autonomous and AI-assisted killing is well underway. Additionally, there are challenges such as the general lack of public knowledge about the development of increased autonomy and ever-growing investments to weaponize AI; there is also the fact that discussions by the international community have been progressing sluggishly, and are consequently fast outpaced by technological developments. Furthermore, there is scant hard evidence of actual harm that we can build upon just yet; in other words, there are no victims of autonomous systems, or widespread atrocities to act upon or to remedy. Nonetheless, in order to restrain the advancement of autonomous weapon systems, AI-assisted in particular, it is worth starting to examine the need:

- To create *common good governance* mechanisms that prohibit the abdication of human control as a global public good under international law; here, new law-making would be necessary in the form of soft law (codes of conduct, political declarations, and so on) and legally binding treaties;
- To clarify existing legal and political frameworks and to then apply them to the challenges presented by the ongoing weaponization of AI—i.e., create global public goods through *common good governance*.

The following are the branches of international law that could constitute the foundational units for the governance of autonomous killing (to address the increasing use of autonomous weapons) and also to govern the militarization of AI. They are listed in Figure 4.1 as well. I will briefly review each in turn, offering more analysis for discussion on IHL, which has been the focus of the discussions at the United Nations:

- Law of State Responsibility
- Law on the Use of Force: *Jus ad bellum*, governing the resort to force

Applicable international law to regulate autonomous weapons and AI

Figure 4.1 Relevant international law to the case of global governance surrounding AI

- IHL: *Jus in bello*. Laws of Armed Conflict/Laws of War
- International Human Rights Law
- International Criminal Law
- Global Commons Law: treaty provisions, principles, and customary law protecting these areas and spaces: Antarctica, outer space, atmosphere (and ozone), high seas; and cyberspace and AI as human-made commons (global commons law is discussed in Chapter 2).

Beyond these branches of international law, other international mechanisms could provide the basis for new law-making or simply new global governance: United Nations General Assembly resolutions, United Nations Security Council resolutions, soft law or politically binding codes of conduct or programs of action, and principles published by companies, states, and civil society.

State responsibility

State responsibility is a fundamental and constitutive dimension of international law.[74] The law of state responsibility has to do with determining when a wrongful act contrary to international law occurs, when the state or other entities are to be held responsible, and what the legal consequences are, along with what types of reparations should follow. Attribution, breach, remedies, and consequences are the key concepts in the law of state responsibility. The United Nations International Law Commission has been examining state responsibility since 1956 and published the articles in 2001. They provide a general codified framework containing the essential rules of international law vis-à-vis the responsibility of states regarding their wrongful acts.[75] The following are the potentially relevant articles of the law of state responsibility that are worth mentioning and that could serve as guidance for new forms of governance to stem the use of algorithmic killing and the march toward weaponizing AI. Article 2 spells out the elements of an international wrongful act, which is usually typified by:

- Conduct consisting of an action or omission that is attributable to the state under international law;
- A breach by a state of an international obligation.

At first glance, the interpretation of this article means that the responsibility for wrongdoing committed with autonomous systems will most likely fall on states. They will also bear the brunt of the responsibility for contravening obligations under treaties and infringing on requirements assumed under other parts of international law, namely human rights law and IHL. Significantly, this part of the law ascribes responsibility to the state for reparations and the payment of compensation for damages to other states. However, a broader interpretation of the law on state responsibility does not exempt other entities of wrongdoing—for instance, the manufacturer or the ones who designed the kill algorithms. When machine learning is employed in autonomous systems, decisions may be taken that were not anticipated by the state employing such systems. Machine learning will mean that the machine will deliver an output, having learned from the input of the trained data:

> AI, and especially machine learning, brings concerns about unpredictability and unreliability (or safety), lack of transparency (or explainability) and bias. Rather than following a pre-programed sequence of instructions, machine learning systems build their own rules based on the data they are exposed to—whether training data or through trial-and-error interaction with their environment. As a result, they are much more unpredictable than pre-programed systems in terms of how they will function in a given situation, and their functioning is highly dependent on quantity and quality of available data for a specific task. These core problems are exacerbated where the system continues to "learn" and change its model after deployment for a specific task. The unpredictable nature of machine-learning systems, which can be an advantage for solving tasks, may not be a problem for benign tasks, such as playing a board game, but it may be a significant concern for applications in armed conflict, such as autonomous weapon systems, cyber warfare, and decision-support systems.[76]

The variable and inscrutable nature of machine learning—which is one of the widespread techniques of AI—will complicate matters extensively: the law on state responsibility, like the other parts of international law, has evolved to deem humans responsible for the actions of their states. If robots make the decisions, who will be responsible for criminal liability? The answer is uncertain. As a result, the path ahead is uncharted. The following state responsibility articles offer further guidance:

- Article 8. "Conduct directed or controlled by a state. The conduct of a person or group of persons shall be considered an act of a State under international law if the person or group of persons is in fact acting on the instructions of, or under the direction or control of, that state in carrying out the conduct."[77]
- Article 15. "Breach consisting of a composite act. 1. The breach of an international obligation by a state through a series of actions or omissions defined in aggregate as wrongful occurs when the action or omission occurs which, taken with the other actions or omissions, is sufficient to constitute the wrongful act. 2. In such a case, the breach extends over the entire period starting with the first of the actions or omissions of the series and lasts for as long as these actions or omissions are repeated and remain not in conformity with the international obligation. Examples include the obligations concerning genocide, apartheid or crimes against humanity [and] systematic acts of racial discrimination."

The use of autonomous systems will likely be used, with varying intensity, in different parts of the numerous functions of the "kill chain." This is a process adopted by the American armed forces (with variations in other militaries), known as the dynamic targeting process, which is the sum of different segments: find, fix, track, target, engage, and assess (F2T2EA). Examination of Articles 8 and 15 make it clear that errors occurring in the "target" or in the "engage" functions using autonomous systems could result in incurring responsibility for wrongdoing. The same applies for what could arise when Article 16 is taken into account to assess the lawfulness of certain actions. Article 16 represents the conceptual core of our discussion on the use and transfer of new arms:

- Article 16: "A State which aids or assists another State in the commission of an internationally wrongful act by the latter is internationally responsible for doing so if: (*a*) That State does so with knowledge of the circumstances of the internationally wrongful act; and (*b*) The act would be internationally wrongful if committed by that State."

Responsibility for wrongdoing is at its gravest and most forbidding in terms of Article 26 on "Compliance with Peremptory Norms." Peremptory norms (*jus cogens*) are "accepted and recognized by the international community of states as a whole as a norm from which no derogation is permitted and which can be modified only by a subsequent norm of general International Law having the same character" (Vienna Convention on the Law of the Treaties 1969: art. 53); examples are genocide and torture.[78] In accordance with Article 53 of the 1969 Vienna Convention, a peremptory norm of general international law is one which is "accepted and recognized by the international community of States as a whole as a norm from which no derogation is permitted and which can be modified only by a subsequent norm of general international law having the same character." If this is contemplated, states would have incurred attributable fault arising not only from the already existing human rights law instruments, but should also bear this customary obligation set by the law on state responsibility.[79]

Governing the resort to force: War made illegal

The central global norms that restrict the use of and recourse to military force in international relations are:

- States may not use or threaten the use of force (United Nations Charter Article 2.4) except in two circumstances:
  - States may use force in self-defense, when responding to an "armed attack" (United Nations Charter Article 51);
- The United Nations Security Council possesses the legal monopoly to authorize the use of force (United Nations Charter Chapter VII) in cases where it deems peace and security are at stake.

These norms were brought about by the codification present in the United Nations Charter (ratified by the 193 member states of the United Nations), which ushered in a paradigm shift in the way foreign politics are conducted in international relations.[80] Before this, wars of conquest through the use of military force were common and frequent.[81] Now, when they occur, as in Ukraine, the violator is met with concerted outrage and relegated to isolation. United Nations Article 2.4 enshrines the prohibition against international wars and had a pacifying effect and has thus far prevented World War III: "All Members shall refrain in their international relations from the threat or use of force against the territorial integrity or political independence of any state, or in any other manner inconsistent with the Purposes of the United Nations." The important element to bear in mind is that the use of force is a *jus cogens* norm (no derogation is permitted). The prohibition of the use of force is of a peremptory nature; therefore, it is a *jus cogens* international norm of overriding weight (reiterated in a decision by the International Court of Justice Nicaragua vs. USA Decision 1986).[82]

   The United Nations Charter made war between states illegal, changing the nature of international affairs. This was a historic shift that heralded a new world order.[83] The charter has several mechanisms to uphold the prohibition against war: a prominent one is contained in Chapter VI on the "pacific" or peaceful settlement of disputes. Central to this set of rules for interstate relations in Chapter VI is Article 33: "The parties to any dispute, the continuance of which is likely to endanger the maintenance of international peace and security, shall, first of all, seek a solution by negotiation, enquiry, mediation, conciliation, arbitration, judicial settlement, resort to regional agencies or arrangements, or other peaceful means of their own choice." Chapter VI is prefaced by the seven principles contained in Article 2, especially paragraph 3: "All Members shall settle their international disputes by peaceful means in such a manner that international peace and security, and justice, are not endangered."[84]

The increased use of autonomy that will be enhanced by the militarization of AI jeopardizes this carefully built edifice that represents the most momentous and weighty change to international law in its history—namely, the prohibition on the use of armed force in international relations—demanding instead that states shall peacefully settle their disputes by means of negotiation, mediation, enquiry, arbitration, and, ultimately, judicial settlement.[85] This means that the resort to armed force is always a last recourse and made under special circumstances—for example, for the purposes of self-defense and under the authorization of the United Nations Security Council (collective action instead of an individual decision by one state). Now, with the progressive development of autonomous systems and the increased militarization of AI and, ultimately, autonomy in the use of force, the concern is that the employment of force will be resorted to more swiftly and at no risk to the troops of those technologically advanced nations.[86]

International humanitarian law

International humanitarian law is the branch of international law dealing with the limits of lethal force and conduct during conflict. The basic treaties are the Geneva Conventions of 1949 and the 1977 Additional Protocols, but many other treaties are also part of this essential aspect of international law, including those that prohibit the use of chemical weapons and blinding laser weapons, as well as laws that protect world heritage sites and cultural property during war.[87] Once war breaks out, IHL is applicable and sets obligations determining what is permissible during hostilities, and what can be done to protect civilians, cultural property, and also the environment. It is worth noting that IHL is universal—it has been ratified by all countries and is considered customary law, which means that it sets up universal expectations and imposes duties of humane conduct for all. From states to rebel groups at war, everyone is under the obligation to respect humane principles limiting the barbarities of war, such as torture, summary executions, the use of inhumane and exceedingly cruel weapons (i.e., chemicals, biological weapons), and arbitrary incarcerations.[88] In sum, most rules of IHL are considered customary and are formally adhered to, despite the many violations. Many customary norms are considered *jus cogens*. States would be best served by focusing on compliance mechanisms to ensure that the law is respected.[89]

One of the principal questions I intend to answer in this book is this: Do IHL and other branches of international law have to be amended, or modified, in the face of new technological developments, or are the existing fundamental principles imposing restrictions on new autonomous systems still valid and sufficiently resilient?

It is essential to observe the chief IHL principles in the light of the use of autonomous killing and to ask whether autonomous systems can be compliant with the following guiding principles, which have been considered by the International Court of Justice as the forming the fabric of international law:[90]

- Distinction: Parties to a conflict must always be able to distinguish and respect lawful targets (combatants) and unlawful targets (civilians and *hors de combat*). This rule is codified in Additional Protocol I to the Geneva Conventions Article 48;
- The choice of weapon is not unlimited: This principle articulates the proscription on weapons that are by nature indiscriminate, and that cause unnecessary suffering or superfluous injury.[91] Several conventions regulate or prohibit the use of specific weapons. These include prohibitions on biological and chemical weapons, antipersonnel mines, cluster munitions, and blinding laser weapons;
- Proportionality: The balance between military necessity and humanitarian needs is safeguarded by a general principle of proportionality in terms of which no force should be used beyond what is needed to achieve a desired military result and to avoid "collateral damage"/additional, incidental loss;[92]
- Precaution: Parties to hostilities are under a solemn duty arising from IHL to minimize the suffering of civilians and therefore to take all necessary precautions accordingly. The choice of (adequate) weapon that would not result in unnecessary suffering and superfluous injury should therefore underpin all actions. The worst violations of this principle may constitute war crimes.[93]

The 1977 Additional Protocol I to the Geneva Conventions of 1949 Article 35 sets out the basic rules pertinent to this discussion:[94]

1) In any armed conflict, the right of the parties to the conflict to choose methods or means of warfare is not unlimited.
2) It is prohibited to employ weapons, projectiles, and materials and methods of warfare of a nature that will cause superfluous injury or unnecessary suffering.
3) It is prohibited to employ methods or means of warfare which are intended, or may be expected, to cause widespread, long-term, and severe damage to the natural environment.

Another centrally important set of rules emanates from Article 36 of the 1977 Additional Protocol I to the Geneva Conventions of 1949; it requires each state party to ensure that the use of any new weapons, means, or methods of warfare that it studies, develops, acquires, or adopts comply with the rules of IHL. This obligation to review weapons leads some experts to categorically affirm that in the light of Article 36 all autonomous weapons fall under this obligation and therefore IHL already governs autonomy.[95] Yes, legally speaking, any new weapon system shall be reviewed and therefore falls under the ambit of this obligation set by Article 36.[96] But arguments that Article 36 is sufficient to regulate autonomous systems are inattentive to the fact that most countries do not conduct such reviews because they are technically difficult and onerous. Only a few—such as the Netherlands, Norway, and other dutiful and technically capable nations—do, which is hardly representative of the world stage.[97]

Additionally, machine learning algorithms will make determining what the output of an action taken by a machine will be uncertain and unpredictable.[98] This unpredictability can rise as different algorithms from different countries are deployed alongside one another in the battlefield.[99] This will make weapons reviews all the more precarious a means of ascertaining the possibility of prevention before the deployment of an autonomous system.[100]

> Many machine learning systems are not transparent, they produce outputs that are not explainable. This "black box" nature makes it difficult—and, in many cases, currently impossible—for the user to understand how and why the system reaches its output from a given input; in other words there is a lack of explainability and interpretability.[101]

Moreover, the ones that are already deployed have not been through the review process, because autonomy was added to already existing components and functions. At the United Nations deliberations, it is those countries that do not want to see any progress in the creation of new global forms of governance which insist that weapons reviews conducted in terms of Article 36 suffice. Finally, AI weapons will not have to be embodied; they can operate in the cyber domain, which will make the traditional forms of testing under Article 36 obsolete and in need of updating. To argue that Article 36 is a sufficient global governance mechanism to stem algorithmic killing and prevent the militarization of AI fails to take account of the pace and scope of the technological challenges presented here.

The possibility of new weapons breaching IHL is acknowledged in the Geneva Conventions (Articles 50, 51, 130, and 147 of Conventions I, II, III, and IV, respectively) and in the Additional Protocol I of 1977 (Articles 11 and 85), which include:

1) Making the civilian population or individual civilians the object of attack;
2) Launching an indiscriminate attack affecting the civilian population or civilian objects in the knowledge that such attack will cause excessive loss of life, injury to civilians, or damage to civilian objects, as defined in Article 57, paragraph 2 (a) (iii);
3) Launching an attack against works or installations containing dangerous forces in the knowledge that such attack will cause excessive loss of life, injury to civilians, or damage to civilian objects, as defined in Article 57, paragraph 2 (a) (iii).

Will new IHL be needed?

The questions as to why and when states should conclude new treaties and to what extent they should opt for informal arrangements of governance when faced with autonomous killing are crucial for enabling us to grapple with how to respond to this global challenge. A generally observed recent trend in international law is resistance on the part of states to enter into new treaties. But what is actually happening? There has perhaps not been an abundance of new formal governance arrangements lately (i.e., new international treaties), but I see two emerging global norms that may contribute to the formulation of new rules of governance on algorithmic killing, be they informal (soft law) or formal (international treaties): 1) IHL applies to states and nonstate actors engaged in international and noninternational armed conflict; and 2) the utilization of disarmament and arms regulation as tools and mechanisms to protect civilians.

The first is an emerging global trend whereby the boundaries set by rules of restraint during war apply equally to international and noninternational armed conflicts. This is part because the foundational norms of protection within IHL are now considered customary and therefore bind all parties to a conflict. Further, it is progressively accepted that human rights law and international criminal law are complementary with regard to the scope of protection offered to the individual by IHL in all types of conflict. It could be argued that this emerging global norm arises from two customary rules. The ICRC Customary Study contains 161 rules of customary IHL. Among these, rules 70 and 71, which are applicable in both international and noninternational armed conflicts, are pertinent to our understanding of the developing norm on the human costs of the availability, use, and misuse of weapons during armed conflict.[102] Rule 70 reads as follows: "The use of means and methods of warfare which are of a nature to cause superfluous injury or unnecessary suffering is prohibited." Practice that can be observed from states' behavior and the judgments of international tribunals show that parties in noninternational conflicts tend to observe the prohibition of weapons applicable to international conflicts. The International Criminal Court and the ICTY have both affirmed the need for actors that are engaged in intrastate conflict to adhere to this principle. The ICTY, in the seminal 1995 *Tadić case*, held that:

> Indeed, elementary considerations of humanity and common sense make it preposterous that the use by States of weapons prohibited in armed conflicts between themselves be allowed when States try to put down rebellion by their own nationals on their own territory. What is inhumane, and consequently proscribed, in international wars cannot but be inhumane and inadmissible in civil strife.[103]

Now, to Rule 71: "The use of weapons which are by nature indiscriminate is prohibited." Weapons that cannot be directed specifically at military objectives are prohibited. This proscription is underpinned by another customary rule: a general prohibition on indiscriminate attacks. In the case of nuclear weapons, the ICJ stated that "States must never make civilians the object of attack and must consequently never use weapons that are incapable of distinguishing between civilian and military targets."[104]

A party's choice of weapons during conflict is not unlimited; Additional Protocol I was the first treaty to articulate this prohibition on weapons that are by nature indiscriminate and cause unnecessary suffering or superfluous injury (cluster bombs or landmines, for instance).[105] Less clear in practice is whether further explicit prohibitions of specific weapon systems are needed. Compounding these factors is the point that, since 1995, all new humanitarian law treaties apply to noninternational armed conflicts (which are more common today, as in Syria, Yemen, etc.). These include:

- the 1993 Convention on the Prohibition of the Development, Production, Stockpiling and Use of Chemical Weapons.
- the 1994 Convention on the Safety of United Nations and Associated Personnel.
- the 1995 Protocol IV to the 1980 Conventional Weapons Convention on Blinding Laser Weapons.
- the 1996 Protocol II to the 1980 Conventional Weapons Convention on the Use of Mines, Booby-traps, and Other Devices.
- the 1997 Convention on the Prohibition of the Use, Stockpiling, Production and Transfer of Antipersonnel Mines and their Destruction ("Ottawa Convention" or the "Mine Ban Treaty").
- the 1998 Rome Statute of the International Criminal Court.
- the 1999 Second Protocol to the Hague Convention of 1954 for the Protection of Cultural Property in the Event of Armed Conflict.
- the 2000 Optional Protocol to the Convention on the Rights of the Child on the Involvement of Children in Armed Conflict.
- October 1980 Convention, amended on December 21, 2001, declaring the Convention on Prohibitions or Restrictions on the Use of Certain Conventional Weapons Which May Be Deemed to Be Excessively Injurious or to Have Indiscriminate Effects as amended on December 21, 2001 (CCW), referred to as the Convention on Certain Conventional Weapons. It is also known as the Inhumane Weapons Convention and all protocols are applicable also in noninternational armed conflicts.
- the 2008 Convention on Cluster Munitions (CCM).
- the 2013 Arms Trade Treaty.[106]

I would argue that there is no stagnation in IHL as it is designed to last and to be resilient. Thus, it continues to constitute a strong basis for building new *common good governance* to limit the danger posed by the deployment of autonomous algorithmic killing and the militarization of AI. Notwithstanding this view, further clarification of IHL is needed, and extra specific prohibitions and regulations are necessary in the light of the challenges raised by the weaponization of AI.

There is a more intense form of governance-making activity, related to the second emerging global norm relevant here: the utilization of disarmament and arms regulation as a mechanism to protect civilians. In this area, the international community will have to think long and hard about how to protect civilians in a world where robots can kill. When the foundations of IHL were established, it was not possible to foresee the nature of today's warfare technology, yet the law is still applicable and functional in regulating the use and development of weaponry. IHL has played a continuous role in either prohibiting or restricting new and existing weapons throughout history, and elements have been created, modified, and refined on several occasions at key global summits held in 1864, 1899, 1907, 1929, 1949, and 1977 in order to enhance the protection of civilian populations, setting limits for conduct during war and limiting armaments by new treaties (1868, 1907, 1925, 1972, 1980, 1993, 1995, 1996, 1997, 2001, 2003, 2008, and 2013—see the list presented above), with clarifications and adaptations to reflect evolving customary law. One can therefore hardly talk of stagnation. IHL is vibrant, but will it need to be clarified in the age of emerging AI?

Despite the fact that informal methods of developing the law, called soft law, are becoming more popular, multilateral negotiations have not quite yet become the exception rather than the rule. It is interesting to see that courts, nonstate groups, and NGOs now influence the making of politically binding agreements, codes of conduct, and more with intense *transnational networked cooperation*, as I argue in Chapter 1. It is important to observe how these processes are formed, whether this is done through legitimate means, and how they fit into the evolution of international law. It is clear that informal processes have mushroomed, moving the evolution of international law away from its traditional sources.[107] Joost Pauwelyn and colleagues have examined this change by utilizing a three-pronged approach: the first line of inquiry is the output that may result—for example, the crystallization of norms or the development of informal agreements; the second is the type of process which is adopted and whether it occurs outside of the framework of international organizations; and third is determining the composition of change makers and groups involved in the process, beyond the state. This new trend in governing global cooperation raises a number of questions: Does it mark an evolution or a regression of international law? What is the impact on accountability in the law-making process? Most importantly, has this trend toward informal governance-making processes reached the realm of IHL? Could it furnish indicators to craft frameworks for the militarization of AI?

The straightforward answer is "yes." And, indeed, the soft law approach has value, though it is seen as voluntary. It may pave the way for further commitments, it may build momentum for further refinements in thinking and action, and it may also provide more time for additional stakeholders to embrace the new development. Examples of informal agreements abound. One is the 2008 Montreux Document on Pertinent International Legal Obligations and Good Practices for States Related to Operations of Private Military and Security Companies during Armed Conflict. This is the first document to specifically address private military security companies at the international level and to outline the applicable international law. In sum, the adoption of soft norms is viewed by some as an incremental approach to law-making. This approach may shape values, but it is not sufficient as it is seen as voluntary. The process may also have ambiguities and entail compromises.[108] Even the Anti-Personnel Mine Ban Convention and the CCM, which are successful IHL treaties, began with declarations of intent that aimed at avoiding causing harm to civilians. Now such treaties have a wide impact not only on the high-contracting parties but also on non-state parties. The influence of the increasing respect for such norms leads to major changes in the behavior of parties and nonparties alike, which are based not only on legal obligations, but also on the power of new normative interpretations.

The legal position and unique role of the International Committee of the Red Cross

The role of the ICRC as the guardian of IHL is unique and means that this branch of international law holds an unusual position compared to others, and so it is essential to examine what role could it play in the changing world order, especially given the weight and centrality of this part of international law in addressing the rise of autonomous killing. The ICRC distinguishes IHL from other branches of international law. The ICRC can influence state behavior because of its moral clout. The ICRC maintains neutrality and takes action only with regard to credible humanitarian challenges in terms of both its mandate and experience. Hence, the opinion of the ICRC is taken with the utmost seriousness by states. The ICRC assists and also reminds states that they are treaty-bound to abide by IHL and that it is in their own interests to do so. Armies that respect IHL are more efficient as a result of increased unity and consistency.

Yves Sandoz wrote about the ICRC as the guardian of IHL and discerned five central functions of the organization. The first is the "monitoring" function, which involves the continuous assessment of the effectiveness of IHL rules and the attempts to adapt and revise them when needed. The second is the "catalyst" function, which involves engaging experts and nongovernmental organizations to contribute their expert knowledge to the understanding and application of IHL, its evolution, and its interpretation. The third is the "promotion" function, which includes advocacy efforts for the dissemination and teaching of IHL. An indicator of the success of this function is how widely IHL is adhered to by countries around the world. This function importantly includes the education of armed forces across the world as well as nonstate actors. The fourth function is that of "guardian angel." This task is to defend IHL from the development of new rules or laws which would weaken, ignore, or undermine its existence. The fifth is the "direct action" function, which is the most important as it relates to the direct and practical application of the law to conflict. The ICRC is able to carry out this function via accessing conflict areas around the world, conducting prison visits, and through the provision of healthcare to the wounded as well as water and sanitation services.[109] Finally, the "watchdog" function the ICRC serves allows it to raise the profile of the most serious violations (i.e., sounding the alarm). However, the ICRC must show restraint in such actions in order to continue to have access to conflict zones and to be able to protect victims from further violations. All these functions energize the processes of *transnational networked cooperation*, thereby furthering the quest to forge global public goods through *common good governance*.

On May 12, 2021—a decade after it first raised the matter—the ICRC issued its position on autonomous weapons. The position presses states to negotiate new international legally binding rules and regulations that will clarify existing responsibilities and create clear obligations for states. Its judicious decision to wait to reveal its position for so long was prudent. The ICRC was one of the key authoritative conveners of meetings, workshops, and reports that led to a thoughtful and cautious approach that guided states in the first decade of the debate. In its position, calling on states to enact legally binding rules, the ICRC presents its definition of autonomous weapon system:

> Autonomous weapon systems select and apply force to targets without human intervention. After initial activation or launch by a person, an autonomous weapon system self-initiates or triggers a strike in response to information from the environment received through sensors and on the basis of a generalized "target profile." This means that the user does not choose, or even know, the specific target(s) and the precise timing and/or location of the resulting application(s) of force.[110]

The absence of human intervention in the process of triggering an autonomous system compounding the twin problems of the lack of precision vis-à-vis the exact target and the inability to know the precise timing of the final application of the use of force led the ICRC to determine its position. According to the ICRC, "A weapon with autonomy in its critical functions that is unsupervised, unpredictable and unconstrained in time and space would be unlawful."[111] The ideal is to ensure proximity between the initial point of the human decision and the final outcomes.

At the heart of the ICRC position are the following considerations: the risks to civilians and combatants, conflict escalation, challenges to compliance with IHL, and human rights law. Moreover, the profoundly poignant ethical questions that arise from the replacement of human control with sensors and software led to the adoption of this position. The ICRC affirms that it stands ready to cooperate with governments, armed forces, the scientific and technical communities, and industry.[112] In the stated position, member states at the United Nations should create an innovative international set of legally binding rules setting limits on autonomous weapon systems that encompass three areas: the first and second would impose prohibitions, and the third would call for regulations. The first area is a prohibition on unpredictable autonomous weapons whose effects cannot be anticipated and whose outcomes cannot be explained. The second area is a prohibition on antipersonnel systems (i.e., they cannot be deployed to target human beings): "an algorithm should not determine who lives or dies, in effect reducing the decision to kill to sensors and data processing, and death by algorithm would be the final frontier in the autonomation of killing."[113] The ICRC position is a reminder that most would support the nondelegation of the final decision to kill to an algorithm: states, the United Nations Secretary-General, civil society, the scientific community, and the technology industry, in line with my arguments about *transnational networked cooperation*.[114] The third area is a subset of regulatory policies to level the playing field:

- Systems should, by design and in use, create rules for limiting the type of target to those that are military by nature;
- Specific attacks should be the result of limits on the duration, geographical scope, and use;
- Human–machine interactions should ensure timely human supervision that would be able to intervene and deactivate.

Autonomy enables weapon deployment to occur based upon initial assumptions and decisions about the mission's objectives as well as the time, target, and location. However, the exact final target, timing, and location are actually determined by a library of algorithms. The final appraisal often occurs without human control and oversight, and does not take into account changed circumstances. Therefore, there is a separation between the initial assumptions and the actual execution of the mission. Instead, the goal of a set of new rules would be to approximate the initial assumptions and the final targeting to reduce risks to life and human dignity, as well as to minimize violations of existing legal, ethical, and moral constraints. In order to ensure that human control remains present, or at least valid (from the initial assumptions and decisions onwards), and to attain the goal of minimizing harm, each of the lifecycle stages of any weapon system—design, development, testing, deployment, monitoring and operation, maintenance, and disposal—should strive to accomplish these goals. Implementation of the goals ensures that the systems with increased autonomy and those that use AI remain under the purview of humans and are human-centered. In other words, the focus of each operational stage of any weapon system shall be on the primacy of human control, and to examine and scrutinize how the level of human involvement is upheld in the operational context of each mission.

The ICRC notes that the military investment in autonomous systems points to the accelerating reliance on AI, which increases the disquiet about unpredictability and concerns over the targeting of people, given the ever-expanding infrastructure of weapon systems that could become autonomous (from sentry guns, to combat aircraft, to ship-hunting underwater drones). Unpredictability could lead to conflict escalation, and the concomitant risk to civilians could be magnified by the longer duration of conflict and the greater likelihood of indiscriminate attacks in densely populated urban areas (as a result of the system's capacity to loiter in place for extended periods of time), aggravated by the lack of precise timing of the final strike. In other words, AI-assisted and AI-controlled autonomous systems magnify the unpredictability and uncertainty of conflict situations because of the inability to explain how the system reached a decision. Current remote-controlled systems are already able to identify, track, and select targets autonomously, and could be updated to apply force without the final consent of a human. It is the user of the weapon who must fulfill this requirement, not the weapon itself; human beings abide by international law and can be deemed responsible. Therefore, the machine process of the functioning of autonomous systems presents a conundrum for assessing compliance with the existing rules.[115] Fundamentally, IHL prohibits indiscriminate systems, and this is why the ICRC recommends in its position the prohibition of unpredictable autonomous systems (the decisions of which cannot be reasonably understood and explained).

In sum, the need for new internationally legally binding rules (prohibitions and regulations) stems from the fact that, according to the ICRC, current IHL does not adequately respond to the breadth of ethical, legal, and humanitarian questions raised by autonomous systems—or, increasingly more so, AI-enabled ones. New rules would clarify areas of uncertainty and imprecision, and would create stability of expectations, along the lines of what I propose in my *common good governance* concept. At the International Committee for Robot Arms Control, we had several discussion with all members across the world, and determined the watershed importance of the landmark ICRC position to galvanize the momentum for initiating new global norms for the common good of humanity.

International human rights protection

The pertinent questions here are: What is the significance of human dignity in the formation of *common good governance*? Are human dignity and the right to life threatened by autonomy in weapon systems? Would the need to preserve human dignity make autonomy in weapon systems illegal per se? Does the weaponization of AI accelerate trends of disrespect for human dignity? More than 100 treaties make up human rights law, but the initial foundational international instruments, after the United Nations Charter are:

- the 1948 Universal Declaration of Human Right (UDHR);
- the 1966 International Covenant on Civil and Political Rights (ICCPR);
- the 1966 International Covenant on Economic, Social and Cultural Rights.

Additionally, it is worth noting the importance of explicitly setting out the legal obligations arising from the 1948 Convention on the Prevention of and Punishment of the Crime of Genocide, and the 1984 Convention against Torture and Other Cruel, Inhumane or Degrading Treatment or Punishment. It is not possible to derogate from many articles contained in the ICCPR that are considered *jus cogens* or peremptory norms—that is, they must be upheld by the high-contracting parties under all circumstances with no exceptions.[116] The effects of *jus cogens* were summarized by the ICTY:

> Because of the importance of the values it [the prohibition of torture] protects, this principle has evolved into a peremptory norm or *jus cogens*, that is, a norm that enjoys a higher rank in the international hierarchy than treaty law and even "ordinary" customary rules. The most conspicuous consequence of this higher rank is that the principle at issue cannot be derogated from by States through international treaties or local or special customs or even general customary rules not endowed with the same normative force.[117]

Of relevance are ICCPR Article 6 (the right to life and the prohibition of genocide) and Article 7 (the prohibition of torture). The right to life and the right to dignity are key guiding principles and represent firm international obligations.[118] This is where IHL and human rights law intersect. The right to bodily security should not be violated. Human rights law has more stringent standards than IHL. Human rights law applies in conflict, concomitantly with IHL, and includes the right to a remedy which presupposes accountability, which would be rendered harder to achieve with autonomous systems.[119] The ICJ, in its Nuclear Weapons opinion, has stated this categorically:

> The Court observes that the protection of the International Covenant of Civil and Political Rights does not cease in times of war, except by operation of Article 4 of the Covenant whereby certain provisions may be derogated from in a time of national emergency. Respect for the right to life is not, however, such a provision. In principle, the right not arbitrarily to be deprived of one's life applies also in hostilities. The test of what is an arbitrary deprivation of life, however, then falls to be determined by the applicable *lex specialis*, namely, the law applicable in armed conflict which is designed to regulate the conduct of hostilities. Thus, whether a particular loss of life, through the use of a certain weapon in warfare, is to be considered an arbitrary deprivation of life contrary to Article 6 of the Covenant, can only be decided by reference to the law applicable in armed conflict and not deduced from the terms of the Covenant itself
>
> (ICJ 1996 para. 25).

- The right to life: According to Article 6 of the ICCPR, every human being has the inherent right to life. This right shall be protected by law.[120] No one shall be arbitrarily deprived of life.
- The rights to liberty and security: According to Article 9 of the ICCPR: 1. Everyone has the right to liberty and security of person. 2. Anyone who is arrested shall be informed, at the time of arrest, of the reasons for his arrest and shall be promptly informed of any charges against him. 3. Anyone arrested or detained on a criminal charge shall be brought promptly before a judge or other officer authorized by law to exercise judicial power and shall be entitled to trial within a reasonable time or to release.[121]
- The prohibition of torture: According to Article 7 of the ICCPR: No one shall be subjected to torture or to cruel, inhuman, or degrading treatment or punishment. According to Article 2 of the United Nations Convention against Torture and Other Cruel, Inhuman or Degrading Treatment or Punishment: 1. Each state party shall take effective legislative, administrative, judicial, or other measures to prevent acts of torture in any territory under its jurisdiction. 2. No exceptional circumstances whatsoever, whether a state of war or a threat of war, internal political instability or any other public emergency, may be invoked as a justification of torture. 3. An order from a superior officer or a public authority may not be invoked as a justification of torture.[122]

Certain norms codified in treaties have historically been considered *jus cogens*.[123] The result is that these norms rank noticeably higher in the order of global norms and therefore cannot be ignored or derogated from. In this sense, it is important to note the effects that such norms have on the behavior of actors in situations of conflict.[124] Two notable *jus cogens* norms are the prohibition of hostilities directed at civilian populations and the prohibition against torture.[125] It is worth considering the effects these prohibitions will have on the creation of *common good governance* to restrain the weaponization of AI and the heightened use of autonomous systems. It is established in state practice and jurisdiction that both human rights law and IHL apply in conflicts, irrespective of their nature or gravity.[126] Taken together, the combined proscriptions contained in IHL and human rights law would impose a higher threshold for the utilization of autonomous weapons and even more so for the weaponization of AI.[127] This is because of the inscrutable nature of machine learning algorithms, and the arising incertitude about the final targeting decisions. The influential reports to the United Nations Human Rights Council by Christof Heyns starting in 2012 brought to light that the definitive issue regarding autonomous weapons is the protection of human dignity.[128] The unregulated use of autonomous systems, especially AI-enabled ones, represents an affront to human dignity, the most basic human right, in that the decision to kill humans is made by an algorithm.

International criminal acts

This branch of international law ascribes criminal responsibility to individuals responsible for violations of IHL and widespread violations of human rights. The central question here is: Who is to be held accountable for a war crime committed by an autonomous weapon system? International criminal law is a complementary branch of IHL. The former criminalizes the worst violations committed in terms of the latter—that is, war crimes committed in the conduct of hostilities may incur international criminal prosecution. Therefore, serious violations of IHL constitute war crimes. Article 8 of the Rome Statute of the International Criminal Court is of particular relevance because it lists the following war crimes: (i) Willful killing; (ii) Torture or inhuman treatment, including biological experiments; (iii) Willfully causing great suffering, or serious injury to body or health; (iv) Extensive destruction and appropriation of property, not justified by military necessity and carried out unlawfully and wantonly. Individuals and not states are prosecuted under international criminal law.[129]

As Rebecca Crootof has noted, autonomous systems test and challenge fundamental assumptions upon which all branches of international law rest: the centrality of human decision-making, attributable wrongdoing for human actions, and protection of human dignity. Algorithmic killing challenges these vital human-centered assumptions. Such uncertainties need to be confronted and existing international law must be clarified. Nowhere is this more evident than in international criminal law, which has evolved since the post–World War II Nuremberg trials to ascribe responsibility to the individual. It is individuals who are prosecuted for violating the worst crimes against humanity, not machines. Who would be held accountable for harm caused by autonomous systems: the manufacturer, the software programmer, the commander, the official in charge of the specific operation? How could personal responsibility be ascribed? Prominent observers, such as Harvard's Bonnie Docherty, warn about a "credibility gap" whereby—given the distributed nature of the design and use of the autonomous systems—it would be hard to assign liability. Compounding the problem, given the opaque characteristics of machine learning systems, it is likely that creators and users could escape responsibility. The distributed nature of the design and the opacity of AI-assisted systems would render attributability of responsibility—a central component of criminal law—unattainable. Docherty says that existing legal accountability mechanisms are insufficient to address the matter at hand,[130] and Thompson Chengeta explains the impossibility of attributing responsibility for a wrongful act committed as a result of the use of an autonomous system.[131]

At this point, it is crucial to bear in mind the basic elements that trigger international criminal responsibility: 1) a serious violation of IHL; 2) a material element which is constituted by the wrongful act itself; and 3) a mental state which is typified by a guilty criminal state of mind (*mens rea*).[132] How could proof of *mens rea* be verified from an act of an autonomous system? Clearly, the manufacturers or the users of the system would have to be aware that it would commit a crime—something that is not possible. As a consequence, the inability to establish a criminal state of mind, or intent, renders the attribution of responsibility impossible. Without a proper assessment of who was responsible for a crime, reparations and justice cannot later be made available for the victims. The remedy for the lack of ability to impose responsibility is the presence of accountable human control.

At the deliberations at the United Nations in Geneva, member states agreed upon the following formulation as one of the 11 politically binding guiding principles: "Human responsibility for decisions on the use of weapon systems must be retained since accountability cannot be transferred to machines. This should be considered across the entire life cycle of the weapons system."[133] However, the difficulty now lies in translating this into achievable ways to evince international criminal responsibility. As the production of autonomous weapons is distributed across many individuals and systems, it may be challenging to materially connect anyone to a criminal act and unlawful conduct.[134] The putative inability to establish *mens rea* remains the most daunting obstacle to bringing justice for potential victims of the use of autonomous systems.

Emerging or desirable international norms: The basis of *common good governance*

After examining the relevant applicable branches of international law, it is evident that the current international legal and political framework will not suffice to confront the challenges posed by the weaponization of AI. The march toward AI-assisted autonomous systems undermines international law's canonic human-centered precepts: cooperation, responsibility, accountability, and attributability. An already ongoing erosion of existing international norms is proceeding unabated and is weakening the legal edifice that underpins international relations. It is a matter of the utmost urgency to strengthen international law to effectively confront the challenges posed by this extraordinary evolution of the technology applicable to war. At stake is the protection of human life itself. Nothing is more urgent than to establish global public goods through *common good governance* to address this monumental peril to human dignity: death by algorithm and digital dehumanization.

The diagram presented in Figure 4.2 encompasses the desired norms for what I call *common good governance*. The lower block of the diagram depicts a firm basic foundational emerging norm that should steer the debate: primarily human control, also called "meaningful human control." This norm is best understood by examining it through the lenses of the aforementioned branches of international law, which would stipulate that human control must be preserved as an enhanced mechanism to protect human life to be enshrined in new international law as a principle. From human rights law we can infer that a "human-centered foundation" must be the basis upon which human dignity must be safeguarded. From these foundational bases, principles can be inferred in the central block. These principles arise from all the germane branches of international law examined. These principles—namely precaution, intergenerational equity, common heritage of humanity, and common concern—along with the foundational bases, will furnish the combined elements of my concept of *common good governance*. The operationalization of *common good governance* is shown on the top of the diagram. An international scientific panel composed of scientists representing many disciplines from each country (in the mold of the Intergovernmental Panel on Climate Change) will ensure that when all the principles are operational and new global public goods are in place within the framework of *common good governance*, it will stand the test of time.

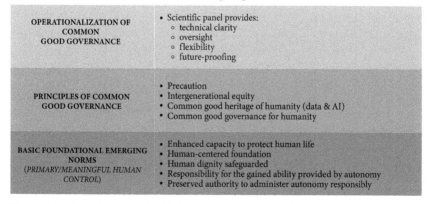

Emerging or desirable international norms
related to common good governance

OPERATIONALIZATION OF COMMON GOOD GOVERNANCE	• Scientific panel provides: ○ technical clarity ○ oversight ○ flexibility ○ future-proofing
PRINCIPLES OF COMMON GOOD GOVERNANCE	• Precaution • Intergenerational equity • Common good heritage of humanity (data & AI) • Common good governance for humanity
BASIC FOUNDATIONAL EMERGING NORMS *(PRIMARY/MEANINGFUL HUMAN CONTROL)*	• Enhanced capacity to protect human life • Human-centered foundation • Human dignity safeguarded • Responsibility for the gained ability provided by autonomy • Preserved authority to administer autonomy responsibly

Figure 4.2 Emerging or desirable international norms related to common good governance

Notes

1. Rüdiger Wolfrum, *Max Planck Encyclopedias of International Law* (November 2006).
2. Mary Ellen O'Connell, "New International Legal Process." *American Journal of International Law*, vol. 93, no. 2 (1999): pp. 334–351.
3. Theodor Meron. *The Humanization of International Law* (Brill Nijhoff, 2006).
4. Anne Marie Slaughter and Gordon LaForge. "Opening up the Order: A More Inclusive International System." *Foreign Affairs*, vol. 100 (2021): p. 154.
5. SIPRI, Vincent Boulanin, et al. "Responsible Military Use of Artificial Intelligence: Can the European Union Lead the Way in Developing Best Practice? Stockholm International Peace Research Institute." https://www.sipri.org/sites/default/files/2020-11/responsible_military_use_of_artificial_intelligence.pdf.
6. Harold Koh, "Transnational Legal Process." *Nebraska. Law Review*, vol, 75 (1996): p. 181.
7. Martti Koskenniemi and Päivi Leino, "Fragmentation of International Law? Postmodern Anxieties." *Leiden Journal of International Law*, vol. 15, no. 3 (2002): pp. 553–579.
8. Antônio Augusto Cançado Trindade, "New Reflections on Humankind as a Subject of International Law." In *Nigerian Yearbook of International Law 2018/2019*, ed. Chile Eboe-Osuji, Engobo Emeseh, and Olabisi D. Akinkugbe (Springer, 2021): pp. 3–25.
9. Louis Henkin, "International Law: Politics and Values." *Developments in International Law*, vol. 18 (1995).
10. Antônio Augusto Cançado Trindade, "Chapter I. The Evolution Towards A New Jus Gentium: The International Law For Humankind." In *International Law for Humankind*. (Brill Nijhoff, 2010): pp. 7–29.
11. Andrew Clapham, "The Role of the Individual in International Law." *European Journal of International Law*, vol. 21, no. 1 (2010): pp. 25–30.
12. See Cecilia M. Bailliet, "Normative Foundations of the International Law of Peace," in *Promoting Peace Through International Law* (Oxford University Press, 2015): pp. 43–65; Diane Marie Amann, "International Law and the Future of Peace." *UGA Legal Studies Research Paper No. 2013–15*, 107th ASIL Proceedings 111 (2014), April 4, 2013; Denise Garcia, *Disarmament Diplomacy and Human Security—Regimes, Norms, and Moral Progress in International Relations* (Routledge, 2011); Mary Ellen O'Connell, "Jus Cogens, International Law's Higher Ethical Norms." In *The Role of Ethics in International Law*, ed. Donald Earl Childress III (Cambridge University Press, 2011): pp. 78–98; Mary Ellen O'Connell, "Peace and War." In *The Handbook of the History of International Law*, eds. Bardo Fassbender and Anne Peters (Oxford University Press, 2012): pp. 272–293.
13. Richard Jolly, Louis Emmerij, and Thomas G. Weiss, *UN Ideas that Changed the World* (Indiana University Press, 2009).
14. Allen Buchanan, *Justice, Legitimacy, and Self-Determination: Moral Foundations for International Law* (Oxford University Press, 2007).
15. Hugo Grotius, *The Freedom of the Seas*, trans. Ralph Van Deman Magoffin (CreateSpace Independent Publishing Platform, 2018).
16. David Freestone, Richard Barnes and David Ong, eds., *The Law of the Sea: Progress and Prospects* (Oxford University Press, 2006).
17. Jan Martenson, "The 1864 Geneva Convention, a link between the ICRC and the United Nations." *International Review of the Red Cross (1961–1997)*, vol. 29, no. 273 (1989): pp. 553–556.

18. Allen Buchanan and Robert O. Keohane, "The Legitimacy of Global Governance Institutions," *Ethics and International Affairs*, vol. 20 no. 4 (2006): pp. 405–437; Hedley Bull, *The Anarchical Society: A Study of Order in International Politics* (Columbia University Press, 1977).

19. Jan Hendrik Verzijl, *International Law in Historical Perspective*. Vol. 3 (Brill Archive, 1970).

20. Antonio Cassese, ed., *Realizing Utopia: The Future of International Law*, (Oxford University Press, 2012); David M Malone, Ian Johnstone, and Simon Chesterman, *Law and Practice of the United Nations: Documents and Commentary, Second Edition* (Oxford University Press, 2016).

21. Olivier Corten, *The Law Against War: The Prohibition on the Use of Force in Contemporary International Law* (Bloomsbury Publishing, 2021).

22. The prohibition against international war is codified in Article 2.4 of the UN Charter, ratified by 193 countries.

23. Oona A. Hathaway and Scott J. Shapiro, *The Internationalists: How a Radical Plan to Outlaw War Remade the World* (Simon & Schuster, 2017); Institute for Economics & Peace, Global Peace Index 2018: Measuring Peace in a Complex World (Sydney, 2018); Jeffrey D. Sachs, "The United Nations at 70," *Project Syndicate*, November 5, 2015, http://jeffsachs.org/wp-content/uploads/2015/08/ProjSynd_The-UN-at-70_821.pdf.

24. Karen J. Alter, Laurence R. Helfer, and Mikael R. Madsen, *International Court Authority* (Oxford University Press, 2018); Karen Alter, *The New Terrain of International Law: Courts, Politics, Rights* (Princeton University Press, 2014).

25. Joshua S. Goldstein, *Winning the War on War: The Decline of Armed Conflict Worldwide* (Plume Books, 2012).

26. Jonathan Israel, *Democratic Enlightenment: Philosophy, Revolution, and Human Rights 1750–1790.* (Oxford University Press, 2013).

27. Thomas Franck, *The Power of Legitimacy Among Nations* (Oxford University Press, 1990); Robert Keohane, "International Relations and International Law: Two Optics." *Harvard International Law Journal*, vol. 38 (1997): pp. 487–502.

28. Louis B. Sohn, "The Human Rights Law of the Charter." *Texas International Law Journal*, vol. 12 (1977): p. 129.

29. Jochen Rauber, "The United Nations—A Kantian Dream Come True? Philosophical Perspectives on the Constitutional Legitimacy of the World Organization." *Hanse Law Review*, vol. 5 (2009).

30. Wade Cole, "Hard and Soft Commitments to Human Rights Treaties, 1966–2000." *Sociological Forum*, vol. 24, no. 3 (Blackwell Publishing Ltd, 2009).

31. Dietrich Schindler, "IHL: Its Remarkable Development and its Persistent Violation." *Journal of the History of International Law/Revue d'histoire du droit international*, vol. 5 no. 2 (2003): pp. 165–188; Denise Garcia, "Humanitarian Security Regimes." *International Affairs*, vol. 91, no.1 (2015): pp. 55–75.

32. Ruti G. Teitel, *Humanity's Law* (Oxford University Press, 2011); W. Michael Reisman, "The Quest for World Order and Human Dignity in the Twenty-first Century: Constitutive Process and Individual Commitment General Course on Public International Law (Volume 351)." In *Collected Courses of the Hague Academy of International Law* (2012). Consulted online on 15 June 2023 <http://dx.doi.org/10.1163/1875-8096_pplrdc_A9789004227255_01>.

33. David Forsythe, "The United Nations and Human Rights, 1945–1985." *Political Science Quarterly*, vol. 100, no. 2 (1985): pp. 249–269.

34. Ingvild Bode, "Reflective Practices at the Security Council: Children and Armed Conflict and the Three United Nations." *European Journal of International Relations*, vol. 24, no. 2 (2018): pp. 293–318.

35. "United Nations Security Council Resolution 688 (1991)," United Nations, https://undocs.org/S/RES/688(1991); Judy A. Gallant, "Humanitarian Intervention and Security Council Resolution S/RES/688: A Reappraisal in Light of a Changing World Order," *American University International Law Review*, vol. 7, no. 4 (1992): pp. 881–920; Dick A. Leurdijk and Stella I.M.L. Beernink, *Decision-Making by Security Council: The Situation between Iraq and Kuwait, 1990-2002: A Survey of Resolutions* (Clingendael Institute, 2002), https://www.jstor.org/stable/resrep05537.

36. United Nations, "United Nations Security Council S/RES/770 (1992)," https://undocs.org/S/RES/770(1992).

37. Schindler, "IHL: Its Remarkable Development and its Persistent Violation."

38. Antônio Augusto Cançado Trindade, *International Law for Humankind* (Martinus Nijhoff Publishers, 2013); Teitel, *Humanity's Law.*

39. International Committee of the Red Cross (ICRC), *"Artificial Intelligence and Machine Learning in Armed Conflict: A Human-Centered Approach,"* (Geneva: International Committee of the Red Cross, 2019): 4. Emphasis is from the original ICRC text.

40. António Guterres, "Message by the Secretary-General to the meeting of the Group of Governmental Experts on Emerging Technologies in the Area of Lethal Autonomous Weapons Systems," United Nations Office at Geneva. https://www.un.org/sg/en/content/sg/statement/2019-03-25/secretary-generals-message-meeting-of-the-group-of-governmental-experts-emerging-technologies-the-area-of-lethal-autonomous-weapons-systems.

41. Daniele Amoroso, *Autonomous Weapons Systems and International Law: A Study on Human-Machine Interactions in Ethically and Legally Sensitive Domains* (Nomos Verlag, 2020).

42. Meron, *The Humanization of International Law.*

43. Matthijs M. Maas, "International Law does not Compute: Artificial Intelligence and the Development, Displacement or Destruction of the Global Legal Order." *Melbourne Journal of International Law*, vol. 20, no. 1 (2019): pp. 29–57.

44. Lyria Bennett Moses. "Recurring Dilemmas: The Law's Race to Keep Up with Technological Change." *University of Illinois Journal of Law, Technology & Policy* (2007): p. 239.

45. Many oppose a preventive ban on the use of autonomous weapon systems, while many others advocate for it. In the first camp, observers warn about the potential stunting of a technology that could be beneficial, while others say that so many autonomous weapon systems are already deployed and operational, what will actually be banned? Careful consideration of the parameters is needed. See: Michael C. Horowitz and Paul Scharre, "Meaningful Human Control in Weapon Systems: A Primer." In *Ethical Autonomy Project* (Center for a New American Security, 2015); Marcel Dickow et al., "First Steps towards a Multidimensional Autonomy Risk Assessment (MARA) in Weapons Systems." Working Paper (Institute for Peace Research and Security Policy at the University of Hamburg, December 2015).

Amongst those who oppose a ban are: Michael N. Schmitt, "Out of the Loop: Autonomous Weapon Systems and the Law of Armed Conflict." *Harvard National Security Journal*, vol. 4, no. 2 (2013): pp. 231–282; Rebecca Crootof, "War, Responsibility, and Killer Robots." *North Carolina Journal of International Law & Commercial Regulation*, vol. 40, no. 4 (2015): pp. 909–933; Kenneth Anderson and Matthew C. Waxman, "Debating Autonomous Weapon Systems, Their Ethics, and Their Regulation Under International Law." In *The Oxford Handbook of Law, Regulation, and Technology*, ed. Roger Brownsword, Eloise Scotford, and Karen Yeung (Oxford University Press, 2017): chp 45; Ron Arkin, "Lethal Autonomous Systems and the Plight of the Non-Combatant." In *The Political Economy of Robots: Prospects for Prosperity and Peace in the Automated 21st Century*, ed. Ryan Kiggins (Springer International Publishing, 2018): pp. 317–326. Observers who are inclined toward implementing a preventive prohibition include: Bonnie Docherty, *Making the Case: The Dangers of Killer Robots and the Need for a Preemptive Ban* (Human Rights Watch, International Human Rights Clinic, 2016); Noel Sharkey, "Saying 'No!' to Lethal Autonomous Targeting," *Journal of Military Ethics*, vol. 9, no. 4 (2010): pp. 369–383; Peter Asaro, "On Banning Autonomous Weapon Systems: Human Rights, Automation, and the Dehumanization of Lethal Decision Making." *International Review of the Red Cross*, vol. 94 (2012): pp. 687–709; Juergen Altmann and Frank Sauer, "Autonomous Weapon Systems and Strategic Stability," *Survival*, vol. 59 (2017): pp. 117–142; John Kaag, "Military Frameworks: Technological Know-how and the Legitimization of Warfare." *Cambridge Review of International Affairs*, vol. 22, no. 4 (2009): pp. 585–607; Heather M. Roff, "The Strategic Robot Problem: Lethal Autonomous Weapons in War." *Journal of Military Ethics*, vol. 13, no. 3 (2014): pp. 211–228; Noel Sharkey, "Why Robots Should not be Delegated with the Decision to Kill." *Connection Science*, vol. 29 (2017): pp. 177–186; Elke Schwarz, "The (Im)possibility of Meaningful Human Control for Lethal Autonomous Weapon Systems." *Humanitarian Law & Policy* (2018); Robin Geiss, "The International-Law Dimension of Autonomous Weapons Systems," International Policy Analysis (Germany: Friedrich-Ebert-Stiftung, October 2015); Caleb Walker, "Prepare for the Flood before the Rain: The Rise and Implications of Lethal Autonomous Weapon Systems (LAWS)." *Canadian Military Journal*, vol. 18 (2018).

46. Noel Sharkey, "Automating Warfare: Lessons Learned from the Drones." *Journal of Law, Information and Science*, vol. 21, no. 2 (2011): pp. 140–154.

47. Rebecca Crootof, "The Killer Robots are Here: Legal and Policy Implications." *Cardozo Law Review*, vol. 36 (2014): p. 1837.

48. Meron, *The Humanization of International Law*.

49. Mary Ellen O'Connell, "Unlawful Killing with Combat Drones: A Case Study of Pakistan, 2004–2009." In *Shooting to Kill: The Law Governing Lethal Force in Context*, ed. Simon Bronitt (Notre Dame Legal Studies Paper 09–43 2009).

50. Antônio Augusto Cançado Trindade, *International Law for Humankind: Towards a New Jus Gentium* (Brill Nijhoff, 2010).

51. Rebecca Crootof, "Autonomous Weapon Systems and the Limits of Analogy." *Harvard National Security Journal*, vol. 9 (2018): pp. 51–83.; Kerstin Vignard, *The Weaponization of Increasingly Autonomous Technologies: Autonomous Weapon Systems and Cyber Operations* (UNIDIR, 2017); Jack Beard, "Law and War in the Virtual Era." *The American Journal of International Law*, vol. 103, no. 3 (2009): pp. 409–445.

52. Louise Doswald-Beck, "Confronting Complexity and New Technologies: A Need to Return to First Principles of International Law." *Proceedings of the ASIL Annual Meeting*, vol. 106 (2012): pp. 107–116.; Denise Garcia, "Lethal Artificial Intelligence and Change: The Future of International Peace and Security." *International Studies Review*, vol. 20, no. 2 (2018): pp. 334–341; Daniel N. Hammond, "Autonomous Weapons and the Problem of State Accountability." *Chicago Journal of International Law*, vol. 15, no. 2 (2015): pp. 652–688.

53. Patrick Lin, "Ethical Blowback from Emerging Technologies." *Journal of Military Ethics*, vol. 9, no. 4 (2010): pp. 313–332; Michael Horowitz, "The Ethics & Morality of Robotic Warfare: Assessing the Debate over Autonomous Weapons." *Daedalus*, vol. 145, no. 4 (2016): pp. 25–36; Robert Sparrow, "Ethics as a Source of Law: The Martens Clause and Autonomous Weapons," *Humanitarian Law & Policy* (blog), November 14, 2017, http://blogs.icrc.org/law-and-policy/2017/11/14/ethics-source-law-martens-clause-autonomous-weapons/.

54. ICRC, *Artificial Intelligence and Machine Learning in Armed Conflict*.

55. Mary Ellen O'Connell, "21st Century Arms Control Challenges: Drones, Cyber Weapons, Killer Robots and WMDs." *Washington University Global Studies Law Review*, vol. 13, no. 3 (2014): pp. 515–534.

56. Kenneth Anderson, Daniel Reisner, and Matthew Waxman, "Adapting the Law of Armed Conflict to Autonomous Weapon Systems." *International Law Studies*, vol. 90 (2014): pp. 386–411.

57. Kenneth Anderson and Matthew C. Waxman, "Law and Ethics for Autonomous Weapon Systems: Why a Ban Won't Work and How the Laws of War Can." In *Jean Perkins Task Force on National Security and Law Essay Series* (Stanford University, The Hoover Institution, 2013), https://papers.ssrn.com/sol3/papers.cfm?abstract_id=2250126.

58. Sarah Kreps and John Kaag, "The Use of Unmanned Aerial Vehicles in Asymmetric Conflict: Legal and Moral Implications." *Polity*, vol. 44, no. 2 (2012): pp. 260–285.

59. William Boothby, *Weapons and the Law of Armed Conflict*, 2nd ed. (Oxford University Press, 2016); Marco Sassoli, "Autonomous Weapons and International Humanitarian Law: Advantages, Open Technical Questions and Legal Issues to be Clarified." *International Law Studies*, vol. 90 (2014): pp. 308–340.

60. Denise Garcia, "Global Norms Governing the Protection of Civilians, Conflict, and Weapons: Formal or Informal Law-Making?" In *Law-Making and Legitimacy in International Humanitarian Law* (Edward Elgar Publishing, 2021): pp. 56–79.

61. O'Connell, "Jus Cogens: International Law's Higher Ethical Norms," pp. 11–19.

62. Heike Krieger and Georg Nolte. "The International Rule of Law—Rise or Decline? Approaching Current Foundational Challenges" In *The International Rule of Law*, ed. Heike Krieger, Georg Nolte, and Andreas Zimmermann (Oxford University Press, 2019): pp. 3–30.

63. Gwendelynn Bills, "LAWS unto Themselves: Controlling the Development and Use of Lethal Autonomous Weapons Systems." *George Washington Law Review*, vol. 83, no. 1 (2014): pp. 176–209; Hammond, "Autonomous Weapons and the Problem of State Accountability."

64. Denise Garcia, "Future Arms, Technologies, and International Law: Preventive Security Governance." *European Journal of International Security*, vol. 1, no. 1 (2016): pp. 94–111.

65. Mary Ellen O'Connell, "Banning Autonomous Killing." In *The American Way of Bombing: Changing Ethical and Legal Norms, from Flying Fortresses to Drones*, ed. Matthew Evangelista and Henry Shue (Cornell University Press, 2014): pp. 224–299.

66. Sharkey, "Saying 'No!' to Lethal Autonomous Targeting."

67. Sharkey, "Automating Warfare."

68. O'Connell, "Banning Autonomous Killing."

69. ICRC, *Artificial Intelligence and Machine Learning in Armed Conflict*, p. 2.

70. Garcia, "Future Arms, Technologies, and International Law"; Rebecca Crootof, "The Varied Law of Autonomous Systems." In *Autonomous Systems: Issues for Defence Policy Makers*, ed. Andrew Williams and Paul Scharre (NATO, February 24, 2015); Crootof, "War, Responsibility, and Killer Robots."

71. Peter M. Asaro, "The Liability Problem for Autonomous Artificial Agents." *2016 AAAI Spring Symposium Series* (2016).

72. Oona A. Hathaway et al., "Which Law Governs During Armed Conflict? The Relationship Between International Humanitarian Law and Human Rights Law." *Minnesota Law Review*, vol. 96 (2012): p. 1883.

73. Asaro, "On Banning Autonomous Weapon Systems."

74. Sean D. Murphy. *The Law of International Responsibility*. Edited by James Crawford, Alain Pellet, and Simon Olleson (Oxford, New York: Oxford University Press, 2010).

75. "Draft Articles on Responsibility of States for Internationally Wrongful Acts, with Commentaries—2001 (International Law Commission A/56/10)," *Yearbook of the International Law Commission*, vol. 2, no. 2 (2001), http://legal.un.org/ilc/texts/instruments/english/commentaries/9_6_2001.pdf.

76. ICRC, *Artificial Intelligence and Machine Learning in Armed Conflict*, p. 10.

77. Boothby, *Weapons and the Law of Armed Conflict*; Marco Sassoli, "Autonomous Weapons and International Humanitarian Law: Advantages, Open Technical Questions and Legal Issues to be Clarified," *International Law Studies*, vol, 90 (2014): pp. 308–340.

78. O'Connell, "Jus cogens: international law's higher ethical norms," pp. 11–19.

79. Elke Schwarz, "Lethal Autonomous Weapons Systems and the Responsibility Gap." In The Routledge Handbook on Responsibility in International Relations, ed. Hannes Hansen-Magnusson and Antje Vetterlein (Routledge, 2021): p. 177.

80. Mary Ellen O'Connell, "The Prohibition of the Use of Force." In *Research Handbook on International Conflict and Security Law*, eds. Nigel D. White and Christian Henderson (Edward Elgar Publishing, 2013): pp. 89–119.

81. Hathaway and Shapiro, *The Internationalists*.

82. Gennady M. Danilenko, "International Jus Cogens: Issues of Law-Making." *European Journal of International Law*, vol. 2 (1991): 42.

83. Mark W. Zacher, "The Territorial Integrity Norm: International Boundaries and the Use of Force." *International Organization*, vol. 55, no.2 (2001): pp. 215–250.

84. Kenneth Watkin, "Controlling the Use of Force: A Role for Human Rights Norms in Contemporary Armed Conflict." *American Journal of International Law*, vol. 98, no. 1 (2004): pp. 1–34.

85. Michael N. Schmitt, "Computer Network Attack and the Use of Force in International Law: Thoughts on a Normative Framework." *Columbia Journal of Transnational Law*, vol. 37 (1998): p. 885.

86. Garcia, "Lethal Artificial Intelligence and Change."

87. To see the full list of IHL treaties, please consult the ICRC database, available publicly at: https://ihl-databases.icrc.org/ihl.

88. Please see the authoritative and seminal study: Jean-Marie Henckaerts and Louise Doswald-Beck, *Customary International Humanitarian Law Volume I: Rules* (Cambridge University Press, 2005).

89. Theodor Meron, "The Continuing Role of Custom in the Formation of International Humanitarian Law." *American Journal of International Law*, vol. 90, no.2 (1996): pp. 238–249.

90. International Court of Justice, *Legality of the Threat or Use of Nuclear Weapons: Advisory Opinion of 8 July 1996* (International Court of Justice, 1996): §78.

91. Codified in Article 35(2) of 1977 Additional Protocol I provides: "It is prohibited to employ weapons, projectiles and material and methods of warfare of a nature to cause superfluous injury or unnecessary suffering."

92. Codified in Additional Protocol I, 51, 57, and 58.

93. Codified in Article 57 of 1977 Additional Protocol I that parties who plan or decide upon an attack shall "take all feasible precautions in the choice of means and methods of attack." Additionally, Rule 17 of the ICRC Customary IHL study states. "Each party to the conflict must take all feasible precautions in the choice of means and methods of warfare with a view to avoiding, and in any event to minimizing, incidental loss of civilian life, injury to civilians and damage to civilian objects."

94. Jonathan Crowe and Kylie Weston-Scheuber, *Principles of International Humanitarian Law* (Edward Elgar Publishing, 2013).

95. Anderson and Waxman, "Law and Ethics for Autonomous Weapon Systems"; Yoram Dinstein, *The Conduct of Hostilities under the Law of International Armed Conflict* (Cambridge University Press, 2004).

96. Thompson Chengeta, "Are Autonomous Weapons Systems the Subject of Article 36 of Additional Protocol I to the Geneva Conventions." *UC Davis Journal of International Law & Policy*, vol. 23 (2016): p. 65.

97. Vincent Boulanin and Maaike Verbruggen, *Article 36 Reviews: Dealing with the Challenges Posed by Emerging Technologies* (SIPRI, 2017); International Committee of the Red Cross Geneva, "A Guide to the Legal Review of New Weapons, Means and Methods of Warfare: Measures to Implement Article 36 of Additional Protocol I of 1977." *International Review of the Red Cross*, vol. 88, no. 864 (2006).

98. Wendell Wallach, "Toward a Ban on Lethal Autonomous Weapons: Surmounting the Obstacles." *Communications of the ACM*, vol. 60, no. 5 (2017): pp. 28–34.

99. Horowitz, "The Ethics and Morality of Robotic Warfare."

100. Frank Sauer, "Lethal Autonomous Weapons Systems." In *The Routledge Social Sciences Handbook of AI*, ed. Elliott Anthony (Routledge, 2021): pp. 237–250.

101. ICRC, *Artificial Intelligence and Machine Learning in Armed Conflict*, p. 10.

102. S. Maslen, N. Weizmann, M. Homayounnejad, and H. Stauffer, *Drones and Other Unmanned Weapons Systems under International Law* (Brill Nijhoff, 2018).

103. *The Prosecutor v. Duško Tadić aka "Dule."* Decision on the Defense Motion for Interlocutory Appeal on Jurisdiction, IT-94-1," International Criminal Tribunal for the Former Yugoslavia, October 2, 1995: § 119.

104. International Court of Justice, *Legality of the Threat or Use of Nuclear Weapons: Advisory Opinion of 8 July 1996*: § 389.

105. Codified in Additional Protocol I, Part III, section I.

106. For a complete list since 1864, please see https://www.icrc.org/en/document/what-treaties-make-ihl-what-customary-ihl. Many observers do not consider the Arms Trade Treaty an IHL document.

107. Joost Pauwelyn, Ramses Wessel, and Jan Wouters, eds., *Informal International Lawmaking* (Oxford University Press, 2012).

108. Kenneth W. Abbott and Duncan Snidal, "Hard and Soft Law in International Governance." *International Organization*, vol. 54, no. 3 (2000): pp. 421–456.

109. Yves Sandoz, *The International Committee of the Red Cross as Guardian of International Humanitarian Law* (International Committee of the Red Cross, 1998).

110. ICRC, Position on Autonomous Weapons Systems, May 12, 2021, Geneva. Position and Background Paper, released by President Peter Maurer.

111. ICRC, International Humanitarian Law and the Challenges of Contemporary Armed Conflicts, 33rd International Conference of the Red Cross and Red Crescent (Geneva, October 2019): p. 31.

112. ICRC, Position on Autonomous Weapons Systems, May 12, 2021.

113. ICRC, Position on Autonomous Weapons Systems, May 12, 2021, p. 8.

114. The ICRC cites: the Future of Life Institute, An Open Letter to the United Nations Convention on Certain Conventional Weapons, 2017, and Future of Life Institute, Autonomous Weapons: An Open Letter from AI & Robotics Researchers, 2015 (4,502 artificial intelligence and robotics researchers, 26,215 other scientists and experts, and the founders and CEOs of 100 artificial intelligence companies in 26 countries signed open letters calling for prohibitions and regulations on AWS); Sundar Pichai, *AI at Google: Our principles* (Google, June 7, 2018), https://blog.google/technology/ai/ai-principles/.

115. ICRC, International Humanitarian Law and the Challenges of Contemporary Armed Conflicts, 33rd International Conference of the Red Cross and Red Crescent (Geneva, October 2019): pp. 22–24.

116. Karen Parker, "Jus Cogens: Compelling the Law of Human Rights." *Hastings International & Comparative Law Review*, vol. 12 (1988): p. 411.

117. Prosecutor v. Anto Furundžija, Judgment of December 10, 1998, Case No. IT-95-17/1, Trial Chamber II.

118. Bruno Simma and Philip Alston, "The Sources of Human Rights Law: Custom, Jus Cogens, and General Principles." *Australian Yearbook of International Law*, vol. 12 (1988): p. 82.

119. Maya Brehm, *Defending the Boundary: Constraints and Requirements on the Use of Autonomous Weapon Systems Under International Humanitarian and Human Rights Law*, Geneva Academy Briefing No. 9 (Geneva Academy, 2017).

120. Elizabeth Wicks, "The Meaning of 'Life': Dignity and the Right to Life in International Human Rights Treaties." *Human Rights Law Review*, vol. 12, no. 2 (2012): pp. 199–219.

121. Christof Heyns, "Autonomous Weapons Systems and Human Rights Law." Presentation made at the informal expert meeting organized by the state parties to the Convention on Certain Conventional Weapons (2014).

122. Peter Asaro, "Autonomous Weapons and the Ethics of Artificial Intelligence." *Ethics of Artificial Intelligence*, vol. (2020): p. 212.

123. Andrea Bianchi, "Human Rights and the Magic of Jus Cogens." *European Journal of International Law*, vol. 19, no. 3 (2008): pp. 491–508.

124. Ingvild Bode and Hendrik Huelss, "Autonomous Weapons Systems and Changing Norms in International Relations." *Review of International Studies*, vol. 44, no. 3 (2018): pp. 393–413.

125. Ulf Linderfalk, "The Effect of Jus Cogens Norms: Whoever Opened Pandora's Box, Did you Ever Think About the Consequences?" *European Journal of International Law*, vol. 18, no. 5 (2007): pp. 853–871; Erika De Wet, "The Prohibition of Torture as an International Norm of Jus Cogens and its Implications for National and Customary Law." *European Journal of International Law*, vol. 15, no. 1 (2004): pp. 97–121.

126. International Court of Justice, *Legality of the Threat or Use of Nuclear Weapons: Advisory Opinion of 8 July 1996*; International Court of Justice, *Legal Consequences of the Construction of a Wall in the Occupied Palestinian Territory: Advisory Opinion of 9 July 2004* (International Court of Justice, 2004); International Court of Justice, *Case Concerning Armed Activities on the Territory of the Congo (Democratic Republic of the Congo v. Uganda): Judgement of 19 December 2005* (International Court of Justice, 2005).

127. Parker, "Jus Cogens: Compelling the Law of Human Rights."

128. Christof Heyns, "Autonomous Weapons in Armed Conflict and the Right to a Dignified Life: An African Perspective." *South African Journal on Human Rights*, vol. 33, no. 1 (2017): pp. 46–71.

129. Casey-Maslen, *Drones and Other Unmanned Weapons Systems under International Law*. I thank Dr. Marta Bo and her project at the Graduate Institute of International Affairs in Geneva, led by Professor Paola Gaeta, for the conversations on this part, and Dr. Stuart Casey-Maslen for the years of conversations with my students at the Geneva Academy for IHL and Human Rights.

130. Bonnie Lynn Docherty, *Mind the Gap: The Lack of Accountability for Killer Robots* (Human Rights Watch, 2015).

131. Chengeta Thompson. "Accountability Gap: Autonomous Weapon Systems and Modes of Responsibility in International Law." *Denver Journal of International Law & Policy*, vol. 45 (2016): p. 1.

132. Chengeta, "Accountability Gap."

133. Group of Governmental Experts on Emerging Technologies in the Area of LAWS, "Report of the 2019 session of the Group of Governmental Experts on Emerging Technologies in the Area of Lethal Autonomous Weapons Systems," CCW/MSP/2019/9, September 25, 2019, Annex III, "Guiding principles" (b).

134. Vincent Boulanin, Laura Bruun, and Netta Goussac. *Autonomous Weapon Systems and International Humanitarian Law* (SIPRI, 2021).

Chapter 5
War, humanity's security, and arms: Existing global norms

Evolutions and revolutions in warfare technologies

Ethical, humanitarian, national security, and public health considerations account for the evolution of the legal and political architecture that today limits armaments—the means and methods of warfare—under international law. Some of the same considerations are also providing the impetus for the deliberations at the United Nations to set limits on autonomous weapons. The evolution of the international law regulatory frameworks for conventional weapons, weapons of mass destruction, and future weapons has been profoundly altering the dynamics of world politics and has helped to protect human beings all over the world. These international law frameworks represent a potent global public good and advance common good governance for all humanity to enjoy.

> "A world free of nuclear weapons would be a global public good of the highest order."
>
> United Nations Secretary-General Ban Ki-moon in his address to the East-West Institute, 24 October 2008.

In this chapter, I discuss the formation of the concept of human security and how it became an ingrained part of disarmament treaties in the last two decades advancing *common good governance*. This discussion is the basis for my concept of *humanity's security* that builds upon the gains brought about by the concept of human security. I first explain its evolution, then elaborate on the concept of *humanity's security* that I introduced earlier in the book. The paramount guiding premise for my argument is that states have an interest in ensuring that weapons are controlled or prohibited. International peace and security are determined in part by the international regulation of armaments, which is a global public good of the highest order.[1] All states will benefit from having weapons either controlled or prohibited. Greater cooperation and compliance with global norms that limit armaments will mean more peace and security, while less coordination and an absence of global public goods will mean a more insecure world and increasingly precarious relations among states. The gains from already existing global cooperation on limiting the methods of warfare, and its success stories, can be utilized to form *common good governance* on military AI.

The AI Military Race. Denise Garcia, Oxford University Press. © Denise Garcia (2023).
DOI: 10.1093/oso/9780192864604.003.0006

Disarmament—a global public good—is indubitably a clear route toward the attainment of *common good governance* to improve *humanity's security*. Several new norms stemming from the prohibition of weapon systems examined here have increased human security across the world, making a difference in people's lives by allowing the possibility of their pursuing gainful livelihoods. Many of these weapon systems did not threaten national security per se but were injurious and deadly to people and communities. This is where new forms of disarmament diplomacy were sought, and succeeded, as in most cases there was scant incentive for the state itself to seek disarmament, as doing so was not imperative for its survival. The more these weapon systems are left unregulated and unconstrained, the more insecure and perilous the international system becomes—and populations are left more vulnerable and insecure. It is worth reiterating that both international geopolitical stability and human security are partly attained by the reduction of armaments.

In the new, post–Cold War world order the concept and practice of security have gradually evolved to also become a common good rather than simply a matter of national interest. In the aftermath of the Cold War, the concept of security was expanded through the flourishing of new ideas and normative frameworks that transcended the state as the pivotal referent in the pursuit of security. Attention to the plight of the individual and suffering in conflict regions or where weapons proliferation abounds became conceivable. During this period, atrocities were committed in new intrastate conflicts from Somalia to the former Yugoslavia, Afghanistan, Myanmar, Rwanda, and Colombia. The proliferation of weapons left over from the Cold War and the circulation of new weapons created a combustible situation as far as human security was concerned. The production and distribution of small arms and light weapons, as well as the threat of nuclear weapons, continued unabated.[2]

New and visionary thinking was needed to address these multiple, interwoven challenges to capture areas that had previously been regarded as discrete, such as achieving human dignity for all, human rights, the observance of international humanitarian law, and ensuring security to advance development. The concept of human security offers the framework for bringing these areas together and enshrining their normative force in new international treaties that are primarily addressed to protect the human being. The formation of innovative treaties focused on human security has an impact on the lives of people across the world.[3] These regimes are designed to protect the living individual and not the abstract state by privileging human security. In the current environment, where the conditions for maintaining international security are deteriorating, reflection on the value and applicability of these humanitarian regimes becomes ever more essential.[4] The Global Peace Index of the Institute for Economics and Peace found that the state of peace in the world has been in constant decline, and has deteriorated rapidly over the last decade.[5] The appearance of the idea of "human security" in the mid-1990s consolidated the trend toward viewing security as a common good where the understanding of security must go beyond the focus on national security and include addressing the notions of "freedom from fear" and "freedom from want."[6] The inclusive developing agenda driven by this notion of human security makes states view and practice the attainment of security in a more all-encompassing way.

One area where states are disinclined to adopt broader ideas about security is the domain of armaments. States equate security with the accumulation of armaments, even if arms have a negligible ability to protect people or to improve the human condition on the planet (Chapters 3 and 4). States tend to protect their power to continue to produce and buy weaponry as freely and as unhindered from any new international treaties as possible. They tend to justify this protectionism and associated expenditure in the name of maintaining national security, and strive to continue building arsenals unconstrained by the imposition of arms reduction and verification.[7] As a result, states may be uninterested about entering into new international agreements and treaties that would restrict their capacity to amass more armaments. Yet, historically, disarmament and the diplomacy aimed at reducing armaments have been central tools at the disposal of states to reduce dangerous levels of armaments, avoid arms races, and ultimately protect human security.[8] Some authors have advanced the view that disarmament diplomacy can serve as an indicator of moral progress in international relations.[9] The more commonly agreed rules and norms there are in this area of security, the more predictability and constancy there will be in the relations involved.

It is essential that we determine how the already existing frameworks regulating or prohibiting certain means of warfare can inform the making of innovative *common good governance* in the area of the weaponization of AI, and establish a benchmark on military AI. In the category of weapons of mass destruction, I focus on the negotiations toward formulating the Treaty on the Prohibition of Nuclear Weapons, referred to as the Nuclear Ban Treaty, which codifies the taboo against the use of nuclear weapons and prohibits them under international law.[10] The treaty entered into force on January 22, 2021, when the 50th member state ratified it. Nuclear weapons have the capacity to annihilate humankind, and it is therefore vitally important to understand the global governing mechanisms that contain and regulate them. I also discuss the global governance of chemical weapons, a landmark framework to protect human beings, and I seek to demonstrate that with every new weapon system and class of weapon that leads to a greater proliferation of arms and harm, a new legal and political architecture of treaties and conventions of containment is needed not only to repair the damage done, but also to limit the current danger and future threats to humans and states, as well as to the well-being of future generations. This architecture is complex enough to construct, but is becoming ever harder to build in the 21st century as states seem to manifest less enthusiasm to negotiate major new international treaties.

As leading AI scientists point out,[11] gunpowder and nuclear weapons represent, respectively, the first and second revolutions in warfare. The intensifying march toward autonomous killing in warfare represents the third revolution. In terms of proliferation, legal and political frameworks are needed to contain the two first revolutions, but we can already predict how destabilizing the third revolution will be for the future of peace and security, both of which are already rather fragile as a consequence of the first two revolutions in warfare.

The first revolution made possible the widespread availability and proliferation of small arms and light weapons, as well as larger conventional weapon systems. Harmful consequences resulted: violence, exacerbation of conflicts, and violations of human rights and international humanitarian law (IHL). Since the member states of the United Nations first started discussing the problem of illicit arms trafficking in 1988, the Arms Trade Treaty—the first legally binding treaty to regulate the transfers of arms—came into force in 2014. A legal political architecture of norms, agreements, and conventions is in place, but it has many shortcomings. I have closely observed the endeavors to create global governing restrictions on small arms and light weapons flows since 1997. I was a student at the Graduate Institute of International Studies and Development at the University of Geneva when discussions on this started in earnest at the United Nations. My advisor, Professor Keith Krause, was entrusted with establishing the Small Arms Survey, the first authoritative research institute to generate data on small arms and light weapons production and proliferation, and the consequences of this proliferation.[12] My first book, *Small Arms and Security: New International Norms*, was the first to link arms and security. This led naturally to my second book, *Disarmament Diplomacy and Human Security*, in which I investigated several processes in this fascinating area, especially the Arms Trade Treaty.[13] I observed the conversations in Geneva and New York, and found those groups leading the Control Arms Campaign, the transnational activist campaign that successfully managed to convince and work with states on the need for an arms trade treaty, to be inspiring.

The second revolution—the creation of nuclear weapons—required the building of another legal political architecture of treaties and global norms, and led to the rise of taboos against their use to contain the possibility of catastrophic proliferation and accidental use.[14] The legal and political architecture to contain nuclear weapons is vast, with several international treaties in many areas from outer space protection and nuclear proliferation to prohibitions of nuclear testing and nuclear-weapon-free zones. Despite some progress, states with nuclear weapons still possess a total of 13,080 such weapons.[15] In 2017, most countries in the world negotiated a new treaty that would make the possession and use of nuclear weapons unlawful under international law. This new impetus is inspired by a human security imperative to disarm based upon humanitarian and public health frameworks. In addition, nuclear-weapon-free zones represent a substantive and often underestimated element in the legal dynamic of limitations of armaments.[16] Most of the planet is covered by such weapon-free zones; the result is that participating countries do not consider nuclear weapons as part of their respective national security strategies, although the agreements do not preclude the use of nuclear technologies (see Table 5.1). The third revolution may be equally costly for peace and security, and will require new global norms under international law to ensure greater predictability and assure all states of each other's intentions. The existing legal and political structures will not suffice to deal with new challenges posed by the development of autonomous weapons, the weaponization of AI, or the ethical and moral implications of using them.

Foundational frameworks for arms limitations

Arms limitation, regulation, and prohibition are essential aspects of national security, a key stabilizer of global security, and a means to achieve peace. Some weapon systems are clearly prohibited under international law, and some are not.[17] Other categories of weapons (such as most conventional arms and nuclear weapons) are only regulated, and so their development, use, and transfer are legal.

Another way of viewing these transformations in the architecture of arms limitations is through the prism of the formation of "humanitarian security regimes," as I have argued earlier,[18] or through an "effects-based humanitarian reframing."[19] These theoretical explanations would advance an understanding of the evolution of the political and legal frameworks in terms of states' attempts to create new security regimes that are humanitarian in their motivation. I define such frameworks as being constituted by altruistic motivations that intend to prohibit destructive behavior and ban lethal technology and weapons. These motivations are animated by humanitarian perspectives to diminish civilian suffering and casualties, and guarantee the protection of victims of armed violence in and out of conflict situations. Within these perspectives,[20] the behavior, technology, and weapons that are the focus of humanitarian efforts include blinding laser weapons, antipersonnel landmines, cluster munitions, arms transfers, nuclear weapons, depleted uranium and other toxic remnants of war, the use of explosive weapons in populated areas, incendiary weapons, and autonomous weapon systems.

Building on these models, I examine arms limitations and dynamics by density of international regulation (see Figure 5.1). All areas of the figure, from left to right—from intensely regulated to barely regulated by international law—are under intense scrutiny from numerous change makers in the international system who want to see progress toward limiting the use of arms and consequently the barbarities that result from such use; these change makers include scientists, transnational civil society movements, and states alike. I argue that the codification of and compliance with international legal regulations on arms reduce the impact of armed violence and prevent the catastrophic use of weapons of mass destruction. The codification of global norms on disarmament through international law signifies progress in international relations and improves human security worldwide. This should be supplemented, I posit, with attention to and national expenditure on social and economic development as well as environmental protection. Two international legal frameworks agreed unanimously by all member states in 2015—the Paris Agreements on Climate Change and the Sustainable Development Goals[21]—provide the appropriate map for states. It gives them a concrete plan for expenditure and investments to promote a

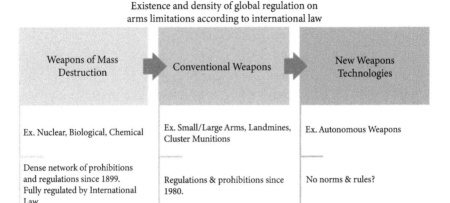

Figure 5.1 Existence and density of global regulation on arms limitations according to international law

future with greater prosperity and security, away from more armaments. The nuclear weapons category has a regulatory structure with the most extensive architecture of treaties, initiatives, and creative political frameworks, such as the nuclear-weapon-free zones. Chemical and biological weapons have been proscribed by international treaties: the 1972 Convention on the Prohibition of the Development, Production and Stockpiling of Bacteriological (Biological) and Toxin Weapons and on Their Destruction, and the 1993 Chemical Weapons Convention.[22]

Conventional weapons are the tools responsible for all the killing in armed conflicts and violence worldwide. There has been increasing regulation and, again, a mix of regulatory and prohibition frameworks. The first comprehensive, legally binding treaty to regulate the transfer of conventional weapons came into force on April 2, 2013: the Arms Trade Treaty.[23] One of the most successful prohibition treaties in the history of disarmament is the 1997 Ottawa Treaty that prohibited landmines.[24] Additionally, the 2008 Cluster Munitions Convention created a framework that bans all aspects of the use and possession of these weapons.[25] Both the landmine and the nuclear weapon ban campaigns were awarded the Nobel Peace Prize, in 2007 and 2017 respectively. These campaigns used exceptional negotiation channels and means anchored in a remarkable partnership between countries, nongovernmental organizations, and scientists. They were inspired by and served to operationalize the human security framework even though states had other motivations beyond improving the state of human security worldwide, such as seeking prestige or maintaining their reputation as law-abiding members of the international community. These prohibitions gave rise to pioneering ways of conducting disarmament diplomacy and fittingly originated new international norms. Future weapons and emerging technologies have fewer or no regulations under international law, except for the constraints imposed upon them by a few branches such as human rights law, IHL, and state responsibility, among others.

Weapons of mass destruction: Focus on nuclear weapons

Nuclear weapons are particularly destructive, indiscriminate, and inhumane, and their accumulation by the highly militarized countries represents an affront to humanity. Their use, no matter how limited, would have devastating humanitarian and environmental consequences.[26] The calculation of the consequences of nuclear warfare on the climate seem to have contributed definitively to the shift toward humanitarian perspectives on disarmament. These scientists modeled the devastating impacts on the Earth's atmosphere and environment, along with the collapse of agriculture and food systems.[27]

The legal framework that governs the limitations on nuclear weapons is vast and is composed of several international treaties and arrangements for nuclear-weapon-free zones. The cornerstone is the 1968 Treaty on the Non-Proliferation of Nuclear Weapons, which set the foundational norm against proliferation and directed states to disarm. Even though progress has been made—from 70,000 nuclear weapons at the height of the Cold War[28] to an estimated 13,080 nuclear warheads at the time of writing—advancement toward total disarmament has stalled over the last 20 years. The nuclear states are the United States, Russia, the United Kingdom, France, China, India, Pakistan, Israel, and the Democratic People's Republic of Korea (North Korea). Ninety percent of the 13,080 existing weapons are American and Russian; of these, 3,825 are deployed at high operational alert levels.[29] Two sets of developments made the 2017 Nuclear Ban Treaty possible. The first is the argument against nuclear deterrence, or global security through the reliance on nuclear weapons, which belongs in the past. This view would claim that nuclear deterrence is obsolete and does not meet the complex security requirements of the 21st century. The second is a move toward a humanitarian and public health approach to eliminate such weapons, which has been taking place over the last five years. These two developments may yet transform world politics. Let us examine each one in turn.

Nuclear deterrence is obsolete

The 2017 Nuclear Weapons Ban Treaty confronts the global nuclear order by explicitly stigmatizing and delegitimizing it, because the treaty tackles head-on the anachronism of nuclear deterrence.[30] Two different arguments make the use of nuclear weapons unthinkable and unjustifiable: the humanitarian consequences as, compared to 1945, most areas on the planet today are densely urbanized and populated; and the public health and environmental after effects.[31] Yet, there are many who still value security by means of nuclear deterrence[32] and thus place nuclear weapons in a special category that provides security and status to the "superpowers."[33]

My views align with those of the overwhelming majority of states in the international community, best expressed as follows: "Limiting the role of nuclear weapons to deterrence does not remove the possibility of their use. Nor does it address the risks stemming from accidental use. The only assurance against the risk of a nuclear weapon detonation is the total elimination of nuclear weapons."[34] Most countries are in nuclear-weapon-free zones, which are parts of the world where countries commit not to manufacture, possess, or test nuclear weapons. There are five nuclear-free zones: Latin America (established in the 1967 Treaty of Tlatelolco), the South Pacific (established in the 1985 Treaty of Rarotonga), Southeast Asia (established in the 1995 Treaty of Bangkok), Africa (established in the 1996 Treaty of Pelindaba), and Central Asia (established in the 2006 Treaty of Semipalatinsk).[35] These nuclear-weapon-free zones represent a firm statement from these states that they do not have nuclear weapons as an aspect of their international relations. Nevertheless, there is resistance against humanitarian security regimes (i.e., human security-shaping treaties), and it comes from a smaller group of states that oppose multilateral interference in their security affairs (i.e., when states are preparing to wage war).

Two international legal structures challenge the legality of the use of nuclear weapons: human rights law and IHL. Taken together, these two global legal frameworks place heavy restrictions on the use of such weapons.[36] The inclusion of these branches of international law into the body of the aforementioned innovative treaties is groundbreaking in several ways. Disarmament treaties are typically about counting the weapon systems and verifying whether the parties are fulfilling their disarmament pledges and obligations. But when human rights law and IHL are incorporated into the treaty-making process, the scope of the states' obligations is broadened to encompass a more humanistic perspective by placing the protection of the individual and human rights at the center of the aspirations in the process of treaty implementation. The tenor of the treaty's goals is also transformed. Many of the principles and rules of human rights law and IHL are not only the most widely adhered to in international law, but are also considered to be customary international law. Therefore, the addition of IHL and human rights law lends credence and moral authority to the endeavor.[37]

Deterrence is fundamentally anachronistic, for three main reasons: first, there is a multitude of alliances and security assurance arrangements (at the regional levels), such as regional agreements and nuclear weapon-free zones, that make the need to maintain nuclear weapons unnecessary. Along the same lines, peaceful settlement of disputes has emerged as a strong international norm in the post–World War II era. This means that nuclear deterrence has fallen out of favor as a crisis stabilizer. The institutionalization of the ability to implement norms peacefully through supranational courts makes the nuclear weaponization of foreign policy unnecessary. The adoption of the 1967 Tlatelolco Treaty, the 1985 Rarotonga Treaty, the 1995 Bangkok Treaty, the 1996 Pelindaba Treaty, and the 2006 Semipalatinsk Treaty (that created the nuclear-weapon-free zones) have revealed the shortcomings and artificiality of the posture of the so-called political "realists," who insisted on the suicidal policy of nuclear deterrence in their characteristic subservience to power politics.[38]

Second, multilateralism has been the prevailing global approach to conducting foreign policy since 1945.[39] It seems, then, that the maintenance of a high-level, unilateral, and risky strategy of maintaining nuclear weapons is uncalled for, as few states have a declared policy hostile to others today. This is all the more the case as the use of military force has been outlawed in international relations by the United Nations Charter (Article 2.4). States agreed to renounce the use of force as their main tool of foreign policy when they ratified the United Nations Charter.[40] When international wars occur today, they are the object of widespread condemnation.

Third, none of the threats that affect humanity today can be eliminated with nuclear weapons. Accumulating nuclear weapons was pointless and ineffectual in dealing with humanity's problems or creating a sense of security. If nuclear weapons are deployed anywhere the effects on the environment and public health will be unconceivable.[41] Such weapons cannot discriminate between civilians and combatants, and their use will be an affront to IHL.[42]

A humanitarian perspective

The 2010 Treaty on the Non-Proliferation of Nuclear Weapons Review Conference expressed "deep concern at the continued risk for humanity represented by the possibility that these weapons could be used and the catastrophic humanitarian consequences that would result from the use of nuclear weapons."[43] This paved the way for what happened next: three state summits marked the beginning of this shift toward a humanitarian and public health approach to nuclear weapons that is transforming the political discourse, which in turn represents progress on building the legal architecture to limit nuclear weapons and eventually eliminate them altogether: in Norway in 2013, in Mexico in 2014, and in Austria also in 2014.

Norway 2013: The Norwegian Minister of Foreign Affairs hosted the International Conference on the Humanitarian Impact of Nuclear Weapons in Oslo that aimed to promote a facts-based discussion of the humanitarian and developmental consequences that would result from a nuclear weapon detonation.[44] In attendance were 127 countries, as well as several United Nations organizations, the International Committee of the Red Cross, and representatives of civil society.

Three streams of argument were evident in the discussions. The first was the inability of any state public health authorities to cope with the catastrophic humanitarian consequences that would result from a nuclear detonation (i.e., they would be unable to provide any assistance).[45] The second was the long-term public health and ecological effects of testing and using nuclear weapons, along with the destruction of infrastructure. The third was the examination of the transnational dimensions of a nuclear weapon detonation: the impact would not be confined to the area within any state's borders, but would have regional and global dimensions.

Mexico 2014: The above arguments were reiterated and a proposal for a new international prohibition treaty was put forward. In addition, there was recognition that there are heightened dangers of accidents as a result of cyber hacking and unintentional erroneous use, along with the potential of use by terrorists.

Austria 2014: 158 states attended, including the United States and the United Kingdom. Vienna crystallized a commitment to devote attention to the humanitarian dimension and the risks of nuclear weapons. Combined, the three conferences produced a groundbreaking compilation of scientific findings on the consequences of a detonation and a clear indication that the risks far outweigh the utility of possessing such weapons. These findings thrust the humanitarian approach to nuclear disarmament to the forefront of the international agenda for negotiations. Vienna provided a full-fledged application of international law beyond the International Court of Justice 1996 opinion on the legality of the use of nuclear weapons[46] and used international environmental law norms, such as precaution,[47] to show that reliance on nuclear weapons was anachronistic. Vienna paved the way for the 2015 Treaty on the Non-Proliferation of Nuclear Weapons Review Conference in which states expressed a desire for a nuclear-free world.

Before I proceed, it is important to review the significance of the International Court of Justice 1996 opinion. The World Health Organization and the United Nations General Assembly (Resolution 49/75 K of December 15, 1994) submitted to the court a request for an advisory opinion on the following question: Is the threat or use of nuclear weapons in any circumstance permitted under international law? On July 8, 1996, the court rendered its advisory opinion that failed to unequivocally condemn nuclear weapons. Instead, it stated that, regretfully, at this stage of the development of international law, it could not conclusively affirm that "the use of nuclear weapons would be illicit under extreme circumstances of self-defense in which the very survival of a state would be at stake."[48]

Antônio Augusto Cançado Trindade fervently criticized the Court's opinion. He became one of the court's judges three years later, in 2009, and was re-elected to a second term in 2018. I also include this quotation because it references the right to life and the anachronistic nature of a state-centric approach to international law.

Two final elements cemented the humanitarian focus on nuclear disarmament and represent a marked evolution in the political debate: the statement by 159 states at the 2015 Nuclear Non-Proliferation Treaty Review Conference, and the views of the International Committee of the Red Cross (ICRC)—the guardian of IHL. At the 2015 conference, 159 states asserted that "awareness of the catastrophic consequences of nuclear weapons must underpin all approaches and efforts towards nuclear disarmament," and that "the only way to guarantee that nuclear weapons will never be used again is through their total elimination" (Joint Statement 2015).[49] These states recognized that the catastrophic humanitarian consequences of the use of nuclear weapons are a fundamental and global concern. The ICRC, the first international humanitarian organization to arrive in Hiroshima in the immediate aftermath of the 1945 bombing, is always neutral on ongoing international negotiations, but it has stated that the "current negotiations of a nuclear weapon ban treaty are the best chance for real progress towards the universal goal of a world free of nuclear weapons. All

States should participate in this endeavor. The future of humanity depends on it."[50] The ICRC had been a pioneer in calling on states to prohibit nuclear weapons under IHL.[51]

The United Nations Charter as a foundational framework for arms limitations

Almost eight decades after the founding of the United Nations and a formal treaty-based normative order with intensive codification of global disarmament norms, urgent challenges, and complexities that need to be addressed remain, especially in the light of the use of autonomy in weapon systems and the militarization of AI. How to best protect the dignity of the individual from the worst atrocities and violations of global humanitarian norms remains a primary concern. The United Nations Charter, the main treaty in international law, was adopted just weeks before detonation of the first nuclear bomb. It does not contain the words "nuclear weapons"; it does not even contain the word "weapons." However, the words "disarmament" and "armaments" do appear, even if in limited form and with constrained scope. It is important to understand their appearance and significance in the charter. The section below outlines where these terms appear in the charter (with my emphases added).

Prima facie, the United Nations Charter is not properly equipped to address further challenges to the legal order posed by autonomous weapons and the weaponization of AI in the ongoing digital revolution. Is this really the case, though? Let us examine the essential and pertinent parts within the charter, which is a guiding instrument for global action.

United Nations Charter, Chapter IV: the General Assembly Article 11:

> The General Assembly may consider the general principles of co-operation in the **maintenance of international peace and security**, including the principles governing <u>disarmament</u> and the regulation of <u>armaments</u>, and may make recommendations with regard to such principles to the Members or to the Security Council or to both.

United Nations Charter, Chapter V: The Security Council, Article 26:

> In order to promote the establishment and maintenance of international peace and security with the least diversion for <u>armaments</u> of the world's human and economic resources, the Security Council shall be responsible for formulating, with the assistance of the Military Staff Committee referred to in Article 47, plans to be submitted to the Members of the United Nations for the establishment of a system for the <u>regulation of armaments</u>.

United Nations Charter, Chapter VII—Action with respect to threats to the peace, breaches of the peace, and acts of aggression. Article 47:

> There shall be established a Military Staff Committee to advise and assist the Security Council on all questions relating to the Security Council's military requirements for the **maintenance of international peace and security**, the employment and command of forces placed at its disposal, the regulation of armaments, and possible disarmament.

The significance of these articles is worth highlighting. Both articles 11 and 47 effectively connect the maintenance of peace and security to disarmament. Therefore, the drafters of the charter made disarmament a tool for the achievement of peace and security. Profoundly, this posited, and accentuated, the idea of channeling the world's human and economic firepower away from over-arming. By doing this, the charter mandates states to maintain peace through the regulation of armaments. Most importantly, it also instructs its chief deliberative body on peace and security, the General Assembly, to be the bellwether in the striving for peace through disarmament; by the same token, the charter charges the Security Council to act upon ensuring the regulation of arms worldwide. The very first United Nations General Assembly Resolution of January 1946, which was adopted by consensus, established a commission "to deal with the problem posed by the discovery of atomic energy."[52] It marked the initiation of mechanisms to deal with disarmament as one of the major preoccupations addressed by the United Nations and created the necessary institutions. Since the terrorist attacks of September 2001 against the United States, the United Nations has been working with renewed creative legislative vigor through the Security Council to stop the proliferation of nuclear weapons.[53] With resolution 1373 of 2001 and then resolution 1540 of 2004, the Security Council used its power for the first time to create legislation to contain a threat to peace and security that emanates from a threat to all—terrorism—and not from one particular state, as this is its remit in terms of the United Nations Charter.

Often, power politics interweaves with international law and robs the latter of some of its power for change and transformation. The case of the prohibition and elimination of nuclear weapons is a case in point and can offer lessons for the formation of *common good governance* on military AI.

The case for prohibition

The 2017 Nuclear Ban Treaty that prohibits nuclear weapons was innovative in that it permanently altered the meaning of security from purely military to lessening the prevalence of the use of force paradigm. In other words, if before disarmament treaties served to strike a balance between military needs and humanitarian concerns, now the treaties are focused in the first place on the protection of the individual. In many ways, this new trend broadens the meaning of security to include other concerns beyond military and state-centered matters. As a result, the beneficiaries are people, and the treaty also generates a public good, reinforcing the *common good governance* that is needed to address not only the multiple threats to global security—principally, climate change, the challenge of autonomous killing, the weaponization of AI, but also annihilation by nuclear weapons. They all pose existential threats to humanity. The prohibition and eventual elimination of nuclear weapons would symbolically and then financially play a part in addressing these and other global problems.[54] Scholars have been questioning the deeply held value of deterrence in defining behavior as well as the significance of nuclear weapons in maintaining stability.[55] An examination of close-call events during the Cold War seems to suggest that it was not the precepts of the strategy of deterrence that prevented catastrophe, but rather other forces and sometimes decisions taken by the right people at the right time.[56]

Nuclear weapons were used before the creation of the United Nations. The new international organization ushered in the formalized human rights era and also gave rise to the codification of most international law that sets constraints on states' behavior. Many would view the continuing reliance on nuclear weapons for the sake of deterrence as obsolete and out of synchrony with the highly complex realities of today's global security landscape.[57]

Adding momentum to the realization of the futility of nuclear weapons, the United Nations Security Council approved Resolution 1887 in 2009. It resolves

> to seek a safer world for all and to create the conditions for a world without nuclear weapons, in accordance with the goals of the Treaty on the Non-Proliferation of Nuclear Weapons, in a way that promotes international stability, and based on the principle of undiminished security for all … *Reaffirming* that proliferation of weapons of mass destruction, and their means of delivery, constitutes a threat to international peace and security.

Significantly, in its operational paragraph five, the resolution

> *Calls upon* the Parties to the Treaty on the Non-Proliferation of Nuclear Weapons, pursuant to Article VI of the Treaty, to undertake to pursue negotiations in good faith on effective measures relating to nuclear arms reduction and disarmament, and on a Treaty on general and complete disarmament under strict and effective international control, and *calls on* all other States to join in this endeavor.[58]

Two notable transnational initiatives illustrate the public discontent with the state of security and peace supposedly maintained by a reliance on nuclear weapons. One is the 2017 Nobel Peace Prize award-winning International Campaign to Abolish Nuclear Weapons (ICAN) and the other is the Global Zero Project.

ICAN won the 2017 Nobel Peace Prize for its leading efforts in bringing the Nuclear Ban Treaty to fruition. Launched in Australia in 2007, it is a coalition of several hundred nongovernmental organizations in more than 100 countries that works toward a nuclear weapon ban treaty, and is composed of bodies ranging from local peace groups to global federations that represent millions of people. The vast majority of countries adopted the Treaty on the Prohibition of Nuclear Weapons on July 7, 2017 in a moving and historic moment at the United Nations in New York. The director of ICAN is Beatrice Fihn. She gave the Nobel Peace Prize lecture on behalf of all the campaigners. She has generously met with my students at the United Nations every year since 2012. It always an honor and very powerful experience to listen to her and my students become ever more convinced of their role in eliminating nuclear weapons.

Global Zero:

Global Zero is the international movement for the elimination of nuclear weapons. Powered by a visionary group of 300 international leaders and experts who support our bold, step-by-step plan to eliminate all nuclear weapons by 2030, the relentless creativity, energy and optimism of young people and half a million citizens world-wide, Global Zero is challenging the 20th-century idea of basing national security on the threat of mass destruction—and together we are making real progress on the road to global zero. Global Zero leaders understand that the only way to eliminate the nuclear threat—including proliferation and nuclear terrorism—is to stop the spread of nuclear weapons, secure all nuclear materials and eliminate all nuclear weapons: global zero. (484)[59]

The international system has been going through profound transformations with heightened interdependence that make the reliance on deterrence perilous.[60] The call toward a *humanity's security* perspective to security issues constitutes the major challenge to arguments in favor of maintaining nuclear weapons and paves the way for a global order that sees no value in creating more tools for humanity's destruction—a world that has more room for the creation of global public goods through *common good governance*. Today, because of the changing strategic geopolitical environment, and with the first major international war of aggression (in Ukraine) since 1945, the structure of nuclear deterrence is less stable and more worrisome than it was at the height of the Cold War. The contemporary global environment includes the dangerous proliferation of nuclear weapons to nonnuclear states, as well as a growing risk of nuclear terrorism and use of nuclear weapons. Nuclear states believe preventing proliferation to some countries is necessary, while they have for years ignored the unacknowledged growth of nuclear arsenals in others. This double standard undermines the universality on which the Treaty on the Non-Proliferation of Nuclear Weapons was constructed.[61]

Under the weight of these developments, the erratic years of Donald Trump in the White House and withdrawal from key stabilizing treaties, such as the 1987 Intermediate-Range Nuclear Forces (INF) Treaty made deterrence more worrisome and precarious. The INF eliminated a whole class of nuclear weapons and was one of the pillars of security for NATO countries. In the absence of further progress toward complete disarmament, and without concrete steps toward a more secure and genuine peace, the nuclear weapon establishment has lost much of its legitimacy.[62] Rapid technological advances in areas of AI that reinforce the current trends toward more autonomy in warfare make the dependence on nuclear technology more perilous, if AI were to enter the realm of nuclear command and control (Chapter 3). Greater scientific understanding of the interlocking systems that make up the functioning of the planet buttress the many civil society and scientific voices stressing that the use of nuclear weapons is unreasonable and morally unjustifiable. To sum up, the role of nuclear deterrence to ensure security is illogical and nonsensical as the real threats confronting humanity cannot be repulsed with these treacherous tools of war. Bearing these considerations in mind, the antecedents I outlined here demonstrate that the weaponization of AI will make very little sense in attempts to maintain the security of future generations.

Legalizing the nuclear taboo

Prominent scholars have argued that it is the taboo against nuclear weapons that deters their use.[63] In other words, since the first use of nuclear weapons in Hiroshima and Nagasaki in 1945, opprobrium against them has intensified, coupled with widespread condemnation because of the horrifying humanitarian consequences of their use. Additionally, powerful campaigning against weapons as tools for conducting foreign policy emerged transnationally, with critical voices from scientists as well as civil society.[64] States started to progressively build a legal and political architecture of treaties and agreements, and eventually nuclear-weapon-free zones that place limits on their use and acquisition, which was in effect a prohibition against further proliferation.

The stigma against nuclear weapons that arises from the taboo does not constitute a legal norm. However, there have been consistent signs of an evolution of the legal and political frameworks that limit nuclear weapons and point toward the legalization of the taboo. A breakthrough occurred when the 2010 Treaty on the Non-Proliferation of Nuclear Weapons Review Conference expressed "deep concern at the catastrophic humanitarian consequences of any use of nuclear weapons" and reaffirmed "the need for all States at all times to comply with applicable international law, including international humanitarian law" (622).[65] A further step provided the necessary ingredient for the acceleration of the evolution of the architecture to address the nuclear issue: on October 27, 2016 member states of the United Nations adopted a General Assembly Resolution to start negotiations toward a new legally binding instrument to prohibit nuclear weapons—or, as it is widely known, the Nuclear Ban Treaty. A core group of countries led the adoption of the resolution: Austria, Brazil, Ireland, Mexico, Nigeria, and South Africa. Fifty-seven nations cosponsored it, and 113 nations voted in favor at the General Assembly in December 2016.[66] Negotiations ended successfully in July 2017.

On the road toward building *common good governance*, enshrined in the Nuclear Ban Treaty, several notable aspects make this resolution particularly groundbreaking in shifting the legal landscape pertinent to nuclear weapons. First, it is based on the recognition that the 1968 Treaty on the Non-Proliferation of Nuclear Weapons remains the cornerstone of the nuclear nonproliferation and disarmament regime, and of its value in providing a framework for peace and security. Second, it builds on the manifest absence of progress in multilateral nuclear disarmament negotiations within the United Nations framework over many decades, even though the Treaty on the Non-Proliferation Article 6 provides the legal framework of negotiations on adopting effective measures toward total nuclear disarmament.[67] Third, essentially, the aim of the Nuclear Ban Treaty is the creation of a world without nuclear weapons through the advancement of multilateral nuclear disarmament negotiations. The Nuclear Ban Treaty codifies the stigma against the use of nuclear weapons. As Beatrice Fihn, the director of the Campaign to Abolish Nuclear Weapons, which won the 2017 Nobel Peace Prize, stated: "Weapons that cause unacceptable harm to civilians cannot remain legal or be considered legitimate options for states in warfare" (45).[68] The negotiations leading to the Nuclear Ban Treaty built upon the existing legal framework created by the Nuclear Non-Proliferation Treaty, under the terms of which 189 out of 195 states are already bound by legal obligations not to acquire or use nuclear weapons for military purposes.[69]

The Nuclear Ban Treaty is having an impact. It could pave the way to building *common good governance* on military AI by eroding previously existing assumptions of what is right.[70] It does so in five ways.

1) It challenges the permissibility of the use of nuclear weapons—under any circumstances—and it strengthens the Treaty on the Non-Proliferation of Nuclear Weapons Article 6 framework for elimination. Additionally, the commitment to remain in "nuclear weapons-free zones" is reinforced. The treaty strengthens the norm of nonproliferation. The Nuclear Ban Treaty is not only a legal tool, it is also a political tool as it creates a new platform for the transnational antinuclear movement to promote change within the nuclear states over time.[71]

2) It establishes a new international norm. The Nuclear Ban Treaty shifted the nuclear nonproliferation global norm toward a no-nuclear-weapons norm. Eventually, plans for the modernization of and continuing reliance on nuclear weapons for security will be regarded with scorn and disapproval. The stakes for the continued reliance on nuclear deterrence will be higher.

3) From strength and prestige to liability: the arguments for elimination and nuclear zero erode the paradigm of strength through nuclear deterrence. It will no longer be regarded as prestigious to continue to rely on an indiscriminate insidious weapon to ensure a place of high status in the international community. An understanding of the disastrous humanitarian consequences subverts

the value of maintaining such weapons. Therefore, the eight states that possess nuclear weapons will be outcasts in a club of high-minded and principled
states that have committed themselves to the terms of the Nuclear Ban Treaty.

4) NATO members feel threated about the new treaty. After the decision to convene negotiations toward the Nuclear Ban Treaty, states participated in an
Open-Ended Working Group. The United States published a letter to its NATO
allies and encouraged them not to vote for the treaty. The reasons put forward for this view were that operational impacts brought by the new Nuclear
Ban Treaty would be numerous. However, in reality the new treaty does not
concretely change existing practice and concentrates mostly on two areas.[72]

   a. First, the United States would not be able to use nuclear weapons on behalf
   of its allies because of the opprobrium associated with the taboo against
   such weapons. The only time that the NATO founding treaty's Article V,
   which stipulates the collective security position, was invoked was after
   September 11, 2001, in the aftermath of the terrorist attacks on the United
   States. At no point during that time was there any mention of the use of
   nuclear weapons.

   b. Second, the nuclear states are not able to station and deploy weapons on
   the High Contracting Party states of the Nuclear Ban Treaty. Yet, it seems
   that most states now no longer favor the stationing of nuclear weapons in
   their territories. For instance, Scotland no longer welcomes the stationing
   of English nuclear weapons on its territory.[73]

5) International financing for nuclear weapons and eroding previously existing
assumptions of what is right: Nuclear weapons investment is a multi-billion
dollar industry. In the United States—with the second largest nuclear arsenal—
$634 billion was allotted for the 2021–2030 period.[74] The prohibition of
nuclear weapons would impact on these financial investments. Divestment
will ensue and change business investments strategies.[75]

To sum up, not only are nuclear weapons unserviceable tools for war—their destructive impact is indiscriminate and would render public health systems unworkable—
but they cost humankind a lot of resources and continue to threaten peace and
security. The building up of nuclear arsenals during the Cold War was a reckless
exercise that imperiled the very existence of life on the planet and diverted vast
amounts of money in unjustifiable ways. In the senseless pursuit of global superiority, the United States and the Soviet Union drove other powers to develop their
own nuclear weapons in search of an elusive parity. The United States had a brief
chance before proliferation to declare that only the good uses of nuclear technology
for the common good of humanity would be acceptable. However, it failed to do so,
and proliferation followed unremittingly.[76] The damage to the environment has been
catastrophic in many regions of the globe where the weapons were tested.[77] Nonetheless, most countries in the world reject the utility of nuclear weapons to maintain

peace and security, and constitute zones of peace free of such weapons.[78] Their continued existence reminds humankind of the high cost, the diversion of human capital, and the ultimate futility of embarking upon the employment of technologies for evil in warfare. Nuclear weapons jeopardize both peace and security, and exposed the flaws and catastrophic consequences of wrong choices. The lessons learned are a monitory signal of what a future in which AI is weaponized could be like.

Prohibition of chemical weapons—the universal model framework

The scientists who create AI have already signaled in their recent letters to the world that they do not wish to see their creation weaponized (Chapter 1). The same applies to chemists and biologists. They participated in raising awareness of the good uses of chemistry and biology, and pointed out the advantages of the prohibition of the use of chemical and biological weapons in warfare. The prohibition of chemical warfare under international law was a turning point for humanity and it represents an extraordinary instance of the way that new norms of common humanity emerge and have a civilizing effect on international relations.[79]

The first norms against chemical warfare were formulated in 1899 and reviewed in 1907 at the first and second major summits of nations when they met at The Hague. The 1899 summit launched the century-long process of prohibiting chemical weapons.[80] The norms written at The Hague at the turn of the 20th century are now considered customary rules of behavior binding on all, high-contracting parties or not, and also on nonstate armed groups; these norms explicitly articulated the prohibition of the use of poison gas as a practice of killing treacherously, which is unlawful under IHL. This latter part of the prohibition is informative. Here we can distinguish the beginning of the stigmatization of chemical weapons. Throughout the expansion of this taboo over the century, the idea that these weapons are insidious and entail a scant possibility of self-defense was underpinned by the association that they were used by "uncivilized nations."[81]

The embryonic and developing stigmatization of chemical warfare suffered a horrific setback when chlorine and mustard gas were widely deployed by Germany and the Allied nations during World War I. Carnage on that scale was unprecedented. These appalling years resulted in hundreds of thousands of casualties and blinded survivors, whose lives were destroyed. This disgraceful conduct in warfare brought dishonor to the countries that had employed these weapons and gave rise to years of pressure and civil society anger and indignation. Consequently, the opprobrium generated by the use of chemical weapons only intensified.

The rising public condemnation led to the 1925 Geneva Protocol,[82] which forbids the use of chemical and biological weapons in war. The use of chemical warfare has been rare since then, although isolated incidents have occurred, such as in the conflict in Syria. The Organization for the Prohibition of Chemical Weapons (OPCW) confirmed the accession of Syria to the OPCW in a pronouncement to the United Nations

Security Council on June 3, 2021.[83] These weapons were not used on the battlefield during World War II, even though all sides continued to build their chemical arsenals to deter potential attacks and Nazi Germany used Zyklon—a form of pesticide that asphyxiates—to perpetrate the genocide it conducted against the Jewish population and other peoples. It is important to note that both the Hague regulations and the 1925 Geneva Protocol banned only the use of the weapons, and not the weapons themselves.

What paved the way for the comprehensive prohibition outlawing all aspects of the use of such weapons (production, transfer, stockpiling, and use), as stated in the groundbreaking 1993 Chemical Weapons Convention, was their use in the 1980s during the Iran–Iraq war and then against the Iraqi Kurds by Saddam Hussein in 1988. These events, when thousands of people were killed, mark the most disreputable uses of chemical weapons in modern times and became symbolic of the inhumane and cruel nature of these weapons.[84] These uses led to the negotiations at the Conference on Disarmament in Geneva. Throughout the Cold War the Americans and the Russians amassed large arsenals of these weapons. North Korea, Egypt, South Sudan, and Israel have not joined the Convention. The use of chemical weapons in Syria and the resulting ignominy signify how strong the proscriptions and the obloquy are. Syria acceded to the convention in response to mounting international pressure.

When the Chemical Weapons Convention entered into force in 1997, it became the first international treaty to eliminate an entire category of weapons, and in particular those that have dual uses: civilian and military. It is regarded as a model for this reason and also because it established a robust monitoring mechanism when it set up the OPCW to rid the world of the threat of chemical warfare. The OPCW is located at The Hague, where the auspicious historic start of the process to ban chemical warfare began. The OPCW marks one of the many new ways to implement global governance with regard to disarmament and nonproliferation. Its efforts were recognized by the award of the Nobel Peace Prize in 2013 to the organization.[85]

The horrific history of the events leading to the institution of a global ban on the use of chemical weapons reminds us that the establishment of a robust *common good governance* mechanism to tackle the threat posed by such sinister weapons came after almost a century of joint efforts. The ICRC, in its statement to the High-Contracting Parties to the Chemical Weapons Convention review of implementation in November 2021, denounces any use as an outrage to common humanity and praises the OPCW for the fact that 98% of declared stockpiles have been destroyed to date under a model monitoring regime that also provides verification. The prohibition on chemical weapons is now universal and considered customary under international law, which means that all parties to conflicts are bound by it.[86]

The *common good governance* narratives of the limitations on nuclear weapons and the creation of an international treaty to outlaw the use of chemical warfare as an insidious practice with no place in a humane and civilized world demonstrate the possibilities for forging international solidarity, and for global public goods to deal with the impending challenges posed by increased autonomy in weapon systems and by the militarization of AI.

Conventional arms: What can we learn from existing legal restrictions?

The trade in conventional arms was the last among the unregulated practices until 2013, when the landmark Arms Trade Treaty was successfully negotiated at the United Nations in New York. The arms trade has serious consequences for human security. Most deaths and mayhem in conflicts today, as well as in transnational crime and in urban violence worldwide, are the result of the utilization of conventional arms, ranging from small arms and light weapons, such as the infamous Kalashnikov, to larger weapon systems such as tanks and airplanes.[87]

The new generation of humanitarian security regimes that I examine here represents a transformation of the way that security is viewed as these treaties have a beneficial impact on human life. I would contend that in combination these treaties are gradually contributing to the dispelling of the deeply held notion that weapons provide security.[88] They have mobilized the world to see the possibilities of real change by reducing the possibility of violence against civilians and the gradual elimination of atrocious weapons by "affirming the collective revulsion of the international community at morally unacceptable weapons of catastrophic destruction."[89] Historically, humanitarian concerns initiated law-making processes in the realm of disarmament, but they were not the predominant motivation that led states to formal treaty-making. The humanitarian impetus dovetailed with national security concerns that, at the time, were of a purely military nature. Not only were conventional arms regulated within the framework created by the Arms Trade Treaty, but the use of landmines and cluster munitions, which were widely used and held in the arsenals of the major powers, was prohibited by the 1997 and 2008 conventions respectively. These prohibitions, especially of landmines, by what is known as the Ottawa Convention of 1997 mark a new way of doing diplomacy.

The Chemical Weapons Convention, for example, was motivated by humanitarian imperatives as well as by military considerations, and was led by states' efforts, in particular France and the United States, to come up with a prohibition. The extraordinary negotiations that led to the conventions which prohibited landmines and cluster munitions—indiscriminate weapons with no capacity to distinguish between civilians and combatants, and in widespread use during the Cold War and in its aftermath—mark a new era for diplomacy, where global governance is fully inspired by considerations to protect human security.[90] The argument that these weapon systems were banned only because they were not useful militarily has no force and needs closer scrutiny. These weapons were useful in military terms and militaries were interested in maintaining them in their arsenals. However, they and their governments were convinced that the devastating humanitarian consequences of their use far outweighed their military advantage in the battlefield. These processes also ushered in a new era for diplomacy because transnational campaigns advocating the need to safeguard humanity were powerful and managed to convince governments to change their national security equation. Many governments in these cases worked closely with the campaigners and ensured that other states became convinced of their cause and also acted as champions for change.

Traditional practices of conventional arms transfers might disrespect essential branches of international law, such as human rights law, the rules on the legality of the use of force, and IHL—think, for example, about the supply of arms from the United States to Saudi Arabia to be used in the conflict in Yemen. The Arms Trade Treaty was intended to rectify these violations and to ensure that global norms and rules are in place to regulate arms transfers from state to state, thus preventing arms transfers that would lead to widespread human rights violations. States agreed to create the first legally binding "humanitarian or responsible arms transfers trade" treaty by an overwhelming majority vote at the United Nations General Assembly on April 2, 2013. The Arms Trade Treaty entered into force on December 24, 2014. It is the first to regulate the conventional arms trade, setting global norms to restrict arms from reaching human rights violators and conflict zones.[91]

The novelty of the Arms Trade Treaty is that it creates a new legal framework that connects two previously seemingly irreconcilable areas: conventional arms transfers and human security—that is, it promotes respect for human rights law and IHL as well setting humanitarian constraints on using armed force in international relations, adding to the already existing architecture instituted by the United Nations Charter against the use of force. Therefore, the treaty successfully created new global norms on arms transfers, which differentiate between lawful and unlawful transfers that can be measured in accordance with common rules. Such transfers will now be carried out in line with legal norms that call for respect for life and restraint of behavior during conflict. A long history of the ideas leading up to the treaty and five years of negotiations created the conditions to make seemingly irreconcilable areas compatible.

Regarding the dynamics of the limitations on armaments, conventional arms in particular, I can put forward three propositions. The first is that, despite the unprecedented normative progress and ideational gains brought about by the Arms Trade Treaty, which combined previously discrete areas in world politics—namely, arms transfers and respect for life—states do not yet observe the new norms arising from the treaty and continue to conduct "business as usual" by transferring arms to gain political advantage and to advance their firmly established pecuniary motives. The second is that, if states do not comply with the new global norms of the Arms Trade Treaty, not only are they acting to their own detriment, they also harm peace and stability. One could reason that, by contravening norms in this area, states will lose legitimacy for not respecting international law (*pacta sunt servanda* is the most fundament principle of international law by which states commit to abide by the universal frameworks created by treaties) and their reputation will suffer. By not observing the norms of the Arms Trade Treaty, states prolong the harm to human security worldwide by carrying out irresponsible arms transfers.[92] The third is that states imperil the future of peace and security by breaching essential global security norms based upon international law. The legal architecture instituted by IHL, human rights law, and the use of force law is essential to uphold peace and security (Chapter 4). Altogether, the treaties examined here advance *common good governance*, one consequence of which is a reconceptualization of the meaning of security. From a purely state-centric conception, security has increasingly come to focus upon the protection of human beings. Not only is the state protected—the traditional conception of national security—but also *humanity*.

How international norms evolve

New international norms often take time to gain a foothold in changing the ways things work in international relations.[93] First, they lay a foundation upon which to build new global governance. Second, they gain prominence and acceptance across a threshold number of states and other entities that come to accept them as the new acceptable forms of behavior.[94] Third, the edifice built upon this initial foundation is geared toward implementing the norms—usually emanating from treaties—and making the words on paper come to life by impacting on people's livelihoods.[95] In many instances, new norms arising from innovative international treaties can serve as prevention platforms for avoiding harm and catastrophic outcomes in the future (Chapter 5, Annex).[96] More often than not, the pathway to norm building and consolidation is circuitous.[97] Therefore, the work of *transnational networked cooperation* is laudable as a means to achieve the change promoted by the rise of new norms (Chapter 1).

For instance, with regard to conventional weapons, a decision by the United Nations Secretary-General, Boutros Boutros-Ghali, gives an indication of how global norms started to emerge:

> I wish to concentrate on what might be called "micro-disarmament." By this I mean practical disarmament in the context of the conflicts the United Nations is actually dealing with and of the weapons, most of them small arms and light weapons, that are actually killing people in the hundreds of thousands.[98]

By coining the term "micro-disarmament," the Secretary-General called for the kind of progress in international regulations in the realm of small arms and light weapons (SALW) as had been achieved in the case of weapons of mass destruction. SALW are a direct threat to human security and to communities within states. They are the cause of an overwhelming number of deaths, and are also harder to monitor as well as being much more widespread than weapons of mass destruction. Only states (so far) possess weapons of mass destruction, whereas just about anybody can own small conventional arms. Also, each country has its own national legislation and cultural perceptions of SALW, which makes small arms control a much more complex question to address.

From the outset, therefore, the overarching emerging international norm was to stop the proliferation and excessive accumulation of arms that were deemed to be destabilizing. This quickly expanded to encompass other norms that started to address various facets of this multilayered problem: weapons destruction, curbing illicit arms brokering, marking and tracing, export controls, transparency in arms transfers, and so forth.[99] The Panel of Governmental Experts on Small Arms published its first report in 1997.[100] This report was influential for two reasons: it defined which weapons are included in the category "small arms and light weapons," and it called for the convening of the first ever multilateral conference on the issue of SALW, to take place under the auspices of the United Nations in 2001. This soft law framework to contain the illicit arms trade on SALW paved the way in the years that followed for the creation of a political and legal framework to address all conventional weapons, with the entry into force of the Arms Trade Treaty in 2014.

The treaty applies human rights law and IHL criteria to transfers of the weapons that are responsible for most of the killings and violence during conflict and in urban armed violence. The treaty is intended to prevent arms flows into destabilizing regions and helps to prevent diversion of arms. It creates express prohibitions on transferring arms that strengthen the existing mechanism of arms embargoes; it also imposes state responsibility vis-à-vis existing obligations, including human rights law commitments, such as the prohibition of torture and genocide; and it connects arms transfer obligations to a duty to refrain from the commission of crimes against humanity and grave breaches of the Geneva Conventions (war crimes). Lastly, the treaty is the first global agreement to interpret the existing rules of IHL and human rights law with reference to arms transfers, with concrete criteria for assessment of transfers, with particular attention to the humanitarian effects of the arms trade on human security. As demonstrated, in all areas of arms limitations, as shown herein, there has been intensive evolution as well as change in the legal and political frameworks. Such transformations have been marked specifically by humanitarian and ethical concerns.

These same considerations drive the *transnational networked cooperation* toward limiting autonomous robotic killing. But will the existing frameworks described here be useful for creating new governing norms to prevent autonomous killing? Autonomous weapons are already here (the Harpy and the Brimstone are autonomous systems and are already being deployed) and autonomous cyber weapons are already being used. This raises the challenge not only to apply global governance to weapons already in use, but also to think preventively about future ones within the scope of common good governance.

We cannot simply graft legal regimes designed to regulate conventional weapons or human combatants onto autonomous weapon systems. Instead, as is often the case when there is no appropriate analogue, it is time to explicitly revise the rules or create entirely new ones to address the specific situations where extant law is insufficient. We need to develop standards for both the training and the legal review of increasingly independently autonomous weapon systems, and we should outline accountability mechanisms to account for the probably inevitable but individually unforeseeable accidents.[101] More broadly, we should be having a larger conversation about the amount of human oversight, control, or judgment necessary in the targeting process for all attacks.[102] As Rebecca Crootof explains, autonomous systems are not a single weapons category, but rather appear in a variety of shapes and forms, from disembodied malware to networked sensors, launch platforms, and robots.[103] Previous treaties tended to address one, two, or more physical systems. If the autonomous system will "learn" in operation by using the AI computational technique—machine learning—how will it fit neatly into a restriction or limitation that had to be decided in advance? Machine learning systems can be deceptive.[104] Back to Crootof, who had presciently contended that there is only so much that one can extrapolate from existing rules to apply to emerging new legal questions.[105]

Humanity's security: Fewer arms, more prosperity

We undoubtedly live in an era of moral and ethical progress; this can be seen in the formation over centuries of commonly agreed global norms of behavior among states through formal treaty-making that limits the barbarities of war and constrains weapons proliferation. Some behaviors that had been considered normal, such as piracy, torture, slavery, and imperial annexation, are now prohibited under international law.[106] The challenges posed by the militarization of AI and its weaponization fly in the face of this progress and further diminish the prospects for building common good governance.

Eliminating nuclear weapons would be a first step toward true *humanity's security*. The idea that nuclear weapons are "expensive" to develop and maintain does not seem to make much headway in convincing states to avoid developing them, or to gain traction as an argument for nuclear weapon states to ratify the Nuclear Ban Treaty. The argument that national security is the guiding priority took precedence over concerns about limiting the expenditure on nuclear weapons. The United Nations Charter Article 26 calls on all states, under the auspices and responsibility of the Security Council, to create a system for the regulation of armaments that will focus on the promotion and maintenance of international peace and security. It also calls on states to ensure that as few as possible of the world's human and economic resources are used to create and maintain armaments. Countries have gone a long way toward fulfilling the terms of Article 26, but much more must be done. There is no doubt that establishing such systems to regulate arms—which are, of course, at the heart of states' national security preoccupations—is costly and controversial. The elaborate legal-political framework to contain the risks and avoid the proliferation of nuclear weapons serves as a useful example. Complying and ensuring that others comply has not only taken up enormous time and resources, but has diverted states' own energies and resources. The United Nations Charter created a rule of law order that can promote equity in international relations, especially when advancing *humanity's security* worldwide.[107]

Therefore, the United Nations Charter guides states toward limiting their military expenditure. And, since 2015, the member states of the United Nations have robustly opened up a path toward economic, social, and environmental development and protection. Two recent major achievements by all member states of the United Nations must be highlighted in order to clarify how the world can tackle economic, social, and environmental problems in a holistic way: the new United Nations Sustainable

Development Goals and the Paris Agreement on Climate Change. Taken together, these two initiatives provide a robust map for finding ways to solve some of the worst economic, social, and environmental problems facing humanity today. The attention and resources of the international community should be focused on this right now.

If autonomous systems and AI-assisted killing are left unregulated or unrestrained, with no common rules under international law, then they are bound to generate insecurity. As a corollary, not only human but also international security is attained in part by the reduction in armaments, or their outright prohibition. The case of autonomous weapons appears to indicate that new international law will be needed pressingly. In this sense, individuals become the ultimate beneficiaries of new rules under international law. This reaffirms the aspiration for peace and stigmatizes wrongful behavior—for instance, by increasing pressure on nuclear-armed states and on those that deploy weapons in vulnerable countries.

Historically, humanitarian concerns initiated global peace-making processes, but they were not the predominant motivation leading states to formal treaty-making. In other words, the motives were mixed between considerations of humanitarian law and national security. The 1968 Nuclear Non-Proliferation Treaty; the 1972 Convention on the Prohibition of the Development, Production, and Stockpiling of Bacteriological (Biological) and Toxin Weapons and on Their Destruction; the 1980 Convention on Prohibitions or Restrictions on the Use of Certain Conventional Weapons Which May Be Deemed to Be Excessively Injurious or to Have Indiscriminate Effects; and the Chemical Weapons Convention are testaments to the laudable attempts to find that balance between humanitarian and military considerations. It is only in recent years that humanitarian concerns have taken center stage and become the driving force, as seen in the 1997 Ottawa Convention on Landmines and the 2008 Convention on Cluster Munitions, behind the overwhelming support for the Arms Trade Treaty. The landmine and cluster munitions bans are the first instruments in IHL not only to ban a weapon, but also to mandate the high-contracting parties to assist present and future victims, while the Arms Trade Treaty is the first treaty to expressly state as its purpose the aim of reducing human suffering. The same trends could be observed in the ongoing negotiations toward the 2017 Nuclear Ban Treaty.

In an intensely globalized world, with more calls for greater transparency, it seems inappropriate for states to continue their expenditure on maintaining nuclear weapons, which I have demonstrated are now subject to an evolving reframing process of delegitimization and prohibition. In summary, another race to militarize yet another technology will make everyone less secure and leave the world worse off. Just as nuclear weapons created a dual power structure in international relations, so autonomous weapons will create a parallel system of state power imbalances. Disrespect for the legal and political architecture shown herein will have a disintegrating effect on the commonly agreed global norms of international law.

Nations today have the greatest opportunity in history to promote a better future by implementing the Paris Agreement and the United Nations Sustainable Development Goals. These are noteworthy legal and political frameworks that will guide and sustain states' actions toward achieving a more humane and sustainable future, with fewer weapons—nuclear or AI-based—and more security and prosperity. Strengthening arms limitations and regulations, and at the same time preventing perilous new applications of otherwise beneficial technology in warfare, are clear indicators that humanity expects a future of peace and security.

The value of previous treaties, in terms of precedent or analogy, is that they outline explicitly, in the way they were drafted and how they evolved, how productive international frameworks on controversial topics or ongoing threats can be designed and serve to promote peace. In the case where an existing treaty's primary subject matter is analogous to a new problem, the earlier treaty can showcase how broad or specific lawmakers need to be when framing the regulations and commitments for member states. Moreover, the drafting processes of previously existing treaties, many of which are well documented, can yield important insights into the making of new regulations. They are the best resource for speeding up the creation of international norms. In the context of disarmament, previously existing treaties, when observed as a group, show a trend away from purely taking into account the national interest that would not be seen otherwise. In this way, they promote peace by proving that prioritizing *humanity's security* in ways that were once inconceivable is now entirely possible.[108] I created the database of treaties in the annex of this chapter to show that prevention to achieve *humanity's security* is possible. This can be attained when countries cooperate to create new rules and norms by concluding treaties that ensure predictability and greater certainty in international relations. The findings here inspire the creation of a *common good governance*-based regulatory framework on AI and view it as a global public good of the highest order.

Annex: Preventive measures in international relations

I utilized four databases to make the assessment of preventive measures through 25 international treaties: the United Nations Disarmament Treaties Database, the United States State Department Diplomacy and Action Treaties and Agreements, the Stockholm International Peace Research Institute (SIPRI) 2021 Yearbook, and the IAEA Treaty Compliance database. I examine 25 instances of precautionary actions toward disarmament that were taken in recent decades.[109]

In an attempt to reflect the scope of policy consequences arising from such preventive actions, I adopted a three-pronged assessment measure that evaluates whether prevention was achieved:

- Full robustness (where the overwhelming majority of states have ratified and/or abide by the norms: prevention was achieved);
- Limited robustness (only half of states—or fewer—have ratified, but norms are still observed and prevention has been achieved);
- Low robustness (no noticeable effect on states' behavior; no prevention achieved).

Table 5.1 Successful preventive action in international relations

Name of Treaty	Preventive Content	Date	Level of Robust-ness	State Parties	Summary
Antarctic Treaty	Prohibition of weaponization and militarization	1959	Full	54	This treaty recognized that it is in the interest of all to keep the region free of weapons deployment and testing, as well as jurisdictional claims. While it prohibits any measures of a military nature, it does not prevent the use of military personnel or equipment for scientific (or any other peaceful) purposes.
The Treaty on Principles Governing the Activities of States in the Exploration and Use of Outer Space, Including the Moon and Other Celestial Bodies (Outer Space Treaty)	Prohibition of weaponization and militarization	1967	Full	109	The Outer Space Treaty is modeled on its predecessor, the Antarctic Treaty, and is considered a nonarmament preventive legal instrument. Its Article IV is considered a basic framework for international space law, and commits states not to: deploy weapons of mass destruction by launching them into the orbit around the Earth, install them on the Moon or any other celestial body, or otherwise station them in outer space. The treaty reserves celestial bodies exclusively for peaceful purposes and strictly prohibits their use for weapons testing, establishment of military bases, installation, or fortifications.
Treaty of Tlatelolco (Treaty for the Prohibition of Nuclear Weapons in Latin America and the Caribbean)	Prohibition of nuclear weapons development	1967	Full	33	This treaty was unanimously adopted based on the principles of the UN Charter. It requires a total prohibition of the use and manufacture of nuclear weapons and weapons of mass destruction of every type. As part of the treaty, member states also agreed to use the already existing nuclear material and facilities under their jurisdiction solely for peaceful purposes. Additionally, contracting parties agreed to refrain from engaging in, encouraging, authorizing, or participating (directly or indirectly) in the testing, usage, manufacturing, production, possession, and control of any nuclear weapon.

Continued

Table 5.1 *Continued*

Name of Treaty	Preventive Content	Date	Level of Robust-ness	State Parties	Summary
Nuclear Non-Proliferation Treaty (NPT)	A monitoring mechanism and prohibition of further proliferation; Legally established aspiration of full disarmament	1968	Limited	191	The core commitment of the NPT appears in Article VI, which requires each party to undertake to pursue negotiations in good faith on effective measures relating to cessation of the nuclear arms race. The treaty also envisions the completion of disarmament under strict and effective international control. Although none of the above has yet been achieved, 190 parties recognized the catastrophic humanitarian consequences of using nuclear weapons. Such an overwhelming recognition led to a change in the international context and governmental discourse on nuclear weapons.
Convention on the Prohibition of the Production and Stockpiling of Bacteriological (Biological) and Toxin Weapons and on Their Destruction	Prohibition of all aspects of development and use	1972	Full	183	This convention became the first multilateral disarmament treaty which banned an entire category of weapons. It effectively prohibited any development, production, acquisition, transfer, stockpiling, and use of biological and toxin weapons. Thus, it is a key legal instrument that serves as a testament to the international community's efforts to address the proliferation of weapons of mass destruction.
Treaty on the Prohibition of the Emplacement of Nuclear Weapons and Other Weapons of Mass Destruction on the Seabed and the Ocean Floor and in the Subsoil Thereof (The Seabed Arms Control Treaty)	Prohibition of weaponization and militarization	1971	Full	94	This is a multilateral agreement banning the emplacement of weapons of mass destruction on the ocean floor beyond a 12-mile coastal zone. It also allows all signatories to observe any seabed activities of other signatories beyond that zone. Similarly to the Outer Space and Antarctic Treaties, the Sea-bed Treaty sought to prevent international conflicts from spreading into "peaceful" territories.

Treaty	Year	Scope	No.	Description
Anti-Ballistic Missile Treaty (ABM)	1972	Limited	2	The ABM Treaty reflects the consensus between the USSR and the United States that mutual restraint of arms would serve as a better balance of power tool than unregulated proliferation. A cornerstone of stability and peace, the treaty prohibited deployment of missiles for the protection of either of these territories; however, it failed to fully renunciate the protection of these territories using antiballistic missiles. The United States withdrew from the treaty in 2001, which is widely considered a mistake.
Prohibits the deployment of missiles as a means of territorial protection				
The Convention on Prohibitions or Restrictions on the Use of Certain Conventional Weapons Which May Be Deemed to Be Excessively Injurious or to Have Indiscriminate Effects.	1980	Full	125	In particular, its *Protocol IV on Blinding Laser Weapons* is considered a major breakthrough. It was only the second time since 1868 that a weapon was prohibited before its full development and deployment. The major achievement of the convention is the stigmatization of deliberate blinding as an aggressive tactic weapon; it could perhaps serve as a model for all future weapon bans.
Prohibits development of blinding laser weapons				
Treaty of Rarotonga (South Pacific Free Zone Treaty)	1985	Full	13	This treaty contains three protocols and is aligned with agreements recorded in the Seabed and Outer Space treaties. Thus, states agreed to keep radioactive waste out of the sea and maintain a clean environment with limited pollution. The treaty also reaffirmed the NPT.
Prohibition of nuclear weapons development				
Intermediate-Range and Shorter-Range Missiles (Intermediate-Range Nuclear Forces Treaty, INF)	1987	Full	2	The treaty between the United States and the Soviet Union required both parties to destroy ground-launched ballistic and cruise missiles with a 500–5,500 km range. Furthermore, it provided for a full inspection system. As a result, a total of 2,692 missiles were eliminated after its entry into force, and remains in place with successor states of the Soviet Union.
Destruction of ground-launched ballistic and cruise missiles Full inspection mechanism				

Continued

Table 5.1 *Continued*

Name of Treaty	Preventive Content	Date	Level of Robust-ness	State Parties	Summary
Missile Technology Control Regime	Proliferation of unmanned delivery systems for nuclear weapons	1987	Full	35	Established among 35 missile technology supplier states, the agreement was created to control the spread of unmanned delivery systems for nuclear weapons—more specifically, systems that could carry a minimum of 500 kg for a minimum of 300 km. The treaty has successfully prevented or ended many ballistic missile programs as delivery systems for weapons of mass destruction, and achieved its objectives through export controls, meetings, dialogue, and outreach.
Agreement between the US and the USSR on Notifications of Launches of Intercontinental Ballistic Missiles and Submarine-Launched Ballistic Missiles	Early-warning mechanism	1988	Full	2	The agreement continued the discussion between the US and the Soviet Union about nuclear war risk reduction. This agreement implemented provisional 24-hour notice of a planned date, launch area, and area of impact for any launch of an ICBM or SLBM. These notices must be provided through Nuclear Risk Reduction Centers.
Treaty on Conventional Armed Forces in Europe	Reduction of conventional arms race (CFE)	1990	Full	30	The CFE[110] limited five major categories of conventional armaments (battle tanks, armored combat vehicles, artillery, combat aircraft, and attack helicopters) from the two Cold War blocs in the area stretching from the Atlantic Ocean to the Ural Mountains. It provides for increased transparency and confidence building among the parties, and prescribed annual exchange of military information, reductions in equipment levels, intrusive inspections to verify reports, and reduction implementations. Due to regional events in the 1990s, the treaty had to be readapted in 1999. The new agreement has not yet entered into force.

Treaty	Purpose	Year	Scope	Number	Description
Strategic Arms Reduction Treaty	Reduction of nuclear arms race	1991	Full	2	A bilateral agreement between the US and the USSR controlled the deployment of more than 6,000 nuclear warheads, prescribing reduction to 1,600 nuclear warheads. This treaty was the most complex and extensive arms treaty of its time. Despite the collapse of the Soviet Union, the treaty resulted in an approximate 80% reduction of all strategic nuclear weapons in existence at the time. It expired on December 5, 2009.
Open Skies Treaty	Limitation of strategic offensive arms deployment	1992	Limited	32	The treaty established a program of unarmed aerial surveillance over the entire territory of all state parties. The main goal of this treaty is to promote confidence, predictability, and stability.
The Chemical Weapons Convention	Prohibition of all aspects of development and use	1993	Full	193	Ratified by 193 state parties, the convention is deemed a success in disarmament. It prohibited military preparations to use chemical weapons and obliged parties to destroy all chemical weapons in their possession or located under their jurisdiction. The treaty has an implementing body, the Organization for the Prohibition of Chemical Weapons (OPCW), and a full monitoring mechanism.
Treaty of Bangkok (Southeast Asia Nuclear Weapon-Free Zone)	Prohibition of nuclear weapons development and use	1997	Full	10	The treaty obliged ten Southeast Asian member states under the auspices of the ASEAN (Brunei Darussalam, Cambodia, Indonesia, Laos, Malaysia, Myanmar, Philippines, Singapore, Thailand, and Vietnam) not to develop, manufacture, or otherwise acquire, possess, or have control of nuclear weapons.
Pelindaba Treaty (African Nuclear Weapon-Free Zone)	Prohibition of nuclear weapons development	2009	Full	41	The treaty prohibited any research, development, manufacturing, stockpiling, acquisition, testing, possession, control, or stationing of nuclear explosive devices on any member's territory. The treaty also prohibited the dumping of radioactive waste originating from outside the continent within the region.
Comprehensive Nuclear Test-Ban Treaty (CTBT)	Prohibition of nuclear testing	1996	Limited (not yet entered into force)	170	This treaty created an effective norm against nuclear testing despite the lack of US ratification, which prevents it from entering into force (the US abides by the norms of the treaty regardless). The CTBT put an end to all nuclear explosive testing and provided an effectively verifiable international monitoring system.

Continued

Table 5.1 *Continued*

Name of Treaty	Preventive Content	Date	Level of Robustness	State Parties	Summary
Convention on the Prohibition on the Use, Stockpiling, Production, and transfer of Anti-Personnel Mines and on Their Destruction (known as the Ottawa Treaty, Mine Ban Treaty, Anti-Personnel Mine Ban Convention)	Prohibition of all aspects of development and use	1997	Full	164	As a result of this treaty, the lowest number of casualties, the largest amount of contaminated land releases, and the highest level of global funding for mine action was recorded in 2012. All European Union member states are parties to the convention. The treaty obliges high-contracting parties to destroy their stockpile of antipersonnel mines within four years of entry into force; make every effort to identify and clear mined areas under their jurisdiction or control as soon as possible, but not later than 10 years after becoming a state party; provide assistance to mine victims and support for mine risk education; and submit annual reports on Mine Ban Treaty implementation activities. Although not all signatories have ratified it, they still abide by all rules and norms.
Treaty of Semipalatinsk (Central Asia Nuclear Weapon-Free Zone)	Prohibition of nuclear weapons development	2006	Full	5	Under this treaty, five Central Asian states pledged not to research, develop, manufacture, stockpile, acquire, possess, or have any control over any nuclear weapon or other nuclear explosive device. This includes nuclear weapon testing, or any other nuclear explosion. Parties must also introduce export controls under which they will not provide any special material or related equipment to any nonnuclear weapon state that has not concluded an IAEA comprehensive precautions agreement and Additional Protocol.
The Convention on Cluster Munitions (CMC)	Prohibition of all aspects of development and use	2008	Limited	110	The treaty has been successful in stigmatizing the use of the weapon. The convention prohibits all use, production, stockpiling, and transfer of cluster munitions; it includes deadlines for clearance of affected areas and the destruction of stockpiled cluster munitions. It also includes articles concerning assistance to victims of cluster munitions incidents.

Treaty	Objective	Year	Scope	Number	Description
New Strategic Arms Reduction Treaty (New START)	Reduce proliferation and importance of strategic offensive weapons deployment	2011	Full	2	This represents a further reduction and implementation of limitations for the Strategic Offensive Arms Treaty. Both the US and Russia have ratified the New START, which will substantially reduce the number of nuclear warheads they deploy. Furthermore, as part of the agreement, NATO and non-NATO states have made commitments to reduce the role played by nuclear weapons in their security policies.
Treaty on the Prohibition of Nuclear Weapons (TPNW)	Prohibition of all aspects of development and use of nuclear weapons leading toward their total elimination	2017	Limited	59	The treaty was negotiated by more than 130 states, and is an attempt to meet responsibilities of signatories of the NPT and the CTBT to pursue effective measures on disarmament. It reinforces states' commitments against the use, development, production, acquisition, transfer, installation, threat of use, stockpiling, manufacture, or possession of nuclear weapons. It also has a number of cooperation and assistance provisions, such as victim assistance. Notably, the treaty also outlines an obligation to take environmental remediation measures in respect of areas that have been contaminated by the testing or use of nuclear weapons. The TPNW has a potential to be foundational in the process of disarming and dismantling nuclear weapons; however, it is currently supported only by states that do not possess nuclear weapons.
Arms Trade Treaty	Regulating the international trade of conventional weapons	2012	Full	110	The ATT was negotiated in New York, adopted with a 154:3 vote, and is the first major multilateral treaty that monitors arms exports to ensure weapons trades adhere to ongoing arms embargoes and abide by IHL and action. It emphasizes the need to prevent these weapons from being used for human rights abuses, whilst also protecting domestic arms trade and varied rights to bear arms among member states. Notable leaders in weapons exports, China and Russia, are absent from the list of treaty signatories, as is the US, whose signature was revoked under the Trump presidency.

The result of the examination of 26 existing treaties that operated within a "preventive framework" to establish new regimes of prohibition or control of weapon systems that had been deemed to be destabilizing has been illuminating (see discussion in Chapter 5). These treaties achieved at least one of three goals:

- they prevented further militarization;
- they made weaponization unlawful; and/or
- they stopped proliferation within cooperative frameworks of transparency and common rules.

Based on the examination of these databases, I contend that disarmament and arms regulations are global public goods to protect civilians and to promote peace and security. They advance common good governance for all humanity.

Notes

1. Nico Krisch, "The Decay of Consent: International Law in an Age of Global Public Goods." *American Journal of International Law*, vol. 108, no. 1 (2014): pp. 1–40.
2. Denise Garcia, *Small Arms and Security: New Emerging International Norms* (Routledge, 2006).
3. Denise Garcia, "Humanitarian Security Regimes." *International Affairs*, vol. 91, no. 1 (2015): pp. 55–75.
4. Institute for Economics and Peace, "Global Peace Index." 2021.
5. The average level of global peacefulness deteriorated by 0.07 per cent in the 2021 Global Peace Index. Although a relatively small deterioration, this is the ninth time in the last 13 years that global peacefulness has deteriorated. Global Peace Index 2021.
6. Gerd Oberleitner, "Human Security." In *Encyclopedia of Human Rights*, ed. David F. Forsythe (Oxford University Press, 2009): pp. 2, 486.
7. Benoît Pélopidas, "Renunciation: Restraint and Rollback." In *Routledge Handbook of Nuclear Proliferation and Policy* (Routledge 2015): pp. 337–348.
8. Åke Sellström, "UNSCOM: A Successful Experiment in Disarmament." Bulletin of the Atomic Scientists, vol. 77, no. 4 (2021): pp. 177–179. Jody Williams, Stephen D. Goose, and Mary Wareham, eds. *Banning Landmines: Disarmament, Citizen Diplomacy, and Human Security* (Rowman & Littlefield Publishers, 2008).
9. Matthew Bolton, *Imagining Disarmament, Enchanting International Relations* (Springer, 2019). Denise Garcia, *Disarmament Diplomacy and Human Security: Regimes, Norms and Moral Progress in International Relations* (Routledge, 2011).
10. Treaty on the Prohibition of Nuclear Weapons. CN.475.2017. Treaties-XXVI-9 of August 9, 2017. The Treaty was adopted on July 7, 2017, by the United Nations conference to negotiate a legally binding instrument to prohibit nuclear weapons, leading toward their total elimination. Nina Tannenwald, "The State of the Nuclear Taboo Today." In *Responding to North Korean Nuclear First Use: Minimizing Damage to the Nuclear Taboo*, eds. Erin Hahn, James Scouras, Robert Leonhard, and Camille Spencer (Johns Hopkins University Applied Physics Laboratory (JHU/APL) Laurel United States, 2019): pp. 6–11, Nuclear First Use.

11. Future of Life Institute, "Autonomous Weapons: An Open Letter from AI & Robotics Researchers," *Future of Life Institute*, available at: http://futureoflife.org/AI/open_letter_autonomous_weapons.
12. Keith Krause. *Arms and the State: Patterns of Military Production and Trade* (Cambridge University Press, 1995).
13. Garcia, Denise, *Small Arms and Security: New Emerging International Norms* (Routledge, 2006). Garcia, *Disarmament Diplomacy and Human Security*.
14. Beyza Unal and Patricia Lewis, "Cybersecurity of Nuclear Weapons Systems." In *Threats, Vulnerabilities and Consequences* (ISD-Chatham House, 2018): pp. 1–26.
15. SIPRI, Stockholm International Peace Research Institute (Oxford University Press, 2021).
16. Gro Nystuen, Stuart Casey-Maslen, and Annie Golden Bersagel, eds., *Nuclear Weapons Under International Law* (Cambridge University Press, 2014).
17. Theodor Meron, "The Humanization of Humanitarian Law." *American Journal of International Law*, vol. 94, no. 2 (2000): pp. 239–278.
18. Garcia, "Humanitarian Security Regimes."
19. John Borrie, "Humanitarian Reframing of Nuclear Weapons and the Logic of a Ban." *International Affairs*, vol. 90, no. 3 (2014): pp. 625–646.
20. Borrie, "Humanitarian Reframing of Nuclear Weapons"; Garcia, "Humanitarian Security Regimes."
21. The Paris Agreement was adopted on December 12, 2015, at the twenty-first session of the Conference of the Parties to the United Nations Framework Convention on Climate Change. United Nations General Assembly, *Transforming our World: The 2030 Agenda for Sustainable Development*, October 21, 2015, A/RES/70/1.
22. Convention on the Prohibition of the Development, Production and Stockpiling of Bacteriological (Biological) and Toxin Weapons and on their Destruction, April 10, 1972. United Nations, Treaty Series, vol. 1975, p. 45; and depositary notifications C.N.246.1994.TREATIES-5 of August 31, 1994: Convention on the Prohibition of the Development, Production, Stockpiling and Use of Chemical Weapons and on Their Destruction ILM 800 (1993).
23. United Nations Treaty Series, vol. 3012. C.N.266.2013.TREATIES.XXVI-8 of May 10, 2013. The Arms Trade Treaty was adopted on April 2, 2013 by resolution 67/234B during the 67th session of the General Assembly of the United Nations.
24. United Nations Treaty Series, C.N.473.1997.TREATIES-2 of December 15, 1997, the 1997 Convention on the Prohibition of the Use, Stockpiling, Production and Transfer of Anti-Personnel Mines and on their Destruction, is the international agreement that bans antipersonnel landmines. It is usually referred to as the Ottawa Convention or the Mine Ban Treaty.
25. Cluster Munitions Convention, United Nations, Treaty Series, vol. 2688, p. 39; depositary notification C.N.776.2008.TREATIES-2 of November 10, 2008. The Convention was concluded by the Dublin Diplomatic Conference on Cluster Munitions at Dublin on May 30, 2008.
26. Alan Robock and Owen Brian Toon, "Local Nuclear War, Global Suffering." *Scientific American*, vol. 302, no. 1 (2010): pp. 74–81. Alan Robock and Owen Brian Toon, "Self-Assured Destruction: The Climate Impacts of Nuclear War." *Bulletin of the Atomic Scientists*, vol. 68, no. 5 (2012): pp. 66–74.

27. Richard Slade, Robert Tickner, and Phoebe Wynn-Pope. "Protecting Humanity from the Catastrophic Humanitarian Consequences of Nuclear Weapons: Reframing the Debate Towards the Humanitarian Impact." *International Review of the Red Cross*, vol. 97, no. 899 (2015): pp. 731–752.

28. Hans M Kristensen and Robert S. Norris. "Global Nuclear Weapons Inventories, 1945–2013." *Bulletin of the Atomic Scientists*, vol. 69, no. 5 (2013): pp. 75–81.

29. "SIPRI Yearbook, Armaments, Disarmament, and International Security" *Federation of American Scientists, Status of the World's Nuclear Forces* (2021).

30. Nick Ritchie, "A Hegemonic Nuclear Order: Understanding the Ban Treaty and the Power Politics of Nuclear Weapons." *Contemporary Security Policy*, vol. 40, no. 4 (2019): pp. 409–434.

31. Robock and Toon, "Local Nuclear War, Global Suffering"; Robock and Toon, "Self-Assured Destruction."

32. Paul K. Huth, "Deterrence and International Conflict: Empirical Findings and Theoretical Debates." *Annual Review of Political Science*, vol.2, no. 1 (1999): pp. 25–48; Brad Roberts, *The Case for US Nuclear Weapons in the 21st Century* (Stanford University Press, 2020); Vipin Narang, *Nuclear Strategy in the Modern Era* (Princeton University Press, 2014).

33. Benoît Pélopidas, "Nuclear Weapons Scholarship as a Case of Self-Censorship in Security Studies." *Journal of Global Security Studies*, vol. 1, no. 4 (2016): pp. 326–336.

34. Government of Austria, *Vienna Conference on the Humanitarian Impact of Nuclear Weapons*, December 8–9, 2014, Chair's Summary.

35. Ramesh Thakur, ed. *Nuclear Weapons-Free Zones* (Macmillan, 1998); Exequiel Lacovsky, *Nuclear Weapons Free Zones: A Comparative Perspective* (Routledge, 2021).

36. Gro Nystuen et al., *Nuclear Weapons under International Law*.

37. Stuart Casey-Maslen, ed. *Weapons under International Human Rights Law* (Cambridge University Press, 2014);Anna Crowe, "Human Rights-Humanitarianism in Disarmament Law." In *Disarmament Law*, ed. Treasa Dunworth and Anna Hood (Routledge, 2021), pp. 80–101.

38. These are the words of my former professor of International Law at the University of Brasilia, now one of the judges of the International Court of Justice: Antônio Augusto Cançado Trindade, *International Law for Humankind* (Martinus Nijhoff Publishers, 2013), p. 409.

39. Lisa L. Martin, "Interests, Power, and Multilateralism." *International Organization* VOL. 46, no. 4 (1992): pp. 765–792.

40. Hersch Lauterpacht and Hans Kelsen. *Rules of Warfare in an Unlawful War* (University of California Press, 2020).

41. Steven L. Simon, and André Bouville, "Health Effects of Nuclear Weapons Testing." *The Lancet* vol. 386, no 9992 (2015): pp. 407–409; Remus Prăvălie, "Nuclear Weapons Tests and Environmental Consequences: A Global Perspective." *Ambio*, vol. 43, no. 6 (2014): pp. 729–744.

42. Borrie, "Humanitarian Reframing of Nuclear Weapons."

43. NPT/CONF.2010/50 (Vol. I) 2010 Review Conference of the Parties to the Treaty on the Non-Proliferation of Nuclear Weapons.

44. Espen Barthe Eide, "Chair's Summary Humanitarian Impact of Nuclear Weapons," March 5, 2013, https://www.regjeringen.no/en/aktuelt/nuclear_summary/id716343/.

45. John Borrie and Tim Caughley, *An Illusion of Safety: Challenges of Nuclear Weapon Detonations for United Nations Humanitarian Coordination and Response* (UNIDIR, New York and Geneva, 2014); Alexander Kmentt, "The Development of the International Initiative on the Humanitarian Impact of Nuclear Weapons and its Effect on the Nuclear Weapons Debate." *International Review of the Red Cross*, vol. 97, no. 899 (2015): pp. 681–709.

46. ICJ Reports, *Legality of the Threat or Use of Nuclear Weapons, Advisory Opinion* (1996): p. 226; International Court of Justice (1996); Louise Doswald-Beck, "International Humanitarian Law and the Advisory Opinion of the International Court of Justice on the Legality of the Threat or Use of Nuclear Weapons." *International Review of the Red Cross (1961–1997)*, vol. 37, no. 316 (1997): pp. 35–55.

47. David Freestone and Ellen Hey, eds. *The Precautionary Principle and International Law: The Challenge of Implementation* (Kluwer Law International, vol. 31, 1996).

48. ICJ Reports, *Legality of the Threat or Use of Nuclear Weapons, Advisory Opinion* (1996), p. 226; International Court of Justice (1996), available at https://www.refworld.org/cases,ICJ,4b2913d62.html, p. 266.

49. The 2015 Review Conference of the Parties to the Treaty on the Non-Proliferation of Nuclear Weapons (NPT) was held at the United Nations in New York from April 27 to May 22, 2015, and was presided over by Ambassador Taous Feroukhi of Algeria. The Treaty, particularly article VIII, paragraph 3, envisages a review of the operation of the treaty every five years.

50. ICRC Statement, 2017: "Urgent Action Needed to Reduce the Risks of Nuclear Weapons, Nuclear Weapon Risks Symposium, United Nations Institute for Disarmament Research (UNIDIR), Geneva, Switzerland, Statement by Yves Daccord, director-general of the ICRC." https://www.icrc.org/en/document/nuclear-weapons-icrc-statement-unidir-2017, p. 5.

51. International Committee of the Red Cross Appeal to the High Contracting Parties Signatory to the Geneva Conventions for the Protection of the Victims of War: Atomic Weapons and Non-Directed Missiles, Geneva, April 5, 1950.

52. UN General Assembly, "Establishment of a Commission to Deal with the Problems Raised by the Discovery of Atomic Energy." *Resolution*, vol. 1, no. 1 (1946).

53. Paul C. Szasz, "The Security Council Starts Legislating." *American Journal of International Law*, vol. 96, no. 4 (2002): pp. 901–905.

54. James E. Doyle, "Why Eliminate Nuclear Weapons?" *Survival* 55, no. 1 (2013): 7–34; Benoît Pélopidas, "Power, Luck, and Scholarly Responsibility at the End of the World(s)." *International Theory*, vol. 12, no. 3 (2020): pp. 459–470.

55. Nick Ritchie, "Valuing and Devaluing Nuclear Weapons." *Contemporary Security Policy*, vol. 34, no. 1 (2013): pp. 146–173; Borrie, "Humanitarian Reframing of Nuclear Weapons"; Didier Chaudet, Florent Parmentier, and Benoît Pélopidas. *When Empire meets Nationalism: Power Politics in the US and Russia* (Routledge, 2016).

56. Benoît Pélopidas, "The Unbearable Lightness of Luck: Three Sources of Overconfidence in the Manageability of Nuclear Crises." *European Journal of International Security*, vol. 2, no. 2 (2017): pp. 240–262.

57. Ward Wilson, "The Myth of Nuclear Deterrence." *Nonproliferation Review*, vol. 15, no. 3 (2008): pp. 421–439; John Mueller, *Atomic Obsession: Nuclear Alarmism from Hiroshima to al-Qaeda* (Oxford University Press, 2009); Benoît Pélopidas, "The Oracles

of Proliferation: How Experts Maintain a Biased Historical Reading that Limits Policy Innovation." *Nonproliferation Review*, vol. 18, no. 1 (2011): pp. 297–314.

58. UN Security Council, Security Council resolution 1887 (2009) [on nuclear non-proliferation and nuclear disarmament], September 24, 2009, S/RES/1887 (2009).

59. Global Zero, https://www.globalzero.org/our-movement/who-we-are. Benoît Pélopidas, "The Birth of Nuclear Eternity." *Futures* (2021): pp. 484–500.

60. Jakob Kellenberger, "Bringing the Era of Nuclear Weapons to an End." Statement, April 20, 2010: www.icrc.org/eng/resources/documents/statement/nuclear-weapons-statement-200410.htm; Kmentt, "The Development of the International Initiative on the Humanitarian Impact of Nuclear Weapons."

61. John Borrie, "An Introduction to Implementing the Treaty on the Prohibition of Nuclear Weapons." *Journal for Peace and Nuclear Disarmament*, vol. 4, no.1 (2021): pp. 1–12.

62. Carl Kaysen, Robert S. McNamara, and George W. Rathjens, "Nuclear Weapons after the Cold War." *Foreign Affairs*, vol. 70 (1990): p. 95. Holy See, Vienna 2014 "Nuclear Disarmament: Time for Abolition," position paper, available at: www.bmeia.gv.at/fileadmin/user_upload/Zentrale/Aussenpolitik/Abruestung/HINW14/HINW14_Holy_See_Contribution.pdf, p. 4.

63. Nina Tannenwald, *The Nuclear Taboo: The United States and the Non-Use of Nuclear Weapons Since 1945* (Cambridge University Press, 2007); Nina Tannenwald, "The Nuclear Taboo: The United States and the Normative Basis of Nuclear Non-Use." *International Organization*, vol. 53, no. 3 (1999): pp. 433–468.

64. Paul, T. Varkey, *The Tradition of Non-Use of Nuclear Weapons* (Stanford University Press, 2009); Frank Sauer, *Atomic Anxiety: Deterrence, Taboo and the Non-Use of US Nuclear Weapons* (Springer, 2015).

65. Louis Maresca and Eleanor Mitchell, "The Human Costs and Legal Consequences of Nuclear Weapons under International Humanitarian Law." *International Review of the Red Cross*, vol. 97, no. 899 (2015): pp. 621–645.

66. A/RES/71/258. Resolution adopted by the General Assembly on December 23, 2016 [on the report of the First Committee (A/71/450)] 71/258; titled "Taking Forward Multilateral Nuclear Disarmament Negotiations."

67. Daniel H. Joyner, *Interpreting the Nuclear Non-Proliferation Treaty* (Oxford University Press, 2011).

68. Beatrice Fihn, "The Logic of Banning Nuclear Weapons." *Survival*, vol. 59, no. 1 (2017): pp. 43–50.

69. Doyle, "Why Eliminate Nuclear Weapons?"

70. Ray Acheson, *Banning the Bomb, Smashing the Patriarchy* (Rowman & Littlefield, 2021).

71. Fihn, "The Logic of Banning Nuclear Weapons."

72. "United States Non-Paper: Defense Impacts of Potential United Nations General Assembly Nuclear Weapons Ban Treaty," October 17, 2016, available at https://www.armscontrol.org/act/2018-10/features/nuclear-weapons-prohibition-treaty-interpreting-ban-assisting-encouraging.

73. Fihn, "The Logic of Banning Nuclear Weapons."

74. Congressional Budget Office, Projected Costs of US Nuclear Forces, 2021–2030. Department of Defense and the Department of Energy. See www.cbo.gov/publication/57130#data.

75. Susi Snyder, *Rejecting Risk: 101 Policies Against Nuclear Weapons* (PAX, 2022).

76. Chaudet et al., *When Empire meets Nationalism*.

77. Howard Hu, Arjun Makhijani, and Katherine Yih, eds. *Nuclear Wastelands: A Global Guide to Nuclear Weapons Production and its Health and Environmental Effects* (MIT Press, 2000).

78. Thakur, ed. *Nuclear Weapons-Free Zones* and Lacovsky, *Nuclear Weapons Free Zones*.

79. I consulted the literature of the ICRC in Geneva, had conversations with ICRC experts in recent years, and reviewed the Organization for the Prohibition of Chemical Weapons history. From the large literature on chemical weapons prohibition, the seminal work of Richard Price is notable, in particular Richard Price, "Syria and the Chemical Weapons Taboo." *Journal of Global Security Studies*, vol. 4, no. 1 (2019): pp. 37–52.

80. Richard Price, "A Genealogy of the Chemical Weapons Taboo." *International Organization*, vol. 49, no. 1 (Winter, 1995): pp. 73–103.

81. Price, "A Genealogy of the Chemical Weapons Taboo."

82. Protocol for the Prohibition of the Use of Asphyxiating, Poisonous or Other Gases, and of Bacteriological Methods of Warfare. Geneva, June 17, 1925.

83. See the Organization for the Prohibition of Chemical Weapons announcement: https://www.opcw.org/media-centre/featured-topics/syria-and-opcw.

84. Javed Ali, "Chemical Weapons and the Iran-Iraq War: A Case Study in Noncompliance." *The Nonproliferation Review*, vol. 8, no. 1 (2001): pp. 43–58.

85. Price, "A Genealogy of the Chemical Weapons Taboo."

86. Twenty-Sixth Session of the Conference of the States Parties to the Chemical Weapons Convention, November 29–December 3, 2021, The Hague, Netherlands Statement by the International Committee of the Red Cross, November 29, 2021.

87. Denise Garcia, "Disarming the Lords of War: A New International Treaty to Regulate the Arms Trade." *Foreign Affairs* (December 2014).

88. Ray Acheson, "Starting Somewhere: The Arms Trade Treaty, Human Rights and Gender Based Violence." *Human Rights Defender*, vol. 22, no. 17 (2013): p. 19; Williams, Goose, and Wareham, *Banning Landmines: Disarmament, Citizen Diplomacy and Human Security*.

89. Ramesh Thakur, "The Nuclear Ban Treaty: Recasting a Normative Framework for Disarmament." *The Washington Quarterly*, vol. 40, no. 4 (2017): p. 71.

90. Garcia, "Humanitarian Security Regimes"; Garcia, *Disarmament Diplomacy and Human Security*.

91. Denise Garcia, "Global Norms on Arms: The Significance of the Arms Trade Treaty for Global Security in World Politics." *Global Policy*, vol. 5, no. 4 (2014): pp. 425–432.

92. Jennifer Erickson, *Dangerous Trade* (Columbia University Press, 2015).

93. Ann Florini, "The Evolution of International Norms." *International Studies Quarterly*, vol. 40, no. 3 (1996): pp. 363–389.

94. Thomas Risse-Kappen, et al., eds. *The Power of Human Rights: International Norms and Domestic Change* (Cambridge University Press, 1999); Martha Finnemore and Kathryn Sikkink, "International Norm Dynamics and Political Change." *International Organization*, vol. 52, no. 4 (1998): pp. 887–917.

95. Mona Lena Krook and Jacqui True, "Rethinking the Life Cycles of International Norms: The United Nations and the Global Promotion of Gender Equality." *European Journal of International Relations*, vol. 18, no. 1 (2012): pp. 103–127.

96. Annika Björkdahl, *From Idea to Norm: Promoting Conflict Prevention* (Lund University, 2002).

97. Denise Garcia "Shifting International Security Norms." *Ethics & International Affairs*, vol. 31, no. 2 (2017): pp. 235–246.

98. United Nations Secretary-General (1995), "Supplement to An Agenda for Peace," A/50/60, S/1995/1, paragraph 60, January 3.

99. Garcia, *Small Arms and Security*.

100. UNGA (1997), "Report of the Panel of Governmental Experts on Small Arms, Pursuant to Paragraph 1 of General Assembly Resolution 50/70 B of 12 December 1995," A/52/298 of August 27.

101. Michael C. Horowitz, "Why Words Matter: The Real World Consequences of Defining Autonomous Weapons Systems." Temple International & Comparative Law Journal, vol. 30 (2016): p. 85.

102. Daniele Amoroso and Guglielmo Tamburrini, "Toward a Normative Model of Meaningful Human Control over Weapons Systems." *Ethics & International Affairs*, vol. 35, no. 2 (2021): pp. 245–272.

103. Rebecca Crootof, "Autonomous Weapon Systems and the Limits of Analogy." *Harvard National Security Journal*, vol. 9 (2018): pp. 51–83.

104. Amanda Sharkey and Noel Sharkey. Sunlight Glinting on Clouds: Deception and Autonomous Weapons Systems." In *Counter-Terrorism, Ethics and Technology*, ed. A. Henschke, A. Reed, S. Robbins, and S. Miller (Springer, 2021): pp. 35–47.

105. Rebecca Crootof, "War, Responsibility, and Killer Robots." *North Carolina Journal of International Law & Commercial Regulation*, vol. 40 (2014): p. 909.

106. Steven Pinker, *Enlightenment Now: The Case for Reason, Science, Humanism, and Progress* (Penguin UK, 2018).

107. Ian Hurd, "The International Rule of Law and the Domestic Analogy." *Global Constitutionalism*, vol. 4, no. 3 (2015): pp. 365–395.

108. Thanks to Emerson Victoria Johnston for this insight.

109. *UNODA Disarmament Treaties Database*. Database accessible at: https://treaties.unoda.org/; https://www.state.gov/depositary-status-lists/ SIPRI Yearbook 2021. Database accessible at: https://www.sipri.org/yearbook/2021; https://www.iaea.org/resources/legal/treaties.

110. While technically the treaty was ratified by 22 states, the USSR and the Warsaw Pact were dissolved in 1991, and Czechoslovakia was in the process of splitting into the Czech Republic and Slovakia.

Chapter 6
A global framework to govern military AI: Transnational networked cooperation and common good governance

The world is at a highly perilous moment and national security must be viewed through different lenses. The grim revival of the unlawful use of military force, often to commit international acts of aggression is evidence that the United Nations must be revitalized and strengthened in the tireless pursuit of peace and security.

Governments have their priorities wrong. Investments and infrastructure based on a narrowly focused type of security—where competition for more power takes precedence—cannot be brought to bear on the global catastrophic risks facing humanity: climate change, future pandemics, nuclear warfare, and artificial intelligence (AI). The proliferation of military AI is leaving the world less safe. The unrelenting pursuit of more militarization does not protect but in fact jeopardizes current and future generations. This book has argued for a return to planetary cooperation whereby all countries can forge global public goods and build humanity's security.

As I finalize this book, a senseless and unlawful international war is taking place—the war of aggression against Ukraine—when such actions should by now be confined to the history books. The war is a testing ground for new autonomous systems and shows that a regulatory framework for military AI is an imperative global public good and must be forged rapidly to contain the ongoing unrestrained race for sophisticated military AI.[1] I have demonstrated that the prohibition or at least regulation of the means and methods of warfare, as well as international legal regulations on military conduct, are powerful global public goods. They have had a pacifying effect in international relations and have minimized human suffering (Chapter 5).[2] As the war currently rages on European soil, the rapid militarization of AI is proceeding, and attempts to incorporate an array of AI technologies in weapon systems continue apace.[3] The prohibition of AI weapons—especially those that target people and are machine-learning-based—is a global public good of the highest order and needs to be

The AI Military Race. Denise Garcia, Oxford University Press. © Denise Garcia (2023).
DOI: 10.1093/oso/9780192864604.003.0007

enacted urgently. The continuing weaponization of AI will create "riskless wars" for the militarized countries as their soldiers will be kept out of harm's way. Riskless wars mean a world where wars occur more frequently as there is a lower risk of casualties for the technologically advanced military powers. The international norm against the use of military force for territorial annexation has thus far prevented World War III, but this norm will be further weakened with the heightened use of uncheked AI. Therefore, it is becoming increasingly urgent to create the means to use AI in ways that are more beneficial than harmful, to serve the whole of humanity, and not for waging war. Instituting *common good governance* norms to limit autonomy in the critical functions of weapon systems is vital. Unrestricted action will bring short-term military advantages that will quickly be overshadowed by disastrous long-term strategic and ethical risks. This will be amplified by the use of AI in autonomous systems.

Military AI is wide-ranging because of the distributed nature of the technology, which means that there are several technologies that fall under the umbrella of AI. These include machine learning, deep learning, image recognition, process automation, and speech translation, among others. The majority of these technologies are created by and for the civilian realm. Nevertheless, the march toward militarizing and weaponizing many of their features continues relentlessly.[4]

The creation of *common good governance* to set rules on the militarization of AI is urgent. A framework on the militarization of AI is a global public good that would benefit all nations and peoples. Even though the discussions at the United Nations started in 2013 in the Human Rights Council, they deal only with autonomy in weapon systems, and merely touch on the uses of AI to enable and enhance such systems. Consequently, they fail to address the broader aspects of the militarization of AI. A growing consensus about the shape and nature of new international law in the form of a treaty on autonomous weapons seems to express that it should be legally binding and would include a few prohibitions (proscriptions) and some regulations. A new treaty on autonomous weapons could inspire new ways to address broader aspects such as the militarization of AI. This would mean that certain modes of autonomy lacking methodical human control and predictability would be prohibited. Furthermore, some systems that target humans would also be unlawful. The regulations—also legally binding—would apply to various other aspects of the use of autonomous systems such as fail-safes, duration and context of operations, and the possibility of deactivation to circumvent errors.

Transnational networked cooperation and common good governance

The *transnational networked cooperation* that I posit can create the forms of *common good governance* that are needed to prevent the eventual widespread weaponization of AI.[5] This is because such cooperation would be global and involve multiple stakeholders, not only countries. Yet technological developments usually outpace diplomacy. Diplomatic attempts to restrain the technologically advanced nations to employ new technologies are even more arduous because of the many interests at play, whereby the militarized countries wish to continue to develop autonomous and AI systems.[6] Nonetheless, the establishment of *common good governance* on the uses of AI in the military is needed to avoid circumstances when AI can be used without regard for international norms of restraint, especially for protecting civilians. The prevention of malicious and deceitful uses of AI should be sought through the creation of *common good governance*. A regulatory framework for military AI is a complex global public good to forge due to the disaggregated and distributed uses and applications across multiple societal levels.[7] Yet it is needed to prevent widespread harm, avoid risk, and be protective of future generations. The idea of *common good governance* presupposes a recognition that most threats to national security today are not only of a military nature, but also economic, societal, and, indeed, planetary in scope. As AI poses a challenge at all these levels, a new framework is all the more essential.

Transnational network cooperation is altering the practice of global cooperation by making it more inclusive and shifting it away from the sole remit of the state. Reshaping the institutions needed to build a nonviolent future is in order so that future generations will hopefully live in a more humane world. This promising outcome requires the mobilization of grassroots or bottom-up connections to change and challenge the unyielding ways of the militarized great powers. The way to achieve global cooperation without the full participation of the major military powers is at the crux of the issue of *transnational networked cooperation*, which starts to emerge precisely when major power championship for change falters in all currently pressing areas: restraining the weaponization of AI, avoiding nuclear warfare, combating climate change, and preventing the next pandemic.

The attempt to establish norms and principles to prevent the uncontrolled race toward greater militarization veering into the rampant weaponization of AI necessitates an all-hands-on-deck approach. This is what *transnational networked cooperation* does by involving and taking into account not only states but also all other relevant stakeholders in attempting to create a regulatory framework—by way of a new international treaty—governing the use of autonomous weapons and AI-assisted systems (Chapter 1). An international treaty on autonomous weapons would be a major component in creating a comprehensive regulatory framework on military AI. A global regulatory framework shall include all actors possible and all countries, not only the technologically advanced, because AI is already ubiquitous and pervasive in people's lives, and will become even more so. The governance of military AI will not only need to be inclusive of various stakeholders, but also preventive, principles-based, and viewed as legitimate and representative.[8]

I identified a rise in *transnational networked cooperation* that is formed by five types of groups: scientific and educational organizations (technology workers, scientists, and academics), members of civil society (individuals, nongovernmental organizations, the media, and religious groups), the private sector (including financial organizations), international and regional organizations, and governments (including some middle and major powers). This *transnational networked cooperation* is occurring not only in an attempt to negotiate a new international treaty on autonomous weapons, but also in creating governance avenues in AI in general (Chapters 1 and 3). But this *transnational networked cooperation* is glaringly less evident in creating a framework for military AI. The composition of this hybrid form of networked cooperation is made up of a complex mosaic where action is taken by a multiplicity of change makers, beyond the formal state level, in several areas of international relations, from climate management to global public health, and even in the domain of security, which is the sphere I investigate. Public–private partnerships are an increasingly dominant feature in allowing alliances for change to occur. In the realm of security, change often occurs slowly unless there is a shock precipitating event. Power politics is the dominant operating principle preserving national security, and there is thus scant motivation for change. Nevertheless, even in the domain of security there are possibilities for a more inclusive multilateral order where many emerging voices are making themselves heard.

Transnational networked cooperation is a realistic way of portraying modes of collaboration that can materialize to build *common good governance*: by means of networks that link and bind together engaged and concerned individuals from different segments of many countries that would not otherwise be able to form alliances in a true collective endeavor. Each segment has its strengths, and they can be mutually complementary. The negotiation of treaties is typically the way to forge solutions to global problems. However, treaties are no longer the sole form of management of global problems. Each node in the network of cooperation reinforces the others by creating innovative forms of global action. These may spearhead powerful debates about what is adequate to shape the future for humanity to benefit more people. Change makers are bound by a belief in more human and secure prospects for future generations.

My five criteria for the rise of *transnational networked cooperation* (Chapter 1) indicate that change makers engage in several steps to achieve their goals of creating change. They generate authoritative knowledge based upon a principled and humanity-based discourse in an attempt to create precautionary arrangements to avoid future harm. They try to influence the highest level on the United Nations agenda to gain traction in international discussions. Momentum and strength developed when a broader array of scientists joined the ranks of those who first raised the alarm against the perils of algorithmic wars where humans lose control; in doing so, they created an epistemic community. The combined moral authority of the scientists who create the technology and the way they express their revolt against the malicious and evil uses of their creation added a compelling dimension to *transnational networked cooperation*.

Everyone will lose in the relentless pursuit of the militarization and weaponization of new technologies, at the same time making international relations more precarious. *Transnational networked cooperation* offers a more inclusive way to find solutions for the contemporary problems of global cooperation. States alone have proven unable or unwilling to forge the path ahead. Two dynamics are at play. First, global cooperation is being constituted by multiple cooperative alliances between different groups in society across many countries in the form of *transnational networked cooperation*. Second, attempts to set rules for, and limits on, the impact of new technologies have been rigorous. New global governing mechanisms will have to be sought. The challenge is that the existing international regulatory architecture will not suffice. Moreover, current international law on bans and regulations of other technologies of warfare cannot fully account for the realm of AI, nor entirely serve as a suitable model for action.[9] This is where *transnational networked cooperation* may point the way forward in inspiring ways because it will more inclusive. With these dynamics in mind, and with the ongoing weaponization of AI, what forms of prevention are in place that evince sufficient precautionary vision to avoid a precarious and perilous future? This book has explored these possibilities and offered a path for coordinated global action through *common good governance*.

If the militarization of AI entails the widespread weaponization of AI and continues without rules, everyone will be worse off: AI wars will extend the list of existential risks humanity faces, along with nuclear warfare, climate change, and pandemics.[10] As soon as the invasion of Ukraine started, Russian president Vladimir Putin threatened to use nuclear weapons by raising Russia's alertness level. Russia boasts the world's largest nuclear arsenal, consisting of 6,255 warheads, followed by the United States with 5,550 (Chapter 3).[11] Nuclear weapons do not deter conflict; instead, they continue to pose an enormous peril to the survival of humanity. The notion of deterrence based upon "mutually assured destruction" is deeply flawed and risks dangerous scalation (Chapter 5). Nuclear weapons continue to pose an existential risk. The lessons drawn from previous limitations on the means and methods of warfare suggest that AI weapons will not deter conflicts either, and will more likely aggravate and escalate them.

The concerted global diplomacy that took place to avert the war in Ukraine demonstrates that most countries wish to have peace and adherence to international law instead of embarking on destructive warfare. The United Nations General Assembly had a historic meeting on March 2, 2022, invoking the "Uniting for Peace" resolution for the 11th time in the history of the organization.[12] Uniting for Peace is a mechanism to uphold peace and security when the United Nations Security Council is stalled due to obstruction by one or more of its members.[13] The historic vote at the United Nations General Assembly took place on March 2, 2022: 141 countries voted against the war on Ukraine, and five voted in favor: Belarus, Eritrea, North Korea, Russia, and Syria.[14] Another historic vote took place on February 23, 2023, marking a year of the war of aggression, and showed 139 countries voting against the invasion and calling for its end. The world is united against the folly of this war.

The war against Ukraine highlights the danger that a few nuclear-armed states continue to pose as existential threats to humanity. Combined, the nine nuclear-weapon states—the United States, Russia, the United Kingdom, France, China, India, Pakistan, Israel, and the Democratic People's Republic of Korea (North Korea)—have an estimated 13,080 nuclear weapons.[15] The unsound logic of excessive militarization in the pursuit of security led to the unconscionable accumulation of 70,000 nuclear weapons during the Cold War.[16] Since 1940, the United States has spent almost $6 trillion in amassing nuclear weapons.[17] Instead of embarking upon another race for militarization, diverting public funds and weaponizing AI, countries must mount a decisive response to the existential risks that continue to imperil their populations. Such risks will be magnified by the long-term impact of the militarization of AI. The response of states in the General Assembly invoking "Uniting for Peace" and guided by the norm against the use of force for territorial annexation demonstrates the power of principles and the norms that sustain peace. There are emerging norms, principles, and precedents that can guide the international community in creating a robust regulatory framework for military AI that is protective of human dignity now and for future generations.[18]

A regulatory framework on military AI would create common good governance and would help fill a gap in an area where there are no commonly agreed regulations. The framework could be based upon the following three pillars that would create *common good governance* to prevent the unrestrained weaponization of AI. These three pillars provide the basis necessary to craft a regulatory framework for the militarization of AI, as discussed throughout and summarized as:

1) The peaceful uses of AI as an emerging international norm: responsible ethical uses and desirable emerging ideas:

   Distributive justice and equity
   Common management—justice for developing countries
   Human-centered and protective of future generations
   AI as a global common
   A new treaty on autonomous weapons advances a framework for
      military AI

2) Risk assessment based upon preventive precautionary action:

   Seeking humanity's security
   Avoiding international instability
   Common concern of humanity

3) Lessons learned from previous successful global cooperation:

   Creation of spheres of peace
   Reduction of suspicion and enhancing trust-building measures
   Conflict-resolution mechanisms and peaceful settlement of disputes

Pillars to create common good governance

Pillar 1. An emerging international norm on the peaceful uses of AI

AI is at the center of the rivalry between China and the United States.[19] The enormous variations in strategic and ethical perspectives adopted by the militarized powers, especially China and the United States, in their search for supremacy in AI (Introduction and Chapter 3) jeopardize the prospects of utilizing AI solely for the common good of humanity.[20] The fundamental criterion to determine the responsible use of military AI is the respect and compliance with international law in all applicable areas (Chapter 4). To further the examination of applicable areas of international law undertaken earlier, it is also key to examine emerging norms and principles.

After surveying emerging initiatives across many countries, civil society, and the private sector (Chapter 1), I argue that there is a rising norm upholding the peaceful uses of AI. This implies that a regulatory framework for military AI can be erected in a more auspicious environment and that it is possible to do so despite the difficulties and geopolitical rivalries.[21] This emerging norm enshrines an understanding of AI as human-centric and trustworthy. A new regulatory framework on military AI must prioritize the attainment of *humanity's security*. This can be accomplished when countries cooperate to create new rules and norms by concluding treaties that ensure predictability and greater certainty in international relations, along with frameworks to protect human dignity. I examined 25 peace and security treaties related to the means and methods of warfare and disarmament, and the way to establish zones of peace, like Antarctica, and the nuclear-weapon-free zones (Chapter 5). I demonstrated that the vast majority of treaties created preventive frameworks that achieved several objectives:

- Prevented (or stopped) further militarization;
- Made weaponization unlawful;
- Controlled proliferation within a common rules framework;
- Created zones of peace, free of nuclear weapons and other armaments;
- Built an environment within which scientific cooperation and exchange could flourish.

These findings affirm and reiterate that an international law rules-based framework to avert excessive militarization and avoid conflict continues to be the most fruitful way to prevent war and lay the foundations for peace for future generations.

I investigated several indicators that point to the emergence of a new norm on the peaceful uses of AI. Let me enumerate a few that mark and galvanize the momentum for global rulemaking in all areas of AI, including the regulation of its military realm. First, since 2015, the foremost AI scientists have written letters alerting the public to the perils of building autonomous weapons and also weaponizing AI. The letters received extensive media coverage, and Elon Musk and the late Stephen Hawking were among the personalities who endorsed the first letter.[22] They have since been joined by almost 5,000 AI and robotics researchers, as well as more than 30,000 other individuals. The scientists advise that AI should be used for the common good of humanity and warn against a military race, which must be prevented through the creation of new global governance mechanisms. In 2018, the scientists' second letter was published and now has almost 2,500 individual and 150 company signatories from 90 countries. In this iteration, the scientists argue that AI is playing an increasingly significant role in military systems. The public should therefore be informed about what are the reasonable and the nonacceptable uses of AI. The scientists' letters present an admonishment and a warning for the future security of humanity. Second, the pioneering Asilomar Principles set out in 2017—in a meeting convened by MIT's Max Tegmark at the Future of Life Institute—have been signed by 1,797 AI and robotics researchers and 3,923 others.[23] AI should enhance and expand humanity's well-being, and for that it must be beneficial, ethical, and human-centered, with systems that are sufficiently robust to prevent the possibility of interference or hacking (safety first) and malfunctioning. The Asilomar Principles warn against an AI military race.

Third, the Institute of Electrical and Electronics Engineers (IEEE)—the world's largest technical professional organization dedicated to advancing technology for the benefit of humanity, with 400,000 members in 160 countries—launched the Global Initiative for Ethical Considerations in Artificial Intelligence and Autonomous Systems (the IEEE Global Initiative) in 2017, the basic principle being "Human wellbeing is our metric for progress in the algorithmic age."[24] The high ethical concerns and general principles guiding it are that all AI and autonomous systems should "embody the highest ideals of human rights, prioritize the maximum benefit to humanity and natural environment, [and] mitigate risks and negative impacts as AI and autonomous systems evolve as socio-technical systems."[25] Fourth, Amazon, DeepMind, Facebook, Google, IBM, and Microsoft, among other technology companies, set out the Partnership on Artificial Intelligence to Benefit People and Society (Partnership on AI), and endorsed the scientists' 2015 letter and cautioned about an AI military race. Fifth, evidence from a large recent survey of machine-learning researchers illuminates the ethics and governance of military AI. The overwhelming majority of researchers oppose AI applications to autonomous weapons. At the same time, they believe the governance of AI for the common good should be led by international organizations and not by militaries or individual governments.[26] Another rich database published by Harvard on the stances of all regions of the world on the development of AI found that an overwhelming majority of governmental national strategies, civil society groups, and companies surveyed found that the promotion of well-being, fairness, and inclusivity should be the key aspiration and that human control should always be a feature of AI applications.[27] Lastly, the AI for Good Movement is underway and comprises initiatives that seek to benefit humanity. The global public flagship platform of the movement is the AI for Good Global

Summits at the United Nations in Geneva, hosted by the International Telecommunication Union (ITU). This platform created a worldwide repository of projects that use AI to advance the implementation of the United Nations Sustainable Development Goals (SDGs) (Chapter 3). The SDGs are a comprehensive plan to promote a livable planet for future generations by achieving a more humane and sustainable world, with fewer weapons—nuclear or AI-based—and more security and prosperity. Strengthening arms limitations and regulations, and at the same time preventing perilous new applications of otherwise beneficial technology in warfare, seem to be the way to pave a path toward peace and security.

AI as a global common

My proposal for global cooperation by implementing a *common good governance*-based framework on military AI and achieving *humanity's security* highlights how AI can be used in the service of humanity, and with a view to protecting future generations. All the commons—human and Earth's—must be safeguarded from human exploitation and the perpetuation of inequality where the technologically advanced countries benefit without regard to sustainability and fairness. Intergenerational equity, which is a principle of international law, must be the guiding precept: it ensures that diplomatic decisions taken today to not weaponize AI are done so in light of the rights of future generations.

Our planet's traditional "global commons"—the high seas (the resources on the deep seabed), outer space, the Moon and other celestial bodies, Antarctica, and the atmosphere (including the ozone layer and the climate system)—offer a fertile laboratory to examine the possibilities for global cooperation in the shifting global order. AI needs to be a shared resource—a public domain for the common good, along with cyberspace—and therefore be considered a global common.[28] Even though there are significant physical differences between the planet's global commons and AI as a human-made common, as well as the challenges posed by each, what they share is the way that they benefit humanity: protecting the planet's common areas and enabling connectivity and representation in the digital revolution.

Recent innovations in AI and its resulting amplified influence in human life are the result of a couple of factors that explain why I hold it should be considered a global common: the increase in computing and processing power at lower cost, and the "big data" produced by billions of people that can be utilized to engender the astonishing development and commercialization of a set of computational techniques such as machine learning.[29] In other words, it is the data generated by people all over the world that is partly enabling the advancements in AI. Therefore, the gains should be returned to the people.[30]

AI will not be useful if it does not uphold and promote human dignity. Its role will be harmful if the algorithms are not fair; they need to be developed by an inclusive and diverse labor force. The creation of AI must occur according to values that are clearly articulated in order to protect human beings—for instance, a prohibition on the weaponization of AI, or clear restrictive measures on facial recognition algorithms. This means that AI can be considered as a global common for two reasons that will also largely help prevent its weaponization. The first is that the "big data" that is furnished to enable the advancements in AI originates from the billions of people who live on the planet and their activities in cyberspace. It is the people who should be able to enjoy the benefits arising from AI. Because of the ubiquity of AI, its large-scale applications will affect everyone in ways that previous societal scientific revolutions did not. Abuse of this development is therefore a matter of concern for the whole of humankind and needs to be confronted in humanity-wide frameworks. Second, software is central to most facets of connected human life today. What enables the interconnections is a digital infrastructure that relies on publicly available code—that is, an "open source" code that is a public good and which is maintained by communities of developers who do so voluntarily.[31] There are 193 countries in the physical world that are members of the United Nations, but billions of networks are connected through the Internet, and AI will only accelerate this trend toward interconnectivity. Most software depends on the unpaid labor of communities of developers who power and maintain much of the web (digital infrastructure needs maintenance as much as physical infrastructure); vast quantities of our data are powering data-driven technologies, such as machine learning. Jennifer Shkabatur contends that data should be considered a global common and managed cooperatively because of its public value.[32]

A new treaty on autonomous weapons advances in military AI

In the diplomatic negotiations at the United Nations on a new treaty on autonomous weapons, the rising norm of keeping AI beneficial and peaceful does not seem to have influenced the course of diplomacy directly. However, there are already desirable emerging norms that would serve as an excellent foundation for a regulatory framework on military AI as well. The rise of these worthy emerging norms that could materialize in the form of actual obligations is observed in the respective statements on positions of most states, and in the legal opinion of the guardian of international humanitarian law (IHL), the International Committee of the Red Cross (ICRC): The rise of these worthy emerging norms that could materialize in the form of actual obligations is observed in the respective statements: humans should maintain control over the use of force (i.e., the nondelegation of decisions over life and death), and profile-based algorithmic targeting of individuals is prohibited to preserve dignity and the right to life. These statements reflect the positions (thus far) of most states, as well as the legal opinion of the ICRC.

The shape and nature of a new international treaty became even clearer when the ICRC publicized its position in May 2021. The ICRC recognizes that prevailing IHL will not be suited to address the challenges posed by AI-assisted autonomous systems. The position advises states to establish new international law in the form of legally binding prohibitions and regulations to limit the increasing levels of autonomy and use of AI in warfare. As a result of the moral clout inherent in the ICRC's position, there is a sense of restored confidence in the prospect of a breakthrough. Still, the ICRC's position, even if compelling, did not quite sway the major powers, who remained obdurate and held onto their respective positions to the exasperation of most other countries.

The ICRC asks states to negotiate an innovative international set of legally binding rules setting limits on autonomous weapon systems that encompass three areas. The first area is a prohibition on autonomous weapons whose effects cannot be predicted and whose outcomes cannot be explained. The second area is a prohibition on antipersonnel systems (i.e., they cannot be deployed to target human beings): "an algorithm should not determine who lives or dies in effect reducing the decision to kill to sensors and data processing, and death by algorithm would be the final frontier in the autonomation of killing."[33] The third area is a subset of regulatory policies to level the playing field:

- Systems should, by design and in use, create rules for limiting the type of target to those that are military by nature;
- Specific attacks should be the result of limits on duration, geographical scope, and use. Human–machine interaction should ensure timely human supervision that would be able to intervene and deactivate.

The ICRC makes the point that it is key to bear in mind that not all autonomous weapons incorporate AI and machine learning:

existing weapons with autonomy in their critical functions, such as air-defense systems with autonomous modes, generally use simple, rule-based, control software to select and attack targets. However, AI and machine-learning software—specifically of the type developed for "automatic target recognition"—could form the basis for future autonomous systems, bringing a new dimension of unpredictability to these weapons, as well as raising concerns about lack of explainability and bias.[34]

This is one more reason why a new treaty to set rules on autonomous weapons use would be a central component in the creation of a framework on military AI.

The ICRC warns that the increasing military investment in autonomous systems is leading to accelerating reliance on AI. Such AI-assisted and -controlled autonomous systems magnify the unpredictability and ambiguity stemming from the inability to explain how the system arrived at a decision. Current remote-controlled systems are already able to identify, track, and select targets autonomously, and they could be updated to apply force without the final consent of a human operator. It is the user of the weapon who must fulfill this requirement, not the weapon itself; human beings abide by international law and can be deemed responsible and held accountable. Therefore, the machine process of the functioning of autonomous systems presents a conundrum for assessing compliance with the existing rules.[35] Fundamentally, IHL prohibits indiscriminate systems, which is why the ICRC recommends in its position the prohibition of unpredictable autonomous systems (the decisions of which cannot be reasonably understood and explained). Current IHL does not sufficiently answer the array of ethical, legal, and humanitarian questions raised by autonomous systems nor, increasingly, by AI-assisted ones. Therefore, new rules would clarify areas of uncertainty and imprecision, and would create stability of expectations, in consonance with what I propose in my concept of *common good governance*.

Pillar 2. Risk assessment based upon preventive precautionary action

The development of a regulatory framework on military AI will be based upon the determination of risks posed by the deployment of the technology.[36] AI applications could rise to the level of a global risk.[37] However, as history has shown with other catastrophic risks for humanity, such as nuclear weapons and pandemics, the severity of the risk is not always what compels global action.[38] The risk of deploying AI in the military is still high as it is prone to accidents.[39] Systems that use machine learning—one of the techniques of AI—learn from data they gather as they operate. The quality and quantity of the data play a role in their functioning and interaction with the environment. As a result, such systems are more unpredictable. Compounding this randomness is the system's lack of transparency and inability to explain outcomes. Such AI systems may also be more unreliable because of the use of biased data.[40] This problem of partial or unfair data was noticed when machine learning was applied to image and facial recognition.[41] AI may not reach the levels of dependability and consistency required by many military applications where life is at risk. What is already happening is that the pursuit of the weaponization of AI is indeed leading to a greater risk of a military race.

The major military powers—mostly states with nuclear weapons—see AI as a critical enabler of their present and future nuclear capabilities. AI's untrustworthiness could make for perilous international relations. The interaction of algorithms from different origins increases the probability of escalatory crises turning into violent conflicts. I contend that the impact of AI will be disruptive of the prevailing, yet volatile, balance of power. Common ground can be found as self-interested states always work toward maintaining their own national security. Every country has an interest in maintaining international stability to carry on commerce and trade, not to mention other human activities.

The weaponization of AI will disrupt military thinking, creating a paradigm shift that will destabilize conditions of peace and security.[42] As Jean-Marc Rickli explained to the World Economic Forum, military strategy to date has prioritized defensive systems, which has deterred the initiation of war and has been conducive to stability. With the use of autonomous systems, the tactic of choice will be swarming, which favors an offensive of several coordinated attacks. Escalation and acceleration of hostilities will ensue and preemption will likely prevail, going against the rules of restraint in the initiation of war under international law.[43] The threshold for starting a war will be lowered, and the existing peaceful settlement of dispute frameworks under international law will be eroded.[44]

AI is not yet as robust as needed for military applications, and the risks are high[45] as a result of the innate unpredictability, bias, and inability to explain and control outcomes, which may result in indiscriminate impacts on civilians, unintended consequences, and malfunctions, especially in complex conflict environments and densely populated areas.[46] Risk assessment should be based upon safety and the ability to control while failure to do so can have disastrous outcomes.[47] The interactions of the systems of different countries, with a diverse range of algorithms deployed, will intensify and heighten concerns of predictability and unreliability. This is the reason why states must cooperate to establish commonly agreed rules.[48]

***

Precautionary action to avoid risk is key to the creation of a *common good governance* framework on military AI. Benefits are more inclusive if all stakeholders are involved. In this regard, not only governments but also scientists and the private sector play a role, along with civil society. Everyone has a platform to cooperate to forge common solutions, building on their distinctive strengths. Ethically informed foresight to avoid harm is at the forefront of preventive action, as no one would benefit from the widespread malicious and evil uses of AI.

> Tech-nationalism, protectionism, and dysfunctional fragmentation might undermine the benefits AI can bring, while increasing the risk of abuse by state and non-state players. We believe that a new technology diplomacy, envisioned as a multi-stakeholder, multi-layer, bottom-up and top-down process, is needed to weave the many existing initiatives into a broader narrative. A critical mass of visionary leaders in government, corporations, non-profit organizations, research institutions, and initiatives on the ground can make a difference. This will not be an easy nor a straightforward process, but it is necessary to realize the full benefits of AI for the largest number possible.[49]

It is in the interests of all countries to take preventive measures and set the benchmarks for what is deemed to be ethically responsible uses of AI.[50] This way, states that adopt this proactive stance can also lead in showing others the way, acting by using international law as a unifying platform. If AI is weaponized and the automation of warfare leads to dehumanization, there is a risk that international law and the functioning of states in international relations will become intensely disordered for three reasons. First, the new technologies of autonomy and AI as they are presently being engaged already evade the global norms for keeping the peace, such as the nonuse of force in international relations and the peaceful settlement of disputes. For example, armed drones are used against entities with whom states are not at war instead of seeking avenues for peaceful resolution. Drones are a step removed from having a human being in the control loop (i.e., the human being is still there but the technological advancement is as such that it could lead to the removal of human oversight in the very near future).[51] There is a disintegrating effect on the most important norms of conduct that maintain global peace. Restraints on the use of force and the peaceful settlement of disputes through negotiation, mediation, and other means are the two main pillars upon which the entire edifice of peace rests.

Second, international law has evolved to be human-centered. Human beings are the creators, adjudicators, benefactors, and beneficiaries of human rights and humanitarian law. If decisions were to be delegated and entrusted to algorithms and robots as their executors, what will happen to the existing legal frameworks that protect human beings and maintain peace?[52] They will most likely be evaded in the name of the expediency provided by the technological convenience of acting more rapidly or in the secrecy of cyberspace. The purpose of common human action as the basis of international law will fade into insignificance and become peripheral.

Third, technological advancements and the rapid pace at which states are already disrespecting the tenor of obligations that afford protection to human beings raises alarm. With no cooperation, humankind is on a dangerous path toward a potentially precarious and uncertain future with more wars where the technologically most powerful may triumph.[53] International relations may go back to a time when the national interest eclipsed the need to safeguard human beings. We want to avoid a shift away from human security-centered law, which now coexists with states' national interests, to an exclusive focus on national security interests, with no regard for human happiness or well-being. International law took centuries to become humanized.[54] The temptation to use an alluring technological advantage offered by autonomous weapons may portend what lies ahead with the weaponization of AI in a more precarious world order. The same logic of a race for technological military superiority in the past led to the accumulation of 70,000 nuclear weapons at the height of the Cold War, with massive diversion of the economic patrimony of nations.

Pillar 3. Lessons learned from previous global cooperation

In this book I have delved into the inspiring concepts and diplomatic avenues that nations and leaders drew on to avert catastrophe, wars, and misuse of the common areas of the planet, and to reduce the dangers to civilians by restricting the means and methods of warfare (Chapters 2 and 5). I draw lessons from the past victories of global cooperation, and take stock of what happened when technological advancements overtook diplomatic initiatives. It was illuminating to inspect the examples of shining and successful global cooperation in several areas that I examined in Chapter 2, from making the continent of Antarctica peaceful and weapons-free, banning nuclear testing, creating the conditions for peace in the Arctic, saving the planet by healing the ozone layer, and forging a constitution (i.e., frameworks of coexistence and avenues for trouble-shooting problems) for the oceans and another for the atmosphere. From the main impacts of earlier global cooperation to maintain and protect the global commons, we can infer some initial principles and apply them to create *common good governance* and a global framework to regulate the rapid militarization of AI.

1) The global commons are beyond any single country's jurisdiction. Therefore, no one can claim jurisdiction: no state, no nation, and no corporation. This restriction set up by the principles of the common heritage of humanity renders ownership legally absent. In this light, I propose AI to be considered a global common. This means that weaponization of AI should be rendered unthinkable as it would not benefit anybody.

2) All states are expected to support efforts toward achieving cooperation within a regime of international management. Herein, I propose the establishment of a permanent and multinational scientific and ethics review board that would oversee the application of AI in the military to ensure (i) that it does not turn into rampant weaponization, and (ii) that utilization of AI meets ethical principles for military uses (Figure 6.1).

3) Benefit sharing (a prospective future basis for regulating military AI): The exploitation of the common areas shall be pursued to further the interests of all of humanity. Therefore, if economic profits should materialize, they are to be shared under a common mandate and authority which is tasked with the equitable distribution of rights and duties, along with serving as a forum for the peaceful settlement of disputes. Within a regulatory framework on AI, this would mean that an international repository of uses is created for peaceful, human-centric purposes for the common good of humanity (Figure 6.2). Such a repository is already evident in the annual AI for Good summits hosted at the UN, which created a means to document projects that use AI for implementing the United Nations SDGs.

4) Common areas are to be used exclusively for peaceful purposes. These areas are not to be weaponized. In outer space, Antarctica, and in nuclear-weapon-free zones across the planet, this principle has taken hold very strongly. An additional element within this realm would be the creation of AI-weaponization-free zones.

5) An international organization can be the site for cooperative scientific research that has to be undertaken in a manner that is transparent. The findings are to be shared to further advance all of humanity. In the case of a framework for military AI, cooperative compliance, technical assistance, and verification options underpinned by published policies at the national level would affirm ethical use by all actors involved (Figure 3.1).

The principle of the common concern of humanity that I investigated could have a significant impact upon the creation of a regulatory framework for military AI considering that AI is a common. The common concern of humanity arose as a principle to give prominence to issues such as climate change, deforestation, and biodiversity loss, which represent pressing problems for all of humanity and as such transcend the interests of states, and solutions to these problems would require humanity to act in terms of a common stewardship and universal solidarity to benefit developing as well as developed countries. To assist in this endeavor, science and technology would be at the forefront.

Technological developments of the 20th century and their consequences—the ever-increasing gap between the rich and poor countries, and the former's attempts to exploit the riches of the latter—were the fundamental motivating dynamics driving the creation of the notion of the common heritage of humanity.[55] The technological capacity of the wealthy nations to exploit certain domains of the planet made their resources accessible only to those nations themselves, to the detriment of the less technologically endowed nations. The common heritage of humanity is thus a mechanism to confront the need for preventing further inequities, which has now become all the more urgent with the development of AI.[56] The following four principles have implications for devising avenues for the militarization of AI:

- The common heritage of humanity: some areas of the planet should not be the object of exploitation or national claims to jurisdiction;
- Common concern: certain issues such as climate change, biodiversity loss, and deforestation would elicit a shared concern that transcends the narrow pursuit of the national interest;
- Intergenerational equity: a concern for the future of the unborn and their rights and reasonable expectation of peace and a healthy environment;
- The precautionary principle—which would advise action to avoid risk even in the face of uncertain future outcomes or scientific confirmation—is all the more urgent given that, on the one hand, AI-related technologies will enhance already existing technologies that will make possible the exploration and exploitation of the global commons, which can have possible harmful consequences (Figure 4.1).

I examined previous cases of effective global cooperation in Chapter 2. In these cases, I identified vast achievements in the creation of global public goods that benefited all of humanity and brought peace by mitigating conflict that I enumerate below. These successes—attained through common good governance—can provide the basic elements for building a military framework for AI, and possibly for AI governance in general.

Cases and lessons learned: (precepts for a military AI framework)

Ocean law

- a constitution for humanity;
- a constitution for the oceans;

- provision of legal order for most of the planet;
- renunciation of purely selfish exploitation and of part of their sovereignty;
- equity between developed and developing countries—technologically advanced and not, under a common management institute (the International Seabed Authority).

Ozone healing

- operationalization of the idea of common concern. The ozone and the climate are common concerns. Other issues include deforestation, climate change and, I argue, AI;
- precautionary action taken in the light of definitive scientific evidence of the problem: the hole in the ozone layer;
- the biggest repair job to save the planet undertaken thus far.

Arctic: cooperation despite all odds

- inclusive and creative diplomacy;
- common desire to preserve peace.

Antarctica: Zone of peace

- scientific cooperation takes precedence over other concerns;
- governing norms and dominant behaviors are cooperation and scientific exchange instead of competition and jurisdictional claims;
- peaceful purposes: no military activities;
- last unclaimed land on Earth.

Outer space cooperation

- achievement of common goals to benefit the planet;
- no weaponization, no arms race;
- cooperation among enemies on Earth.

Prohibition of nuclear tests

- scientific cooperation for monitoring and enforcement of rules;
- creation of a strong norm that repudiates nuclear testing;
- example of a robust verification mechanism.

All the cases examined here provide precepts that could guide a framework to regulate military AI:

- creation of spheres of peace;
- cooperation is possible and can prevail even among rivals;
- frameworks for the reduction of distrust;
- transnational networked cooperation is essential;
- comity for peace;
- precautionary frameworks to avoid war and heal the planet;
- detailed conflict solving and peaceful settlement of disputes mechanisms;
- role of science—scientific community is charting the course.

West and Allen advocate for a regulatory framework on military AI to follow the tenets of the biological, chemical, and nuclear weapons treaties of the past and adopt well-tried principles. First is the incorporation of human rights and holding decision-makers accountable for their responsibility to protect civilians. The adoption of a principles-based approach will prevent a technological race to attain military superiority from trumping basic human values. Second is the need to maintain a human being in the control loop. These two authors say that good judgment cannot be automated and that it is not possible to incorporate the necessary ethical principles into AI algorithms. Third, the adoption of a norm in terms of which AI algorithms are banned from command-and-control systems is imperative to prevent existential threats to humanity. Fourth is the creation of a common definition of what constitutes critical infrastructure and commonly agreed mutual respect among all countries. Fifth is the need to develop frameworks for making AI systems more robust and predictable. This can reassure the public, and ensure that greater predictability and stability are safeguarded. Finally, the development of oversight and inspection mechanisms to ensure compliance with international agreements is central to allow for expert assessment of technical and information exchange to verify compliance.[57] In Figure 6.1, I align my common good governance framework (as discussed throughout the book) with the views of West and Allen.

***

One of the main drivers for me to write this book was to investigate whether current international law must be amended or modified in the face of new technological developments in the realm of AI, and specifically in the face of the heightened automation of the means and methods of warfare. The other questions I set out to examine are as follows: Are the existing international legal fundamental principles still serviceable and adequate to meet the current challenges? How can we learn from the brightest examples of global cooperation in the past to instill a sense of what to safeguard for a less violent world for future generations? How can the weaponization of AI be restrained by the creation of a regulatory framework for military AI? In what ways can the dehumanizing impact of war be contained by setting rules for the use of autonomous systems in warfare?

Elements for a Governance Framework on Military AI

Permanent Scientific Panel & Ethics
Review Board

AI: Global Common

Cooperative Compliance
technical assistance and verification options

International Treaty
*on autonomous weapons and AI-assisted systems with a
secretariat in Geneva*

International Repository
*peaceful and human-centric user for the common
good of humanity*

Published Policies at National & Regional Level
*emerging norms and principles on responsible ethical
uses by a range of actors*

Precautionary & Risk Assessment
Frameworks

Figure 6.1 Transnational networked cooperation for military AI

I undertook a detailed examination of the germane parts of international law as applicable to the heighted use of autonomous systems in order to create a legal framework for military AI. It is evident that the current international legal and political framework will not suffice to confront the challenges posed by the weaponization of AI. The march toward AI-assisted autonomous systems undermines the canonic human-centered precepts of international law: cooperation, peaceful settlement of disputes, responsibility, attributability, and accountability. The ongoing erosion of existing international norms is proceeding unabated and is weakening the legal edifice that underpins international relations. It is a matter of the utmost urgency to strengthen international law to effectively confront the challenges posed by this extraordinary evolution of the technology applicable to war. At stake is the protection of human life itself. Nothing is more urgent than to safeguard human life and dignity against death by algorithm.

Autonomous systems challenge the basic assumptions upon which all branches of international law rest: the centrality of human decision-making, attributable wrong-doing for human actions, and the protection of human dignity. Algorithmic killing tests these central human-centered assumptions. Such uncertainties need to be confronted and existing international law must be clarified. Existing international legal regulatory and prohibition frameworks on means and methods of warfare provide guidelines and serve as foundations. However, their utility is limited. The lessons derived from the global governance of nuclear weapons are valuable, but their role in the creation of a framework for military AI is incomplete.[58] As Matthijs Maas explains, AI systems will be ubiquitous in the battlefield and, in a way that is different from nuclear weapons, AI technologies will not be employed in one weapon (as a nuclear warhead is, for example) but rather integrated across different functions and parts of different systems and operations.[59] Additionally, the development and acquisition of nuclear weapons has been confined to a small group of states, and this is still the case. AI, on the other hand, is pervasive and individuals play a role in using the technology as well. Most of the talent and inventions are located in the private sector. Most people benefit from these inventions and can use image recognition, language processing on their smart phones, and beyond. AI will be increasingly more accessible in multiple sectors, from the individual to the governmental levels. As Stuart Russell tells us, "many hands hold AI cards."[60] The creation of *common good governance* is hence vital.

Current diplomatic attempts to address and curb the development of autonomous weapons and the heightened militarization of AI are qualitatively different from past initiatives. The centrality of software in autonomous systems makes them less reliant on traditional, quantitative, weapons-counting forms of arms control. At stake is not the banning or prohibition of a single weapon system, but rather a whole range of technologies. This is not about a single or particular weapon system, but rather about multiple functions, in particular autonomous functionality in military systems, already existing or yet to be invented. One can discern distinct types of weaponry in nuclear, chemical, and conventional weapons. It is possible to count them. However, with autonomous systems we are talking about adding autonomy to different functions. If they happen to be the "critical functions" of selection and engagement, or target and attack (focus to kill or destroy), then the concern is whether human oversight is maintained during the performance of the function. Therefore, in autonomous systems, a qualitative rather than a quantitative analysis is essential in the technical and operational aspects, as Figure 6.2 indicates.

Earlier processes to regulate and prohibit weapons were remarkable, involving different groups of change makers who effectively persuaded and worked with states to create international law that ended up improving *humanity's security* worldwide in concrete terms. Currently, militaries of the technologically highly advanced countries are actively pursuing and already deploying AI to enhance their military operations. Projects that seek to enhance "man–machine teaming" or "hybrid intelligence" are in vogue. Still, responsibility for the use of AI and the consequences for future generations rests with the highly militarized countries. They are the ones that are

How to operationalize common good governance

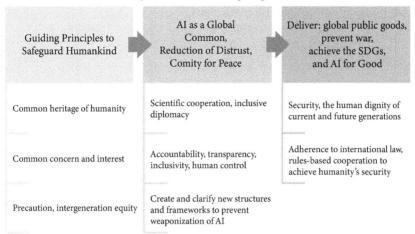

Figure 6.2 How to operationalize common good governance

attempting to weaponize the technologies utilizing AI. Therefore, the creation of common good governance to manage the militarization of AI, and the prohibition of most weaponization of AI, is in order. New thinking is required for the magnitude of the change that AI will bring to military affairs.[61] The colossal proliferation of nuclear weapons that reached its zenith of 70,000 during the Cold War shows that proliferation can be extremely costly and potentially dangerous. The International Atomic Energy Agency (IAEA) is the focal point for global nuclear cooperation and the uses of atomic energy for peace. A combination of the Intergovernmental Panel on Climate Change (IPCC) and the IAEA would be ideal. The IAEA has already started discussing the role of AI in nuclear applications in nuclear science for the benefit of a broad spectrum of human affairs including global public health, water resource management, and nuclear fusion research.[62]

Lessons from previous prohibitions on means and methods of warfare

From the lessons derived from previous prohibitions and limitations on means and methods of warfare examined here (Chapter 5, Annex), there are five features that seem particularly relevant to inform the formation of a *common good governance*-based framework for military AI. Previous instances of global cooperation—from banning cluster munitions and landmines, to the prohibition of nuclear and chemical weapons, to restricting conventional weapons transfers—were more impactful and robust when they endeavored to include the following attributes:

- prevention of bodily harm;
- accounted for the dual civil–military aspect;

- prohibited further development of harmful technology;
- regulated or prohibited certain behaviors;
- created a framework for scientific cooperation and technical exchange.

Altogether, the treaties examined here advance *common good governance*, one consequence of which is a new way of thinking about and implementing security. From a purely state-centric perspective, security has increasingly come to focus upon the protection of human beings. Not only is the state protected—the traditional conception of national security—but so too is *humanity's security*. The *common good governance* narratives on the limitations on nuclear weapons and the creation of an international treaty to outlaw the use of chemical warfare as an insidious practice with no place in a humane and civilized world demonstrate the possibilities for forging international solidarity to deal with the impending challenges posed by increased autonomy in weapon systems and by the militarization of AI. Legal regimes that offer fruitful examples of success are the Chemical Weapons Convention, the Biological Weapons Convention, and the Ozone Protocol known as the Montreal Protocol. Some of their elements could inform a new regulation—for example, a scientific board to monitor technological developments and provide guidance for implementing. These five features made these treaties successful and resilient. These attributes also offer an incentive for a new international treaty and require states to transcend the technical dimensions of the discussion on human–machine interactions and consider the normative perspectives, given the fundamental ethical and legal questions raised.[63] The Chemical and Biological Weapons Conventions restricted dual-use chemicals and controlled harmful activities by eradicating the possibility of weaponizing chemistry and biology. They did so by fostering the peaceful uses of such chemicals and by promoting scientific cooperation. The Montreal Protocol was the first to codify the principles of precaution and took decisive preventive action to avoid further future harm to the ozone layer. These instruments, now almost universally ratified, are flexible enough to continue to include technological developments as they evolve and hence stand the test of time. A treaty must therefore be broad enough to encompass all present and future systems that select and engage sensor-based targets. In other words, every time the target has been identified by sensors and not human observation, the firmest prohibition would be eliminating the possibility to target people.

The foundational underpinning of a new treaty on autonomous weapons would be the positive obligation to maintain human control throughout all the phases and stages of the design and operations. A positive obligation strengthens a more preventive stance in the promotion of human well-being. A purely negative obligations-based treaty would not necessarily put in place the conditions for long-term comprehensive ways to keep the treaty relevant in the light of further technological advancements that include AI. This new treaty could serve as a basis for more regulations and *common good governance* to set rules for the militarization of AI without endorsing its weaponization.

At this critical juncture at which the utilization of AI technologies remains largely unregulated globally, the probability is high that they will be used in ways that will exacerbate current inequalities. This is one more powerful reason to create *common good governance* for military AI with a preventive purpose, as a force promoting equity for all humans and not as just one more technological advance that will not be scaled up to benefit the largest number of people.

The need for common good governance

In this book, I have attempted to devise *common good governance* avenues for a global framework on military AI based upon existing and new international law in the pursuit of global public goods to benefit all, and the protection of future generations. In this endeavor, I expressed a degree of alarm and attempted to warn readers about the portentous and potentially menacing unrestrained utilization of autonomous weapons with no human control, and the hostile and unregulated use of militarized AI. There was therefore a cautionary message in the appraisal of the investment already being made in militarizing AI. My contention is that such investments could be reallocated to averting the societal, environmental, and planetary threats humanity now faces. The same over-investment in weaponizing a technology that could have been harnessed solely for the common good has happened before. The accumulation of nuclear arsenals during the Cold War was a reckless pursuit that risked the very existence of life on the planet and diverted vast amounts of money in unwarrantable ways. In the pointless pursuit of global superiority, the United States and the Soviet Union drove other powers to develop their own nuclear weapons in search of an elusive parity. The damage to the environment has been catastrophic in many regions of the globe where the weapons were tested.[64] The United States had a brief opportunity before proliferation to declare that only the use of nuclear technology for the common good of humanity would be acceptable. Nonetheless, most countries in the world reject the utility of nuclear weapons to maintain peace and security, and constitute zones of peace that are free of such weapons. Their continued existence reminds humankind of the high cost, the diversion of human capital, and the fundamental futility of weaponizing technologies that humanity could use for beneficial purposes. Nuclear weapons jeopardize both peace and security, and they exposed the flaws and catastrophic consequences of wrong choices. The lessons learned are a cautionary signal of what a future in which AI is weaponized could be like. Vast investments in intellectual and financial resources were channeled into building a massive arsenal of nuclear weapons. Did this accumulation bring peace and security? Hardly. And the risk of malevolent uses remains high.

If autonomous systems and AI-assisted killing are left unregulated or unrestrained, with no common rules under international law, then they are bound to generate insecurity. As a corollary, not only individual human but also international security is attained in part by the reduction in the proliferation of armaments, or by their outright prohibition. The case of autonomous weapons appears to indicate that there is a pressing need for new international law. In this sense, individuals become the ultimate beneficiaries of new rules under international law. This reaffirms the aspiration for peace and stigmatizes wrongful behavior, for instance by increasing pressure on nuclear-armed states and on those that deploy weapons in vulnerable countries.

Today, nations have an unparalleled chance in history to foster a better future by implementing the Paris Agreement on climate change and the United Nations SDGs. These are comprehensive landmark legal and political frameworks that will guide actions toward achieving a more humane and sustainable future. Fewer weapons—conventional, nuclear, and AI-based—mean greater security and prosperity. Reinforcement of arms limitations and regulations, and at the same time preventing perilous new applications of otherwise beneficial technology in warfare, are strong signs that humanity expects a future of peace and security.

A regulatory framework for AI is desirable, given the exigencies created by the ongoing third revolution in warfare—epitomized by an ever-heightening use of autonomous weapons, and increasingly assisted by AI—at the intersection of the rapidly progressing fourth industrial revolution that is blurring the lines between the biological, digital, and physical realms, affecting all people on the planet in ways that the previous revolutions did not. The rapid development of AI will be an established characteristic of these transformations. The power and ingenuity of humanity must prevail to create a healthier world for future generations by containing autonomous algorithmic killing, which is a monumental affront to human dignity. By surveying the vast inspiring array of previous successes of global cooperation in limiting the proliferation of weaponry, prohibiting chemical, biological, and nuclear weapons, along with reviewing extraordinary concrete cases where all nations and hard-fought victories managed to forge peace and limit violence, I hope to elucidate the role of global cooperation through international law as an indispensable tool to address and confront the challenges, and as providing both the means and the language for nations to gain perspectives and pave the way for *common good governance* toward a nonviolent future and a global order wherein peace shall prevail. In this world, AI must realize its potential to be employed for the common good of humanity, as a global public good, and be protective of the dignity and well-being of present and future generations alike to attain *humanity's security.*

Notes

1. Denise Garcia, "Stop the Emerging AI Cold War." *Nature*, vol. 593, no. 7858 (2021): pp. 169; Gregory Allen and Elsa B. Kania. "China is Using America's Own Plan to Dominate the Future of Artificial Intelligence." *Foreign Policy*, vol. 8 (2017).
2. Jeffrey Arthur Larsen, ed. *Arms Control: Cooperative Security in a Changing Environment* (Lynne Rienner Publishers, 2002); Lloyd Axworthy, "Human Security and Global Governance: Putting People First." *Global Governance*, vol. 7 (2001): p. 19. Stuart Maslen, *Commentaries On Arms Control Treaties* (Oxford University Press, 2005).

3. Stuart Russell, "AI Weapons: Russia's War in Ukraine shows why the World Must Enact a Ban." *Nature*, Comment: February 21, 2023.

4. Shaza Arif, "Militarization of Artificial Intelligence: Progress and Implications." In *Towards an International Political Economy of Artificial Intelligence*, ed. Tugrul Keskin and Ryan David Kiggins (Palgrave Macmillan, 2021): pp. 219–239.

5. Reinmar Nindler, "The United Nation's Capability to Manage Existential Risks with a Focus on Artificial Intelligence." *International Community Law Review*, vol. 21, no. 1 (2019): pp. 5–34.

6. Elvira Rosert, et al., *Norm Dynamics in Multilateral Arms Control: Interests, Conflicts, and Justice* (University of Georgia Press, 2013): pp. 109–141.

7. Claudio Feijóo, et al., "Harnessing Artificial Intelligence (AI) to Increase Wellbeing for All: The Case for a New Technology Diplomacy." *Telecommunications Policy*, vol. 44, no. 6 (2020): 101988.

8. Eugenio V. Garcia, "Multilateralism and Artificial Intelligence: What Role for the United Nations?" *International Governance of AI* (2020). Allan Dafoe, "AI Governance: A Research Agenda." In *Governance of AI Program, Future of Humanity Institute, University of Oxford*, 1442 (2018): p. 1443.

9. The work of Rebecca Crootof from Yale is very instructive; in particular, see Rebecca Crootof, "Autonomous Weapon Systems and the Limits of Analogy." *Harvard National Security Journal*, vol. 9 (2018): pp. 51–83.

10. Nathan Alexander Sears, "International Politics in the Age of Existential Threats." *Journal of Global Security Studies*, vol. 6, no. 3 (2021). Nick Bostrom, "Existential Risks." *Journal of Evolution and Technology*, vol. 9, no. 1 (2002): pp. 1–31.

11. SIPRI Yearbook 2021, *Armaments, Disarmament and International Security* (Oxford University Press, 2021).

12. Andrew J. Carswell, "Unblocking the UN Security Council: The Uniting for Peace Resolution." *Journal of Conflict and Security Law*, vol. 18, no. 3 (2013): pp. 453–480.

13. Rebecca Barber, "Uniting for Peace Not Aggression: Responding to Chemical Weapons in Syria Without Breaking the Law." *Journal of Conflict and Security Law*, vol. 24, no. 1 (2019): p. 39.

14. United Nations General Assembly, A/ES-11/L.1, Eleventh Emergency Special Session, 1 March 2022 (and vote on the following day).

15. SIPRI Yearbook 2021, *Armaments, Disarmament and International Security*.

16. Robert S. Norris and Hans M. Kristensen, "Global Nuclear Weapons Inventories, 1945–2010." *Bulletin of the Atomic Scientists*, vol. 66, no. 4 (2010): pp. 77–83.

17. Stephen I. Schwartz, *Atomic Audit: The Costs and Consequences of US Nuclear Weapons Since 1940* (Brookings Institution Press, 2011).

18. Urs Gasser, and Virgilio A. F. Almeida, "A Layered Model for AI Governance." *IEEE Internet Computing*, vol. 21, no. 6 (2017): pp. 58–62.

19. Vincent Boulanin et al., *Responsible Military Use of Artificial Intelligence—Can the European Union lead the Way in Developing Best Practice?* (SIPRI, 2020).

20. Feijóo et al., "Harnessing Artificial Intelligence (AI) to Increase Wellbeing for All," p. 10.

21. Eugenio V. Garcia, *The Peaceful Uses of AI: An Emerging Principle of International Law* (The Good AI Newsletter, 2021).

22. Daniel Victor, "Elon Musk and Stephen Hawking Among Hundreds to Urge Ban on Military Robots," *The New York Times*, July 28, 2015, https://www.nytimes.com/2015/

07/28/technology/elon-musk-and-stephen-hawking-among-hundreds-to-urge-ban-on-military-robots.html.

23. See https://futureoflife.org/ai-principles/. The story of how the Asilomar Principles came into being are told in detail in Max Tegmark, *Life 3.0* (Knopf, 2018). Numbers of signatories from January 2022.

24. IEEE, *Ethically Aligned Design: Version 1* (Institute of Electrical and Electronics Engineers, 2016): p. 2.

25. Ibid., p. 5.

26. Baobao Zhang, et al, "A. Ethics and Governance of Artificial Intelligence: Evidence from a Survey of Machine Learning Researchers." *Journal of Artificial Intelligence Research*, vol. 71 (2021): pp. 591–666.

27. Jessica Fjeld, et al., "Principled Artificial Intelligence: Mapping Consensus in Ethical and Rights-Based Approaches to Principles for AI." *Berkman Klein Center Research Publication* (2020): pp. 2020–2021.

28. The AI Commons: https://aiforgood.itu.int/introducing-ai-commons-a-framework-for-collaboration-to-achieve-global-impact/

29. Kate Crawford, *The Atlas of AI* (Yale University Press, 2021).

30. Jennifer Shkabatur, "The Global Commons of Data." *Stanford Technology Law Review*, vol. 22 (2019): p. 354; Shkabatur considers that data should be considered as a "global common."

31. Nadia Eghbal, *Roads and Bridges: The Unseen Labor Behind Our Digital Infrastructure* (Ford Foundation, 2016).

32. Jennifer Shkabatur, "The Global Commons of Data." *Stanford Technology Law Review*, vol. 22 (2019): p. 354; Shkabatur considers that data should be considered as a "global common."

33. ICRC, Position and Background Paper, "Position on Autonomous Weapons Systems" (2021). Available: https://www.icrc.org/en/document/icrc-position-autonomous-weapon-systems: p. 8.

34. International Committee of the Red Cross (ICRC), *Artificial Intelligence and Machine Learning in Armed Conflict: A Human-Centered Approach* (International Committee of the Red Cross, 2019): p. 4. Emphasis is in the original ICRC text.

35. ICRC, "International Humanitarian Law and the Challenges of Contemporary Armed Conflicts." In *33rd International Conference of the Red Cross and Red Crescent* (Geneva, October 2019): pp. 22–24.

36. Araz Taeihagh, "Governance of Artificial Intelligence." *Policy and Society*, vol. 40. no. 2 (2021): pp. 137–157.

37. Eliezer Yudkowsky, "Artificial Intelligence as a Positive and Negative Factor in Global Risk." *Global Catastrophic Risks* (2008): p. 184.

38. Seth Baum, et al., "Lessons for Artificial Intelligence from Other Global Risks." In *The Global Politics of Artificial Intelligence*, ed. Maurizio Tinnirello (Chapman & Hall, April 25, 2022).

39. Zachary Arnold and Helen Toner, "AI Accidents: An Emerging Threat: Center for Security and Emerging Technology Policy Brief." *Center for Security and Emerging Technology* (2021).

40. ICRC, "Artificial Intelligence and Machine Learning in Armed Conflict: A Human-Centred Approach." International Review of the Red Cross, vol. 102, no. 913 (2020): pp. 463–479.

41. Matthew Hutson, "Hackers Easily Fool Artificial Intelligences." *Science*, vol. 361, no. 6399, July 20, 2018: pp. 215.

42. Vincent Boulanin, The Impact of Artificial Intelligence on Strategic Stability and Nuclear Risk: Euro-Atlantic Perspectives (SIPRI, 2019); Denise Garcia, "Lethal Artificial Intelligence and Change: The Future of International Peace and Security." *International Studies Review*, vol. 20, no. 2 (2018): pp. 334–341.

43. Jean-Marc Rickli, "Artificial Intelligence and the Future of Warfare." In *World Economic Forum, Global Risks Report*, 12th Edition (2017): p. 78. Available here: https://www3. weforum.org/docs/GRR17_Report_web.pdf

44. Garcia, "Lethal Artificial Intelligence and Change."

45. Stuart Russell, et al., "Ethics of Artificial Intelligence." *Nature*, vol. 521, no. 7553 (2015): pp. 415–416; Kenneth Payne, "Artificial Intelligence: A Revolution in Strategic Affairs?" *Survival*, vol. 60, no. 5 (2018): pp. 7–32.

46. ICRC, *Autonomy, Artificial Intelligence and Robotics: Technical Aspects of Human Control* (Geneva, 2019).

47. UNIDIR, "Safety, Unintentional Risk and Accidents in the Weaponization of Increasingly Autonomous Technologies" (UNIDIR, 2016).

48. Paul Scharre, "Autonomous Weapons and Operational Risk." *Center for New American Security* (2016): p. 2019.

49. Feijóo et al., "Harnessing Artificial Intelligence (AI) to Increase Wellbeing for All," p. 13.

50. Boulanin et al., "Ethics of Artificial Intelligence."

51. Noel Sharkey, "Automating Warfare: Lessons Learned from the Drones." *Journal of Law, Information and Science*, vol. 21, no. 2 (2011): pp. 140–154.

52. Rebecca Crootof, "The Killer Robots are Here: Legal and Policy Implications." *Cardozo Law Review*, vol. 36 (2014): p. 1837.

53. Mary Ellen O'Connell, "Unlawful Killing with Combat Drones: A Case Study of Pakistan, 2004–2009." In *Shooting to Kill: The Law Governing Lethal Force in Context*, Simon Bronitt, ed. (Notre Dame Legal Studies Paper, 2009): pp. 09–43.

54. Antônio Augusto Cançado Trindade, *International Law for Humankind: Towards a New Jus Gentium* (Brill Nijhoff, 2010).

55. Bradley Larschan and Bonnie C. B. Brennan, "The Common Heritage of Mankind Principle in International Law." *Columbia Journal of Transnational Law*, vol. 21 (1983): pp. 305–333; Mohammed Bedjaou, *Towards a New International Economic Order* (UNESCO, 1979); Nagendra Singh, "Right to Environment and Sustainable Development as a Principle of International Law." *Studia Diplomatica*, vol. 41, no. 1 (1988): pp. 45–61.

56. Surabhi Ranganathan, "Global Commons." *European Journal of International Law*, vol. 27, no. 3 (2016): pp. 693–717.

57. Darrell M. West and John R. Allen, *Turning Point: Policymaking in the Era of Artificial Intelligence* (Brookings Institution Press, 2020).

58. Waqar Zaidi and Allan Dafoe, *International Control of Powerful Technology: Lessons from the Baruch Plan for Nuclear Weapons* (Center for the Governance of AI, 2021).

59. Matthijs M. Maas, "How Viable is International Arms Control for Military Artificial Intelligence? Three Lessons from Nuclear Weapons." *Contemporary Security Policy*, vol. 40, no. 3 (2019): pp. 285–311, p. 289.

60. Stuart J. Russell, *Human Compatible Artificial intelligence* (Viking, 2019): p. 249; I am grateful for my conversations with the always prescient Benoît Pélopidas.

61. Kenneth I. Payne, *Warbot: The Dawn of Artificially Intelligent Conflict* (Oxford University Press, 2021).
62. Elodie Broussard, "The Future of Atoms: Artificial Intelligence for Nuclear Applications." *IAEA Bulletin*, vol. 61, no. 4 (2020).
63. Daniele Amoroso, *Autonomous Weapons Systems and International Law A Study on Human-Machine Interactions in Ethically and Legally Sensitive Domains* (Napoli Nomos, 2020).
64. Howard Hu, Arjun Makhijani, and Katherine Yih, eds. *Nuclear Wastelands: A Global Guide to Nuclear Weapons Production and its Health and Environmental Effects* (MIT Press, 2000).

Index

For the benefit of digital users, indexed terms that span two pages (e.g., 52–53) may, on occasion, appear on only one of those pages.